CONTENTS

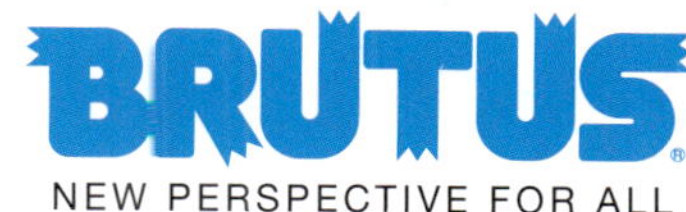

features

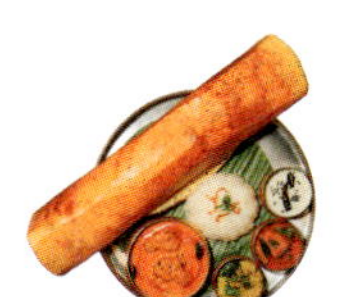

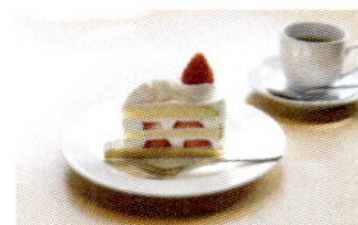

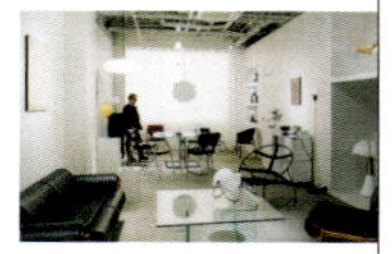

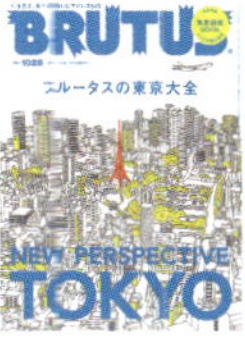

This English-language publication is a revised and re-edited version of articles featured in BRUTUS April 15, 2025 issue "BRUTUS no Tokyo Taizen. (BRUTUS Tokyo Encyclopedia)."

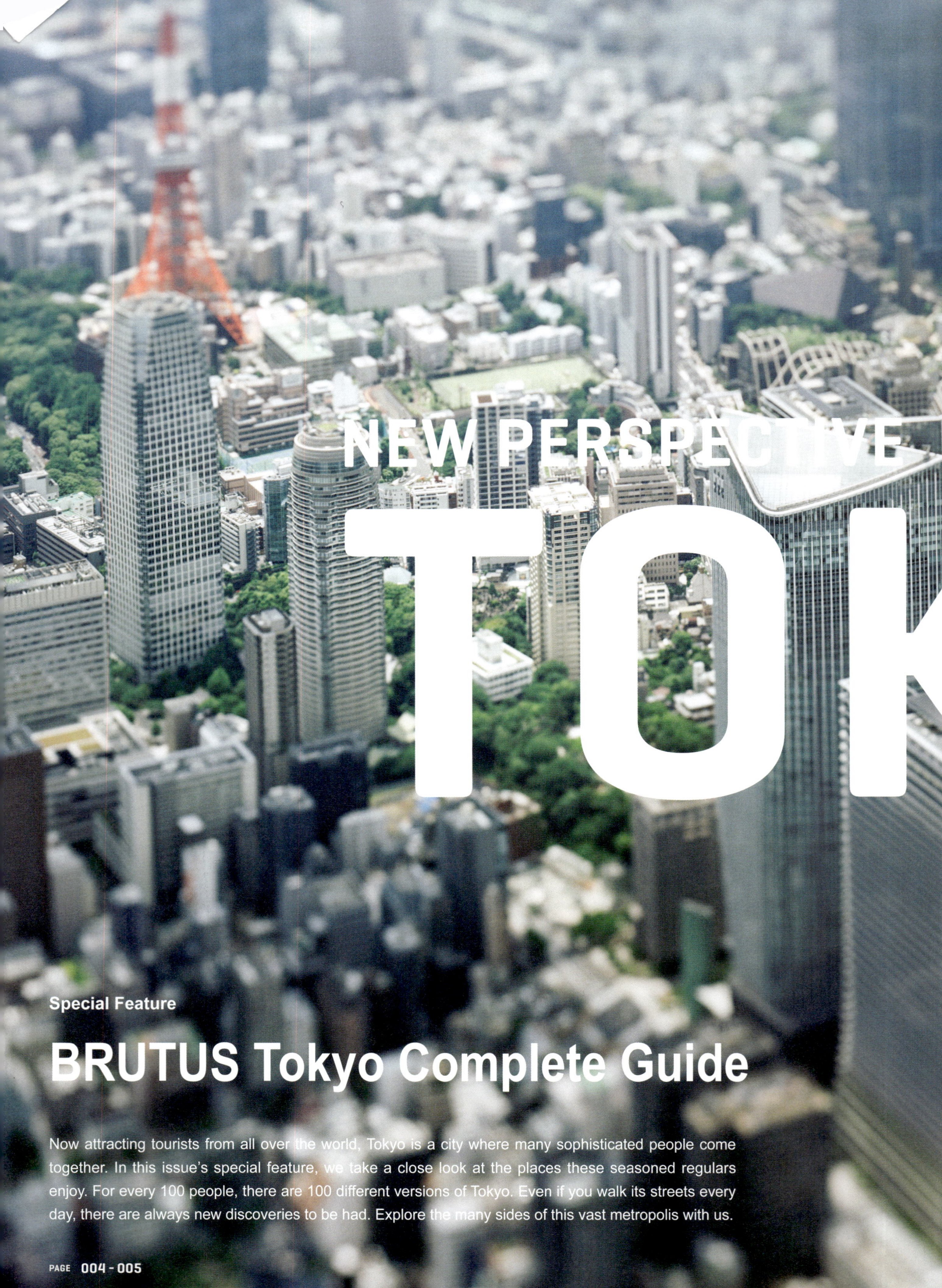

Special Feature

BRUTUS Tokyo Complete Guide

Now attracting tourists from all over the world, Tokyo is a city where many sophisticated people come together. In this issue's special feature, we take a close look at the places these seasoned regulars enjoy. For every 100 people, there are 100 different versions of Tokyo. Even if you walk its streets every day, there are always new discoveries to be had. Explore the many sides of this vast metropolis with us.

PAGE 004 - 005

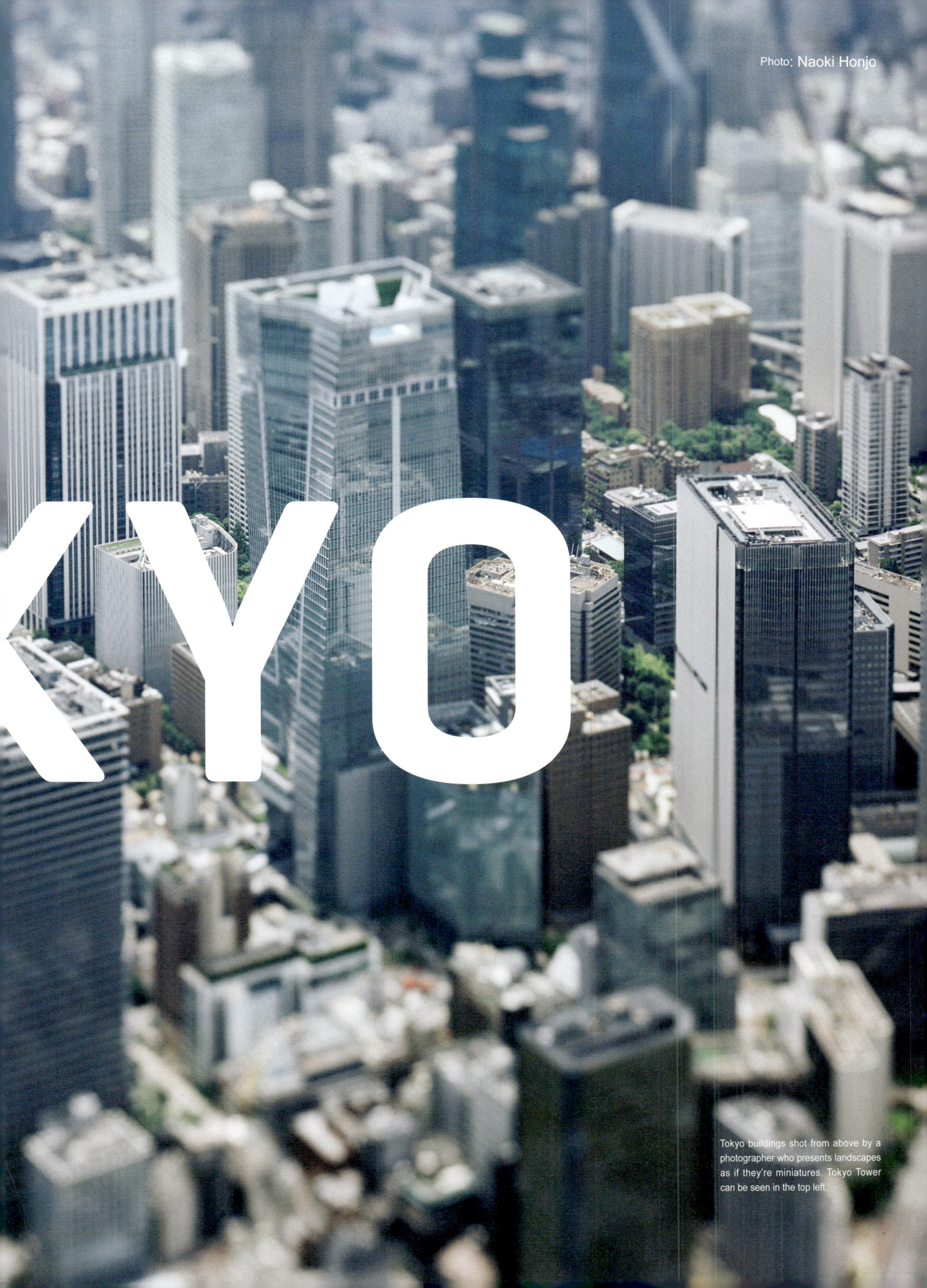

Photo: Naoki Honjo

Tokyo buildings shot from above by a photographer who presents landscapes as if they're miniatures. Tokyo Tower can be seen in the top left.

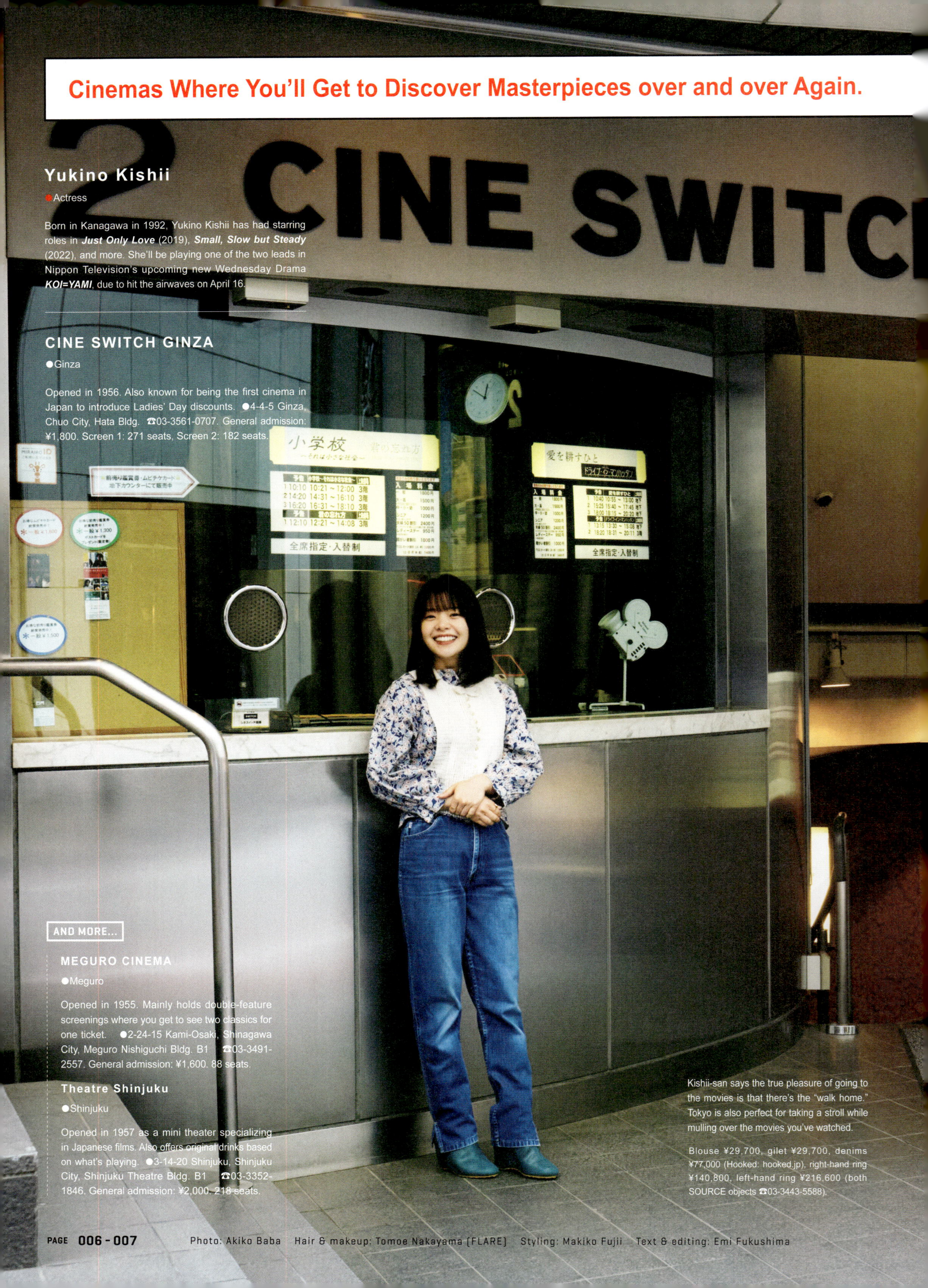

Cinemas Where You'll Get to Discover Masterpieces over and over Again.

2

Yukino Kishii

Actress

Born in Kanagawa in 1992, Yukino Kishii has had starring roles in ***Just Only Love*** (2019), ***Small, Slow but Steady*** (2022), and more. She'll be playing one of the two leads in Nippon Television's upcoming new Wednesday Drama ***KOI=YAMI***, due to hit the airwaves on April 16.

CINE SWITCH GINZA

●Ginza

Opened in 1956. Also known for being the first cinema in Japan to introduce Ladies' Day discounts. ●4-4-5 Ginza, Chuo City, Hata Bldg. ☎03-3561-0707. General admission: ¥1,800. Screen 1: 271 seats, Screen 2: 182 seats.

AND MORE...

MEGURO CINEMA

●Meguro

Opened in 1955. Mainly holds double-feature screenings where you get to see two classics for one ticket. ●2-24-15 Kami-Osaki, Shinagawa City, Meguro Nishiguchi Bldg. B1 ☎03-3491-2557. General admission: ¥1,600. 88 seats.

Theatre Shinjuku

●Shinjuku

Opened in 1957 as a mini theater specializing in Japanese films. Also offers original drinks based on what's playing. ●3-14-20 Shinjuku, Shinjuku City, Shinjuku Theatre Bldg. B1 ☎03-3352-1846. General admission: ¥2,000. 218 seats.

Kishii-san says the true pleasure of going to the movies is that there's the "walk home." Tokyo is also perfect for taking a stroll while mulling over the movies you've watched.

Blouse ¥29,700, gilet ¥29,700, denims ¥77,000 (Hooked: hooked.jp), right-hand ring ¥140,800, left-hand ring ¥216,600 (both SOURCE objects ☎03-3443-5588).

Photo: Akiko Baba Hair & makeup: Tomoe Nakayama (FLARE) Styling: Makiko Fujii Text & editing: Emi Fukushima

Let's Ask These Folks How to Enjoy Tokyo.

Unfamiliar sights constantly unfold around you even on familiar streets you walk every day. Here, connoisseurs living in this metropolis share tips on places to go theme by theme, and how to explore and enjoy them.

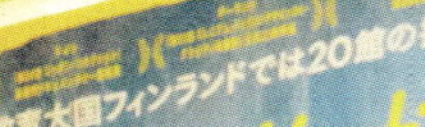

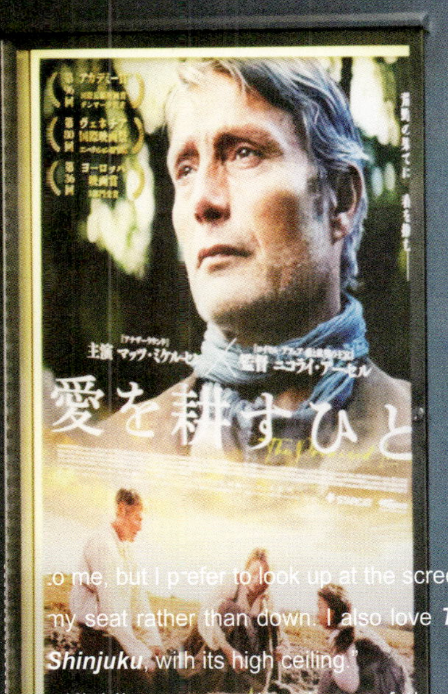

Yukino Kishii loves films both as an actress and as a moviegoer. As she wanders among its unique cinemas, what quintessentially "Tokyo" movie experience does she enjoy herself?

"Actually, I was here just a couple of weeks ago," says Kishii-san as she stands in front of ***Cine Switch Ginza***'s large signboard. Since moving to Tokyo in her early twenties, she's gotten into the habit of going to the movies a few times a month—and still keeps it up even now she's a familiar face on the big screen herself. "What surprised me when I first moved to Tokyo was that there are movies you can only get to see in certain cinemas. I was used to just having multiplexes, so the variety of mini theaters where everything was different—the movies, the atmosphere, and even the smell—was really fresh."

While the movies are a "factor as well," it's the wonderful theaters themselves that keep her coming back. The comfort of the theater space, including on the way to your seat, makes the whole moviegoing experience that much richer. "Screen 1 in ***Cine Switch Ginza*** has balcony seats. I love how it feels so open, like it's spreading the world of the movies all around you. And then there's ***Meguro Cinema***, where you take a staircase down into the basement. It really feels like you're entering an extraordinary world. Maybe it's because movies are sacred to me, but I prefer to look up at the screen from my seat rather than down. I also love ***Theatre Shinjuku***, with its high ceiling."

Kishii-san says the charm of these mini theaters lies in also getting to discover a wide variety of classic movies. "It's amazing to see on the big screen movies that were made before I was born, and ones I thought I'd never get to see again. For example, I go see Guillaume Brac's films whenever they're playing again. The appeal of movies is that despite being made in different eras and countries, they still have universal things to show you. I want people to go unique cinemas and discover movies that make the world look different on the way home."

A Small Stage He Continues to Adore.

SMALL THEATERS

Jiro chooses small theaters for Sissonne's solo live shows. What kind of Tokyo-ness does that place hold that he went to back in his twenties, right after moving to the city?

What prompted Jiro to move to Tokyo was seeing a City Boys stage show in Osaka when he was in junior college. "I wanted to do something like the City Boys but wasn't sure what, so for the time being, I just bought the magazine ***Engeki Book.*** It often had articles about small theaters and Otona Keikaku, and I developed a vague sense that theaters were sacred places for me."

The first theater he went to see a show at was the now-closed ***Ginza Shogekijo***. Later, he took to the stage himself for the first time at the very same venue. "The first play I saw was a double performance, one of which was like a comedy skit. Finding it really entertaining, I immediately contacted the theater via its magazine ad. I made my own stage debut at around 22. When I got my first offer to perform at ***Honda Theater***, I cried to myself while I was on my motorbike. I mean, a Yoshimoto comedian like me getting to perform at ***Honda Theater***?"

Sissonne now regularly do multiple solo shows at ***Honda Theater***, but achieving the rare feat of giving comedy performances there is likely thanks to Jiro's love for small theaters. What's more, June will see him making his debut as an actor in an Otona Keikaku production. "My dream of performing at ***Honda Theater*** with Otona Keikaku has come true, and I can't wait. It's a great venue for both giving performances and watching them. I like to use small props in our gags, but that's hard to pull off in a large theater. ***Honda Theater*** is small enough for even the folks right at the back to have a decent view, so it's really easy to perform at. I often visit ***Shogekijo B1*** for Shiroyagi no Kai performances. The intimacy and warmth are like you're eavesdropping on everyday chit-chat—a special feeling only small theaters can provide. Moreover, the luxury of going to ***THEATRE TRAM*** exclusively to watch plays is simply out of this world. For a bumpkin from Aomori, Tokyo's theater density is amazing, and being able to go see a show every day is an option you'll only get in the capital."

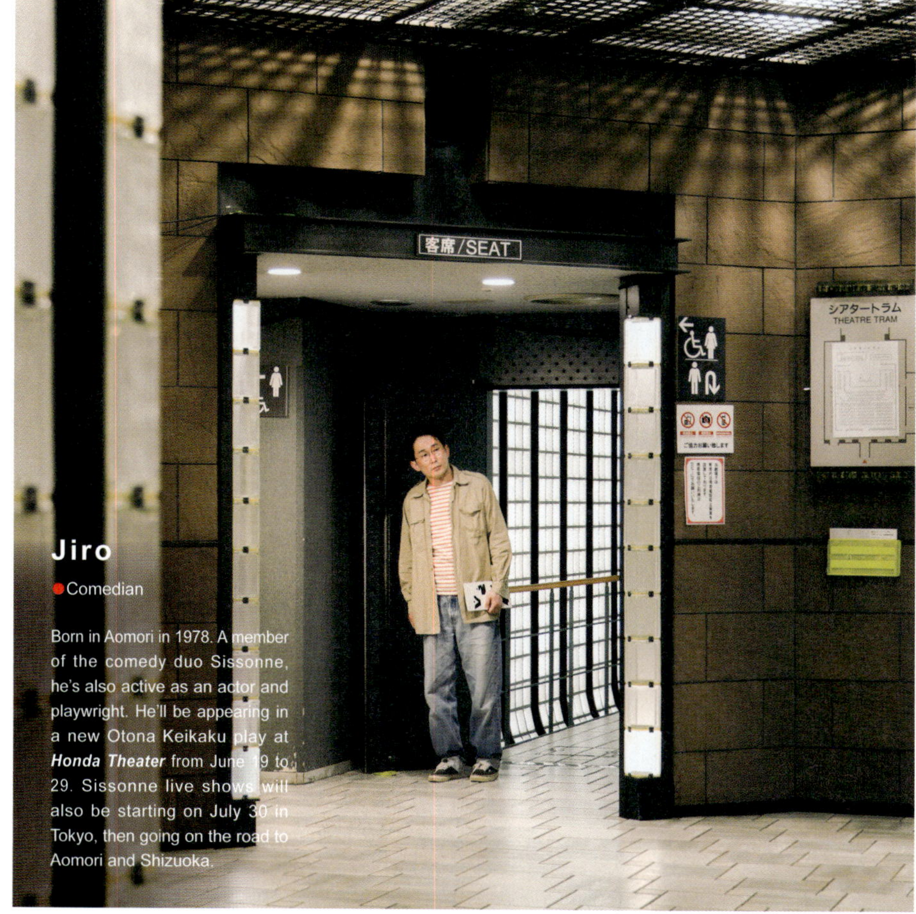

Jiro

●Comedian

Born in Aomori in 1978. A member of the comedy duo Sissonne, he's also active as an actor and playwright. He'll be appearing in a new Otona Keikaku play at ***Honda Theater*** from June 19 to 29. Sissonne live shows will also be starting on July 30 in Tokyo, then going on the road to Aomori and Shizuoka.

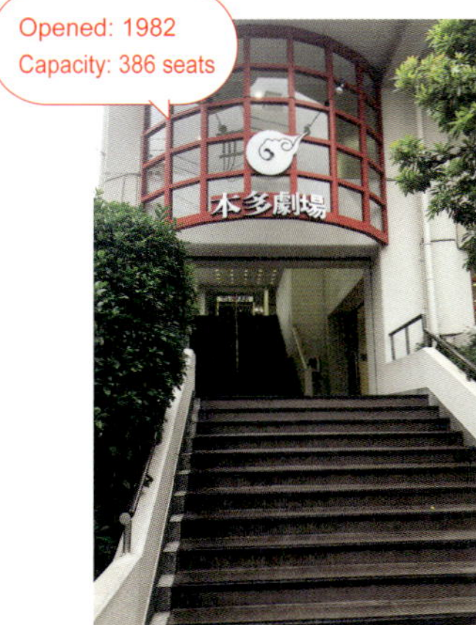

Opened: 1982
Capacity: 386 seats

Honda Theater ●Shimo-kitazawa

Shimo-Kitazawa's iconic playhouse is a leading venue in the theatrical world. It hosts many performances by renowned troupes like Otona Keikaku and Nylon 100°C, with regular chances to see popular actors up close, too. ●2-10-15 Kitazawa, Setagaya City ☎03-3468-0030. Irregular closed days.

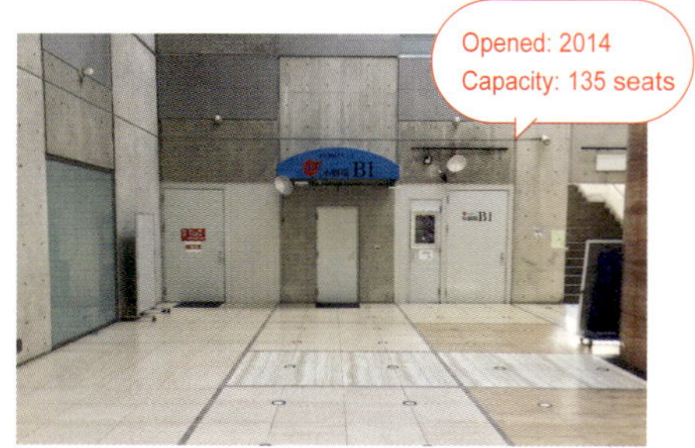

Opened: 2014
Capacity: 135 seats

Shogekijo B1 ●Shimo-kitazawa

Features an intimate space that brings the audience and performers into close proximity. Also used for dance and music performances. ●2-8-18 Kitazawa, Setagaya City, Kitazawa Town Hall B1 ☎03-6416-8281. Irregular closed days.

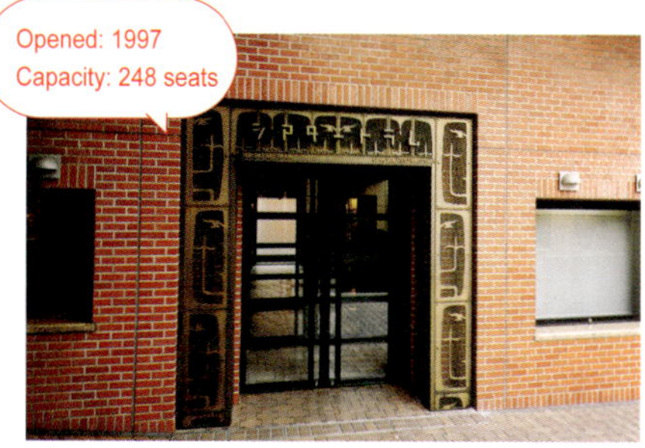

Opened: 1997
Capacity: 248 seats

THEATRE TRAM ●Sangen-jaya

An experimental theater that focuses on contemporary performances and dance and explores new performing arts. Also features the flexibility to set up the audience seating and stage in proscenium, floor, and other formats. ●4-1-1 Taishido, Setagaya City ☎03-5432-1526. Irregular closed days.

The modern, luxurious entrance to ***THEATRE TRAM***'s audience seats. Your portal to the world of stories.

Photos: Masanori Kaneshita Text: Asuka Ochi Editing: Emi Fukushima

A Botanical Garden for Walking and Thinking.

Shibuya native Rei Nagai says this garden was once her only place to escape the noise and be alone. It was also a space for immersing herself in diverse thought.

A regular at the ***SHIBUYA CITY BOTANICAL GARDEN FUREAI*** since university, Nagai was amazed at its soaring popularity after the renovation. "I also used to like how its vibrant plants and rustic, countryside community center-like charm were at odds with Shibuya, but it's more refined and beautiful now. I love how botanical gardens remind me of human's efforts to create greenery in urban areas where nature has been lost, and also underline our need for it. Plants look so much greater, and humans so small. Being overwhelmed feels lovely."

This botanical garden inspired her to check out others as well. Due to her work, she often comes for a stroll when she has a mental block. "Walking and thinking go well together. More than clearing my head, it's about widening my view by touching the unknown through plants and nature. This small garden contrasts with larger ones like the ***Institute for Nature Study*** or ***Shinjuku Gyoen***, where I can walk more and be amazed by their vastness, too. That means more room to think."

She also likes how, unlike typical commercial facilities, botanical gardens are public spaces with no fixed purpose. "Besides looking at all the plants, it's nice to focus on one favorite species, or read a book. With public spaces vanishing from the city, I hope readers visit them to remember how important they are."

AND MORE...

Institute for Nature Study

●Meguro

Over 1,400 plant species. ●5-21-5 Shirokanedai, Minato City ☎03-3441-7176. 9 a.m. to 4:30 p.m. (to 5 p.m. in summer; last admissions: 4 p.m. all year round). Closed on Mon. (or next day if Mon. is a holiday) and the day after a holiday (but open if a Sat. or Sun.). General admission: ¥320.

Shinjuku Gyoen

●Shinjuku-gyoemmae

Established in 1906. One of Tokyo's largest (58.3 hectares). ●11 Naitomachi, Shinjuku City ☎03-3350-0151. 9 a.m. to 6 p.m. (to 7 p.m. in summer and 4:30 p.m. in winter; last admissions: 30 min before closing). Closed on Mon. (or next weekday if Mon. is a holiday). General admission: ¥500.

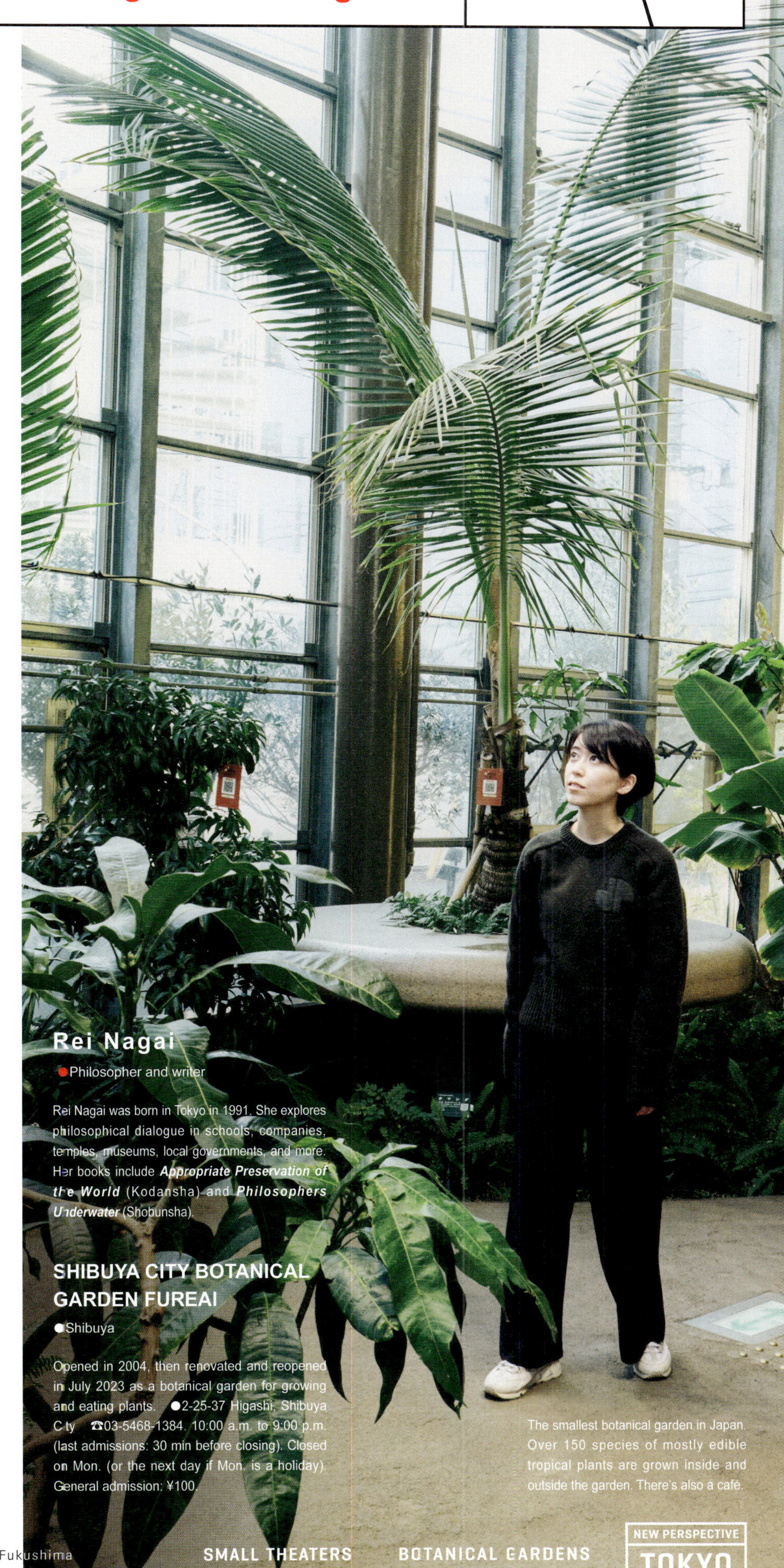

Rei Nagai

●Philosopher and writer

Rei Nagai was born in Tokyo in 1991. She explores philosophical dialogue in schools, companies, temples, museums, local governments, and more. Her books include ***Appropriate Preservation of the World*** (Kodansha) and ***Philosophers Underwater*** (Shobunsha).

SHIBUYA CITY BOTANICAL GARDEN FUREAI

●Shibuya

Opened in 2004, then renovated and reopened in July 2023 as a botanical garden for growing and eating plants. ●2-25-37 Higashi, Shibuya City ☎03-5468-1384. 10:00 a.m. to 9:00 p.m. (last admissions: 30 min before closing). Closed on Mon. (or the next day if Mon. is a holiday). General admission: ¥100.

The smallest botanical garden in Japan. Over 150 species of mostly edible tropical plants are grown inside and outside the garden. There's also a café.

Photos: Akiko Baba Text: Asuka Ochi Editing: Emi Fukushima

The Joy of Finding Your Own Style in a Rotating Microcosm.

Kaitenzushi, one of Japan's most iconic pieces of culture. Only in Tokyo can you compare restaurants that offer affordable, delicious options and evolve every day!

Gatten Sushi, Shinjuku Nishi-Ochiai Branch

●Ochiai-minami-nagasaki

High quality, while still keeping it all nice and casual. The "toro-bincho" made with fatty bincho tuna and the rare New Zealand "king salmon" are among the toppings carefully selected by the exclusive buyers. Daily specials using fresh fish from various ports showcase each restaurant's individuality. ●3-22-4 Nishi-Ochiai, Shinjuku City ☎ 03-6771-7377. 11:00 a.m. to 8:45 p.m. (last orders). No closed days.

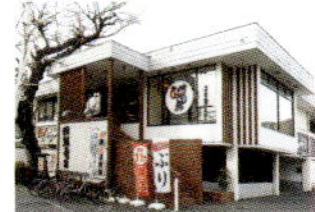

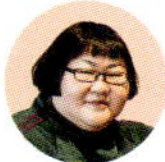

In addition to the sushi, the fried food is top-notch as well. Try rock salt for white-meat fish and squid!

It was a high school classmate who inducted Natsu Ando into the world of kaitenzushi despite her aversion to raw fish. A kaitenzushi-lover and former kaitenzushi part-timer, that classmate went on to become the stylist for Maple Chogokin, and whenever the two get together, sushi always ends up on the agenda. "For me, eating out means kaitenzushi. There's just no other choice," she says. Of course, she loves the sushi at high-end restaurants with no conveyor belts as well. But the reason her feet nevertheless lead her kaitenzushi-wards is because "pretty much anything goes" there. "I'm hooked on squid at the moment, and it often accounts for eight out of ten plates of sushi I have. I'd definitely get strange looks if I did that at a classy place."

The high level of freedom is evident in more than just the sushi. "Don't you ever feel like having fried food when you're having sushi? And then, I get a craving for melon soda. It's also nice to be able to indulge those little vices, too." In Tokyo with its fierce competition between popular restaurants, each one having signature dishes like ***Gatten Sushi***'s "toro-bincho" means that just like Ando, you'll always find a reliable flavor anytime, anywhere. "Some of them even make things that aren't on the menu if I ask." The seasoned vibe of someone who enjoys..... Are you brave enough to give it a try!?

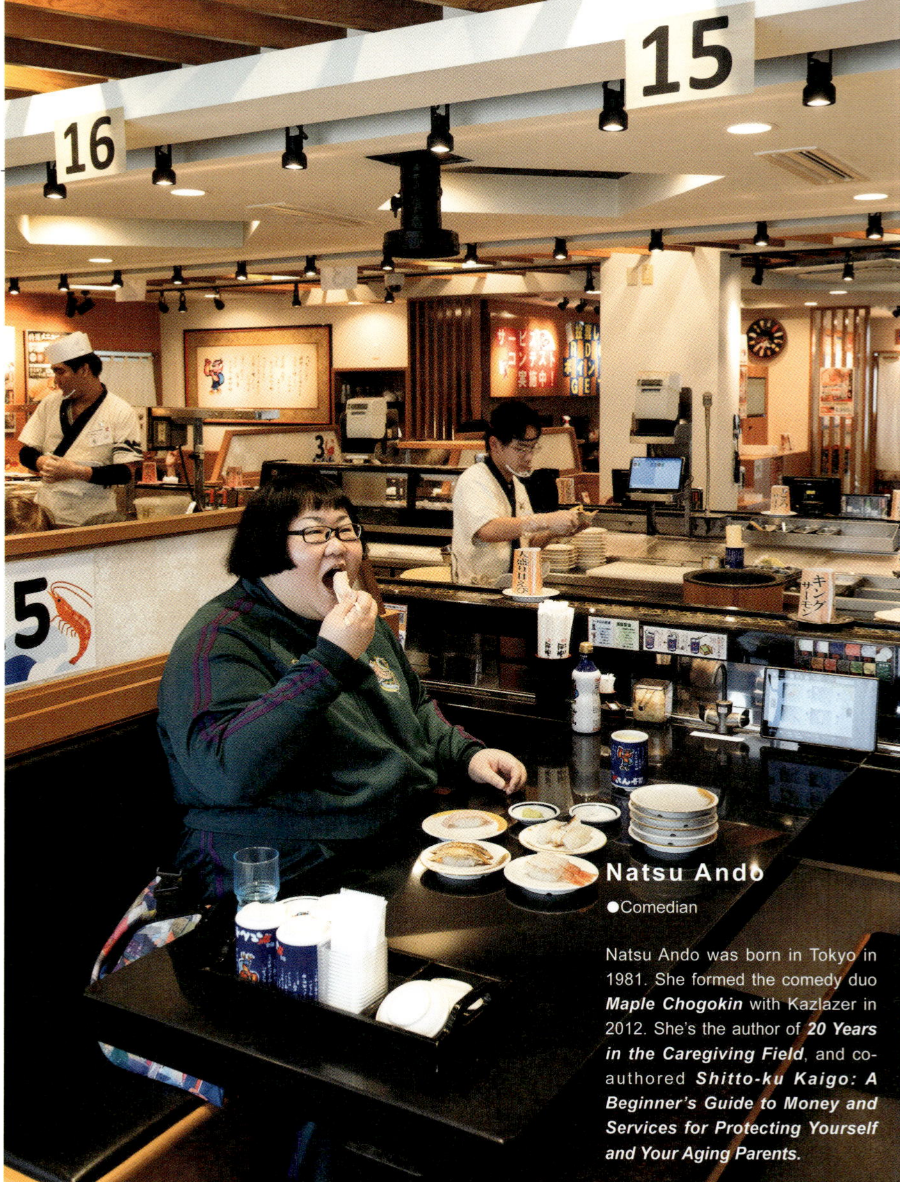

Natsu Ando

●Comedian

Natsu Ando was born in Tokyo in 1981. She formed the comedy duo ***Maple Chogokin*** with Kazlazer in 2012. She's the author of ***20 Years in the Caregiving Field***, and co-authored ***Shitto-ku Kaigo: A Beginner's Guide to Money and Services for Protecting Yourself and Your Aging Parents.***

"I always eat squid, octopus, and shrimp, even ordering them multiple times." Never mind about the proper order and stuff: just go freestyle!

AND MORE...

Sushi Choshimaru, Toyotama-Minami Branch

●Toritsu-Kasei

Starting with Choshi Port featuring in its name, this restaurant sources fresh sushi toppings from all around the world, and serves sushi expertly prepared by skilled chefs. A sushi restaurant in a residential area and with parking spaces to boot, it attracts people who enjoy having sushi in a casual setting. Designed with a "theater" concept, its high entertainment value is its main draw. ●3-29-2 Toyotama-Minami, Nerima City ☎03-5912-5900. 11:00 a.m. to 8:30 p.m. (last orders). No closed days.

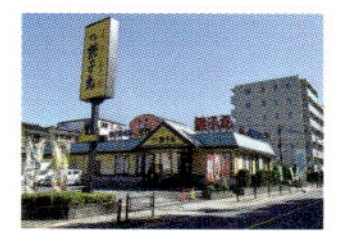

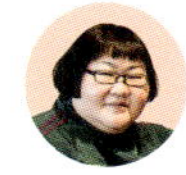

Based on my own research, the sushi toppings are on the large side. The fish head soup is free at lunchtime on weekdays!

Kaitenzushi Misaki, Koenji Pal Shopping Street

●Koenji

Located in the arcade shopping street south of the station. The main feature here is casually enjoying the traditional Edomae sushi "aka-shari rice" that's often served in high-end restaurants. They use red vinegar made from sake lees aged over two years. The signature tuna and seasonal toppings from Toyosu are enhanced by the mellow, vinegary acidity. ●4-25-7 Koenji-Minami, Suginami City ☎03-5305-3920. 11:00 a.m. to 10:00 p.m. (last orders). No closed days.

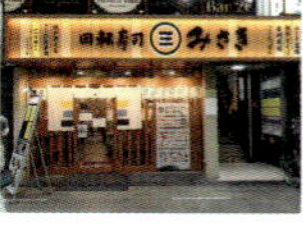

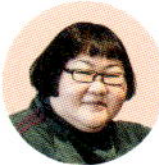

Regular limited-period fairs, like "Oni Neta"—humongous sushi toppings!

Photos: Kazufumi Shimoyashiki Text: Ikuko Hyodo

Delicious Mixed: Warp to South India.

SOUTH INDIAN FOOD

Pour curry, soup, or yogurt over the rice, then mix to produce your favorite flavor. Four South Indian set meals, each with new discoveries!

U-zhaan visits India almost every year, and is well versed in its local cuisine. He once spent several months in Chennai, learning the classical instrument called the kanjira. There, he encountered "meals," a South Indian set meal consisting of rice, curry, sambar (spicy soup), and more, all served on one plate. "South Indian cuisine uses tangy tamarind and coconut for a light finish, so it often has a lighter flavor and texture compared to the rich food of the north. The ingredients are mostly vegetables, yet somehow, you never get tired of eating it every day."

After returning to Japan, he toured Indian restaurants in search of the same culinary experience. There are also restaurants where native chefs faithfully recreate dishes from the old country, like the rice-rich Thanjavur region's cuisine at ***Thanjaimeals*** and the Mangalore fish dishes at ***Bangera's Kitchen***. Run by a Japanese person who got captivated by Tamil Nadu's flavors, ***Nandri*** rivals restaurants in India. "***Srimangalam A/C*** offers flavors so close to what you get in Chennai that it feels like you've warped to India. Tokyo has lots of spots offering 'authentic' South Indian cuisine, so find your favorites, and keep coming back for more."

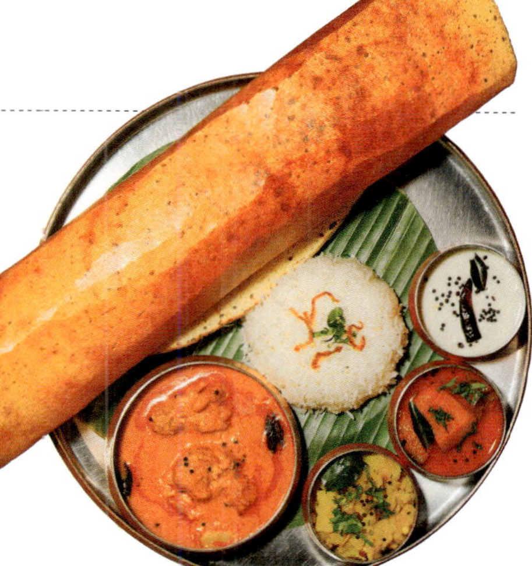

Bangera's Kitchen

●Yurakucho

A restaurant where you get to savor the flavors of Mangalore, a city renowned for its fine cuisine. Features spices that enhance seafood's umami, with a menu ranging from à la carte dishes to full-course meals. Perfect for both casual dining and banquets. Masala dosa thali: ¥1,500. ● 2-2 Ginza-Nishi, Chuo City, Ginza Inz2 2F ☎03-3561-5516. 11:00 a.m. to 11:00 p.m. No closed days.

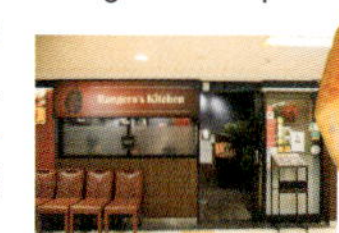

Nandri

●Arakawa-yuenchimae

The name comes from "nandri," which means "thank you" in Tamil. Many of the dishes are vegetable-based, gluten-free, and easy on the stomach. Serves casual, homestyle dishes. Lunch meals: ¥1,300 (¥1,500 on Sat. and holidays). ●7-29-9 Nishi-Ogu, Arakawa City ☎ 03-3800-6494. Check the social media for the opening hours. X: @nandri_tokyo

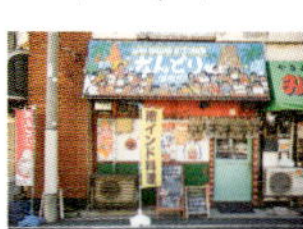

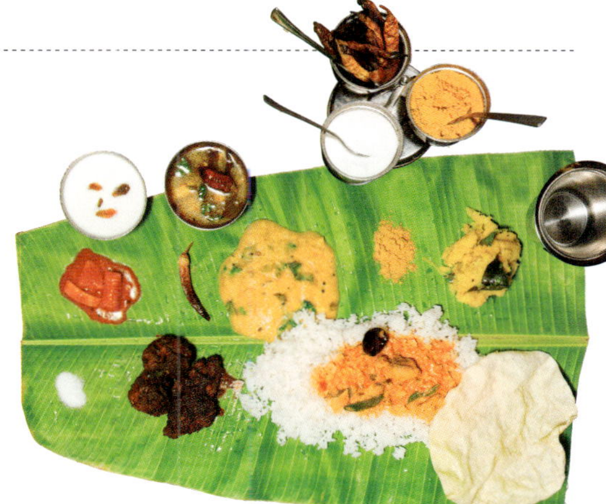

Srimangalam A/C

●Soshigaya-Okura

Serves cuisine from Chettinad, a region that boasts a highly distinctive food culture even in India. The meals served on banana leaves are generously served with unlimited seconds. Renovations in March 2025 doubled the seating capacity from 30 to 60. Non-veg meals: ¥2,000. ●3-33-2 Soshigaya, Setagaya City, Sanko Bldg. B1 ☎03-6676-2812. 11:00 a.m. to 3:00 p.m. and 6:00 p.m. to 10:00 p.m. No closed days.

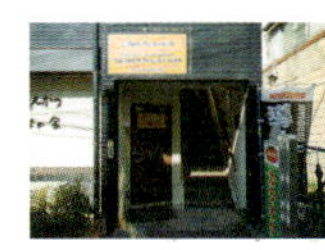

Thanjaimeals

●Hatagaya

Offers meals with simple flavors that recreate the taste of the chef's home region of Thanjavur. You can get seconds of rice, sambar, and rasam once for free. Also offers a wide variety of "tiffin" snacks. Vegetarian meals: ¥1,450. ●2-7-10 Hatagaya, Shibuya City, Matsumoto Bldg. 2F ☎03-5352-8055. 11:00 a.m. to 3:00 p.m. and 6:00 p.m. to 10:00 p.m. No closed days.

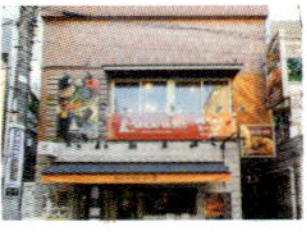

U-zhaan

●Musician

U-zhaan was born in Saitama in 1977. He plays the North Indian percussion instrument called the tabla, and has been traveling to India regularly since he was 20. He supervised the recipe books ***Bengali Food Is Delicious*** and ***I Want to Eat Bengali Food***, which were created with sitar player Tadao Ishihama.

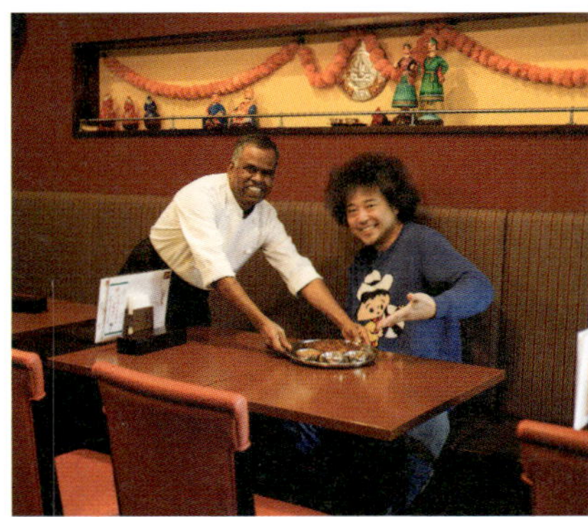

With the head chef (left) at ***Thanjaimeals***.

Photos: Koh Akazawa Text: Sho Kasahara

A Little Slice of Happiness Found in a 38°C Bath and a Bottle of Milk.

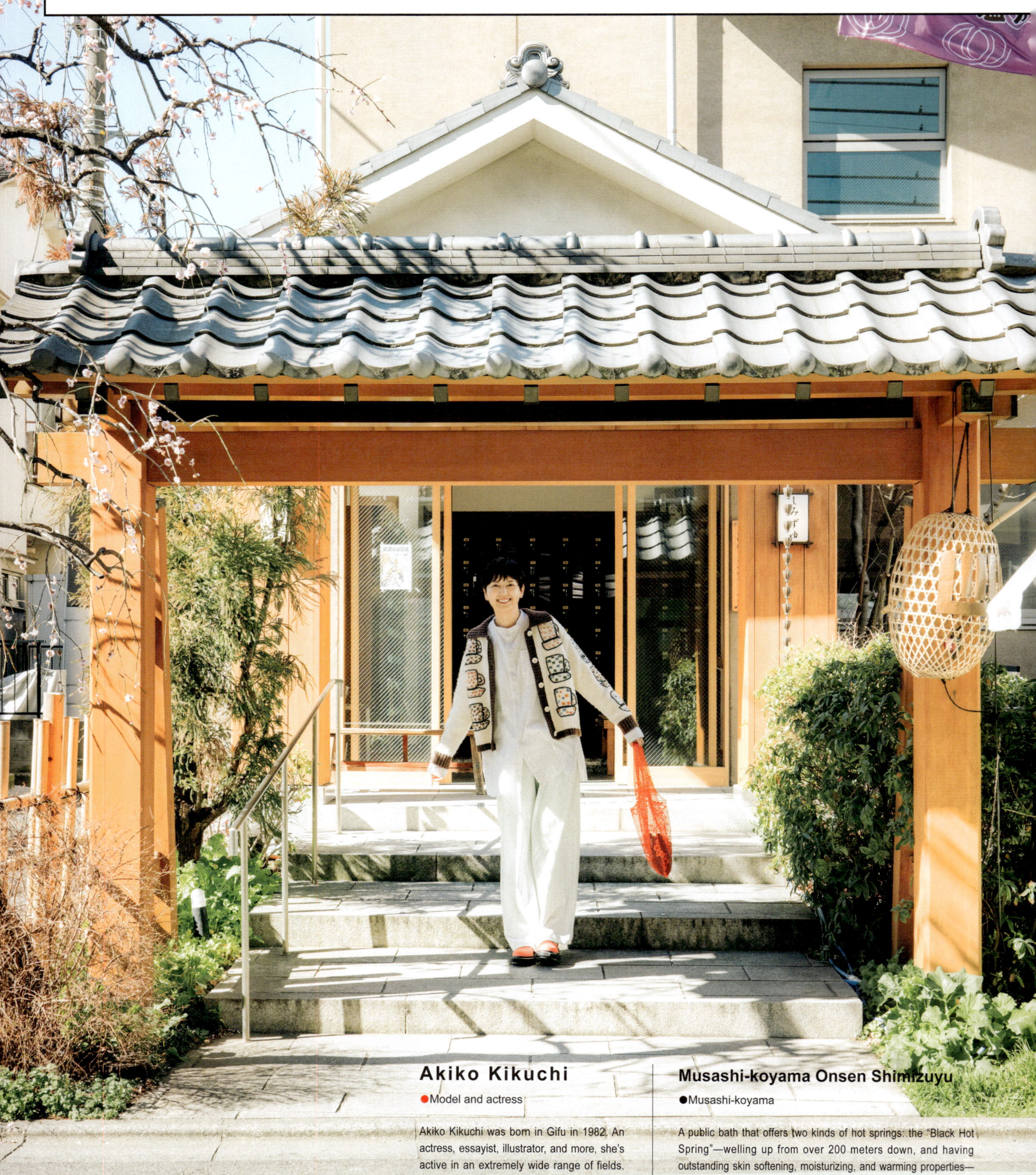

Go check out Musashi-koyama Onsen Shimizuyu—it's just a five-minute walk from Musashi-koyama Station!

Akiko Kikuchi

●Model and actress

Akiko Kikuchi was born in Gifu in 1982. An actress, essayist, illustrator, and more, she's active in an extremely wide range of fields. ***Akiko Kikuchi's "Show Me Your 10 Favorite Clothes!"*** (Fusosha) is in bookstores now. Catch her in the TBS Sunday Drama ***Caster*** when it starts in April.

Musashi-koyama Onsen Shimizuyu

●Musashi-koyama

A public bath that offers two kinds of hot springs: the "Black Hot Spring"—welling up from over 200 meters down, and having outstanding skin softening, moisturizing, and warming properties—and the "Golden Hot Spring"—sourced from even deeper layers, and said to be good for cuts and grazes. ●3-9-1 Koyama, Shinagawa City ☎03-3781-0575. 12:00 p.m. to 12:00 a.m. (from 8:00 a.m. on Sun.). Closed on Mon. (open on holidays).

 Photos: Ayumi Yamamoto Styling: Kaho Yamaguchi Hair & makeup: Misako Nitta Text: Koji Okano

A traditional bathhouse found in the bustling city. Relax in a spacious bath, and let the fatigue of daily life melt away.

A childhood spent in a nature-filled town in Gifu. Akiko Kikuchi grew up with hot springs and public baths nearby, and there were even places to drop in for a bath along the hiking trails nearby, too. So for her, having a soak in hot water every weekend was a family routine. She says she kept up the habit even after moving to Tokyo and starting to live alone, walking or biking to a public bath several times a week.

She says the appeal lies in "stretching out in a spacious bath and soaking in hot water. Gazing at the rising steam while I'm taking a bath makes me feel completely relaxed and free from the hectic pace of Tokyo."

For busy people, she recommends ***Musashi-koyama Onsen Shimizuyu***. "It's close to the city center, and has two hot springs and an outdoor bath for you to enjoy, all for Tokyo's standard public bath fee of just ¥550. The "Golden Hot Spring" rising up from deep underground is a soothing 38°C, so it's perfect for a long soak."

She recommends small trips to public baths around the 23 wards for a quick getaway. ***Jindaiji Natural Hot Spring Yumori no Sato*** "offers 12 baths, including separate and mixed-gender options. It's a day-trip natural hot spring, but the rest area has picture books and pet rabbits. The nostalgic atmosphere means you can have a relax after getting out of the bath, too."

Another spot gaining attention lately is ***Komae-yu***. The interior design makes abundant use of graphic design, and there's a wide selection of drinks and food for after. "It has a café-like, welcoming atmosphere, making it perfect for public bath novices."

1. First, put your shoes in the locker (for which you need a ¥100 coin, which you get back when you leave). 2. Go through the curtain and head to the baths. 3. After your bath, have a nice drink. The recommended choice is a bottle of milk. 4. The second floor also has a relaxing space where you can lie down.

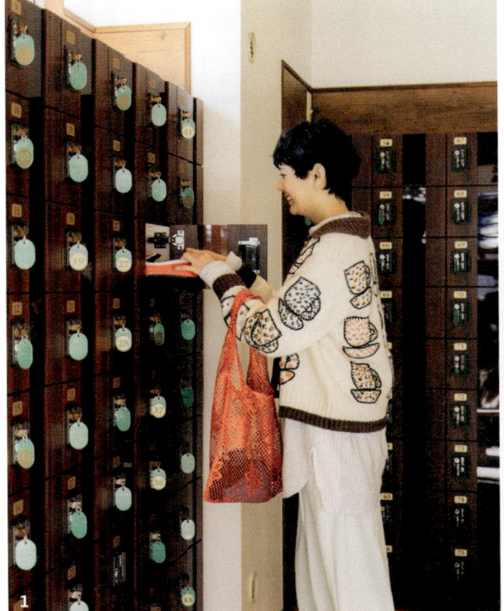

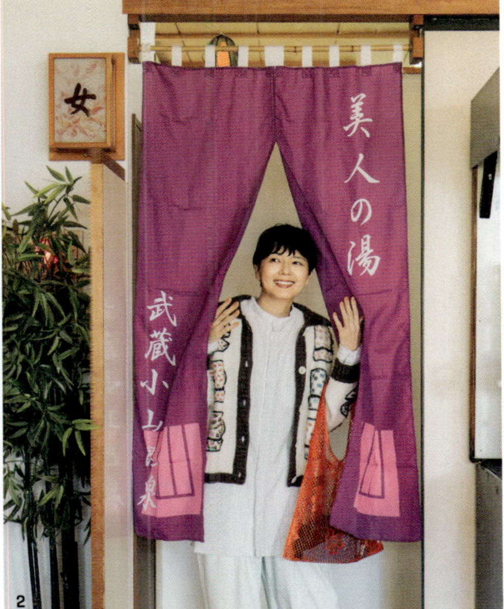

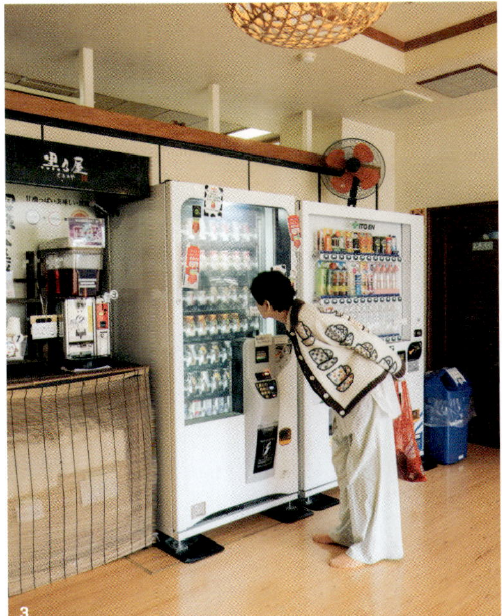

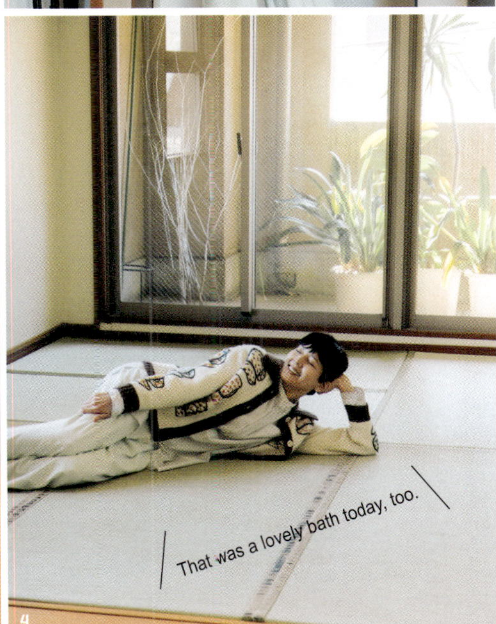

AND MORE...

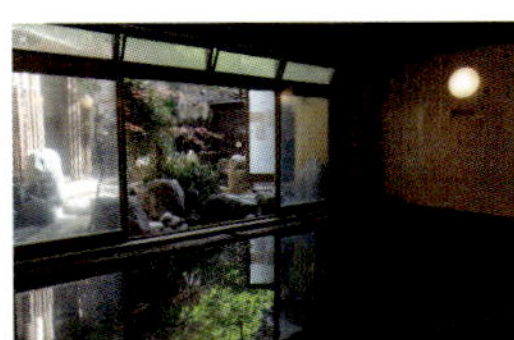

Jindaiji Natural Hot Spring Yumori no Sato

●Chofu

A day-trip hot spring that uses the pure spring water as is. The natural spring water has virtually the same salinity as the human body, making long soaks less taxing. ●2-12-2 Jindaiji -Motomachi, Chofu City ☎042-499-7777. 10:00 a.m. to 10:00 p.m. No closed days. (Occasionally closed for maintenance.)

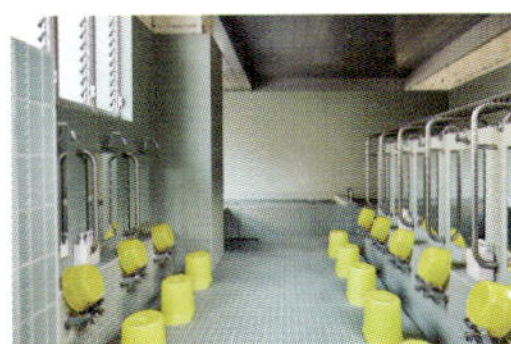

Komae-yu

●Komae

Renovated and reopened in 2023. Has hot baths, carbonated springs, and cold baths, and a Finnish sauna, too. The on-site café bar's menu includes soft drinks, craft beer, and Taiwan-style lu rou fan. ●1-12-6 Higashi-Izumi, Komae City, Hasegawa Bldg. 1F ☎03-3489-3881. 1:00 p.m. to 11:00 p.m. Closed on Tue.

Cardigan ¥100,100 (Sea New York / Brand News ☎03-6421-0870), shirt ¥55,000 (HANNOH WESSEL / Journal Standard Luxe OMOTESANDO ☎03-6418-0900), pants ¥29,700 (Graphpaper / Graphpaper Tokyo ☎03-6381-6171), bag ¥2,750 (Tuuli / Bow Inc. ☎070-9199-0913), shoes ¥78,100 (Adieu / Bow Inc.). The socks are the stylist's own.

Quality Souvenirs For Your Travels.

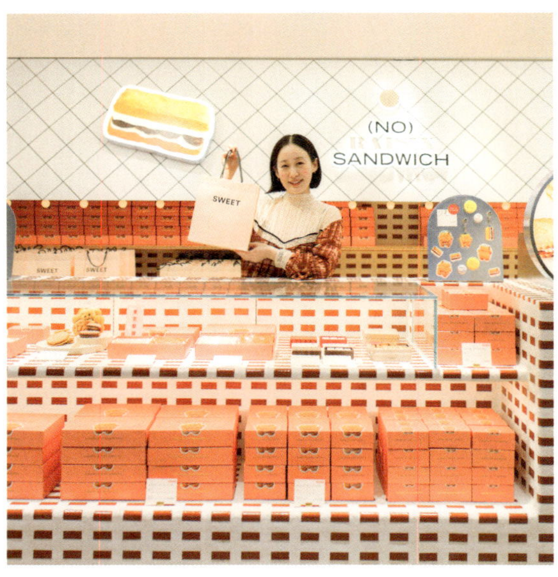

Caramel Butter Sandwich

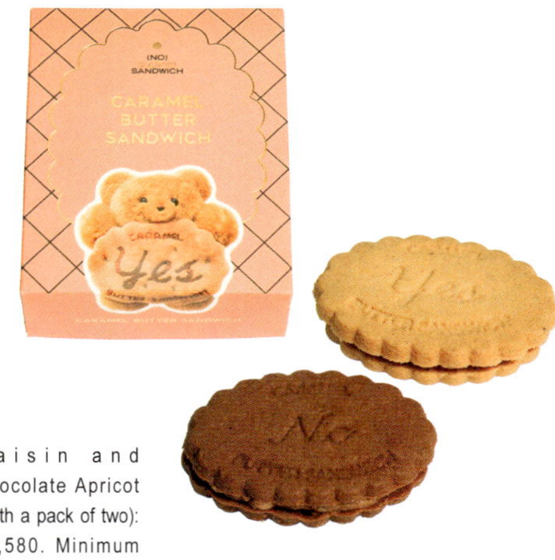

Raisin and Chocolate Apricot (both a pack of two): ¥1,580. Minimum purchase: two packs.

(NO) RAISIN SANDWICH GRANSTA TOKYO

●Marunouchi

The confectionery brand launched in 2018 with the concept of "raisin and other sandwich sweets" has opened its first permanent store. It offers raisin, seasonal fruit, and Tokyo Station-exclusive caramel butter sandwiches that are okay to stroll around with at room temperature. ●1-9-1 Marunouchi, Chiyoda City, GRANSTA TOKYO 1F, atrium area in JR Tokyo Station ☎ 03-6206-3615. 8:00 a.m. to 10:00 p.m. (to 9:00 p.m. on Sun. and holidays). No closed days.

A new era of station & airport sweets! With more and more independent players entering the game as well, there's a huge range of seasonal sweets that make perfect on-the-go snacks, too.

Sakiko Hirano

●Essayist and food director

Born in 1991, Sakiko Hirano is the representative of ***(NO) RAISIN SANDWICH***. She's been keeping a food diary since she was in elementary school, and has numerous article series and writing contributions to her name. Recently authored books include ***Delicious, Thanks: Flavor Commentary Tracks*** and For ***Shortcakes, Start with the Back.***

Sakiko Hirano leads the confectionery shop ***(NO) RAISIN SANDWICH***. Here, she tells us about the sweets at Tokyo gateways like GRANSTA TOKYO and Haneda Airport's "HANEDA STAR & LUXE." "The big stage for confectionery shops, Tokyo Station, is now home to a ***(NO) RAISIN SANDWICH*** store! The exclusive caramel butter sandwich features soft caramel and buttercream between sablé cookies. At Haneda Airport, try the palm-flavored white warabi mochi from ***Kagurazaka Ishikawa***. Digging through the snow-like coconut powder reveals warabi mochi infused with coconut milk—an otherworldly treat. Using fat-free milk to delicious effect, 'Butter no Itoko' has a trusted flavor overseen by pastry chef Yuichi Goto. The akasand cookie tin features just one type of cookie, making it charmingly simple. Glistening crimson strawberry jam and buttery cookies, sprinkled with wasanbon sugar. I don't think there's any way anyone could fail to like this flavor. Four items that are perfect for souvenirs or for snacks on the Shinkansen or plane."

Palm-flavored white warabi mochi

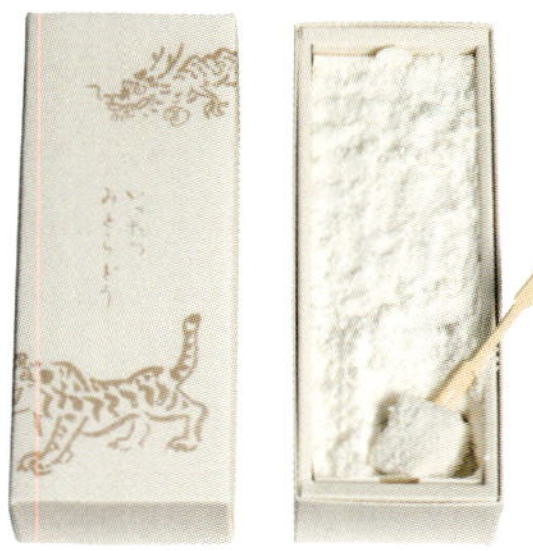

Ittatsu Mitora Do, Haneda Airport Store

●Haneda Airport

Coconut-flavored warabi mochi crafted by Michelin three-star restaurants ***Kagurazaka Ishikawa*** and ***Kohaku***, using their mastery of paste foods. Also sold at the Imperial Hotel Tokyo Gargantua and via the official website. ¥3,888 for 330 g. ●3-3-2 Haneda Airport, Ota City, Haneda Airport Terminal 1 2F, inside the market place HANEDA STAR & LUXE ☎Not disclosed. 6:00 a.m. to 8:00 p.m. No closed days.

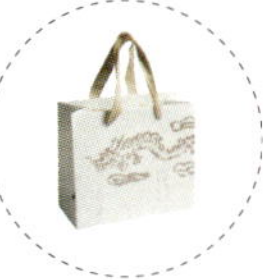

Butter no Itoko

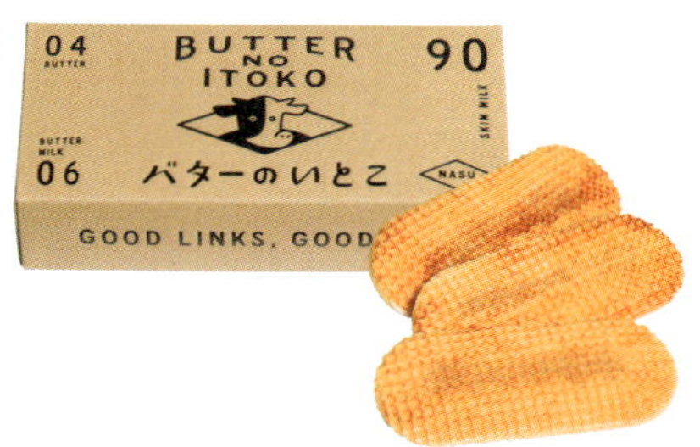

GOOD NEWS TOKYO, ecute Shinagawa Store

●Shinagawa

A confectionery designed to cut down on food waste by adding new value to fat-free milk that's a byproduct of making butter. Special fat-free milk jam sandwiched between buttery gaufrettes—a delightful texture. At nine locations in Tokyo (stations, airports, department stores, etc.). Box of three: ¥972. ●3-26-27 Takanawa, Minato City, inside the ticket gates at JR Shinagawa Station ☎03-5424-6200. 10:00 a.m. to 8:00 p.m. No closed days.

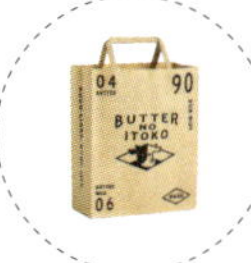

akasand cookie tin

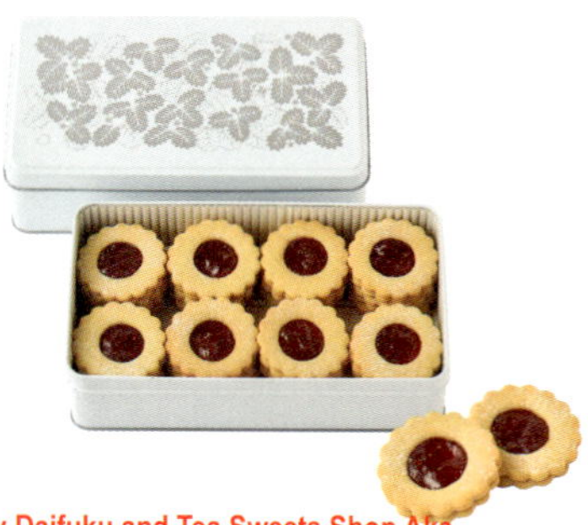

Strawberry Daifuku and Tea Sweets Shop Aka, Shibuya Hikarie ShinQs Store

●Shibuya

Fresh Nyoho strawberry jam from Kagawa, sandwiched between cookies with soft wasanbon sugar from Tokushima. These handmade, additive-free treats made with carefully selected ingredients are also sold online. Box of 24: ¥4,800. ●2-21-1 Shibuya, Shibuya City, Shibuya Hikarie ShinQs B2, Toyoko Norengai Sweets ☎03-6427-3715. 11:00 a.m. to 9:00 p.m. (to 8:00 p.m. on Sun. and holidays). No closed days.

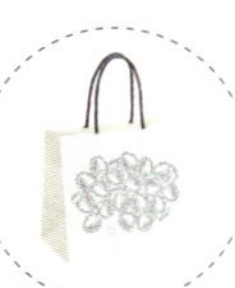

Photos: Koh Akazawa, Hikari Koki Text: Hikari Torisawa

Classic Cream and Strawberry Treats You'll Crave.

SHORTCAKES

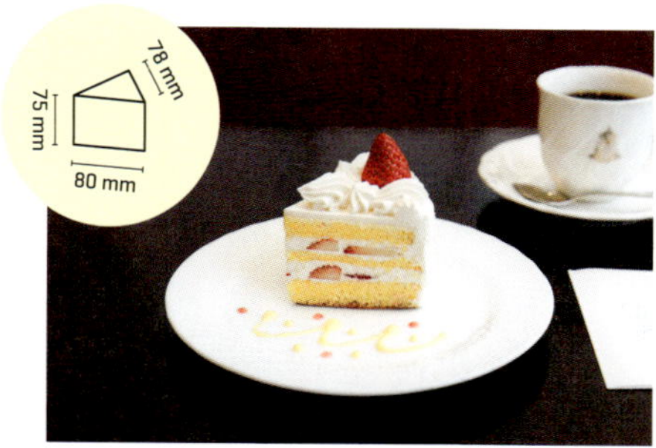

Colombin Harajuku Salon ●Meiji-jingumae

Closed temporarily for the Shibuya redevelopment, and reopened in 2024 (its centenary). Lunch and afternoon tea in the retro interior too. The sponge cake with 1:1 eggs and yolks is fluffy like castella. ¥605. ●6-34-14 Jingumae, Shibuya City, Harajuku Omotesando Bldg. 1F ☎03-6450-5175. 10:00 a.m. to 9:00 p.m. (to 8:00 p.m. on Sun. and holidays). No closed days.

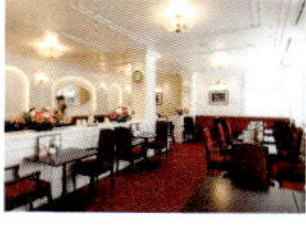

Gazing softly at her cake in the classically styled interior of ***Colombin Harajuku Salon***.

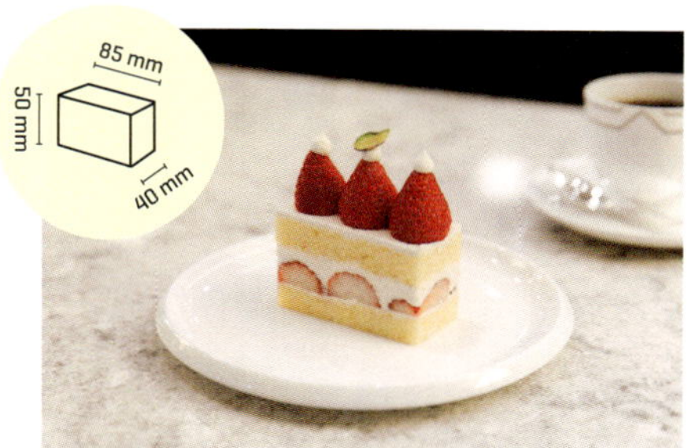

Gargantua ●Hibiya

Opened in 1971 as a pioneering hotel shop in the Imperial Hotel. The lineup includes sweets, deli food, and more. The cake infused with Maraschino cherry liqueur is a hit with older folks too. ¥1,350. ●1-1-1 Uchisaiwaicho, Chiyoda City, Main Bldg. 1F ☎03-3539-8086. 8:00 a.m. to 8:00 p.m. (The pastry, bakery, and deli wares are available from 11:00 a.m. to 7:00 p.m.). No closed days.

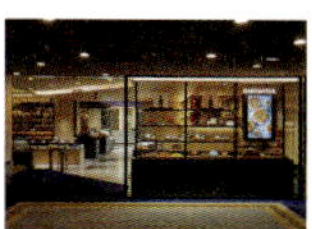

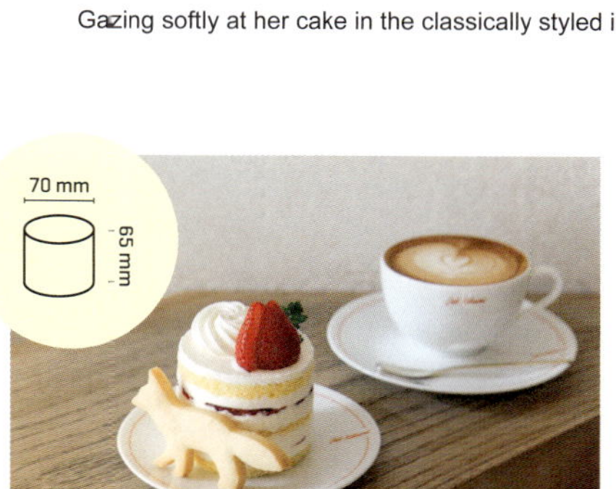

Café Kitsuné Aoyama ●Omotesando

A café produced by the lifestyle brand ***Maison Kitsuné***. The interior is a Japanese-style space that gives a respectful nod to traditional architecture. The classic choice is to have the milky cake made with condensed milk together with the separately sold fox-shaped cookie (¥400). ¥900. ●3-15-9 Minami-Aoyama, Minato City ☎03-5786-4842. 9:00 a.m. to 8:00 p.m. Irregular closed days.

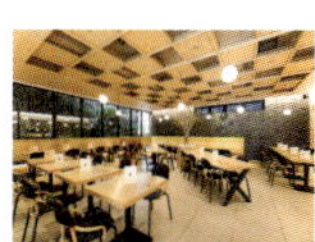

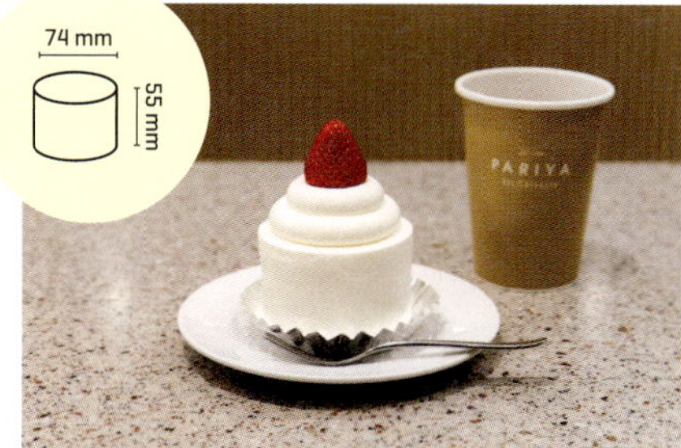

PARIYA DELICATESSEN ●Roppongi

Founded in Aoyama in 1996. Has six stores in Tokyo, each purveying deli food, sweets, and more. Eating-in comes with unlimited-refill self-service drinks. The signature cake features a finely mixed sponge with a smooth, melt-in-the-mouth texture. ¥1,058. ●9-7-3 Akasaka, Minato City, Tokyo Midtown Galleria B1 ☎03-6434-7671. 11:00 a.m. to 9:00 p.m. No closed days.

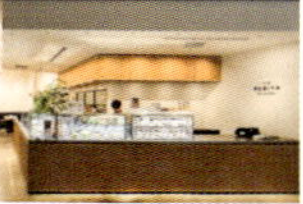

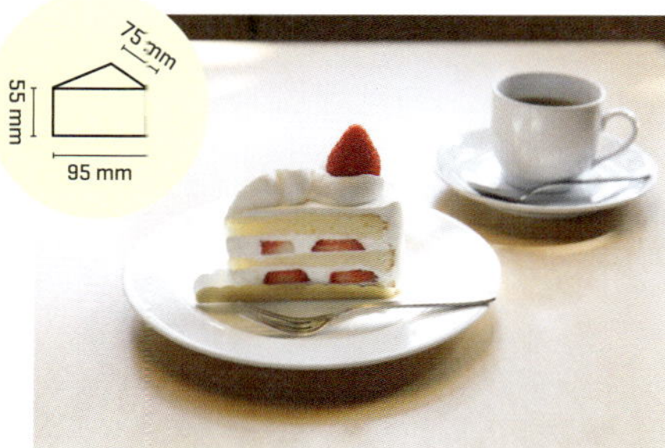

Fujiya Restaurant, Nishi-Eifuku Store ●Nishi-eifuku

A restaurant that's been much loved by three generations since 1979. Frequented by many locals, who come in groups ranging from a couple of friends to the whole family. The premium shortcake with Chantilly cream and tangy strawberries is a Fujiya long-seller. ¥594. ●4-19-15, Eifuku, Suginami City ☎03-3317-0051. 10:00 a.m. to 9:00 p.m. No closed days.

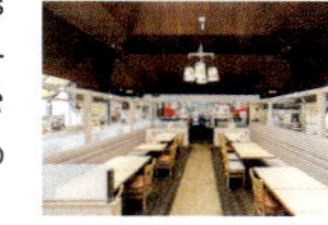

Minori Kai tours around confectionery shops all over Japan, and calls shortcakes "idols." Here are five special spots you'll want to head to, no matter the occasion.

Minori Kai

●Writer

Minori Kai was born in Shizuoka in 1976. Her writings cover travel, souvenirs, architecture, daily life, and more. Her books include ***Walking and Eating: A Guide to Tokyo's Delicious Landmarks*** (X-Knowledge) and ***Maiden's Guide to Tokyo*** (Sayusha).

"It's so cute!" exclaims Kai as her cake arrives. "Shortcakes really are cute, aren't they? I bet everyone longed to have them when they were children." These cakes with strawberries atop white cream come in a wide variety of styles. "***Colombin*** and ***Fujiya*** have classic triangular shortcakes, while ***Café Kitsuné Aoyama*** adds condensed milk for a fresh twist. ***Gargantua***'s and ***PARIYA***'s have charming shapes, too." Insatiable when it comes to her favorites, Kai spends her days off strolling from café to café, taking in several in a session. "What's there today might not be tomorrow. That's why I pay shops a visit as soon as they catch my eye. If I 'like' something when I'm on a walk, I often take it home and have it as a 'morning snack' the next day, too. I don't just want people who live in Tokyo to have these cakes: I want folks here on a trip to have them in their hotel room, too. Having a treat that brings you a bit of joy every morning lets you start the day in a good mood."

Photos: Kenya Abe Text: Mutsumi Okazaki

Note: The sizes shown are for the base only.

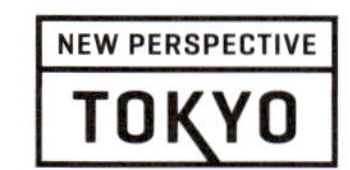

The Landscape Is the Biggest Criterion When Choosing a Hotel.

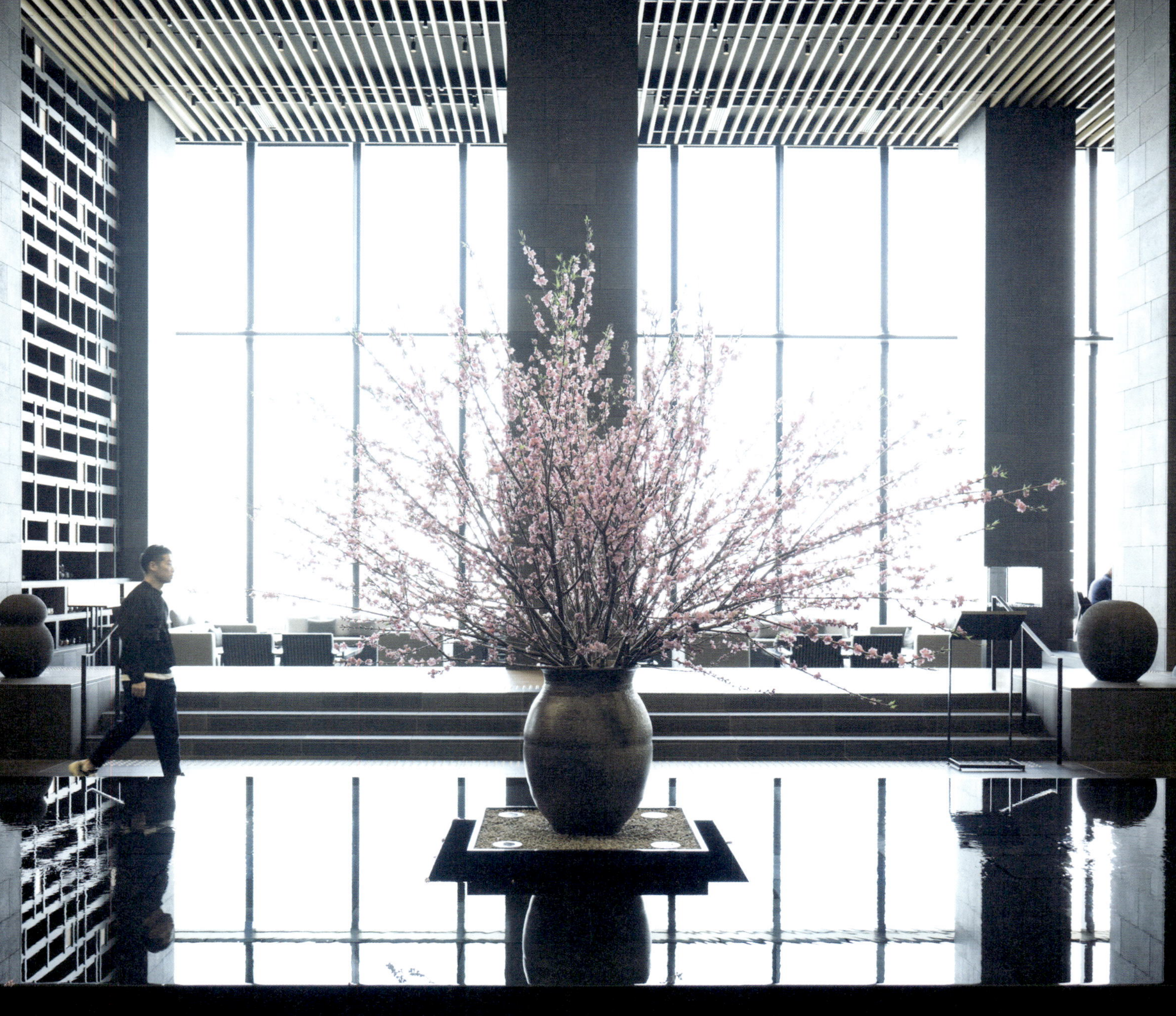

New hotels are opening up one after another in Tokyo. With so many features and services, how to choose? Here's a new criterion revealed by an architect.

"I always remember that while I can create buildings, I can't create landscapes. What truly impresses people when they enter a building is the scenery. When choosing a hotel in Tokyo, my criterion is how the location is presented," says architect Makoto Tanijiri. An example he gave was ***Aman Tokyo*** in Otemachi. Located on the 33rd floor, the lobby has a 30-meter-high ceiling and stunning views through large windows. The glass windows offer a panoramic view of Meiji Jingu Gaien and the Shinjuku Subcenter skyscrapers. He also loves the swimming pool here. One of the two 8-meter-tall windows offers views of Gaien's forest, skyscrapers and Mount Fuji, while the other overlooks Tokyo Bay. The same goes for the guest rooms. All of these are over 71 m^2, and the bedroom design gives you an unobstructed outside view when you wake up. "It's a right-brain emotion, with no need for logical analysis by the left brain. I design building interiors to be darkish so as to enhance the beauty of the landscape."

Bvlgari Hotel Tokyo in Yaesu and ***JANU TOKYO*** in Azabudai have a similar appeal. Besides the view from the hotel, how it blends into the city is important. ***K5*** in Nihombashi Kabutocho preserves the city's memory through its renovated bank, while ***TRUNK (HOTEL) YOYOGI PARK*** maximizes the effect of its green surroundings. What truly moves people is the unexpected scenery that unfolds before them.

Makoto Tanijiri

Architect

Makoto Tanijiri is a cofounder of ***SUPPOSE DESIGN OFFICE***. In recent years, he's been expanding beyond architecture and bridging business and design in a wide range of fields, examples being ***tecture***, ***DAICHI***, ***yado***, and ***Mietell***.

 Photos: Atsushi Kondo Text: Fumio Ogawa

Aman Tokyo

●Otemachi

While ***Aman*** has become renowned for blending seamlessly with nature, ***Aman Tokyo*** inspires in you a sense that the whole world—including the city—is a form of nature. Opened in 2014. ●1-5-6 Otemachi, Chiyoda City, Otemachi Tower ☎03-5224-3333. From ¥278,700 for two people per night.

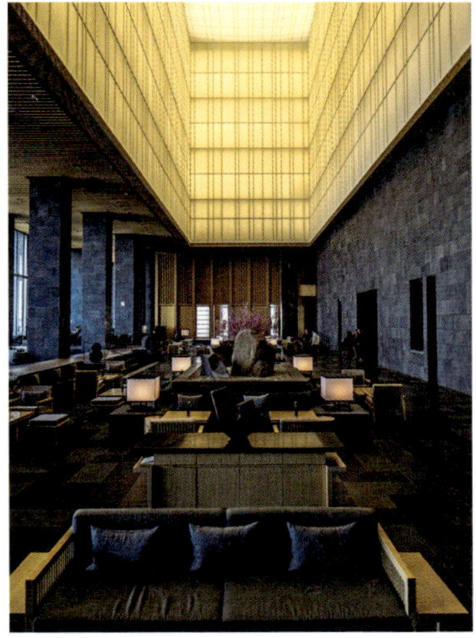

The impressive design's high ceilings and views from large windows give a wonderful sense of height, depth, and space.

← The 33rd floor has a bar lounge with a dining service and a view that changes from morning to night.

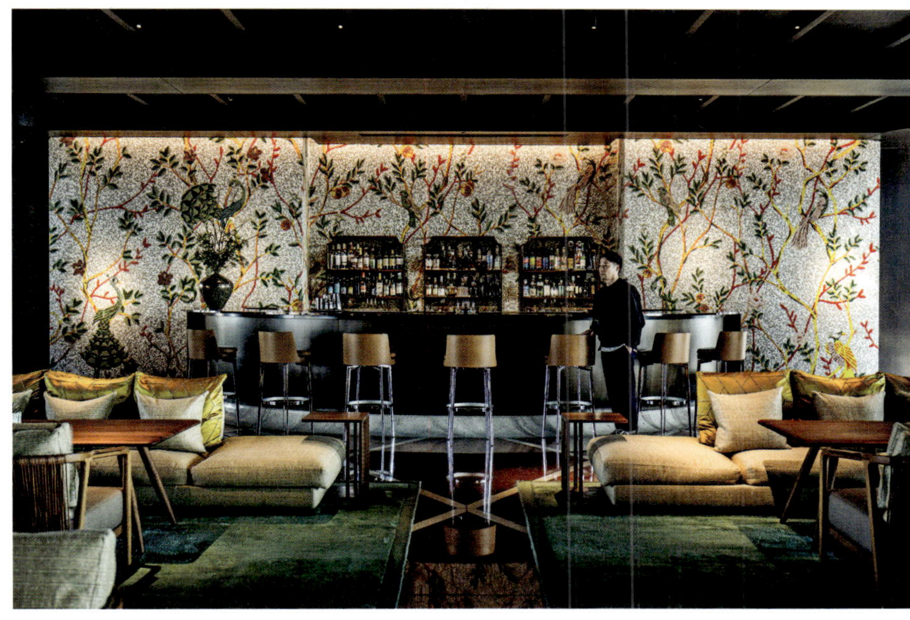

Bvlgari Hotel Tokyo

●Yaesu

Opened in April 2023 as the first hotel in Japan run by Bvlgari Hotels & Resorts. Excelling in design, space, and service, and one of the restaurants has earned a Michelin star for two years in a row. The glass-tile wall behind the bar counter on the 45th floor is a must-see. There's also a fantastic view of Tokyo from the vast terrace. ●2-2-1 Yaesu, Chuo City, Tokyo Midtown Yaesu, 40-45F ☎ 03-6262-3333. From ¥250,000 per room per night.

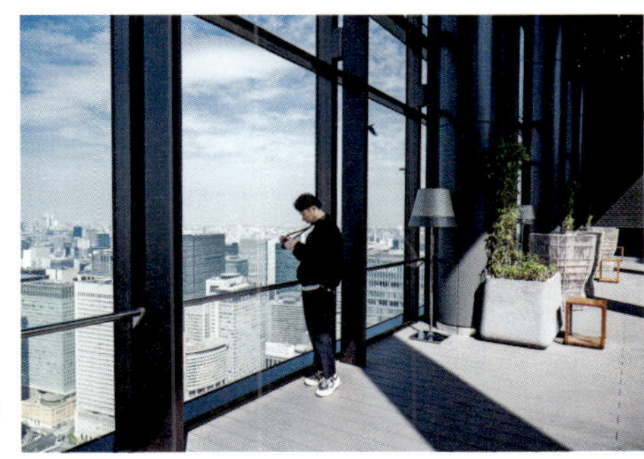

Tanijiri-san capturing the view with his Leica from the ***Bvlgari Bar*** terrace on the 45th floor.

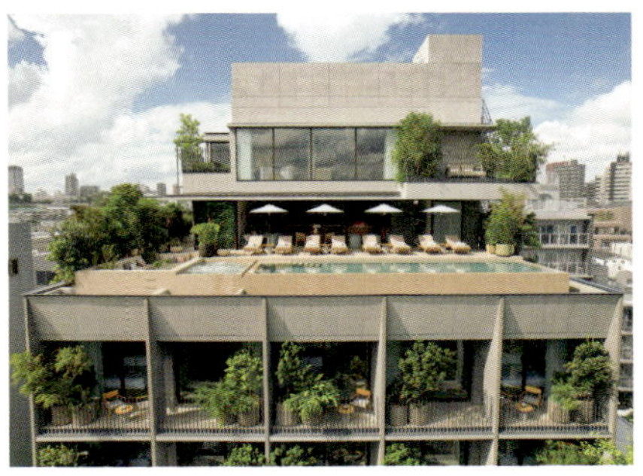

TRUNK (HOTEL) YOYOGI PARK

●Yoyogi-koen

Lying adjacent to Yoyogi Park, this hotel embodies balance between city life and nature. The exterior wall has a traditional Japanese wash finish, while the interior blends in Nordic modern elements. The top floor includes a heated infinity pool and jacuzzi for staying guests, offering a rich experience and seasonal views. Opened in September 2023. ● 1-15-2 Tomigaya, Shibuya City ☎03-5454-3210. From ¥79,800 per room.

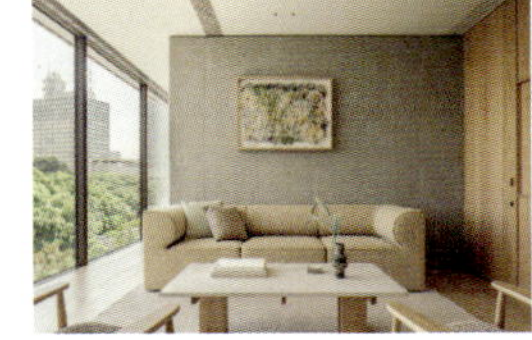

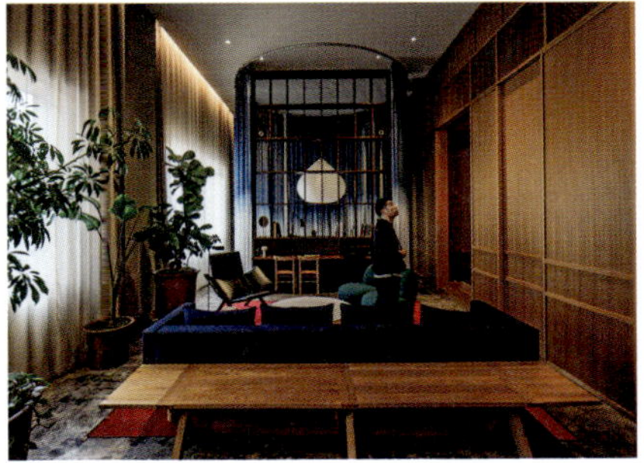

K5

●Kayabacho

Kabutocho has been a financial hub ever since Japan's oldest bank was founded by Eiichi Shibusawa. A bank annex built in 1923 has been renovated by a Swedish architectural unit. Unique features include the high-ceilinged "K5 SUITE." Recline on the quality bed, and your thoughts will naturally turn to Tokyo's history. ● 3-5 Nihombashi-Kabutocho, Chuo City ☎03-5962-3485. From ¥45,000 for two people per night.

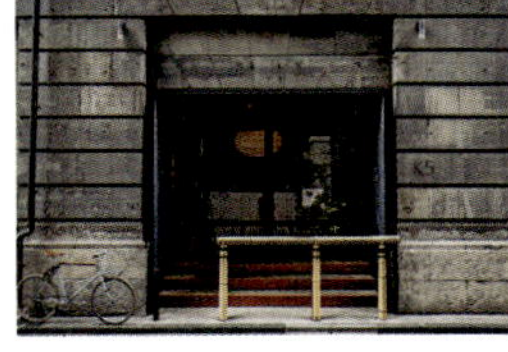

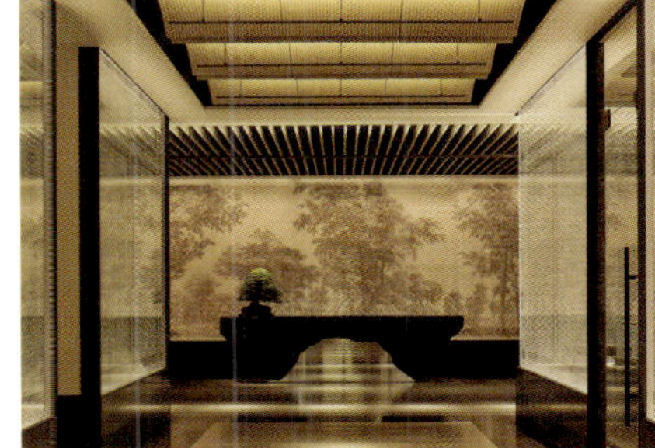

JANU TOKYO

●Azabudai

This hotel was established in 2024 as the first hotel of the ***JANU*** brand. The room design by Belgian designer J-M Gathy's blends traditional Japanese and European elements. It also offers an energetic and dynamic atmosphere—something different from the tranquility of sister brand ***Aman***. ● 1-2-2 Azabudai, Minato City ☎03-6731-2333. From ¥164,850 for two people per night (with breakfast).

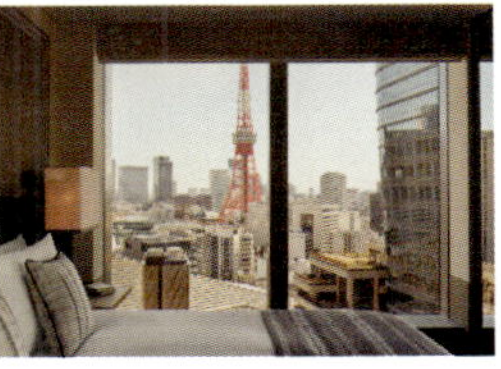

The "Dough" Is the Key to Mexico's National Dish.

Though called simply "tacos," their styles vary widely, from traditional Mexican ones to innovative creations. A new trend in Tokyo tacos.

Koichiro Yoshikawa

●Taco navigator

Koichiro Yoshikawa was born in Tokyo in 1979. He runs ***Tacos Mercado*** and ***Tortilla Mill*** in Kodaira. As a taco navigator and tortilla expert, he also promotes Mexican cuisine.

"The key to deliciousness is, above all, the 'shell'—the tortilla," says Koichiro Yoshikawa, who's sampled countless tacos. "In the past, Americanized wheat tortillas were common in Japan. But recently, places like ***TACOSUAVE*** and ***KITADE TACOS*** have embraced the traditional Mexican method of "nixtamalization"—boiling corn in lime water—so now, we can enjoy the authentic flavors. It takes effort, but creates a fragrant aroma and moist texture." The arrival of the tortilla specialty store ***NEW CLASSIC TORTILLA CLUB***—a rarity in Japan at the time—also symbolizes this movement. With Japanese- and Chinese-inspired spots like ***FUKUMEN*** and ***Tokyo Tacos ChaChaCha*** and Okinawan-style ones like ***TACOS BEAM***, the variety is expanding. "In fact, tacos are very flexible. No limits on the ingredients or methods means individuality can really shine through. I want lots of people to discover how fun they are."

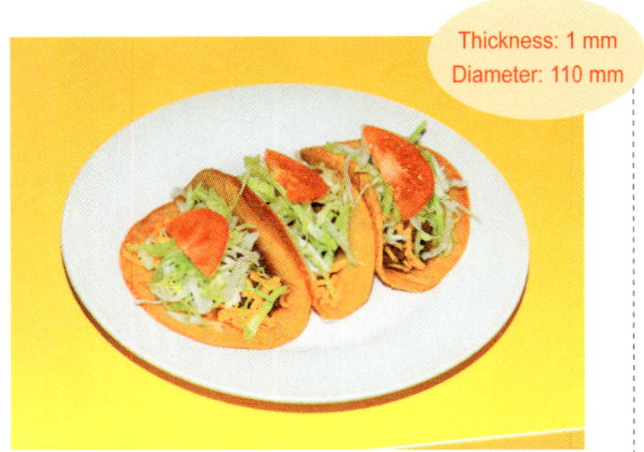

Thickness: 1 mm
Diameter: 110 mm

TACOS BEAM

●Kami-itabashi

Authentic Okinawan tacos loved by locals, now in Itabashi. Packed with 100% beef, plus lettuce, and plenty of tomatoes. Made from a corn and flour mix, the homemade shell is crispy yet soft, so it goes down easy. Have it with spicy red salsa and refreshing yogurt sauce. ¥770 for three. ●3-21-15 Sakuragawa, Itabashi City ☎03-6906-5794. 11:00 a.m. to 8:30 p.m. No closed days.

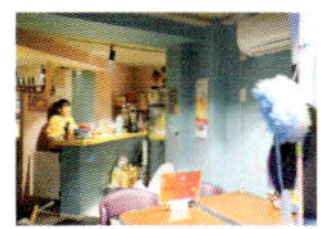

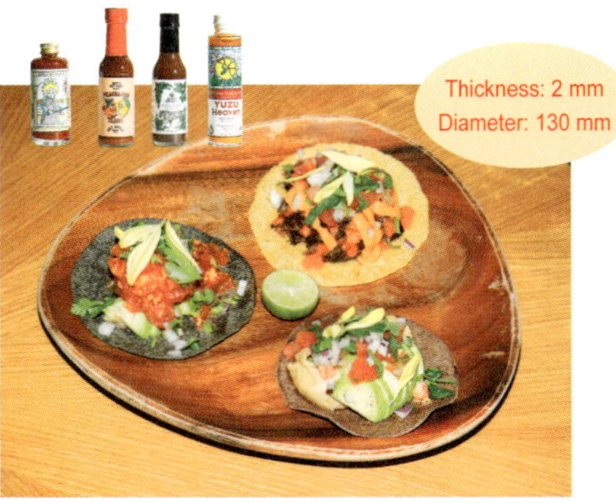

Thickness: 2 mm
Diameter: 130 mm

Tokyo Tacos ChaChaCha

●Hiro-o

Using ingredients like shrimp in chili sauce and baby octopus—creative thinking befitting a former Italian chef. Soft, moist tortillas, seasoned with olive oil and salt, and hand-pressed one by one. Customize your tacos with hot sauces from all around the world. From ¥550 each. ●2-8-1 Moto-Azabu, Minato City ☎070-1734-9165. 11:00 a.m. to 10:00 p.m. Closed on Tue.

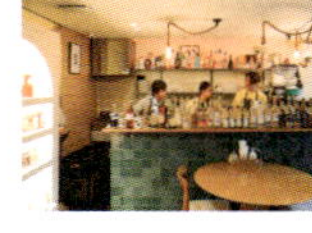

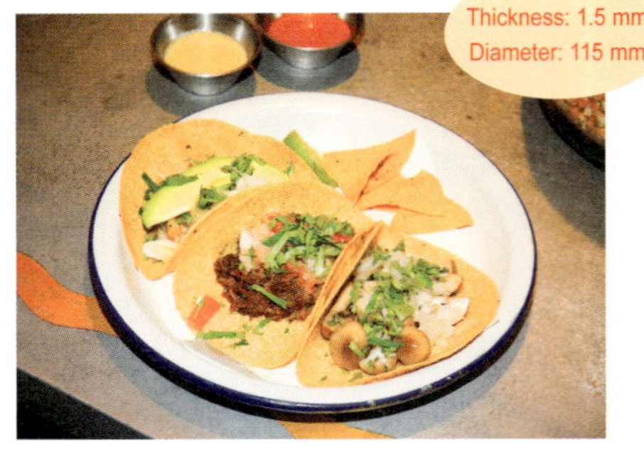

Thickness: 1.5 mm
Diameter: 115 mm

Kitade Tacos COMMISSARY

●Nihombashi

Made every day in the shop-factory in Nihombashi with 100% Hokkaido corn. Always freshly ground tortillas. Currently seven locations in Tokyo (Tokyo Station, Shimokitazawa, Gotanda, etc.). Great for taco beginners. Three classic tacos: ¥1,480. ●3-11-5 Nihombashi-Honcho, Chuo City, Life Science Bldg. 2 1F ☎03-3527-3277. 11:00 a.m. to 9:00 p.m. (last orders). No closed days.

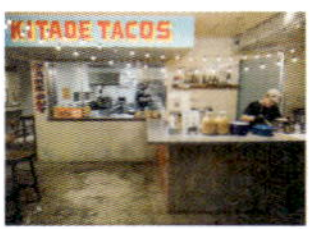

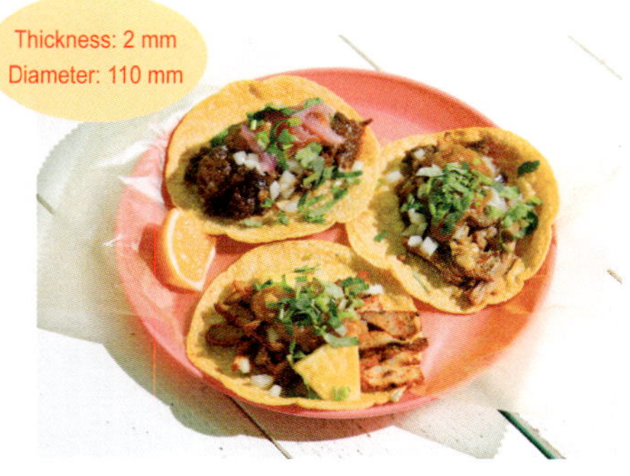

Thickness: 2 mm
Diameter: 110 mm

TACOSUAVE

●Hachioji

Tortillas made from the native Hokkaido variety "Hachiretsu corn," offering an authentic taste of Mexico. They mainly use organic ingredients, including pasture-raised pork and local Hachioji vegetables. The aim is to serve dishes that are safe for all ages to enjoy. Set of three: from ¥1,280. ●12-14 Honcho, Hachioji City ☎042-649-7686. 4:00 p.m. to 9:00 p.m. Closed on Mon. and Tue.

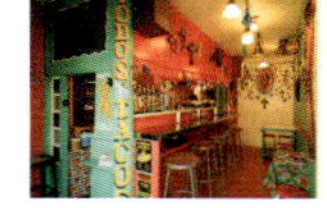

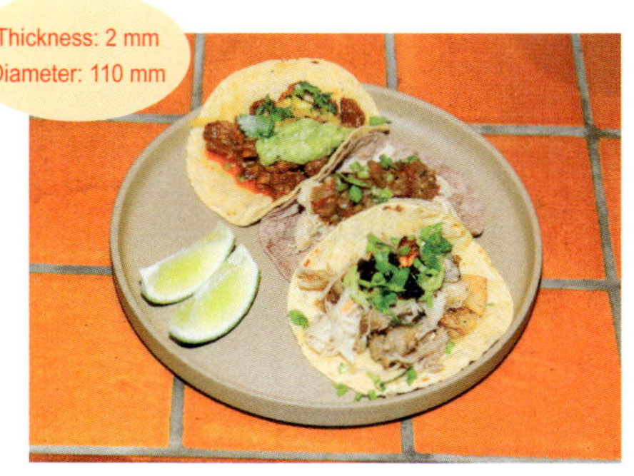

Thickness: 2 mm
Diameter: 110 mm

NEW CLASSIC TORTILLA CLUB

●Yoyogi-Uehara

A shop specializing in corn tortillas, Mexico's staple food. The main feature is selling "masa" dough by weight. Rare tortilla dishes like sopes, tostadas, and tetelas are also available. Crowdfunding to build a new factory is underway, too. From ¥1,100 for two. ●1-32-3 Uehara, Shibuya City, CABO uehara 1F ☎03-6804-9712. 11:00 a.m. to 6:00 p.m. Closed on Mon. and Tue.(unless they're holidays).

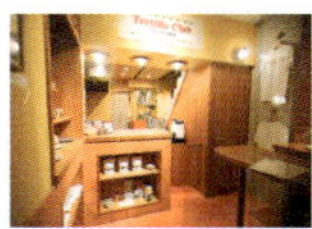

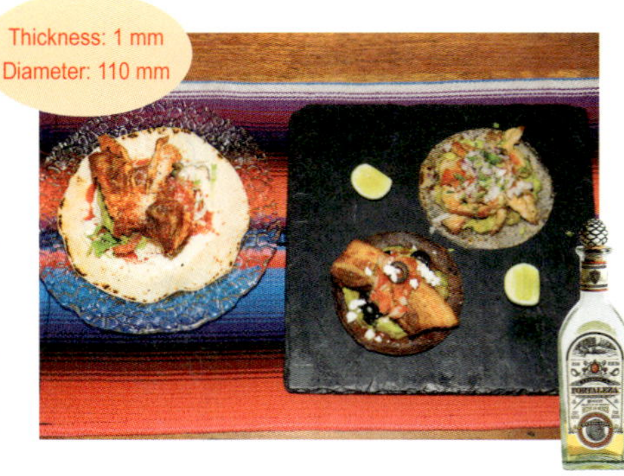

Thickness: 1 mm
Diameter: 110 mm

FUKUMEN

●Asakusa

Owner went to Mexico for its wrestlers. A tequila bar with many tacos, from authentic Mexican to creative. Tortillas are corn or flour to suit the dish. Unique fillings like "wasabi chicken neck" and "crab tempura." From ¥500 each. ●2-14-13 Asakusa, Taito City, 1F ☎03-4361-0440. 5 p.m. to 11:00 p.m. (from 1:00 p.m. on Sat., and from 1:00 p.m. to 9:00 p.m. on Sun. and holidays). Closed on Tue.

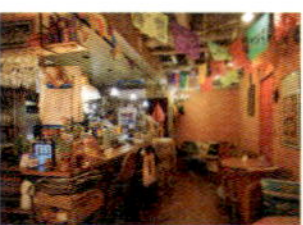

Photos: Koh Akazawa Illustrations: Yoshifumi Takeda (p. 18, 19, 20, 21, 24, 25, 26, and 27) Text: Sho Kasahara

Meat, Cuts, and Sauces Pros Admire.

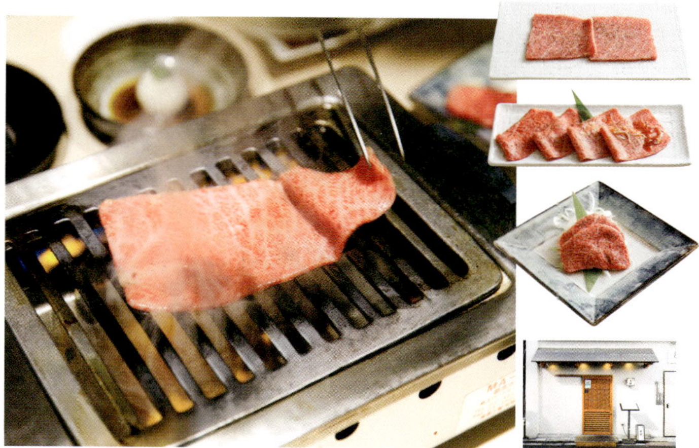

Asakusa Yakiniku Kimura

●Asakusa

Uses only female Kuroge Wagyu beef, for lean cuts with fine marbling, sweetness, and a rich aroma. Based on availability and preference, "Kimura's Lean Meat Assortment" (¥3,480) combines two slices each of four cuts—e.g., sirloin cap and chuck flap. Fresh, premium offal like beef tongue and skirt steak, direct from Shibaura. ●2-13-13 Asakusa, Taito City, 1F ☎03-5830-6676. 5:00 p.m. to 11:00 p.m. (last orders). Closed on Mon.

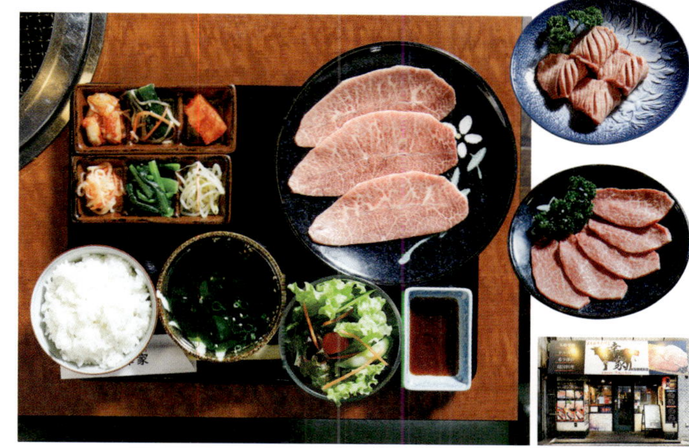

Yakiniku SACHIYA

●Shinjuku-gyoemmae

Yakiniku lunch sets from a mere ¥1,200. "A5 Premium Sirloin Set" comes with namul, kimchi, seaweed soup, and salad for ¥2,000. There's a rich variety of meats as well, including thick-cut salted tongue and A5 oyster blade. A highly satisfying spot both for flavor and price. ●1-18-9 Shinjuku, Shinjuku City, 1F ☎03-6457-7006. 11:00 a.m. to 2:30 p.m. and 5:00 p.m. to 10:00 p.m. (11:00 a.m. to 10:00 p.m. on Sat., Sun. and holidays). "To" times are all last orders.) No closed days.

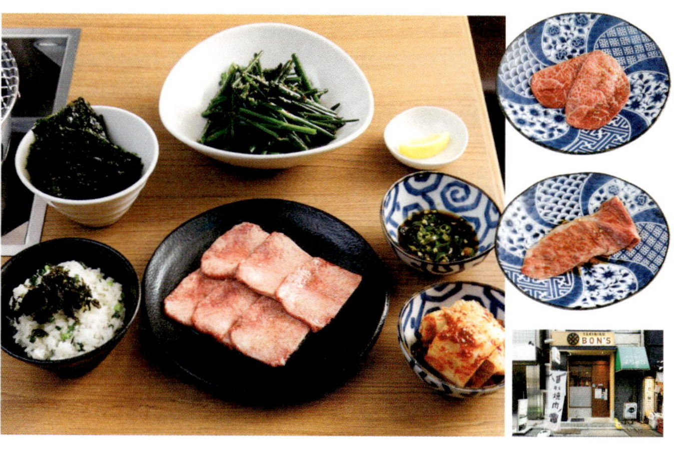

YAKINIKU BON'S

●Suitengumae

Known for its careful, seasonal selection, storage, and precise cuts. Half portions are also available for Omi Beef Sirloin Yaki Shabu (¥4,850) and more. Try it with sides like seaweed rice, Korean seaweed, green onion salad, and kimchi.●1-15-6 Nihombashi-Ningyocho, Chuo City, Gobangai Kyodo Bldg. A 1F ☎03-6810-8730. 6:30 p.m. to 1:00 a.m. (from 1:00 p.m. on Sun. and holidays). Irregular closed days.

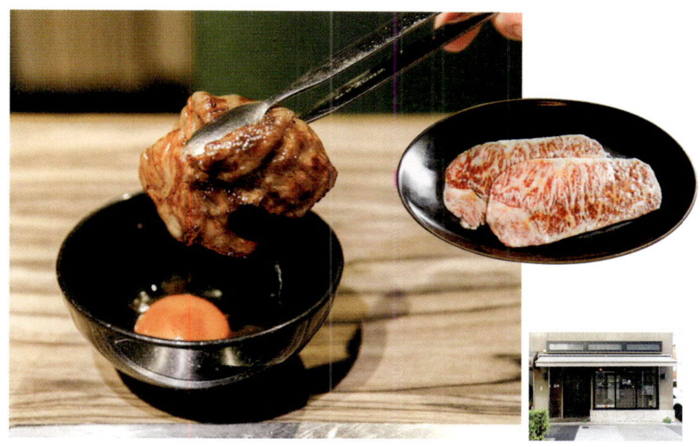

Yakiniku Jumbo Hanare

●Hongo-sanchome

One signature dish, "Nohara Yaki" (from ¥2,300 for one, depending on the weight), features large sirloin slices flash grilled and coated in savory fat and a sweet, sukiyaki-style soy-based sauce. For a blissful flavor, dip it in a raw egg (sold separately). ●3-27-9 Hongo, Bunkyo City, Anritsu Bldg. 1F and B1 ☎03-5689-8705. 5:00 p.m. to 11:30 p.m. (last orders). Irregular closed days.

A restaurant Tokyo's yakiniku cognoscenti choose. From the ingredients to the seasonings and side dishes, everything teaches you how deep yakiniku's flavors are, and how to savor them.

Isami Takayama

●Chef

Trained in restaurants in Italy and Tokyo. Opened meat Italian restaurant ***ANTICA OSTERIA CARNEYA*** in Ushigome-kagurazaka in 2007, and reservation-only charcoal-grill steakhouse ***NASQUILLO*** in Shinjuku-gyoemmae in 2021.

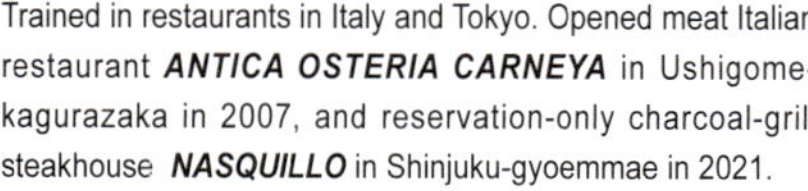

There's a chef whose dedicating his life to meat. He's Isami Takayama, he learned his craft in the long-running yakiniku restaurant ***Fumiya*** in Asakusa, and he's now the owner-chef of the charcoal-grill steakhouse ***NASQUILLO***. "Always being delicious as a given is really difficult. Knowing your strengths is vital," he says, and sure enough, individuality is key to being considered a "good restaurant" in Tokyo.

In particular, he recommends ***Yakiniku Kimura*** for its "high-quality meat and beautiful presentation," and praises ***Yakiniku Jumbo Hanare***'s signature "Nohara Yaki" for its "perfect balance of sweet sauce and aftertaste." For everyday use, choose ***SACHIYA***. He loves the fragrant, umami-rich Kuroge Wagyu beef lunch set, offered at an unbeatable price of around ¥2,000. At ***YAKINIKU BON'S***, try the Takayama-style set, which pairs sauced meat with sides.

"Tokyo yakiniku also draws inbound visitors, but should aim to please Japanese diners first," says Takayama. Eating yakiniku at spots chosen by pros will expand your enjoyment vastly.

Photos: Kenya Abe Text: Ayano Yoshida

An Art City That Keeps Evolving.

Tokyo's vibrant art scene, constantly bustling with museum renovations and the birth of new facilities. We asked a chief editor about what the must-visit spots are now.

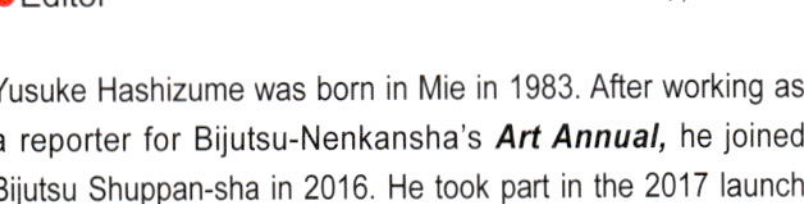

Yusuke Hashizume

●Editor

Yusuke Hashizume was born in Mie in 1983. After working as a reporter for Bijutsu-Nenkansha's ***Art Annual,*** he joined Bijutsu Shuppan-sha in 2016. He took part in the 2017 launch of the web version ***Bijutsu Techo***, and is now its chief editor.

Tokyo—Asia's top art city, where unique museums, galleries, and public art abound. We asked Yusuke Hashizume, chief editor of the web version ***Bijutsu Techo***, about Tokyo's recent art scene. "The ***Mitsubishi Ichigokan Museum, Tokyo***'s renovation and gallery ***Pace Tokyo***'s Japan debut were impactful topics. The ***UESHIMA MUSEUM*** opened last year by a contemporary art collector is also interesting. The new ***Jil Sander*** store with its exhibition space harmonizes artworks, interior design, and products, showing particular respect for art among luxury brands." Tokyo, a place where unmissable art spots are popping up continually, is also seeing large-scale urban developments. "In the past year or two, large-scale developments like ***Azabudai Hills*** and ***TODA BUILDING*** have been notable for incorporating art right from the start. A form where the private sector directly engages with art is emerging, driven by developers." For example, ***TODA BUILDING*** is currently leading a project to display public art in its entrance lobby, making it a space for up-and-coming artists to present their works. "A major benefit of public art is that it even creates connections with people who haven't come there with that in mind. That must surely add value to the location as well."

Mitsubishi Ichigokan Museum, Tokyo

●Marunouchi

RENOVATED Nov. 2024

Opened in 2010. Restored building designed by Josiah Conder (completed in 1894). Lovely small exhibition room was added during last year's renovation. Holds small exhibitions focused on its core collection. ***From Edo to Tokyo*** is on until May 11. (Admission included with special exhibition.) ● 2-6-2 Marunouchi, Chiyoda City ☎050-5541-8600 (Hello Dial). 10:00 a.m. to 6:00 p.m. Closed on Mon.

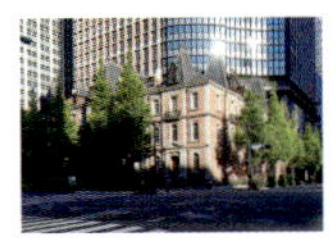

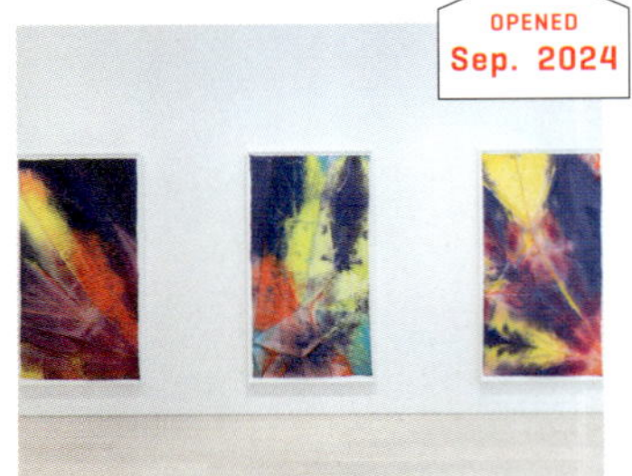

Pace Tokyo

●Azabudai

OPENED Sep. 2024

One of the eight bases worldwide of a gallery founded in Boston, USA in 1960. The interior by architect Sou Fujimoto is also a highlight. Works by artists rarely seen in Japan are also shown. There's currently a Sam Gilliam exhibition running until May 6. ●5-8-1 Toranomon, Minato City, Azabudai Hills Garden Plaza A 1 & 2F ☎03-6681-9400. 11:00 a.m. to 8:00 p.m. Closed on Mon.

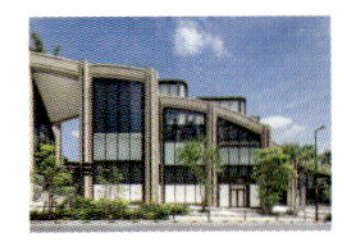

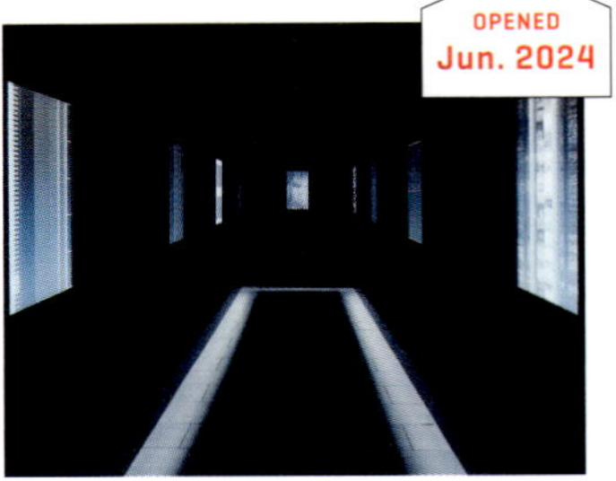

UESHIMA MUSEUM

●Shibuya

OPENED Jun. 2024

Museum showing contemporary art collected by entrepreneur Kankuro Ueshima since 2022. The six floors from B1 to 5F have works by renowned artists like Olafur Eliasson and Ryoji Ikeda. Catch up on the latest trends in the art scene. ●1-21-18 Shibuya, Shibuya City, Shibuya Kyoiku Gakuen Ueshima Tower ☎03-6271-5359. 11:00 a.m. to 5:00 p.m. (last admissions at 4:00 p.m.). Closed on Mon.

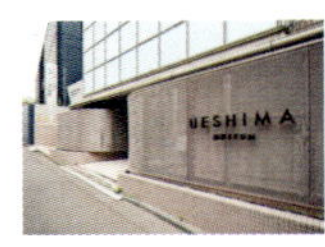

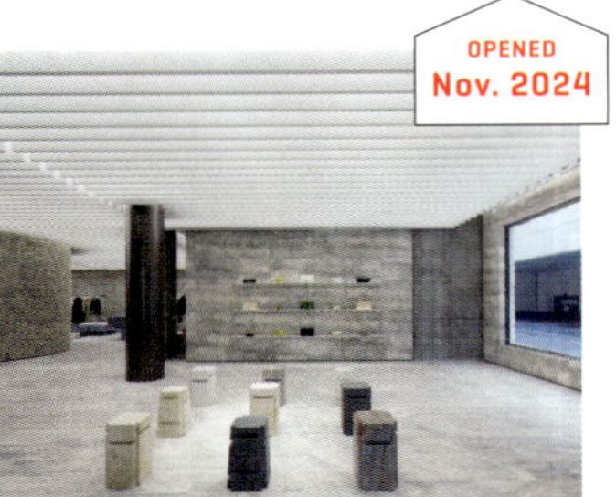

JIL SANDER GINZA

●Ginza

OPENED Nov. 2024

The world's largest flagship store. The exhibition space for art permanently shows works by British sculptor Rachel Whiteread. The interior was designed by the renowned architectural firm ***Casper Muller Kneer Architects***, uses natural materials like travertine, and shapes the space beautifully. ●3-4-1 Ginza, Chuo City ☎03-3528-6278. 11:00 a.m. to 8:00 p.m. Irregular closed days.

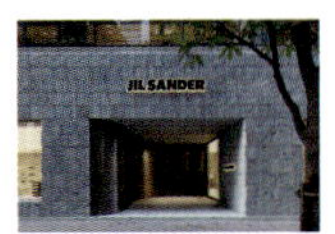

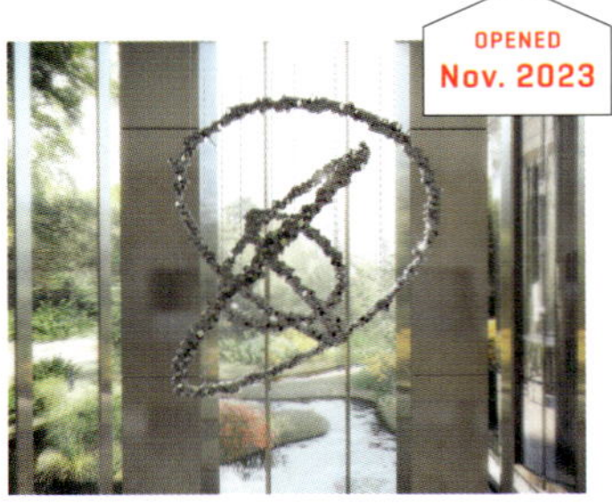

Azabudai Hills

●Azabudai

OPENED Nov. 2023

A "compact city" combining commercial facilities, residences, and offices. Also includes multiple galleries, and public art by Olafur Eliasson and Yoshitomo Nara. ●1-3-1 Azabudai, Minato City ☎03-6433-8100. Opening hours vary by facility. No closed days.

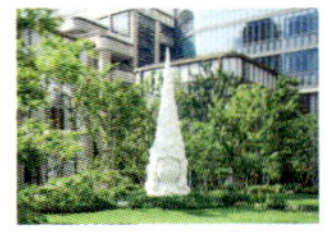

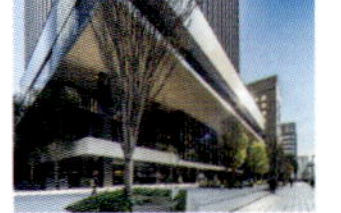

Right: Olafur Eliasson (Denmark), ***A harmonious cycle of interconnected nows***, 2023, Mori JP Tower Left: Yoshitomo Nara, ***Miss Forest in Tokyo***, 2023, bronze, urethane coating, 762.0 x 243.0 x 234.0 cm Photo: Mie Morimoto

TODA BUILDING

●Kyobashi

OPENED Nov. 2024

Office building fusing art and cultural facilities. Hub for Japan's leading galleries. Entrance has public art overseen by major curators from Japan and abroad. Currently showing works by four artists, Atsuko Mochida being one. ●1-7-1 Kyobashi, Chuo City ☎No phone number. Opening hours and days vary by facility.

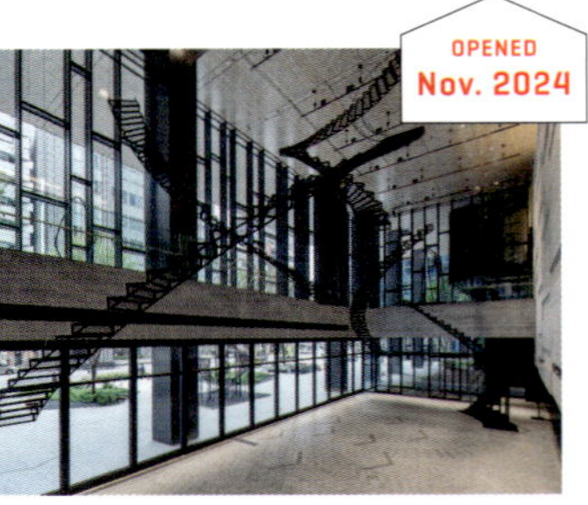

Right: Atsuko Mochida, ***Steps***, 2024 Photo: ToLoLo studio Left: ©Kawasumi-Kobayashi Kenji Photograph Office

Text: Anna Abe

Discover the Stories Behind Famous Furniture.

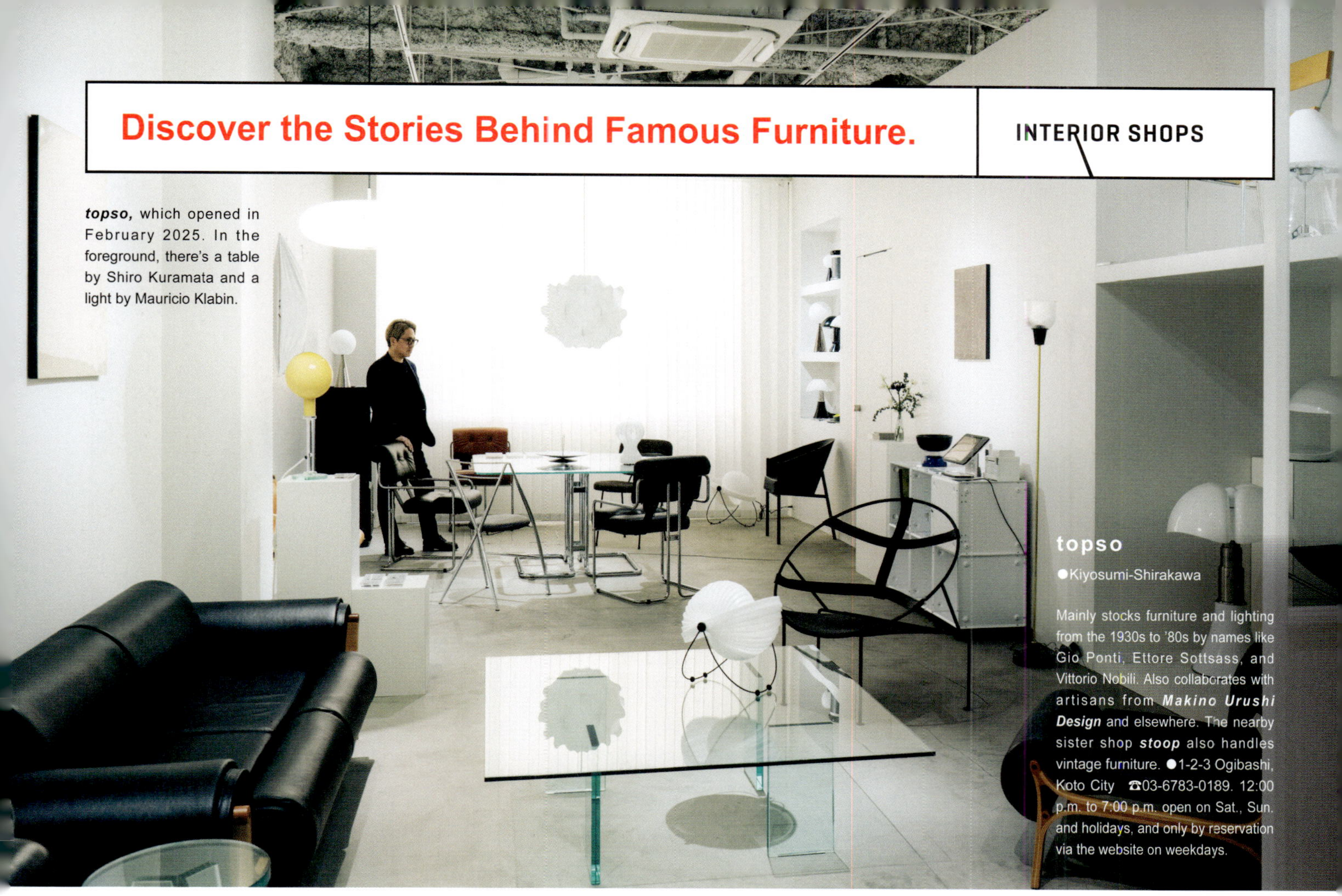

topso, which opened in February 2025. In the foreground, there's a table by Shiro Kuramata and a light by Mauricio Klabin.

topso

●Kiyosumi-Shirakawa

Mainly stocks furniture and lighting from the 1930s to '80s by names like Gio Ponti, Ettore Sottsass, and Vittorio Nobili. Also collaborates with artisans from ***Makino Urushi Design*** and elsewhere. The nearby sister shop ***stoop*** also handles vintage furniture. ●1-2-3 Ogibashi, Koto City ☎03-6783-0189. 12:00 p.m. to 7:00 p.m. open on Sat., Sun. and holidays, and only by reservation via the website on weekdays.

Eyewear designer Yuichi Toyama says, "Chairs and glasses are similar." Here are three shops recommended by an interior design and art connoisseur.

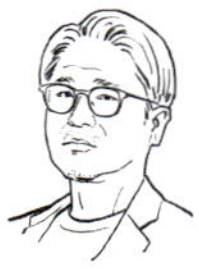

Yuichi Toyama

●***YUICHI TOYAMA.*** designer

Yuichi Toyama was born in Tokyo in 1971. In 2017, he launched ***YUICHI TOYAMA.***, an eyewear brand with Japanese craftsmanship and innovative design at its core. The stylish interior of the Omotesando flagship store is also a hot topic.

"As with glasses, when I look at chairs or cutlery, I focus on design and comfort related to the human bone structure," says Yuichi Toyama. He recommends ***topso***, newly opened near the ***Museum of Contemporary Art Tokyo***. It offers rare furniture brands found only here in Japan, including Shiro Kuramata tables, Philippe Starck's latest works, and Guido Faleschini leather chairs. "The appeal of the furniture and lighting at ***topso*** lies in the stories behind their designs and the craftspeople's devoted pursuit of comfort. The staff's deep knowledge and passion for the pieces are also reasons to highly recommend the store. They share brand stories tuned to your interests and let you touch or sit on masterpieces, leaving a lasting impression. It's an irreplaceable experience."

He feels the same joy at ***Crafts, Tableware & Tools SML*** and ***pejite Aoyama***, which handle Japanese tableware. "I hope people experience that fulfilled feeling of having gained some great input after leaving the store."

AND MORE...

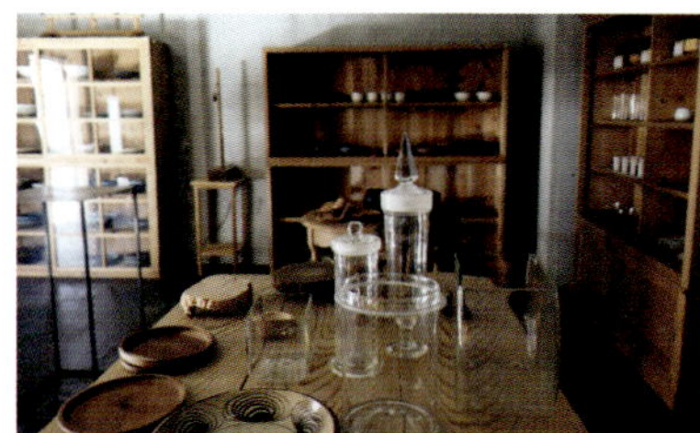

pejite Aoyama

●Omote-sando

Original tableware from a pottery studio in Mashiko, Tochigi, Tadao Akutsu and Naoto Hirata ceramics, and cutlery by woodworker Shinnosuke Akutsu. Solo exhibition every month. Antique furniture you can buy. Opened antique shop ***Hakutousha*** in Kiyosumi-Shirakawa in March. ●5-6-9 Minami-Aoyama, Minato City, South Aoyama Mansion, Room 102 ☎03-6427-6131. 12:00 p.m. to 7:00 p.m. Irregular closed days.

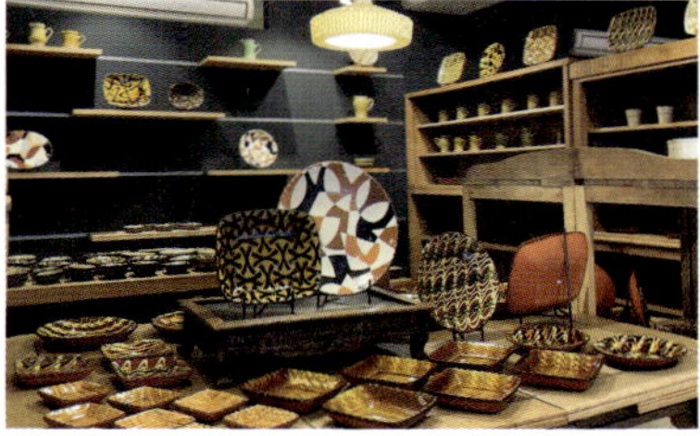

Crafts, Tableware & Tools SML

●Naka-meguro

Shop for tableware and tools trusted by professional chefs. Besides folk-art works, has Tetsuya Otani porcelain, Shinya Kakiuchi glassware, ***Tobimatsu Toki*** lighting, and other contemporary tools and products. Also well known for cooking and tool workshops and events. ●1-15-1 Aobadai, Meguro City, AK-1 Bldg. 1F ☎03-6809-0696. 12:00 p.m. to 7:00 p.m. (from 11:00 a.m. on Sat., Sun., and holidays). Irregular closed days.

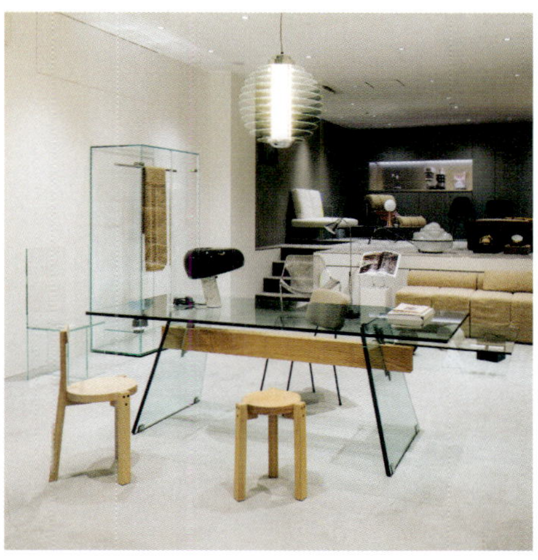

Shop interior renovated from a former auto repair factory. The glass table by Philippe Starck is from 2024. The chairs are by Lina Bo Bardi.

Photos: Ayumi Yamamoto Text: Masae Wako

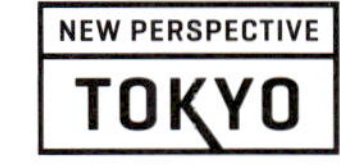

Renowned Shops That Are Sure to Sate Your Coffee Cravings.

Yarlens' Junnosuke Dei loves coffee as much as he loves manzai comedy. It was Tokyo that sparked his passion for the drink.

Influenced by his father working in the coffee business, Dei-san has been on familiar terms with coffee since early childhood. He moved from Osaka to Tokyo in 2014, looking to break through as a comedian. This move also further fueled his love for coffee. "It was after coming to Tokyo that I began to focus on flavor. I used to like bitter, round dark roasts, but the Ethiopian Alaka Washed at ***COUNTERPART COFFEE GALLERY*** surprised me with its fruity, bright acidity. Like, 'Light roasts can be delicious, too.' My world expanded. Back then, I used to bike everywhere to save money, so I'd jot down any shops that caught my eye along the way."

He's been exploring coffee shops with an open mind and savoring both dark and light roasts ever since. "I'm drawn to shops that reveal their philosophy and passion. For example, there's ***swamp*** behind Nishishinjuku Narugeki. I first went there before I was due to go on stage. Having three coffee grinders really reveals their dedication—and of course, the flavor is flawless. I drop by there from time to time."

Dei-san's "coffee craving" now rivals the basic human drives. Even now he's a popular star, he still finds time to frequent coffee shops. "Tokyo packs top-grade bean specialists and long-running cafés into a compact area. If I have even just an hour to spare, I'll take a taxi simply to have some coffee. I've gotten a bit rounder since I stopped biking (laughs). There's no better city for enjoying coffee."

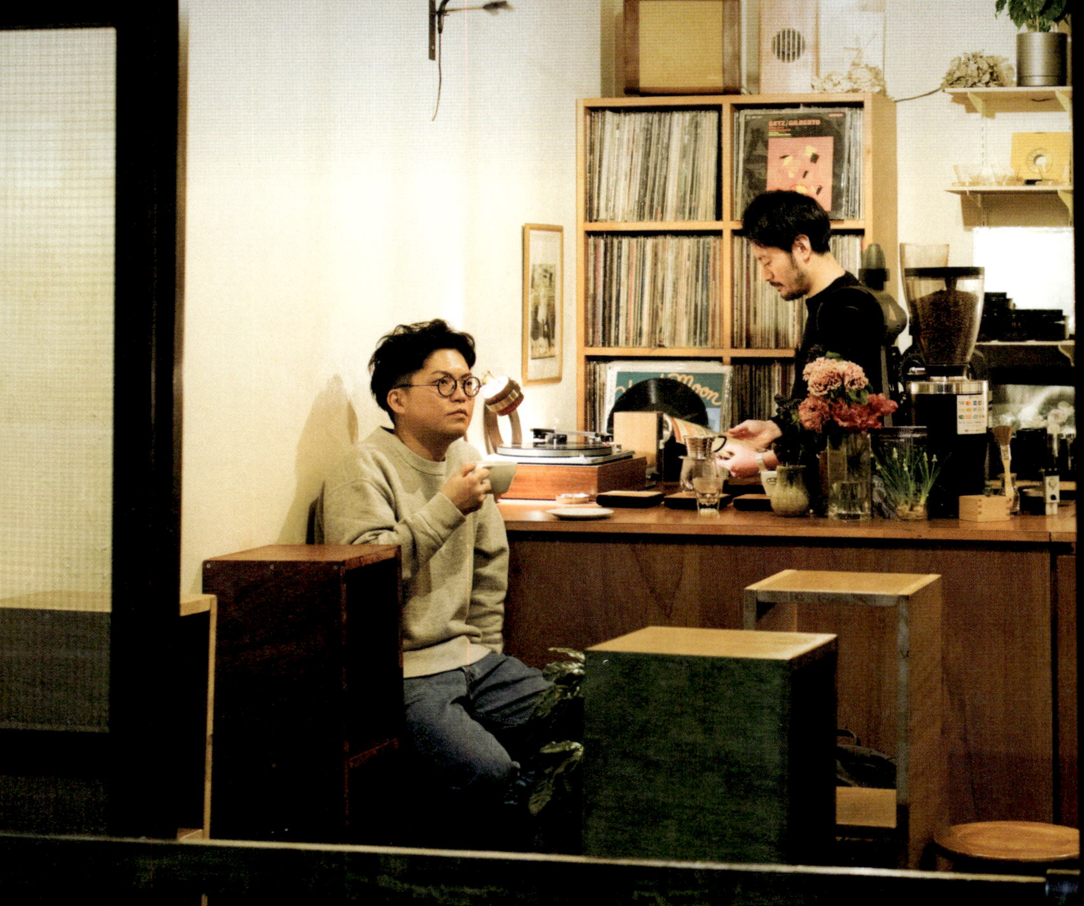

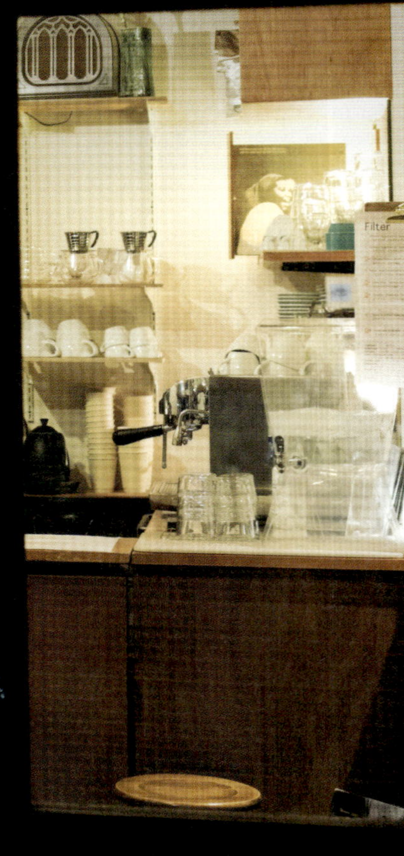

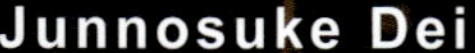

Junnosuke Dei

●Comedian

Junnosuke Dei was born in Kanagawa in 1987. He's one half of the comedy duo ***Yarlens***, which was a runner-up in the M-1 Grand Prix 2023. You can currently catch him in ***Yarlens' All Night Nippon 0***, which is airing on Nippon Broadcasting System once a month.

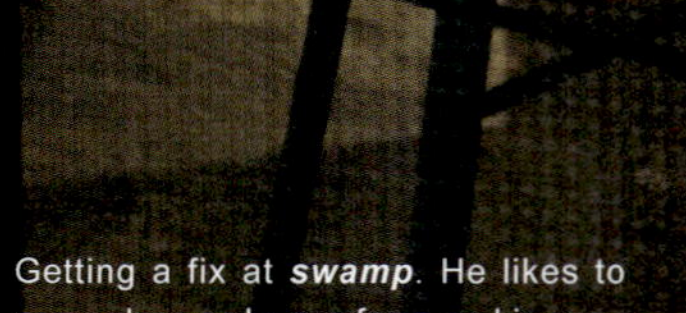

Getting a fix at ***swamp***. He likes to come alone so he can focus on his cup.

Photos: Kazuharu Igarashi, Anna Abe (shops) Text & editing: Emi Fukushima

Hot tips from Dei-san! Eight shops you don't want to miss.

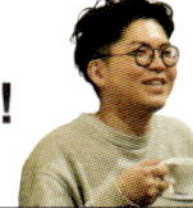

Dark Roasts

G☆P COFFEE ROASTER

●Hatsudai

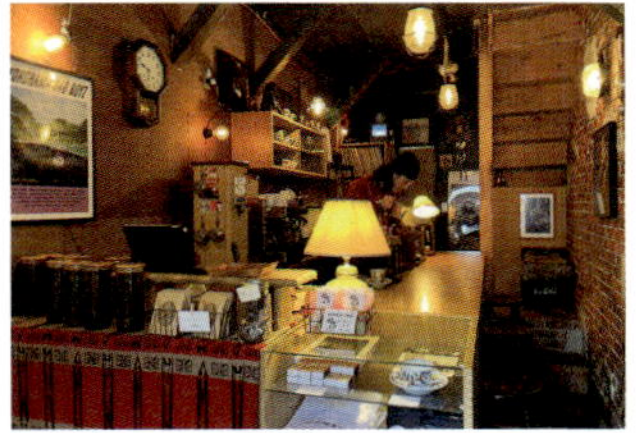

Their dark roasts have a bold bitterness with a gently sweet undertone.

Always has eight to ten kinds of house-roasted beans. They use a direct-heat "Fuji Royal 103" roaster to reduce the bitterness and off-flavors and to bring out the subtle sweetness. In addition to paper drip, you can also choose nel drip, which will really highlight the beans' unique character. Served in Arita ware Genemon Kiln cups. One cup: from ¥594. Beans: 100g from ¥1,080. ●2-28-4 Hommachi, Shibuya City ☎080-5324-0548. 11:00 a.m. to 8:00 p.m. Closed on Wed.

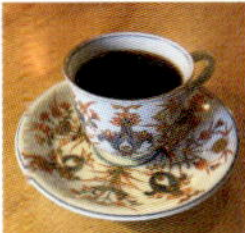

Sujigane Coffee Baisenjo

●Shimo-Kitazawa

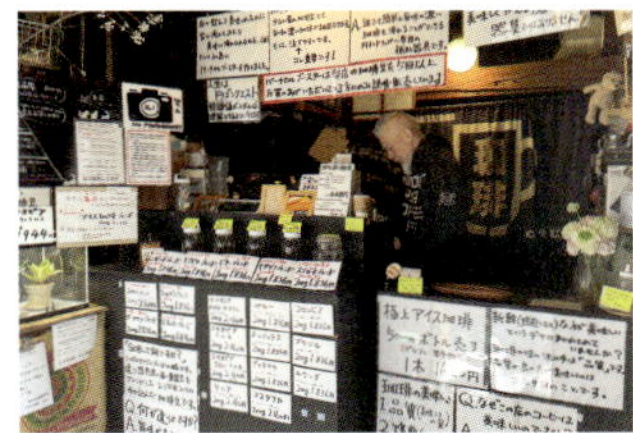

The sheer number of handwritten signs conveys their passion loud and clear, too. Try the signature Sujigane Blend.

This dark-roast specialty shop was opened in 2004 by owner Atsushi Furuichi—who says originally, he didn't even used to like coffee. Top-quality beans are carefully roasted to draw out their full flavor. For the takeout coffee, 30g of beans are brewed for over 5 minutes for each cup. The cheesecake made with Calpis butter is also popular. One cup: ¥648. Beans: 200g from ¥1,836. ●3-31-3 Kitazawa, Setagaya City ☎No phone number. 10:00 a.m. to 9:00 p.m. Closed on Mon.

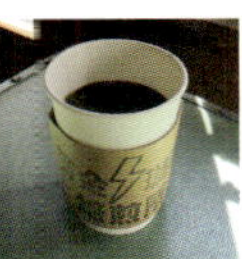

Coffee Dojo Samurai

●Kameido

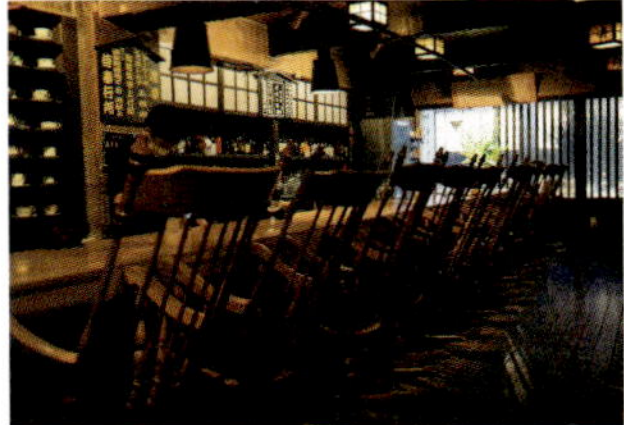

All the counter seats are these unbelievably comfy rocking chairs.

Established in 1978. Serves Dutch coffee (cold-brewed) percolated for eight hours, blends, and around ten single-origin coffees, including specialty varieties. Also charming is the diverse collection of cups and saucers first-and second-generation owners Takayuki and Kotaro Kondo have amassed on their travels. One cup: from ¥600. Beans: 100g from ¥800. ●6-57-22 Kameido, Koto City ☎ 03-3638-4003. 8:00 a.m. to 9:30 p.m. (to 11:00 p.m. on Fri. and Sat.). Closed on Sun.

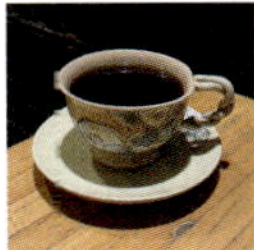

cafe Bach

●Minami-Senju

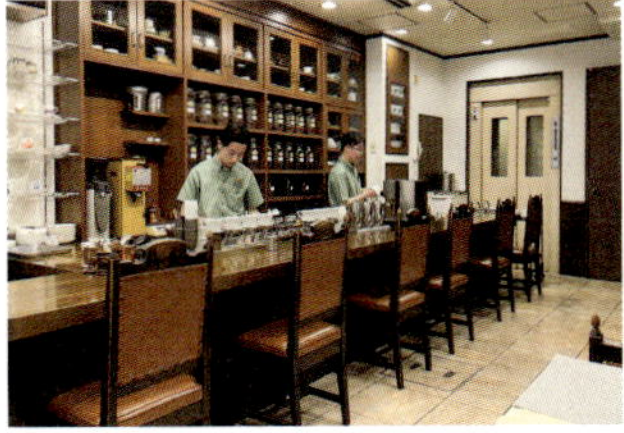

A legendary shop founded by the "God of Coffee." The flavors, service, and everything else are all flawless.

Founded in 1968 by Japanese coffee pioneer Mamoru Taguchi and currently run by general manager Koichi Taguchi. Freshly roasted beans straight from an original roaster. They serve their signature medium-dark Bach Blend, plus everything from light to dark roasts—whatever suits the beans' character best. One cup: from ¥680. Beans: 100g from ¥880. ●1-23-9 Nihonzutsumi, Taito City ☎03-3875-2669. 10:30 a.m. to 6:30 p.m. Closed on Tue. and the 2nd & 4th Wed.

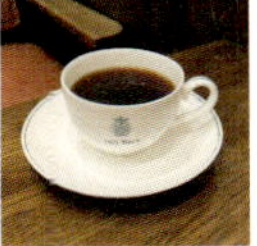

Light Roasts

swamp

●Nishi-shinjuku

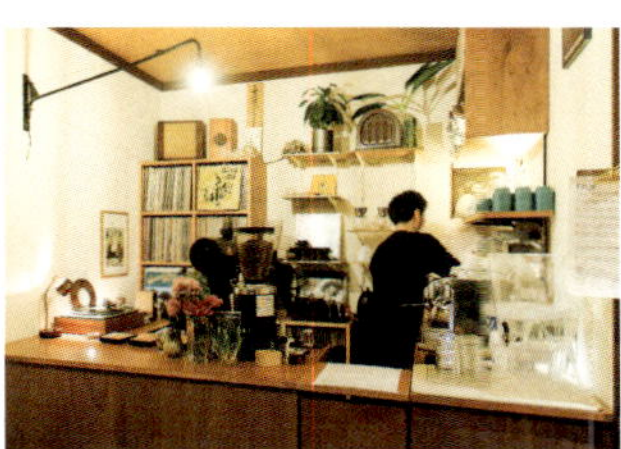

The calm vibe with records playing in the background is just as appealing as the flavor of the coffee.

Opened in August 2022. Always has eight types of beans in stock (including Ethiopian washed and natural). Also has three different ***Mahlkönig*** grinders, using them to suit the brewing method. The jazz and blues music picked by owner Atsuki Ishikawa is great, too. One cup: from ¥600. Beans: 100g from ¥1,150. ●7-21-12 Nishi-Shinjuku, Shinjuku City, Rengeso, Room 105 ☎No phone number. 7:00 a.m. to 3:30 p.m. (Closed from 11:00 a.m. to 12:00 p.m.). Irregular closed days.

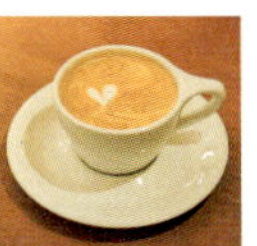

Acid Coffee Tokyo

●Yoyogi-uehara

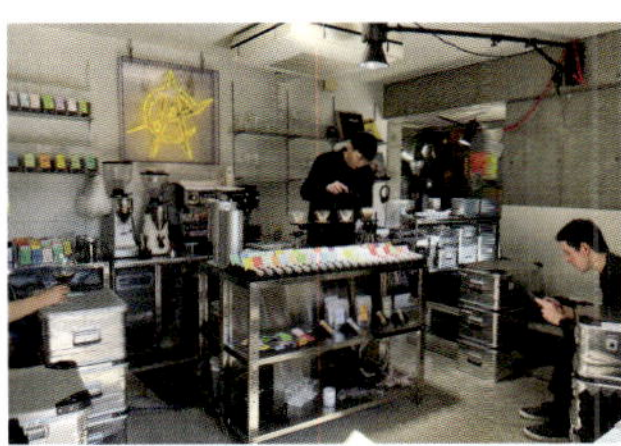

The highly skilled baristas gently guide newbies, too.

You'll find over 30 varieties of beans labeled "super fruity" lining the shelves in this shop, whose interior design brings to mind a science lab. The coffee cards are all assigned a color inspired by the flavor, so you get to enjoy choosing based on color, aroma, origin, and variety. One cup: from ¥480. Beans: 100g from ¥1,500. ●1-29-5 Uehara, Shibuya City, BiT-Yoyogi-Uehara, Room 101 ☎ No phone number. 8:00 a.m. to 6:00 p.m. No closed days.

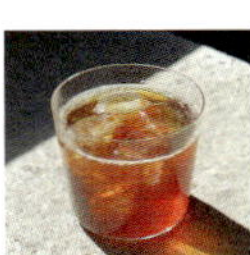

COUNTERPART COFFEE GALLERY

●Nishi-shinjuku gochome

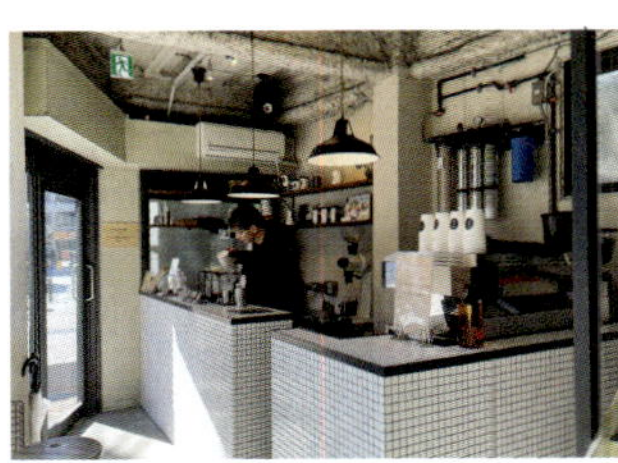

One of the shops that baptized me into the world of light roasts. I love the atmosphere here, and have been coming for years.

This shop serves at least three fully traceable varieties of beans, the main source being the renowned ***GLITCH COFFEE & ROASTERS*** in Jimbocho. Besides classics like Ethiopian washed, it also offers varieties like peach-and oolong-flavored beans from YUAN YI YUAN farm in China. One cup: from ¥1,000. Beans: 100g from ¥2,200. ●3-12-16 Hommachi, Shibuya City ☎No phone number. 9:00 a.m. to 6:00 p.m. (to 2:00 p.m. on Fri.). Closed on Mon. and Thu.

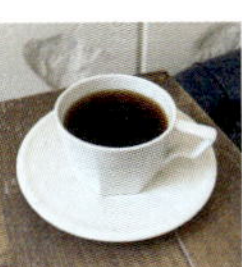

Definitive. Kichijoji

●Kichijoji

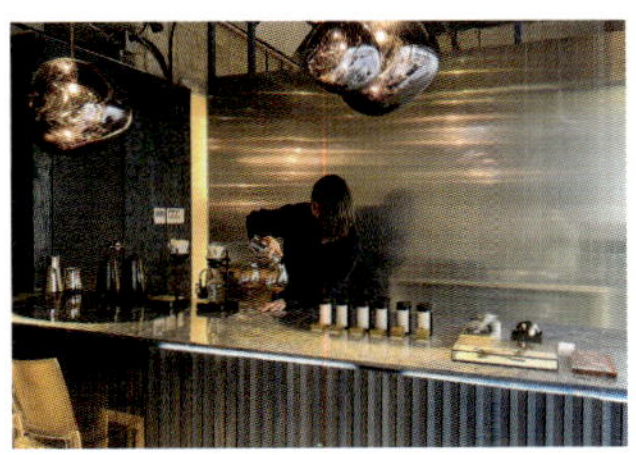

No compromise in either flavor or ambience—the owner's passion for Panama really shines through!

Specializes in the world's best Panama coffee. Opened in November 2024. Each of the 15 to 20 varieties offered are top-tier Panama beans—some of them award winners—all showcasing each farm's individual character. Served in glasses whether hot or iced, to boost the flavor. One cup: from ¥1,500. Beans: 85g from ¥5,000. ●2-6-4 Kichijoji-Honcho, Musashino City, Rufure Kichijoji 1F ☎No phone number. 1:00 p.m. to 10:00 p.m. Irregular closed days.

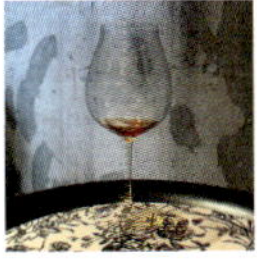

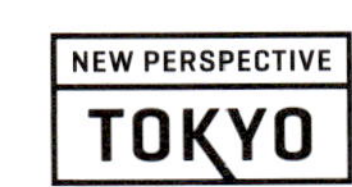

Gyms You Don't Have to Sign up For.

"I want to hit a gym every once in a while!" A gym that fulfills that desire is one that allows visitors. Here are seven recommended by a top trainer.

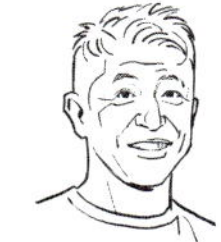

Takuya Shirato

●Personal trainer

With 30 years' experience in program development at a major fitness club, Takuya Shirato is now the director of the MS Group's fitness division. Someone who knows all there is to about fitness, he's a "legendary trainer" both in Japan and around the world.

After dropping during the COVID-19 pandemic, the demand for fitness is now even surpassing its former peak. "The image of gyms dominated by muscular regulars is already a thing of the past. With muscle training also gaining popularity among women and a wide range of other groups as well, the atmosphere in them has become brighter and more open," says Takuya Shirato, a personal trainer with deep knowledge of the industry. Even beginners are welcome to drop in casually as a visitor.

"First and foremost, we can't miss ***GOLD'S GYM***, which is called 'Disneyland for trainees.' Next, there's ***TIP.X TOKYO Shibuya***, located in a prime area. Both gyms are very spacious and also let you break a sweat through studio programs and agility training. For machine-focused gyms, places like ***LÝFT GÝM*** in Omotesando Hills and ***WONDER LIFE*** with its Instagram-worthy spaces have a stoic atmosphere that ups your motivation."

If you're looking for a more casual workout, there are also boutique gyms with time-based group lessons. "Sessions last an hour to 90 minutes, and you just follow the instructions and move to the music. So, no expertise needed. It's really refreshing! Please do experience the pleasure of working up a sweat at your favorite gym."

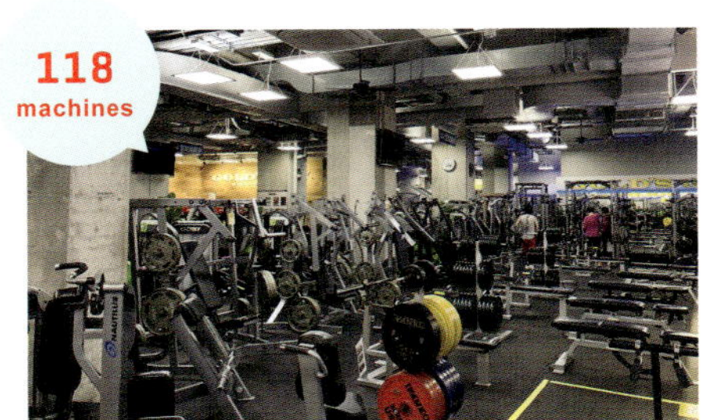

118 machines

GOLD'S GYM HARAJUKU ANNEX

●Harajuku

Features a spacious floor that includes a gym area, women-only section, and machine Pilates, all on one floor. After training, you can soothe your fatigue in the on-site semi-natural hot spring and sauna. ●1-5-8 Jingumae, Shibuya City, Jingumae Tower Bldg. 1F ☎03-3408-7474. 6:00 a.m. to 11:30 p.m. (from 6:30 a.m. on Mon., and from 7:00 a.m. to 9:00 p.m. on Sun.). Closed on the 2nd Mon. Visitor fee: ¥3,520.

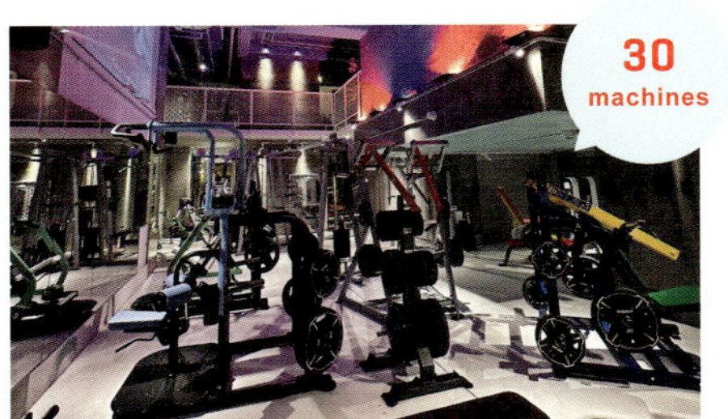

30 machines

WONDER LIFE

●Myogadani

A photogenic gym whose colorful machines, unique lighting, and "OK" policy on going shirtless and having tattoos lend it a real overseas vibe. Visitors get a drink on the house, providing a perfect protein pick-me-up for muscle care. ●4-2-5, Kohinata, Bunkyo City, Kohinata Yasuda Bldg., Room 101 ☎03-6801-8303. 10:00 a.m. to 10:30 p.m. (to 9:00 p.m. on Sun.). Irregular closed days. Visitor fee: ¥2,500 (for 4 hours).

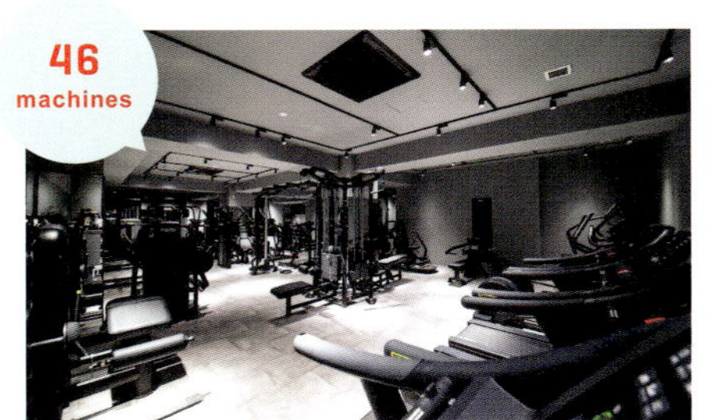

46 machines

HERO GYM

●Zoshigaya

A top-tier gym that's popular with famous bodybuilders and offers an authentic American training environment. While its machine lineup will even impress advanced users, beginners and casual users are warmly welcomed as well, so there's no need to feel intimidated. ●2-5-27 Mejiro, Toshima City ☎03-6914-0683. Open 24 hours. No closed days. (For visitors, the hours are from 10:00 a.m. to 9:00 p.m., with irregular closed days.) Visitor fee: ¥3,500.

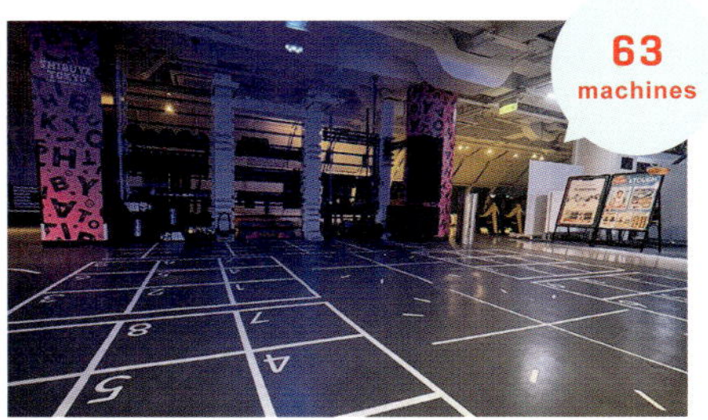

63 machines

TIP.X TOKYO Shibuya

●Shibuya

Located in the heart of Shibuya, this gym features a gym area, a studio, and a 25-meter pool. With its wide variety of studio programs, if in doubt, just come here for some guaranteed sweaty workout fun. The best time to go is in the evening when it's less crowded. ●16-4 Udagawacho, Shibuya City ☎03-3770-3531. 7:00 a.m. to 11:00 p.m. (from 9:30 a.m. to 10:00 p.m. on Sat., and from 9:30 a.m. to 8:00 p.m. on Sun. and holidays). Closed on Fri. Visitor fee: ¥2,420.

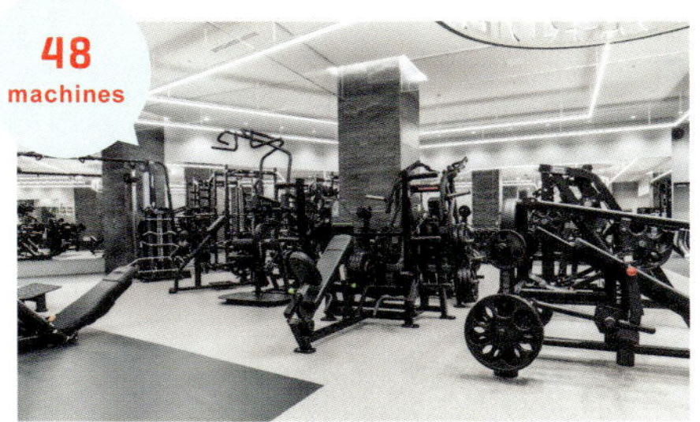

48 machines

LÝFT GÝM

●Omote-sando

A luxury gym with 50+ state-of-the-art machines and a 3-meter ceiling despite its basement location. Visitors can get a one-week pass—handy for traveling or business trips. ●4-12-10 Jingumae, Shibuya City, Omotesando Hills Main Bldg. B3 ☎03-5843-0280. 7:00 a.m. to 11:00 p.m. Closed on the 4th Wed. and when the building is closed. Visitor fee (week pass): ¥22,000 for men, ¥16,500 for women.

Try an enthusiastic workout at a boutique gym.

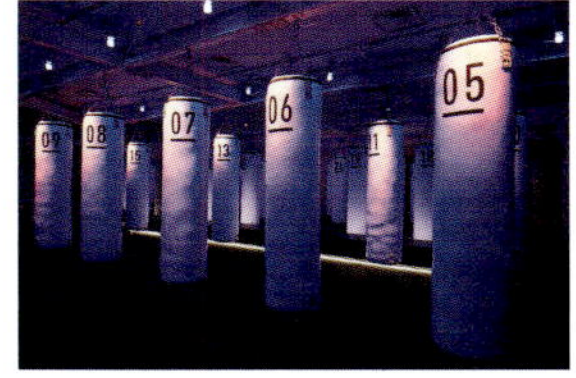

b-monster Shinjuku Studio

●Shinjuku

The pioneers of dark boxing in Japan. That exhilarating feeling of hitting a bag to music is getting more and more people hooked. ●7-1-1 Nishi-Shinjuku, Shinjuku City, Shinjuku Kaleido Bldg. 5F ☎ 0570-097-700. 6:30 a.m. to 10:45 p.m. Irregular closed days. Visitor fee (single-session ticket): ¥4,950.

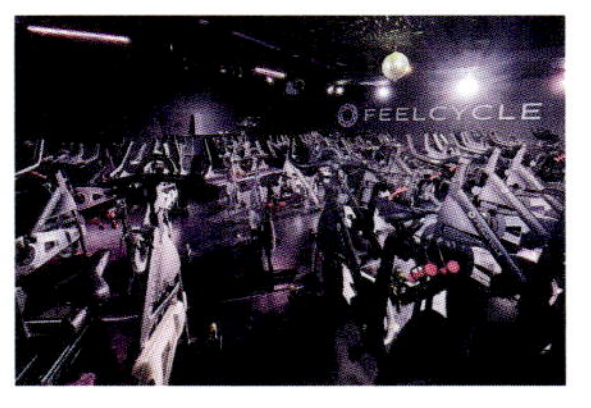

FEELCYCLE Shibuya

●Shibuya

Workout combining cardio and muscle training with dark cycling. Burns about 800 kcal in 45 min. Over 200 programs to choose from. ●20-11 Udagawacho, Shibuya City, Shibuya Mitsuba Bldg. 3F ☎No phone number. 6:30 a.m. to 11:00 p.m. (7:00 a.m. to 9:30 p.m. on Sat., Sun., and holidays). Closed on Fri. Visitor fee: ¥6,000.

Text: Ryo Ishii

Buddies You Can Count on Out in the Wild.

If you're looking for tough outdoor gear that'll prepare you for the unexpected as well, what stores does outdoor enthusiast Naoto Isawa recommend for reliable finds?

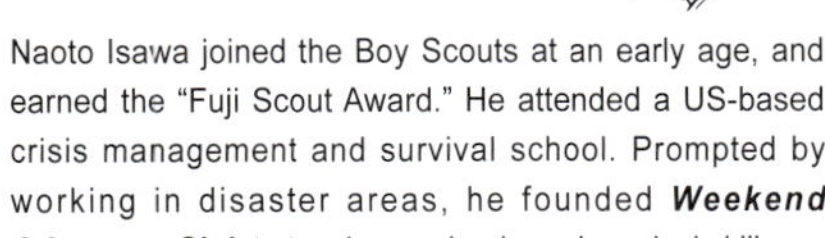

Naoto Isawa

●Outdoor enthusiast

Naoto Isawa joined the Boy Scouts at an early age, and earned the "Fuji Scout Award." He attended a US-based crisis management and survival school. Prompted by working in disaster areas, he founded ***Weekend Adventure Club*** to teach camping-based survival skills.

"In the vastness of nature, all you can rely on is yourself and your gear. So, choose dependable gear you can trust with your life."

So says ***Weekend Adventure Club*** founder Naoto Isawa, who runs survival camping schools at the base of Mts. Yatsugatake. Light enough not to hinder movement, reliable sturdiness, and versatile functionality. These three are Isawa-san's absolute musts for gear.

"When choosing new gear, get advice from experienced staff while examining it in person. For example, ***BOZEMAN***'s experienced mountaineer owner reflects his own expertise in his selection of wares. Knife experts ***Matrix-AIDA*** carefully help you choose the right blade for you, including the steel and handle materials."

Isawa-san emphasizes finding "buddies" you can bond with. With buddies by your side, anywhere—be it an unfamiliar forest or your own backyard—becomes an adventure. Enjoy the outdoor world that your gear opens up for you.

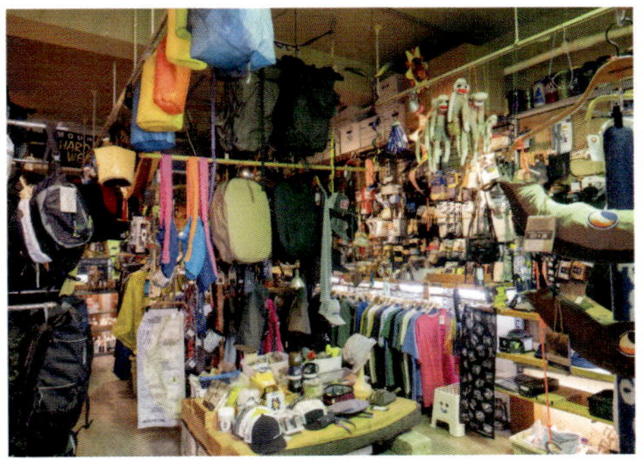

BOZEMAN

●Shimo-kitazawa

The goods selected by the outdoor enthusiast owner, who spends two days a week in Niigata's mountains, go beyond just mountain gear. Based on the flexible attitude that "everything is outdoor except slippers," the store has lots of unique outdoor items. It's a must-visit for gear enthusiasts, and you'll want to explore every corner like it's a treasure hunt. ●2-33-6 Kitazawa, Setagaya City, Fujiwara Bldg. B1 ☎03-3481-9250. 1:00 p.m. to 7:00 p.m. No closed days.

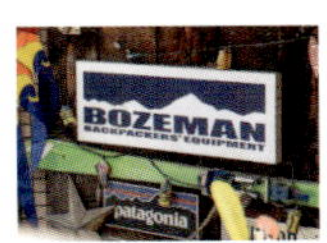

From the right: ***FIELD RECORD*** FR Sleeping Mat AL10 ¥8,690, ***TAR(P) MENT*** HOUR Sacoche ¥14,300, ***SylvanWorks*** Grippin' Gator ¥8,800.

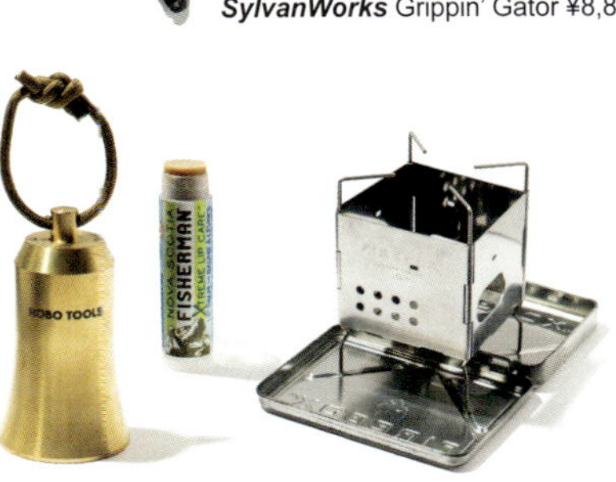

From the right: ***Firebox*** GEN2 Nano Stove ¥10,890, ***Nova Scotia*** Fisherman Lip Balm ¥935, ***HOBO TOOLS*** Bear Bell ¥16,500.

sokit

●Nerima

From ultralight gear to garage brands and artisan-made items. A mountain select shop that's the only place in Tokyo you'll find many of the goods. Offers functional wear that's made from the latest fabrics and great to wear around town as well as in the mountains. The owner's kind nature makes for comfortable shopping. ●1-34-11 Nerima, Nerima City ☎03-3994-3822. 12:00 p.m. to 6:00 p.m. Closed from Mon. to Thu., and on other irregular days.

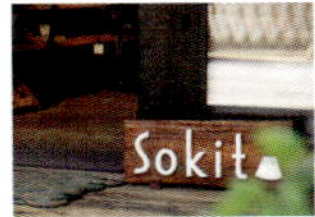

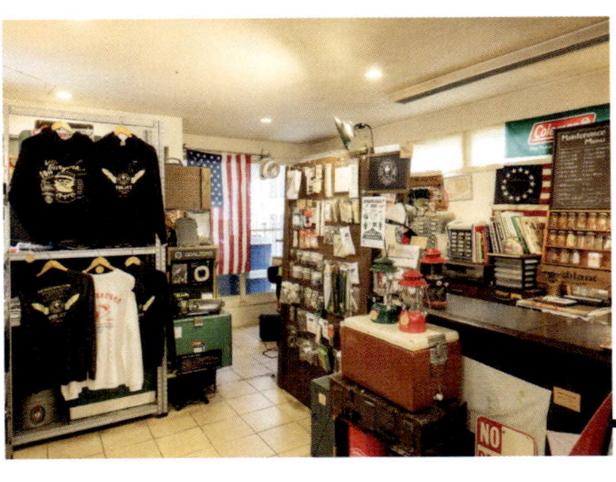

viblant

●Futako-tamagawa

A store specializing in vintage lanterns for core enthusiasts. The selection of goods encompasses century-old models to recent rare pieces, with a focus on ***Coleman***. The simple structure means repairs are easy, so even old models can be used without any issues—and the store also offers full repair services. ●2-15-13 Tamagawa, Setagaya City, Varenna Futakotamagawa 2F ☎03-6805-6366. 11:00 a.m. to 8:00 p.m. Closed on Tue.

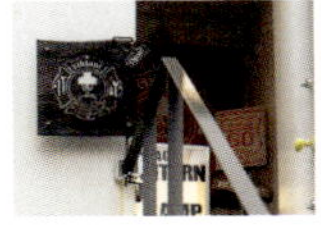

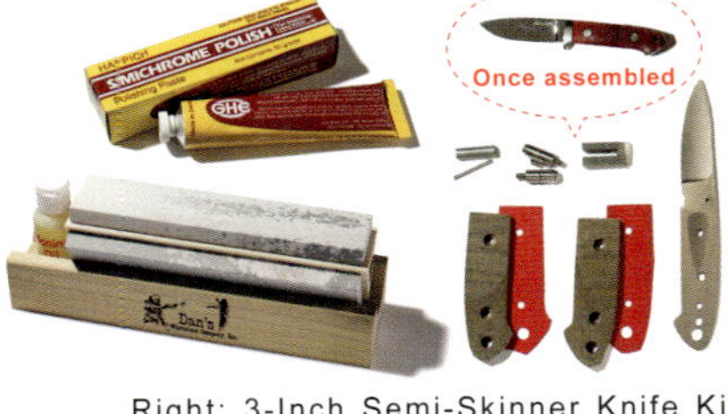

Right: 3-Inch Semi-Skinner Knife Kit ¥27,500. Top left: ***Simichrome*** Metal Polisher ¥2,750. Bottom left: ***Dan's*** Arkansas Triple Stone ¥9,900.

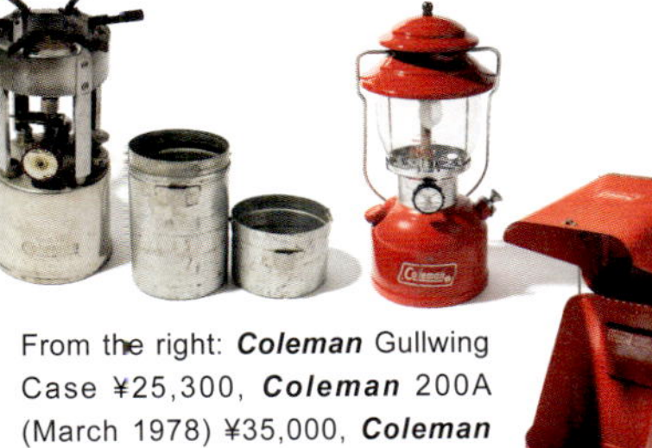

From the right: ***Coleman*** Gullwing Case ¥25,300, ***Coleman*** 200A (March 1978) ¥35,000, ***Coleman*** Coleman 530 Stove (known as the GI Stove) ¥44,000.

Matrix-AIDA

●Narimasu

Founded in 1914, this specialty store has long been producing its own blades, and is now recognized as a world-class custom knife maker. Packed with steel and handle materials and other knife making goods, it also carefully teaches beginners looking to try their own hand at the craft. ●2-26-18 Narimasu, Itabashi City, Casa-Aile 1F ☎03-3939-0052. 10:00 a.m. to 6:00 p.m. Closed on Sun.

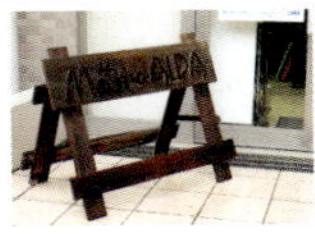

Photos: Mai Hokari Text: Ryo Ishii

A Bar Culture Where World-Class Cocktails Converge.

A city-center bar scene where global bartenders and diverse drinks create new cultures. Four must-visit spots for savoring drinks in culturally rich settings.

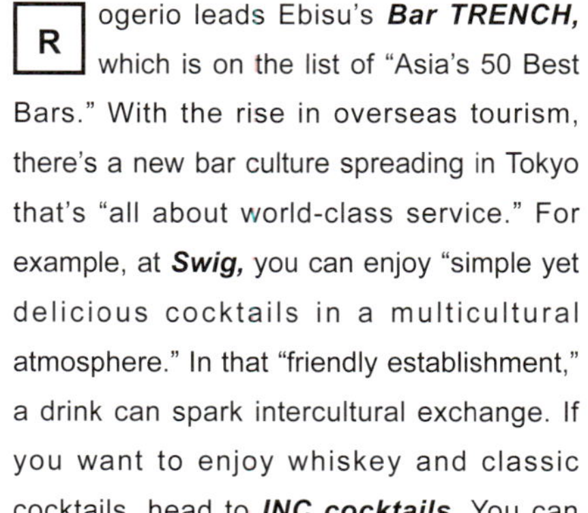

Rogerio Igarashi Vaz

●Bartender

Bar TRENCH co-owner and head bartender Rogerio Igarashi Vaz also oversees the menu at ***Bar Tram*** and ***Bar TRIAD.*** He's renowned for cocktails that combine delicate details with a playful touch.

Rogerio leads Ebisu's ***Bar TRENCH,*** which is on the list of "Asia's 50 Best Bars." With the rise in overseas tourism, there's a new bar culture spreading in Tokyo that's "all about world-class service." For example, at ***Swig,*** you can enjoy "simple yet delicious cocktails in a multicultural atmosphere." In that "friendly establishment," a drink can spark intercultural exchange. If you want to enjoy whiskey and classic cocktails, head to ***INC cocktails.*** You can enjoy house-aged whiskey while listening to jazz music playing from the ***ALTEC*** speakers. For more unique cocktails, head to the hotel bar ***VIRTÙ.*** Rogerio himself endorses it, saying, "Nothing beats a drink enjoyed with premium service." If you're looking for a relaxing evening, we recommend ***Flying Bumblebee*** in Daikan-yama. Enjoying "carefully crafted drinks" at the open counter makes a great time-out from everyday life.

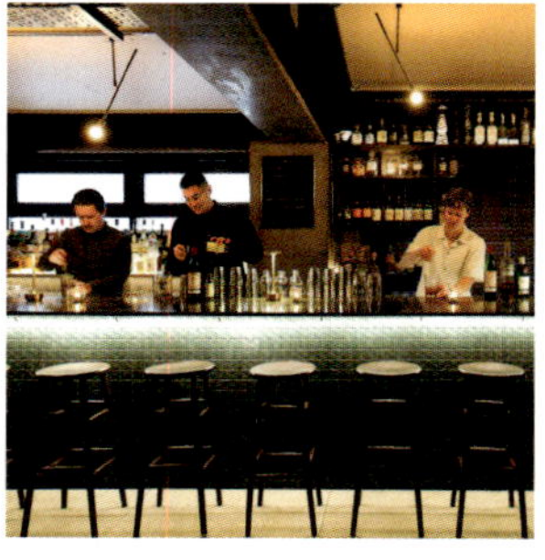

Swig ●Shibuya

A casual and friendly spot run by three bartenders—Fred, Jack, and Inuk—who met at the Naka-meguro bar ***Berry.*** English is spoken freely inside, creating a warm space where locals and travelers interact naturally. Every weekend, the place gets as lively as a party. ●1-6-3 Shibuya, Shibuya City ☎No phone number. 7:00 p.m. to 1:00 a.m. Closed on Sun. and Mon.

SIGNATURE

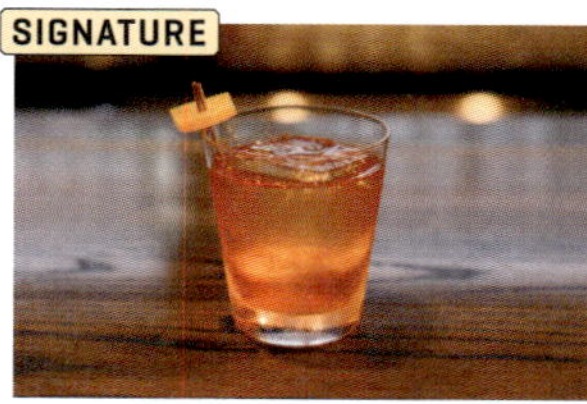

Penicillin Milk Punch

A twist on the Scotch-based cocktail "Penicillin." Its milky taste belies its clear appearance. ¥1,500.

SEASONAL

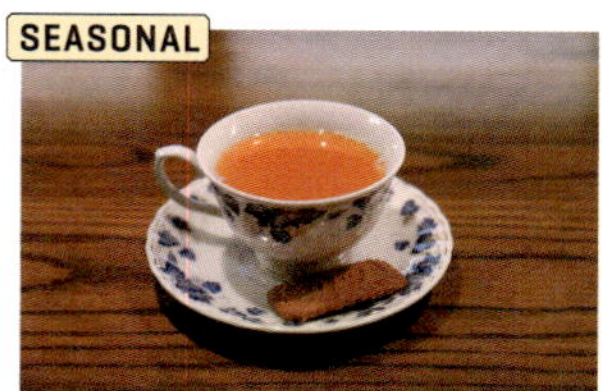

High Tea

A warm drink made with Finnish gin and apple juice. Infused with the aroma of cinnamon and cloves. ¥1,400.

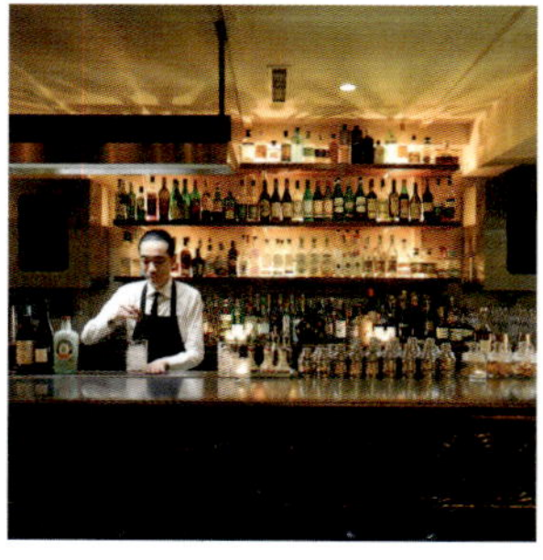

INC cocktails ●Shibuya

Known for cocktails crafted by owner Kenji Morioka with great respect for the classic styles. Named the "silver box," the ALTEC 612A is the bar's symbol. High-quality vinyl music, with guest DJs on weekends. ●1-5-6 Shibuya, Shibuya City, La Collina Shibuya B1 ☎ 03-6805-1774. 6:00 p.m. to 2:00 a.m. No closed days. Cover charge: ¥500.

SIGNATURE

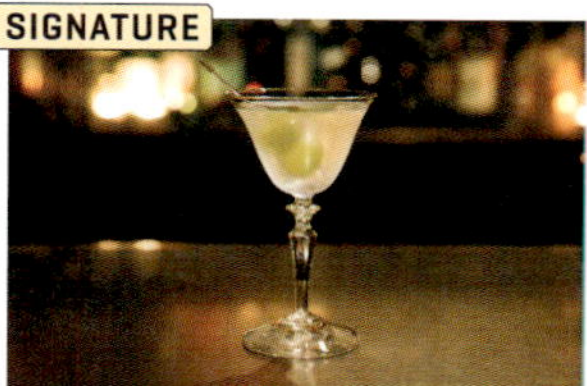

The INC Cocktails Martini

A twist on the classic martini, made with Plymouth gin, Spanish vermouth, and a touch of sherry for added aroma. ¥1,540.

SEASONAL

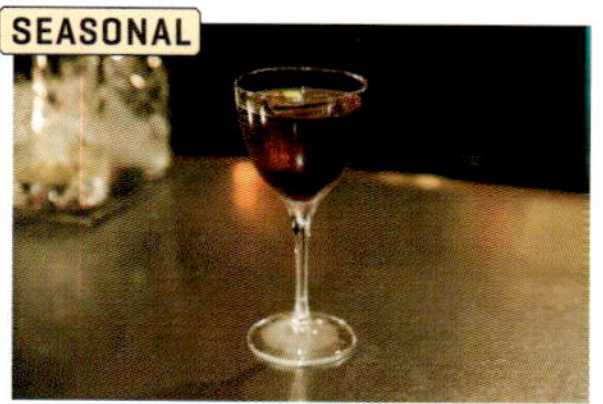

Green Sleeves

A mellow short cocktail made with single malt and sweet sherry with a caramel flavor. ¥1,870.

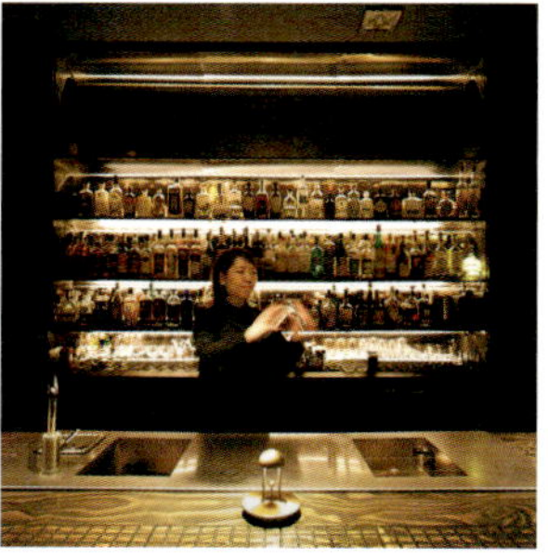

Flying Bumblebee ●Daikan-yama

Impressive central 7-meter island counter. Dark, moody-yet-open interior with a comfortable ambience of warm wood and soft lighting. 30 cocktails permanently served. ●13-7 Daikan-Yamacho, Shibuya City, Belvie Daikan-Yama B1☎03-6455-1185. 5:00 p.m. to 12:00 a.m. Irregular closed days. Cover charge: ¥600.

SIGNATURE

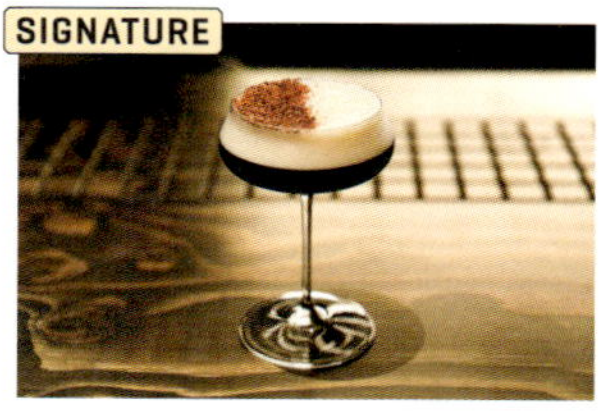

1942 Espresso Martini

Made with a lavish dose of "Don Julio 1942." Dark-roasted coffee boosts the rich flavor of the tequila. ¥2,000.

SEASONAL

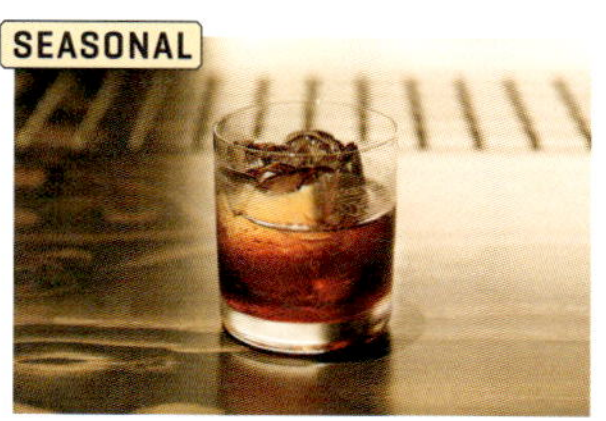

Mezcal Negroni

A twist on the classic cocktail using the increasingly popular mezcal. The smoky flavor is really addictive. ¥1,900.

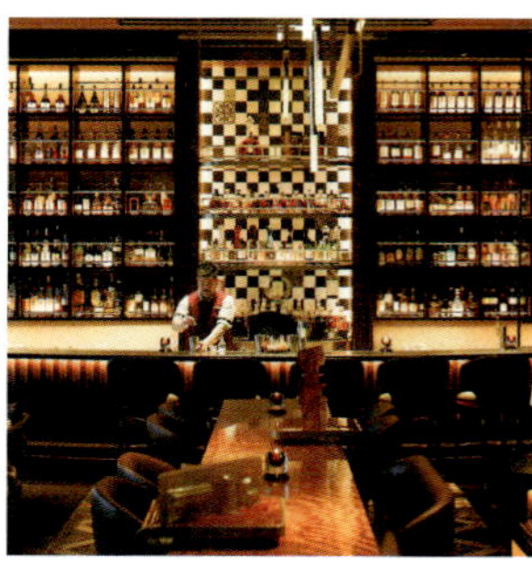

VIRTÙ ●Otemachi

A selection of cocktails that blend classic French styles with Japanese ingredients and new techniques. The elegant space fuses Art Déco and Nishijin brocade, and offers a view of Tokyo's nightscape. ●1-2-1 Otemachi, Chiyoda City, Four Seasons Hotel Tokyo at Otemachi 39F ☎03-6810-0655. 5:00 p.m. to 12:00 a.m. (to 12:30 a.m. on Thu., Fri., and Sat.). No closed days.

SIGNATURE

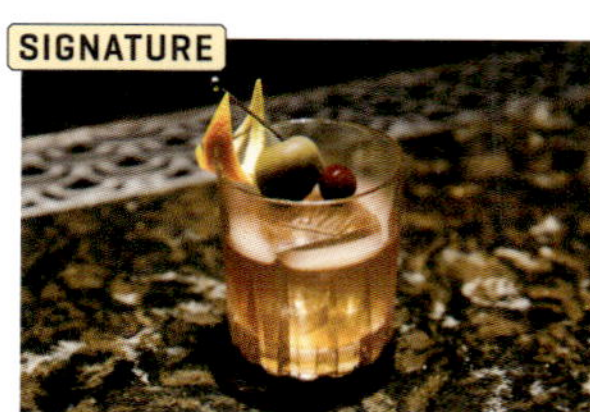

Smoked Ume Fashioned

A twist on the classic cocktail with homemade plum wine. A smoky drink enclosing a cherry wood chip aroma. ¥4,000.

SEASONAL

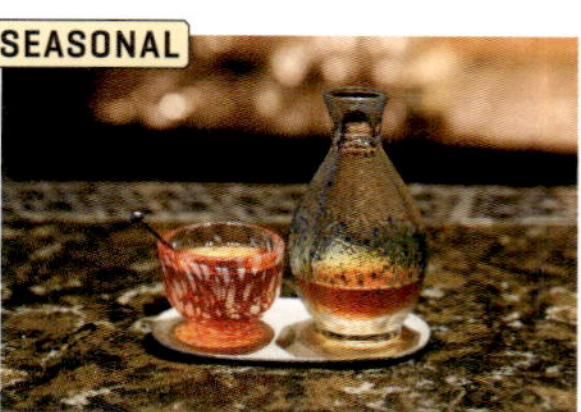

Sakura Sazerac

A slow-sipping drink with rye whiskey's spiciness and a hint of cherry blossom. A twist on the oldest cocktail. ¥4,100.

Photos: Kenya Abe Text: Chisa Nishinoiri

Enjoy "Layers" of Ice, Sauce, and Extra Ingredients.

Kanako Murakami's shaved ice awakening happened 10 years ago. After Mao Asada took her to the famous ***Kuriya Kurogi***, she got so into shaved ice that she even went on to open her own shop. The shaved ice of the recent boom isn't like the "traditional" kind—there are different reasons for craving it every season. "For example, various shops offer sakura-flavored shaved ice every April, but how the ice is shaved, the extra ingredients, and the layers all differ from place to place. From first bite to last, each layer tells a carefully crafted tale." In order to enjoy shaved ice at any time, she says she's also careful to keep warm. Why would an ice skater want shaved ice even in winter? "Maybe it's a bit like how beer-lovers will have a cold one even when it's chilly out. The season doesn't matter. I love the feeling of the cold ice melting inside me. Once you can appreciate that, you're a true shaved ice devotee."

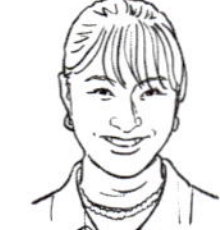

Kanako Murakami

●Professional figure skater

Kanako Murakami was born in Aichi in 1994. She started skating at the age of three, won the 2010-11 GP Series US Cup, and competed in the Sochi Olympics in 2014. Since retiring, she's been appearing in ice shows and on TV.

Ice skating tiredness, soothed away with ice. Kanako Murakami has had as many as 500 bowls of shaved ice in a year. Here, she shares some tips on how and where to enjoy it all year round.

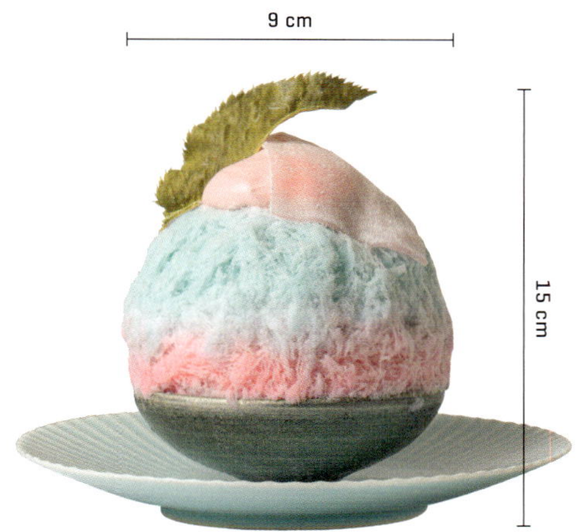

Sakura Chocolate Mint

Iced-Tea Room Tsukisome ●Ginza

A shaved ice shop run by a bartender. "Sakura Chocolate Mint" (¥1,600) features mint and sakura milk, with chocolate sauce inside. The salty taste of sakura leaves adds a nice accent. There's also "Potato Mentaiko," with a hint of rosemary. The menu is packed with innovative ideas, and changes every week. ●8-7-19 Ginza, Chuo City, 2F ☎ No phone number. 3:00 p.m. to 9:00 p.m. (last orders at 8:30 p.m.). Irregular closed days.

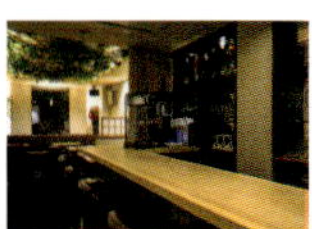

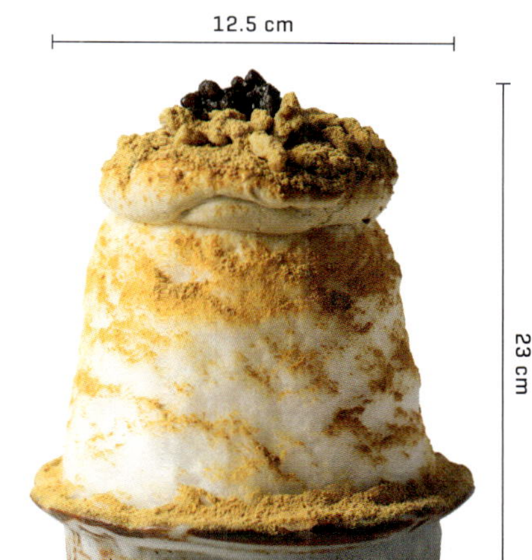

Kuromitsu and Golden Soybean Flour

Kuriya Kurogi ●Ueno-hirokoji

A shaved ice shop run by Japanese restaurant ***Kurogi***. The sauce with Japanese cuisine-inspired touches like adding soy sauce is divine. The classic "Black Syrup & Soybean Flour" (¥1,750) is shaved ice topped with syrup cream and soybean flour. Slowly mix in the cream, and the ice's texture evolves deliciously. ●3-24-6 Ueno, Taito City, PARCO_ya Ueno 1F ☎03-6284-2796. 10:00 a.m. to 9:00 p.m. (last orders at 8:00 p.m.). No closed days.

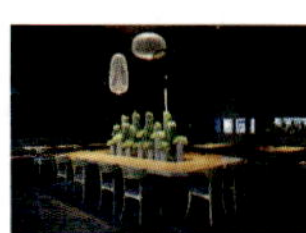

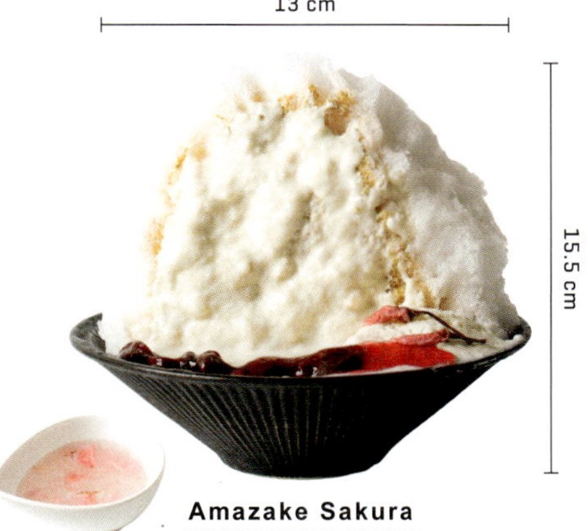

Amazake Sakura

Sabo Okuno Shibuya ●Shibuya

Shaved ice shop run by a former Japanese sweets artisan. The cliff-like "Amazake Sakura" (¥1,980, ends mid-April) uses mascarpone, plus homemade amazake solely made with highly polished rice. Playful shaved ice with cherry sauce and strained bean paste hidden within. Sakura syrup pops up to switch the flavor, too. ●7-15 Kamiyamacho, Shibuya City, Whiteheim Otake, Room 102 ☎03-6804-9889. 10:00 a.m. to 7:00 p.m. (last orders at 6:30 p.m.). Closed on Tue.

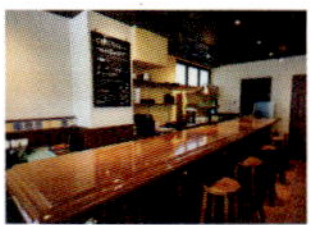

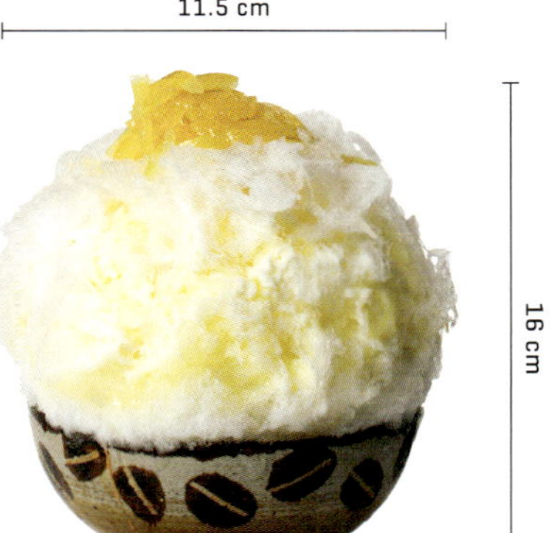

Shonan Gold Citrus & Rare Cheese

Hyoshya mamatoko ●Shin-nakano

A shop by shaved ice boom pioneer Asako Harada. Every detail, from the shaving technique to the layering, is carefully designed to enhance the ice's texture. You can also customize the sauce combinations. The photo is of the limited-period "Shonan Gold Citrus & Rare Cheese" (¥1,800). ●6-31-2 Honcho, Nakano City ☎No phone number. 2:00 p.m. to 6:30 p.m. (from 1:00 p.m. to 5:30 p.m. on Sat., Sun., and holidays). Irregular closed days.

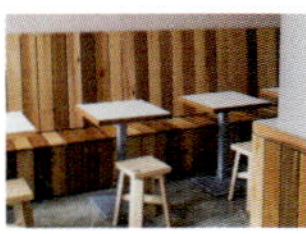

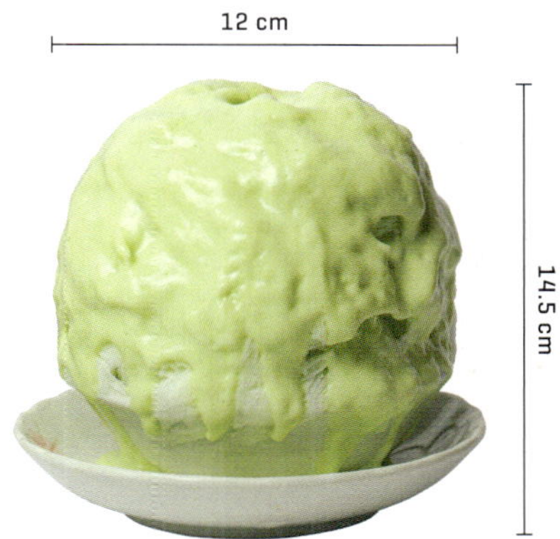

Avocado Milk

Kobe Minatoya ●Sasazuka

Owner trained at the long-running Osaka store ***Takoya Dotonbori Kukuru***. Takoyaki and akashiyaki dumpling shop that serves sublime shaved ice. Always around 14 flavors to choose from, like "Avocado Milk" (¥1,100). A refreshingly simple combo of just one fresh sauce and ice. You'll want to keep coming back. ●2-41-20 Sasazuka, Shibuya City, Okada Bldg. 1F ☎03-6383-3120. 11:00 a.m. to 6:30 p.m. Closed on Wed.

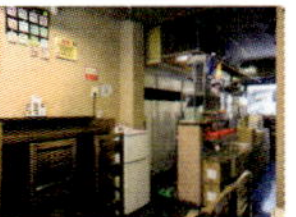

Note: The shaved ice sizes are as measured by our editorial team.

Photos: Mai Hokari, Shu Yamamoto Text: Anna Abe

Sate Your Desire for Food and Culture in This Busy City.

The movie starts in 30 minutes. Time for a quick, tasty bite. Utamaru shares some Tokyo spots that offer that, and some culture to boot.

Utamaru stopped by at ***Susan's MEAT BALL*** on the B1 floor of Tokyo Midtown Hibiya. "I love the unique idea of a 'meatball specialty store' and the authentic American diner vibe, so I've been coming here a lot ever since it opened in 2018. Besides the super-speedy service, the choice of meatballs and pasta stirs up my inner child. It takes me right back to the pure-hearted boy dreaming of movies who I once was."

He usually enjoys food like that either before a movie or right before getting on the Shinkansen when he's on tour. His favorites are ***Sekiya Spaghetti EXPRESS*** in Shinagawa, ***Indian Curry, Marunouchi Store*** in Marunouchi, and ***Acacia, Shinjuku Main Store*** in Shinjuku. Even if he's only got 30 minutes to spare, he still carefully chooses each order.

"***BLESS COFFEE, Kyobashi Store*** is a café across from the National Film Archive of Japan, where I often go for screenings. The shop's vintage vibe feels like it really goes with the movie I'm about to watch. Fast food is fine, but I think the unique coffee and sandwiches are a very Tokyo-like pleasure."

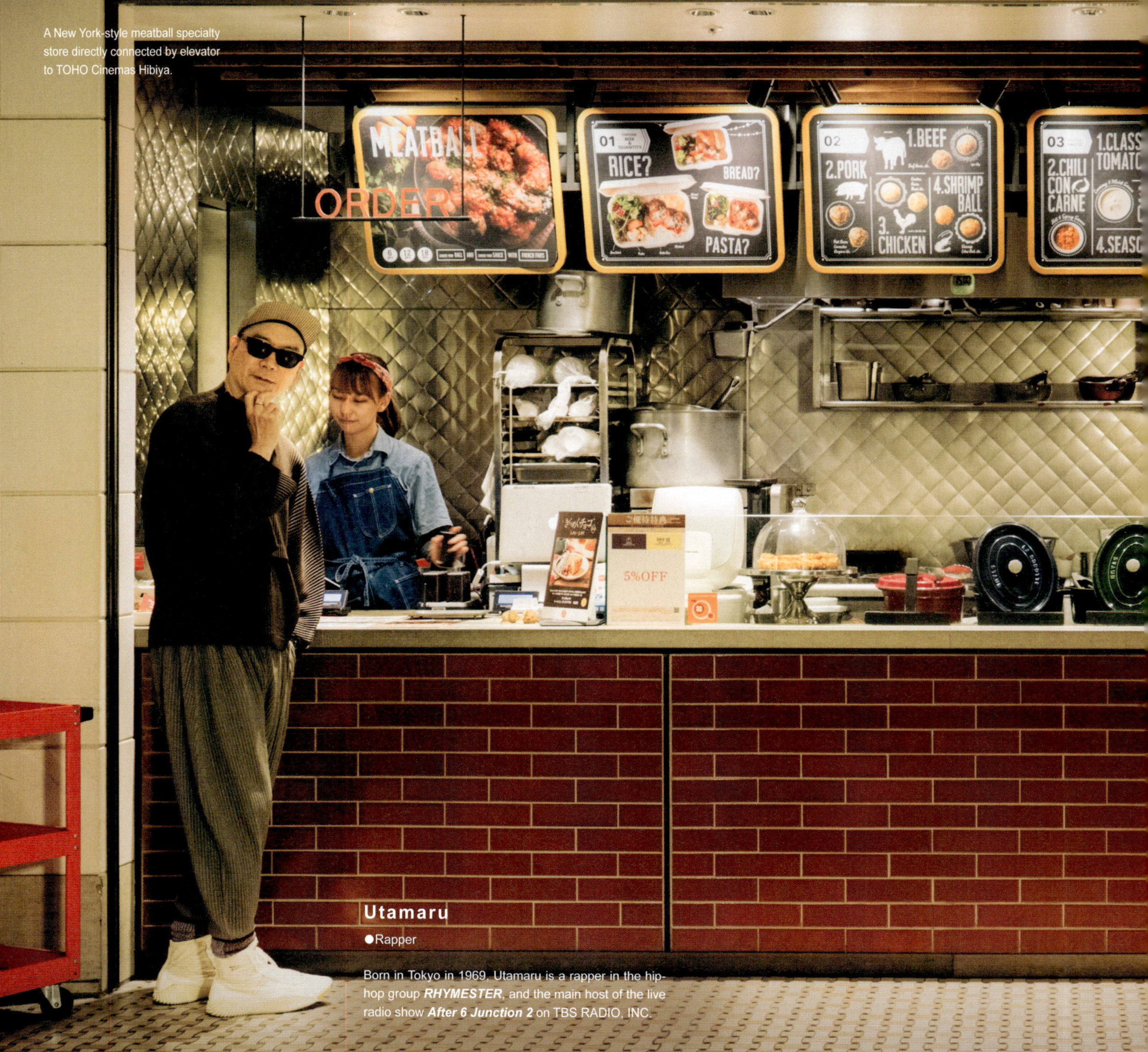

A New York-style meatball specialty store directly connected by elevator to TOHO Cinemas Hibiya.

Utamaru

●Rapper

Born in Tokyo in 1969, Utamaru is a rapper in the hip-hop group ***RHYMESTER***, and the main host of the live radio show ***After 6 Junction 2*** on TBS RADIO, INC.

Photos: Ayumi Yamamoto Text: Kohei Hara

And he doesn't simply wolf it down in seconds, either, never forgetting to enjoy the city even when he's in a rush.

"If they end up being just something to consume, both food and movies lose their charm. A mindset of connecting the history and context is crucial. This city still has plenty of unique cultures besides the usual ones. Discovering these is what makes going out in Tokyo such a unique pleasure."

Susan's MEAT BALL Tokyo Midtown Hibiya

●Hibiya

Customizable meatballs and sauce. ●1-1-2 Yurakucho, Chiyoda City, Tokyo Midtown Hibiya B1 (Inside HIBIYA FOOD HALL) ☎03-3519-7311. 11 a.m. to 9:30 p.m. (to 10 p.m. on Fri., last orders in both cases). No closed days.

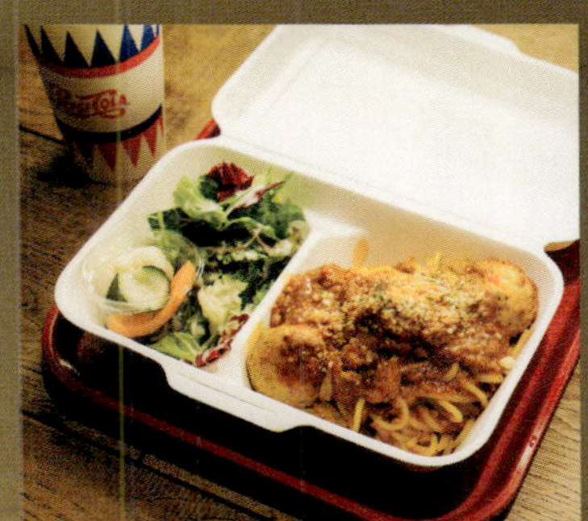

Right: The ¥1,250 box with pasta, spicy pork meatballs, and chili con carne sauce is his standard choice.

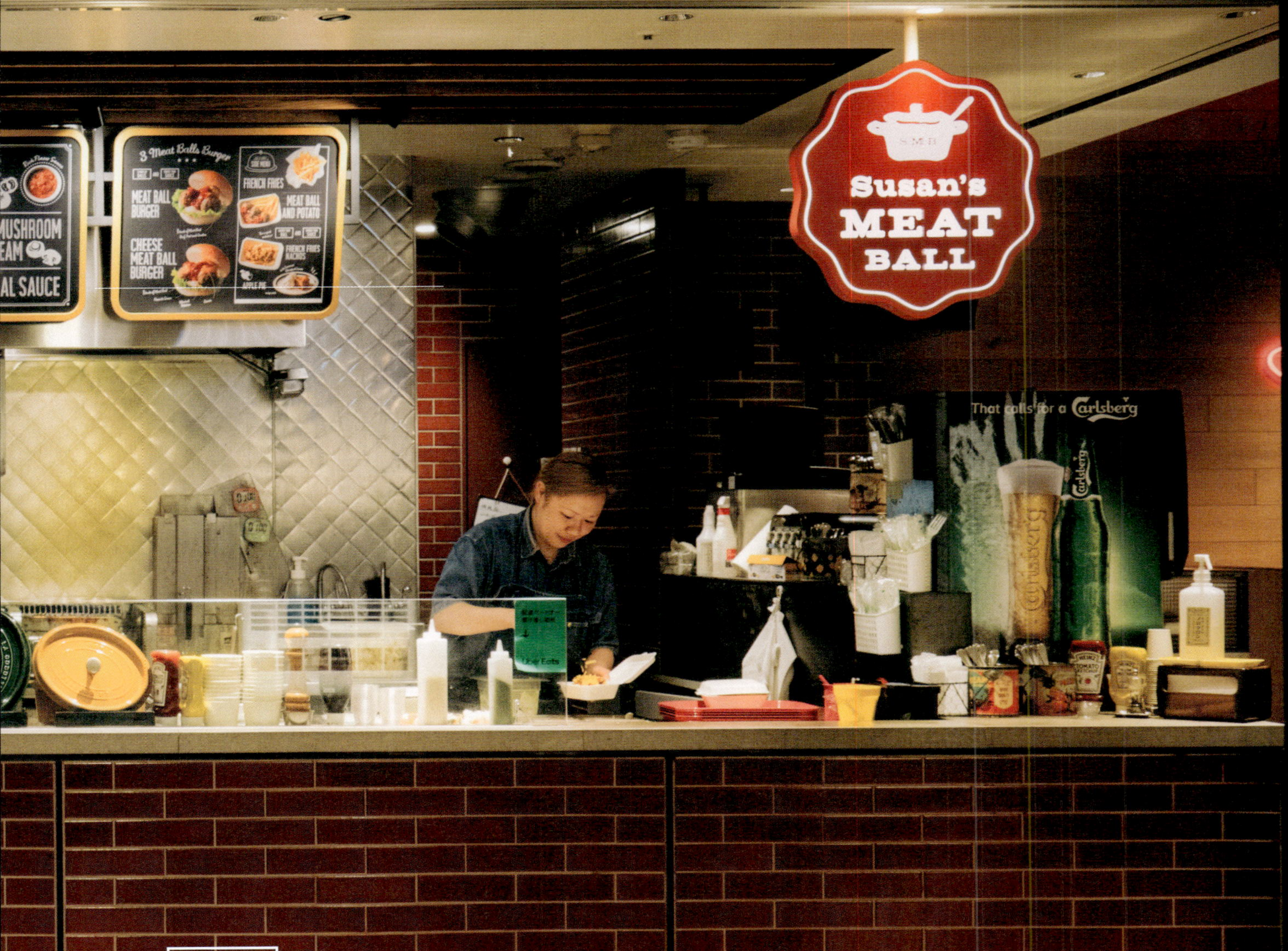

AND MORE...

Sekiya Spaghetti EXPRESS

●Shinagawa

Serves classic spaghetti with a focus on "stir-fry." ●3-26-27 Takanawa, Minato City, ecute Shinagawa inside JR Shinagawa Station ☎03-6450-3309. 7:00 a.m. to 9:30 p.m. (last orders) (from 8:00 a.m. on Sun.). No closed days.

INDIAN CURRY, Marunouchi Store

●Marunouchi

Tokyo's first branch of the 70-year-old Osaka curry shop. Delightfully traditional flavors. ●2-7-3 Marunouchi, Chiyoda City, Tokyo Bldg. TOKIA B1 ☎03-3216-2336. 11:00 a.m. to 9:45 p.m. (last orders). Irregular closed days.

Acacia, Shinjuku Main Store

●Shinjuku

Japanese home cooking-style Western food. Specialty dish: cabbage roll stew with homemade roux. ●3-22-10 Shinjuku, Shinjuku City ☎03-3354-7511. 11 a.m. to 8:30 p.m. (to 9 p.m. on Fri., Sat. and Sun., last orders in all cases). No closed days.

BLESS COFFEE, Kyobashi Store

●Kyobashi

Besides Ethiopian coffee beans, there's also a wide variety of sandwiches and sweets. ●2-5-17 Kyobashi, Chuo City, Kyobashi SK Bldg. 1F & 2F ☎03-3563-5580. 7 a.m. to 9 p.m. (9 a.m. to 6 p.m. on Sat., Sun., and holidays). Irregular closed days.

The Fun of Tokyo, Seen from Kansai.

Yoriko Sakata

●Owner of baked sweets shop ***SAKATA YAKIKASHI TEN***

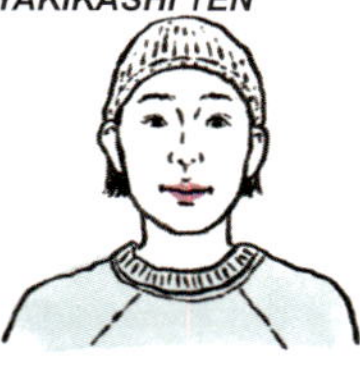

Born in Kyoto in 1980 and spent her early years in Canada, where she fell in love with her mother's baked sweets. Since 2015, she's been running ***SAKATA YAKIKASHI TEN*** near Kyoto's Kitano Tenmangu, where she bakes fresh, all-natural sweets.

Tokyo wagashi that are light but richly flavorful.

Kyoto's bean paste is great, but Tokyo's is tasty in a different way. After visiting a friend's grave, I buy ***TAIYAKI WAKABA***'s taiyaki, which are crisp and bursting with bean paste—a rarity in Kansai. ***Seijuken***'s dorayaki have a moist skin and sweet bean paste. Elegance in unity. Also a sweet potato fan, I love ***Funawa***'s imo yokan. They bring out the deep sweet potato flavor to the full, hinting at careful craftsmanship behind the simple appearance.

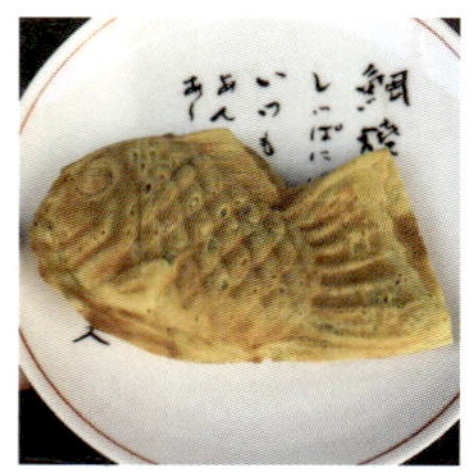

TAIYAKI WAKABA

A beloved Yotsuya shop since 1953 that sells around 3,000 taiyaki a day. Crammed in all the way to the tail, the lightly salted homemade bean paste goes down easy. ¥210. ●1-10 Wakaba, Shinjuku City, Ozawa Bldg. 1F ☎03-3351-4396. 9:00 a.m. to 5:00 p.m. Closed on Wed. and Sun.

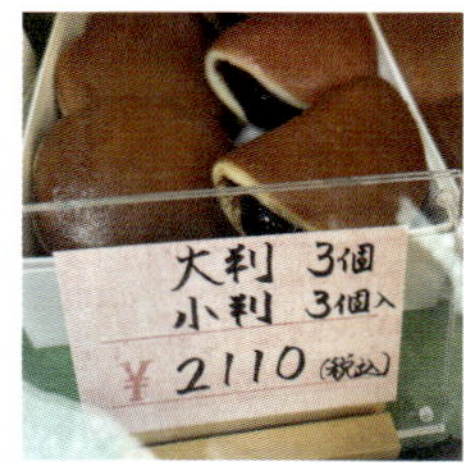

Seijuken

Founded in 1861, at the end of the Edo period. Their rich bean paste dorayaki with a hand-grilled skin often sell out by noon, so phoning to reserve them is advised. Koban: ¥300. ●1-4-16 Nihombashi-Horidomecho, Chuo City, Pcos Nihombashi Bldg. 1F ☎03-3661-0940. 9:00 a.m. to 5:00 p.m. Closed on Sat. and Sun.

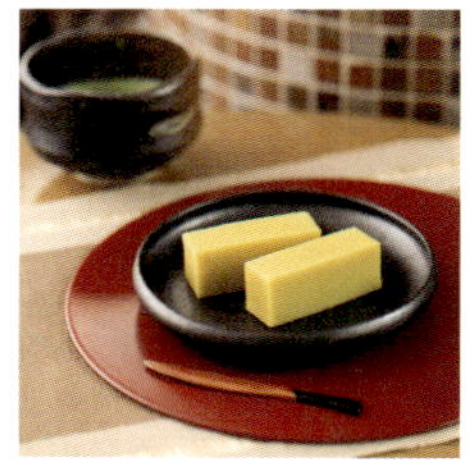

Funawa

A long-running wagashi shop founded in 1902. Their simple imo yokan made from sweet potato, sugar, and salt have been a staple since they first opened their doors. Also great toasted. Pack of five: ¥864. ● 1-22-10 Asakusa, Taito City ☎ 03-3842-2781. 10:00 a.m. to 7:00 p.m. No closed days.

Yoshitaka Haba

●Book director, and representative of ***BACH***

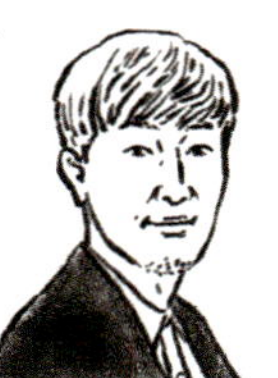

Born in Aichi in 1976, Yoshitaka Haba creates libraries in public spaces like hospitals, schools, hotels, and offices, and also curates ***The Waseda International House of Literature (The Haruki Murakami Library)***.

I only go occasionally, but they're real comfort places.

My life is split between Kyoto and Tokyo, and these three are my go-to spots when I'm in the latter. I've known ***MA STORE***'s owner for years and feel really attached to it, having known it right from the start. ***Shiomachi*** shows deep love for seafood and sake, serving izakaya fare like natto yakisoba and crab zha cai fried rice. Popular with global guests, ***HIBANA Roppongi*** wins my heart every time with its owner Atsushi Nagashima's wonderful service.

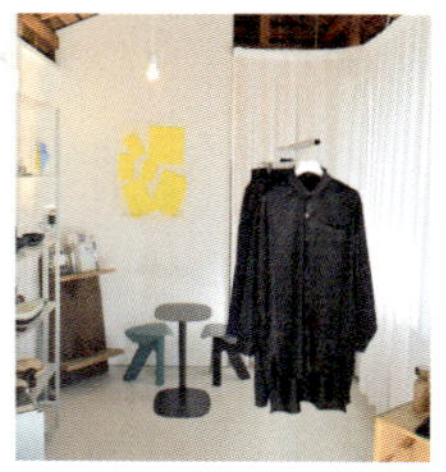

MA STORE

A Shoin-jinja-mae select shop that sells modern Japanese folk and craft goods and respects the classics. Opened in 2024 by Tsubasa Matsuo, an owner in his 30s. ●4-13-18 Setagaya, Setagaya City, KUMI-HOUSE 2F ☎No phone number. 1:00 p.m. to 7:00 p.m. Irregular closed days.

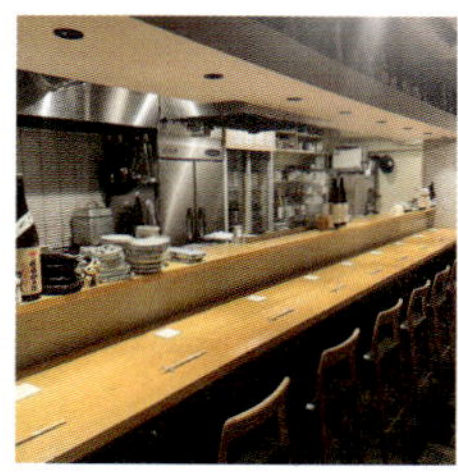

Shiomachi

The owner sources fresh seafood from The Toyosu Shijou and serves it as sashimi, simmered, or grilled. The sake is also delicious, and is mainly selected not for its fame, but how well it goes with the food. ●1-34-10 Uehara, Shibuya City, Shigaya Bldg. 2F ☎03-6804-8484. 5 p.m. to 10 p.m. Irregular closed days.

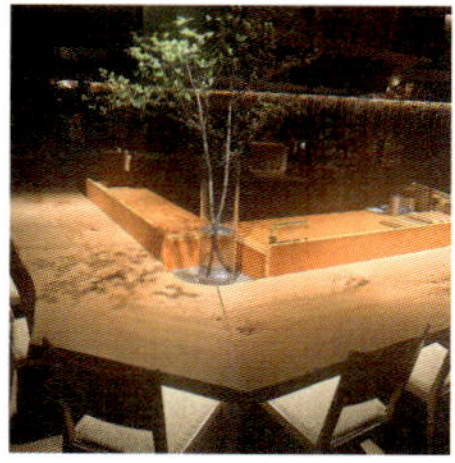

HIBANA Roppongi

A wine bar that moved from Yotsuya to Roppongi in 2024. Aiming for a freer, livelier drinking style ever since, they offer global wines, hot sake, spirits, and more. ●6-1-7 Roppongi, Minato City, Osawa Bldg. 6F ☎050-1808-7540. 6:30 p.m. to 11:30 p.m. Irregular closed days.

Yasuko Kohira

●Culinary expert

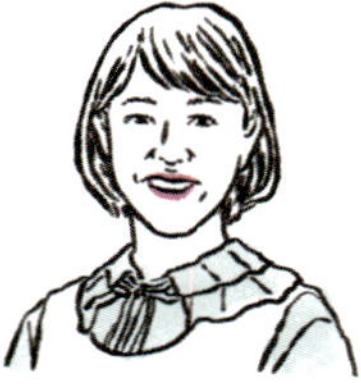

Born in Kyoto in 1977. Runs cooking classes in Kyoto's Karasuma and Kyotanbacho and Tokyo's Nihombashi—a life split between east and west. Delivers obanzai dishes nationwide. See her Instagram (@yasukokohiragokan) for details.

A thoughtful souvenir with a lingering afterglow.

I'm envious of how many shops Tokyo has for souvenirs like that. ***call***'s wines, sweets, and spices are carefully selected and beautifully packaged. ***AU BON VIEUX TEMPS*** features classic French confectioneries and a strong charcuterie selection. I like buying both and serving them at home like afternoon tea. A nice touch at ***LAMMAS*** is how they beautifully plate your chosen cheeses. The truffle brie is a must—my family all love it, too.

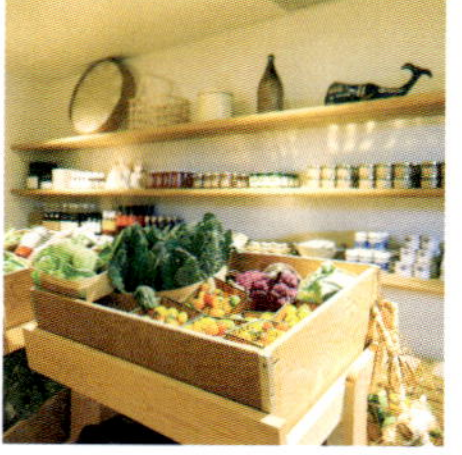

call

A ***minä perhonen*** flagship with lifestyle items that encompass fashion, food, and home goods. Handles groceries, kids' clothes, and global crafts. ● 5-6-23 Minami-Aoyama, Minato City, Spiral 5F ☎03-6825-3733. 11:00 a.m. to 7:00 p.m. (to 8:00 p.m. on Fri., Sat., and Sun.). No closed days.

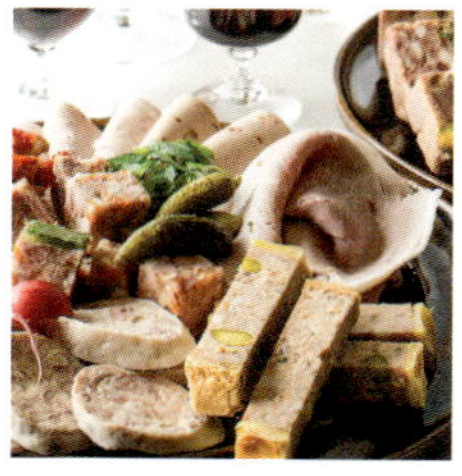

AU BON VIEUX TEMPS

Founded in 1981 by Katsuhiko Kawata, a pioneer of French pastry in Japan. The wide charcuterie selection is the work of his son, Rikiya. ●2-1-3 Todoroki, Setagaya City ☎ 03-3703-8428. 10:00 a.m. to 5:00 p.m. Closed on Tue. and Wed.

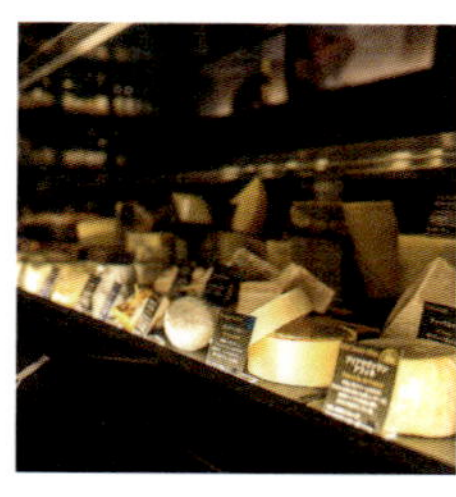

LAMMAS

Imported cheeses aged by affineurs, and natural wines. Main store in Sangen-jaya, plus locations in ***Roppongi Hills*** and ***Toranomon Hills***. ●2-20-5 Shimouma, Setagaya City ☎03-6453-2045. 1:00 p.m. to 7:00 p.m. (from 12 p.m. on Sat., Sun., and holidays). Closed on Mon., Tue., and the day after holidays.

Photos: Masahiro Sambe [call], Norio Kidera [MOGI Folk Art] Illustrations: naohiga Text: Shoko Yoshida

Comparison-prone Tokyo and Kansai. There's no place like home, but there's fun to be had away, too. Which Tokyo spots do these six Kansai-based connoisseurs recommend?

Shigeki Hattori

●Representative of ***graf***

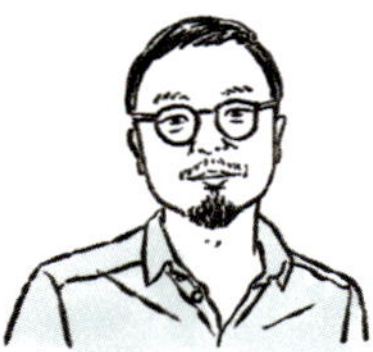

Born in Osaka in 1970. After working at interior shops and design firms, he founded ***graf*** in Osaka in 1998. They handle architectural and interior design, and also branding direction.

Three memorable spots I encountered at key junctures.

The Japanese-Western dishes at ***Nomiya Parole*** felt like a special dinner adorning the table. Barhopping often ended with being taken along to ***VELVET OVERHIGH'M d.m.x*** by painter Shinro Otake and Shinichiro Nakahara from ***THE CONRAN SHOP***. ***wellk*** was opened by a former staff member. Photographer Yayoi Arimoto brings me sweets from here when she's in Kansai. Despite all the countless shops Tokyo has, only a few have left a real mark on me. Strangely, they all appeared at turning points in my life.

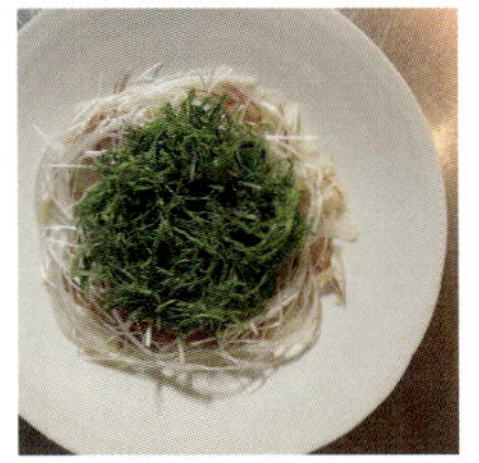

Nomiya Parole

Homey bar opened by the late Emiko Sakurai at age 71, now run by her daughter. White-themed space and dishes are unchanged. Photo: carpaccio with lots of condiments (¥2,500). ●2-22-14 Minami-Aoyama, Minato City ☎ 03-6434-5959. 6:00 p.m. to 9:00 p.m. (last orders). Closed on Sat., Sun., and Mon.

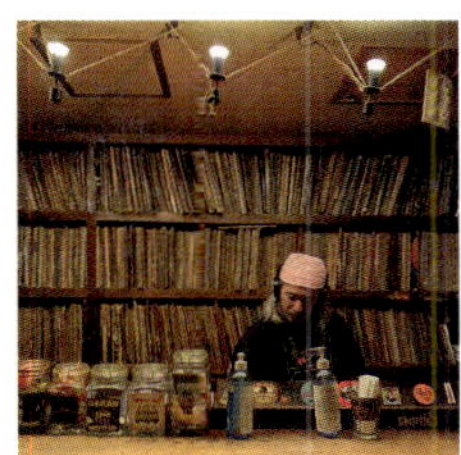

VELVET OVERHIGH'M d.m.x

A long-running record bar nestling deep in Shinjuku 2. The second-generation rock 'n' roller owner is nice to newcomers, too. ●2-14 Shinjuku, Shinjuku City ☎ 03-5379-3220. 6:00 p.m. to 3:00 a.m. Closed on Wed.

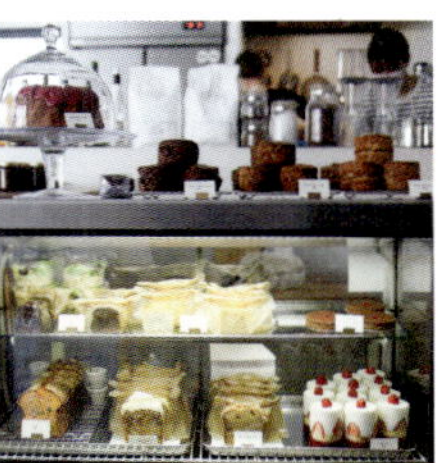

wellk

Café and restaurant run by pastry school graduate and former ***graf*** employee Hirofumi Ishihara. Popular seller is the ¥560 spiced carrot cake. ●2-5-11 Mita, Meguro City, Yoshida Bldg. 2F ☎03-6303-2411. 10:00 a.m. to 6:00 p.m. (from 8:30 a.m. to 5:00 p.m. on Sat. and Sun.). Closed on Mon. and Tue.

Yoriko Hoshi

●Manga artist

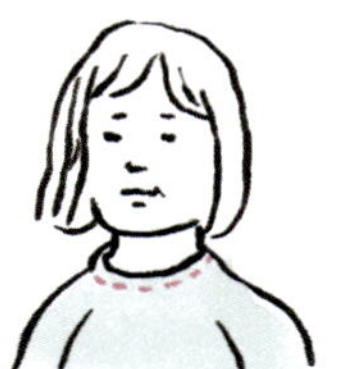

Born in 1974. Based in Kansai. Posting one panel of ***Today's Ms. Nekomura 1*** online daily since 2003. First collected volume published in 2005. Later adapted into a live-action drama. Has captivated the whole of Japan.

Places that make me think, "Ah, I'm in a big city."

Yakitori Takechan exudes Edo vitality with its cool atmosphere and brisk, sharp service. ***Picon Ber*** is a regular haunt for customers of all genders and ages—including dogs. The master's casual care is cool, and both the food and wine are rugged yet refined. I found out about ***HOOTERS GINZA*** when I heard it was a favorite of Ed Sheeran's while I was working on a music video of his. The lively cheerleader service will send your spirits into the stratosphere. Hope they bring back the merch T-shirts.

Yakitori Takechan

Behind ***Ginza Mitsukoshi***. Founded in 1953. Popular yakitori restaurant, busy every night. Two-choice menu: 5 skewers (¥3,000) or 8 (¥4,000). Specialty: "Miso Dengaku with Duck." Can add individual skewers. ●4-8-13 Ginza, Chuo City ☎03-3561-6889. 5 p.m. to 9 p.m. Closed on Mon., Sun., and holidays.

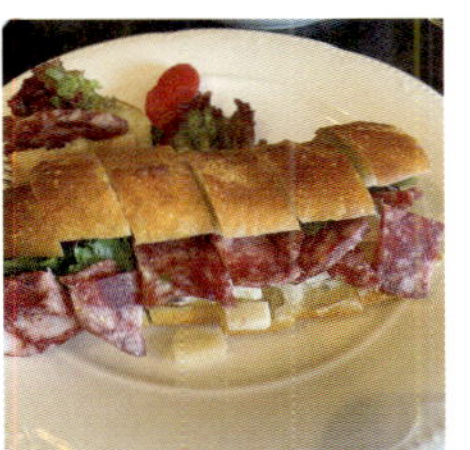

Picon Ber

Back-alley French spot in Gotokuji that serves as a café, bar, and bistro. Known for its chic food, amaro, and owner. Now in its 30th year. Photo: lunchtime-only sandwich (¥1,100). ●1-45-2 Gotokuji, Setagaya City ☎03-3420-9977. 1 p.m. to 11 p.m. (from 12 p.m. to 9 p.m. on Sun.). Closed on Tue.

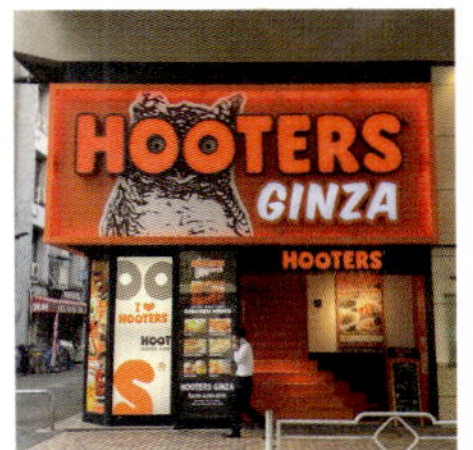

HOOTERS GINZA

An American restaurant & sports bar from Florida. The interior features orange and white, and the staff wear cheerleader-style tank tops and shorts. ●8-5 Ginza, Chuo City, Ginza Nine 1st Bldg. 2F ☎03-6280-6318. 11:30 a.m. to 11 p.m. No closed days.

Shoichi Tamaru

●Owner of ***dieci***

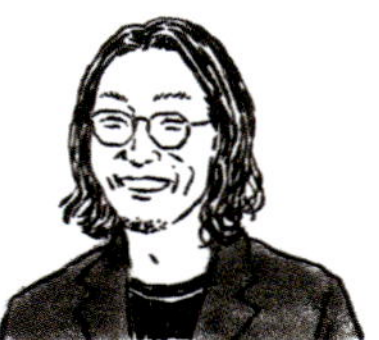

Born in Osaka in 1975. In 1999, he opened ***dieci***, an interior shop offering various goods sourced in Japan and overseas. He now runs three stores in Osaka.

Interiors that reflect the owners' sensibilities.

The two owners of ***MOGI Folk Art*** used to work at ***BEAMS***, so every product feels fashionable. Formerly a gallery and folk craft shop, ***Kanmi Okame Kojimachi*** has stylish fixtures that convey the owner's tastes. ***Swimsuit Department*** offers creative original goods crafted by Takahiro Goko, a connoisseur of global crafts. Tokyo is such a cornucopia, so it's a great place to find shops designed around their owners' unique sensibilities.

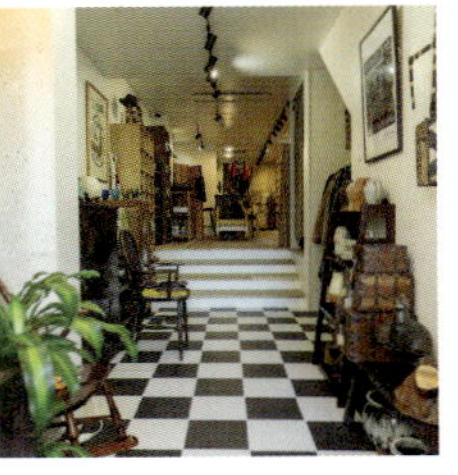

MOGI Folk Art

Run by Terry Ellis and Keiko Kitamura, who launched ***BEAMS***'s label ***fennica*** and excelled as skilled buyers. Offers global tableware and crafts, original knitted goods, and vintage clothes. ●3-45-12 Koenji-Minami, Suginami City ☎080-8058-1761. 12:00 p.m. to 7:00 p.m. Closed on Tue. and Wed.

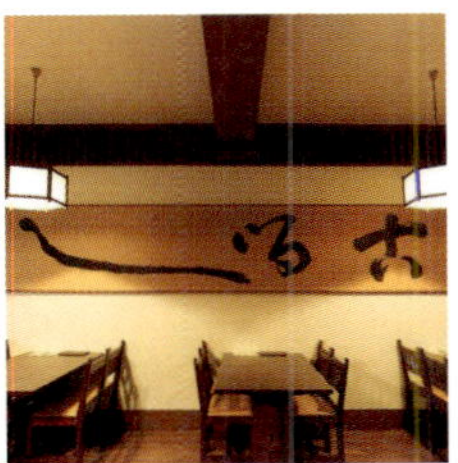

Kanmi Okame Kojimachi

Opened under its current name in postwar 1946. Mizuyadansu cabinets by ***Matsumoto Mingei Kagu***, stencil dyeing by Keisuke Serizawa, seasonal folk craft tableware, and regional toys. ●1-7 Kojimachi, Chiyoda City ☎03-5275-5368. 10:30 a.m. to 6:00 p.m. Closed on Sat., Sun., and holidays.

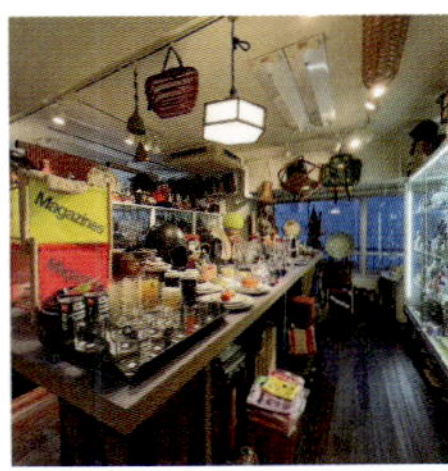

Swimsuit Department

Brimming with vintage and interior goods chosen from an unlimited range of genres and regions by keen-eyed owner Takahiro Goko. ●3-36-26 Jingumae, Shibuya City, Villa Uchikawa, Room 201 ☎03-6804-6288. 1:00 p.m. to 6:00 p.m. (Appointment required from Mon. to Wed.). Irregular closed days.

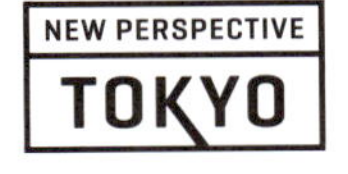

7 TOKYO HOT SPOTS

JIMBOCHO

Food, books, and comedy.
A town where young talents hone their craft.

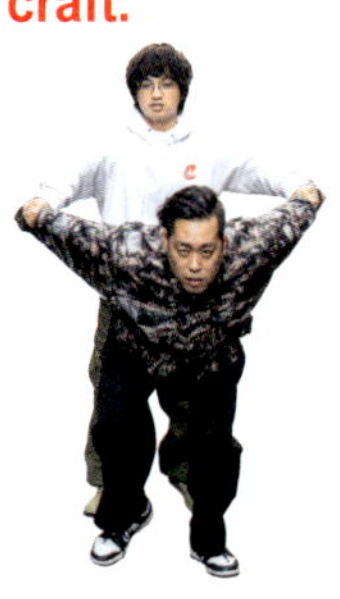

Evers

●Comedians

Formed in 2015, this comedy duo consisting of funny man Takafumi Sasaki (top) and straight man Kazuki Machida (bottom) was a finalist in the ***M-1 Grand Prix 2024***. To celebrate their tenth anniversary of teaming up, they kicked off their first national tour ***Soredemo, Wind-Up*** in April.

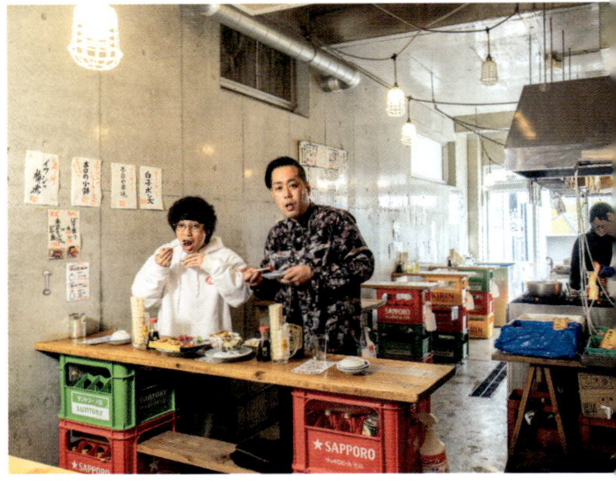

Uokuma Sengyo Ten to Tachinomi Botefuri 1

Stand-up bar & fish shop. Great sashimi and shellfish. Pick food from showcase. Self-service drinks. Pay after. Tank seafood: method requestable. Bluefin tuna eyeball stew: ¥638 (top). Bote Asstd. Platter (large): ¥2,480 (bottom). ●1-20-7 Kanda-Jimbocho, Chiyoda City ☎03-5577-6996. 5 p.m. to 11 p.m. Closed on Sun.

Jimbocho Yoshimoto comedians' go-to spots!

Bumpodo 2

I use flip charts in solo performances, but I've never seen a store with such a variety of paper, easels, and paint! A super gyaru-esque street where various vibes mix and coexist like a zebra's stripes!!!!

Plus a café. Art supply store founded in 1887.●1-21-1 Kanda-Jimbocho, Chiyoda City.

MAME KOH BOH, Jimbocho Shop 3

Every comedian in Jimbocho hangs out here cup in hand, and no exaggeration! Wide variety of beans, plus cocoa and acai juice. Be sure to stop by after lunch!!

2 daily coffee types for breakfast, lunch, and p.m. ●1-39-9 Kanda-Jimbocho, Chiyoda City.

Elf

Arakawa (left) and Haru (right). Formed in Osaka in 2016. Came 2nd in 2023 ***Women Comedians No. 1 Contest THE W*** thanks to Arakawa's gyaru-rich comedy. 1st podcast show: ***Elf no Torima Shugo Radio!*** (every Wed.).

NEKI 6

I'm from Hiroshima, so a store where you can watch Carps games on a huge screen over some tasty okonomiyaki is great. I recommend the "Grilled Green Onion & Salt Okonomiyaki." By the seen here so far.

Antenna shop for Fuchu City, Hiroshima. ●1-3-1 Kanda-Ogawamachi, Chiyoda City, 1F.

TOBICHI 7

A store that sells ***Hobonichi*** goods. They also handle goods to do with my favorite game "EarthBound", so even just browsing the shelves is great fun. Please do come to the Manzai Theater, too.

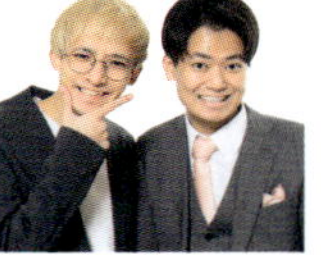

A store and gallery run by ***Hobonichi***. ●3-18 Kanda-Nishikicho, Chiyoda City, Hobonichi Kanda Bldg. 1F.

Pute

Point (left) and Tomoya Takeuchi (right). A duo formed in 2019 by 22nd-generation classmates from NSC Tokyo. Point is also the actor Shohei Murata. Like Nansui's Tsurumaru, Takeuchi is also a member of the trio ***Itabashi House***.

Kotoki 4

A Chinese restaurant on Kanda-Suzuran-dori Avenue. It stays open late, so we often go after our theater performances. We've gotten so friendly with the lady owner that we've swapped contact info with her. Give it a try.

Famous for lamb skewers and seafood stone hotpot mapo tofu. ●1-11-6 Kanda-Jimbocho, Chiyoda City.

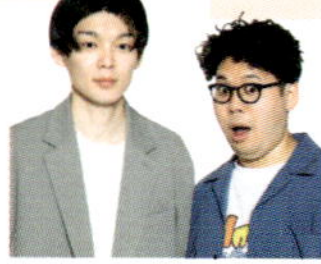

Bánh Mi☆Sandwich 5

The "Crispy Pork Bánh Mi" and "lotus tea" are recommended. The lotus tea is lovely, but I always forget how it tastes, so every time I have it, I'm like, "Oh yeah, it's this flavor."

The bánh mi and pho set is also popular. ●2-4-29 Kanda-Jimbocho, Chiyoda City, Matsumoto Bldg. 1F.

Nansui

Satoshi Okawauchi (left) and Tsurumaru (right). Classmates from NSC Osaka's 35th gen. Formed in 2013. A trio at first, then became a duo in 2016. Tsurumaru also performs as a member of the trio ***Itabashi House***, who share a house in Itabashi.

Wine Shochu 208 8

I went with two juniors, and we were awestruck by our first taste of the fried chickpeas called "panis." We've gotten so into them that whenever we're all together backstage, we're like, "Shall we go for panis?" "Sounds good."

Specialty: "Kobore Wine." (It's brimming!) ●2-14 Kanda-Jimbocho, Chiyoda City, 2F.

Jinza 9

I just kind of wandered in, but I'll never forget my excitement when I had the "Meat, Egg & Soy Sauce Udon." I didn't want to say this, but I also order it at home on Uber Eats. I've spent over half my career in this town. Welcome.

Big hit: homemade noodles topped with pork. ●3-2 Kanda-Nishikicho, Chiyoda City, 1F.

Nightingale Dance

Nakarutin Nakano (left) and Yasu (right). Met through university comedy. Formed a duo in 2016. Graduated top of NSC Tokyo's 22nd gen. Won the 2023 ***Tsugikuru Geinin Grand Prix***. First show: ***Naichingai Retro*** (3 a.m. every Sat.).

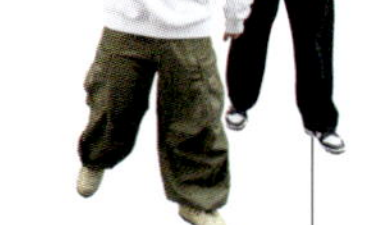

Photos: Kazufumi Shimoyashiki, Shu Yamamoto Illustrations: Adrian Hogan Text: Sho Kasahara

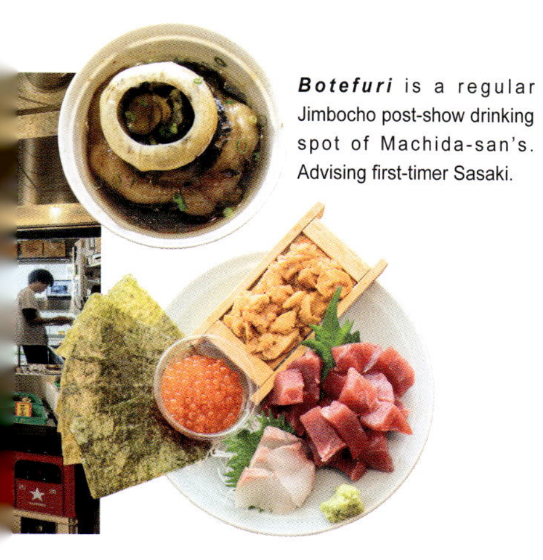

Botefuri is a regular Jimbocho post-show drinking spot of Machida-san's. Advising first-timer Sasaki.

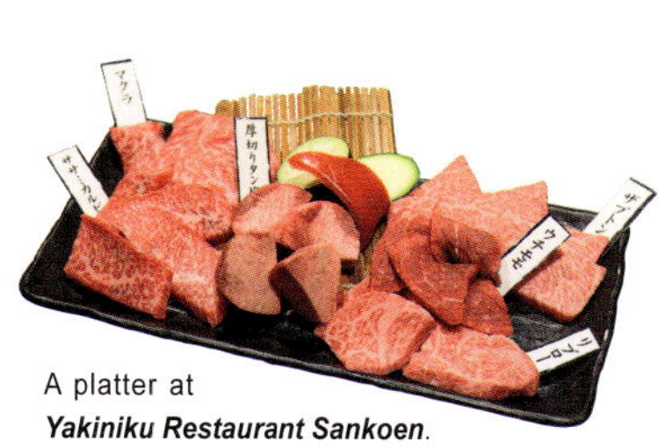

A platter at ***Yakiniku Restaurant Sankoen***.

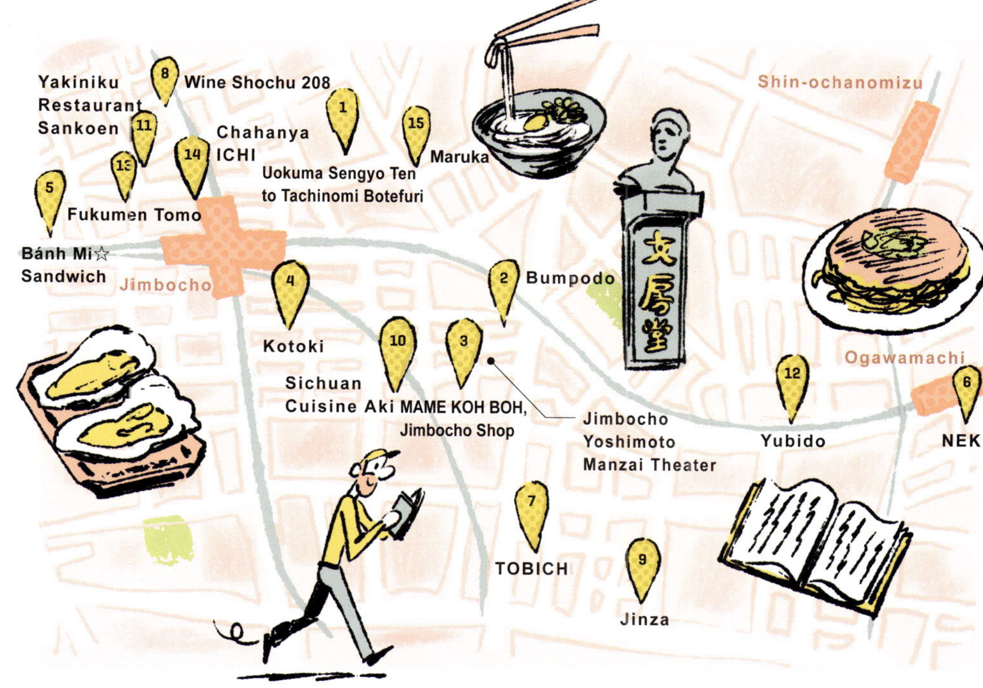

Sichuan Cuisine Aki 10

Top-tier all-you-can-eat-and-drink, with every dish absolutely delicious. The staff are really friendly, and ask after Ai, too. Like, "Where's that big friend you're always with? Is she okay?"

Great all-you-can-eat Sichuan at a nice price. ● 1-37-3 Kanda-Jimbocho, Chiyoda City, B1.

Yakiniku Restaurant Sankoen 11

Making props for a skit alone one night, I suddenly felt really hungry. Wanting something better than convenience store food, I ended up here until late. Try the stone-baked bibimbap as well.

Specialties: grilled shabu-shabu & aged-meat platter. ●2-14-2 Kanda-Jimbocho, Chiyoda City.

Yoneda 2000

Makoto (left) and Ai (right). Got to the ***M-1 Grand Prix 2022*** finals just two years after forming. Unique comedic banter is a hot topic. Solo live tour ***We are Yoneda 2000 Da*** coming up in June (Tokyo, Osaka, and Fukuoka).

When the Jimbocho Yoshimoto Manzai Theater opened in 2020 as a venue for young comedians, it got smaller audiences than the others at first. But then it gained recognition year by year, and attracted more young fans. With a movie theater downstairs as well, older customers sometimes drop by, too, so I think it's a great town. I don't drink alcohol, so I often go to cafés to come up with ideas. I like how it's laid-back and not too bustling. Before moving to Tokyo, I thought of it as an "unreal world" that only existed on TV, but I'm fully used to it now. (Sasaki)

When I'm done at the theater, I often stop by Uokuma Sengyo Ten to Tachinomi Botefuri. A senior comedian recommended it to me, and you can help yourself to drinks, sides, and fish, so you can take it at your own pace. Jimbocho is definitely a "town for grown-ups." No matter where I go to eat, I rarely feel like "I've made a mistake." I always get to have a quiet drink and go home feeling good. When I drink with seniors or juniors, the talk always turns to money. Since I'm a "grown-up" who Jimbocho suits well (laughs). (Machida)

Cold udon with tempura shrimp at ***Maruka***.

Yubido 12

I sometimes pop in before a live show. There's a kotatsu and even an Akita dog there, too, so in winter, I feel right at home. Jimbocho isn't hectic, so it's a great place to spend a relaxing whole day.

Art space. Formerly a picture frame shop. ● 2-4 Kanda-Ogawamachi, Chiyoda City, Yubido.

Fukumen Tomo 13

Recommended by a ramen-loving writer, so I went first thing in the morning. Top tip: "Fukumen Ramen." Jimbocho has books and great food everywhere. Books! Gourmet food! Books on gourmet food!

The soup changes every day. Members-only on Wed. ●2-2-12 Kanda-Jimbocho, Chiyoda City

Kingyo Bancho

Tomoyuki Minowa (left) and Yusuke Furuichi (right). Formed in 2018. Graduated top of NSC Tokyo's 24th gen. Name is a fusion of "Kingyo-bachi" (Minowa's idea) and "Monster Bancho" (Furuichi's).

Chahanya ICHI 14

A real memory lane of a spot that a senior comedian first took us to back when we'd only just joined the theater, saying, "You call yourselves ***Kazoku Chahan***, so let's go have some fried rice." I recommend the lettuce fried rice.

Over ten fried rice dishes - even one with crab sticks. ●2-2 Kanda-Jimbocho, Chiyoda City, 1F.

Maruka 15

I was brought here by Kashiwagi-san from ***Sutekijanaika***. I remember being really happy, because it was back when I still hadn't really settled in. It's a great town, and I'll be even happier if you come to the theater, too.

Famously chewy udon, and a perpetual line. ●3-16-1 Kanda-Ogawamachi, Chiyoda City, 1F.

Kazoku Chahan

Oishi (left) and Egashira (right). Both from the 25th gen. at NSC Tokyo. Teamed up in 2023. An ex-NEET and an ex-member of theater troupe ***Bungakuza***. Got to the ***M-1 Grand Prix 2024*** semifinals in just their 2nd year. Great skit comedy.

Come to the ***Jimbocho Yoshimoto Manzai Theater***, too. We'll give you a laugh!

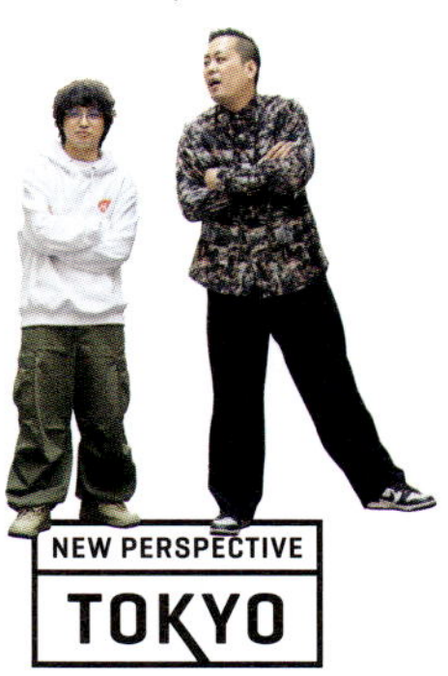

GAKUGEI-DAIGAKU

Just six minutes from Shibuya on the Toyoko Line, Gakugei-daigaku is a new area, but hints of the Showa-era remain.

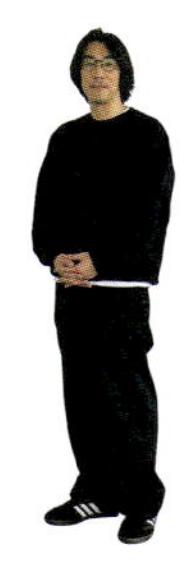

Osamu Kawata

●Owner of ***BOOK AND SONS***

Osamu Kawata was born in Hyogo in 1976. In 2002, he established the design office ***full size image inc***. He's currently working as a curator and web designer. With its main focus on design and photography, the selection of books attracts a lot of attention—and customers from overseas, too.

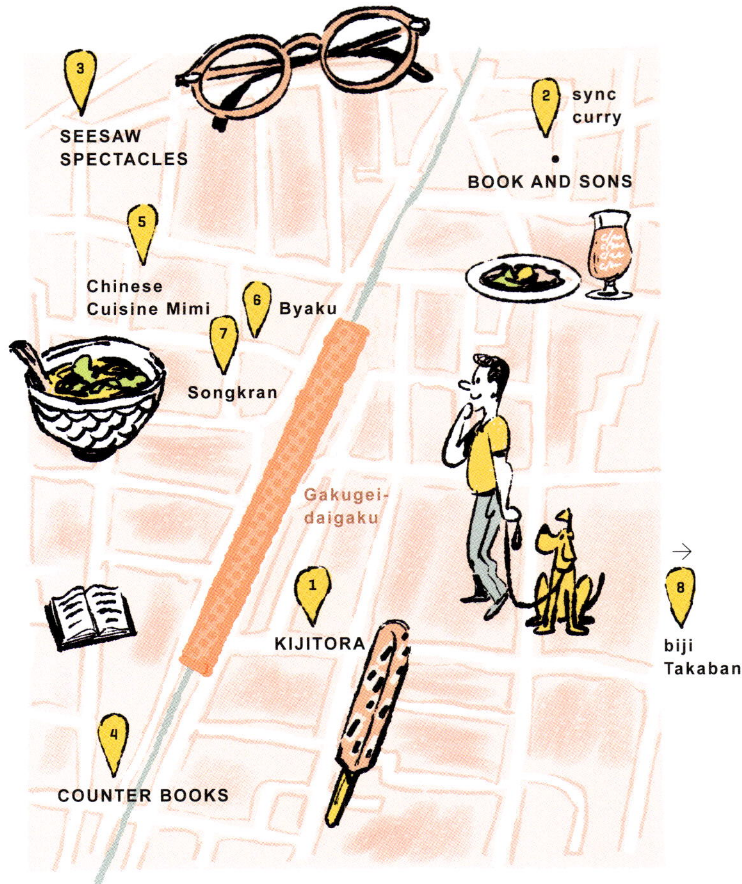

KIJITORA 1

Gluten-free baked sweets. Minimal additives, so they're kind to the body and have a subtle sweetness and flavor. Pheasant and tiger in the logo symbolize the love of children, and the hope that people of all ages can enjoy the sweets free from worry. Fig and walnut brownies: ¥482. ●3-3-9 Takaban, Meguro City ☎03-3793-0222. 11 a.m. to 6 p.m. No closed days.

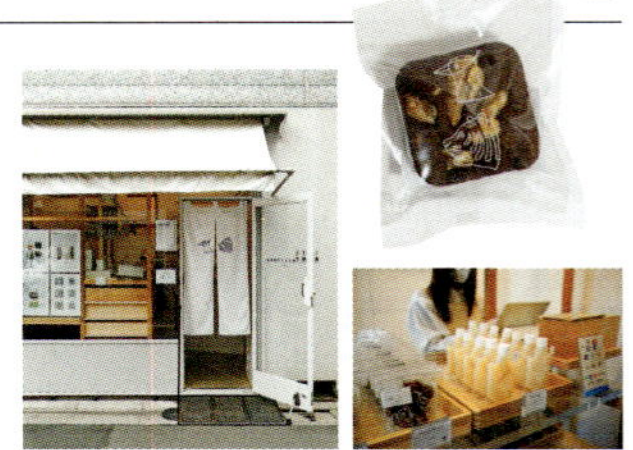

sync curry 2

Owner loved doing curries at another restaurant, so took over this place. Signature dish: soups with onion and spices. Also does seasonal specials. Oyster & watercress curry: ¥1,700. Nam pla egg topping: ¥150. ●2-13-9 Takaban, Meguro City, Rojiura Cultural Hall C/NE 1F ☎03-6452-3617. 11:30 a.m. to 2:30 p.m. (last orders). Irregular closed days.

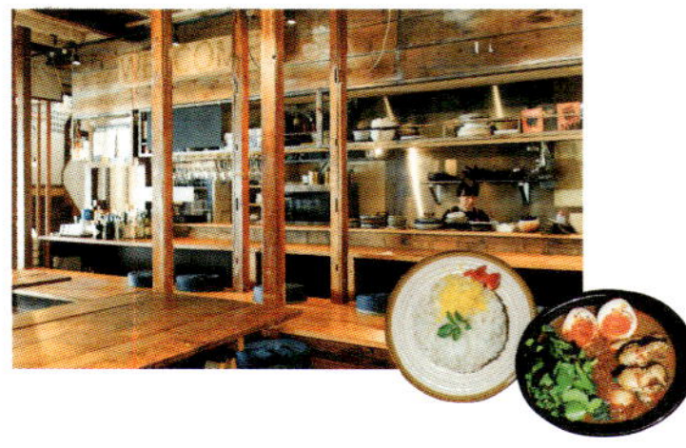

SEESAW SPECTACLES 3

Glasses store with a new concept: "fun with glasses based on size." Besides thinking about the shape, they also write the sizes as simple S, M, and L. Plus, they suggest frames based on the position of your eyes, to offer glasses that truly suit you. Also show select brands for limited periods. ●2-40-8 Chuocho, Meguro City ☎03-6303-4337. 11 a.m. to 7 p.m. Closed on Wed.

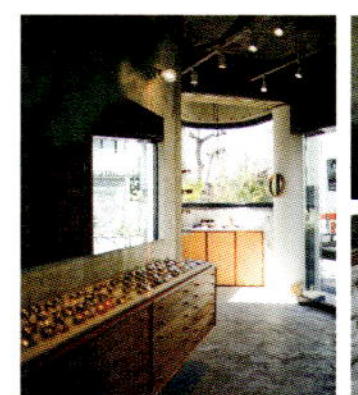

Gakugei-daigaku has been featured in "Time Out" magazine's ranking as one of the "coolest neighborhoods in the world," but it doesn't really feel that way. That said, it's true that for a town that still retains a Showa-era vibe, stylish storefronts are definitely on the increase. The rent is cheaper than in Nakameguro, so I think it's an easy environment for young people to open a store in. When we first opened ours, people asked us why we'd gone for a place like this, too, but now, we also get a lot of customers from overseas. While urban shops like ***COUNTER BOOKS*** and ***SEESAW SPECTACLES*** are on the rise, there are long-running ones like ***Mimi*** dotted around as well. It's lively, but it doesn't try too hard. Maybe that sense of imbalance gives the place a real Japanese people's daily lives kind of feel.

COUNTER BOOKS 4

A bookstore with a café bar, opened under an elevated railroad in 2024. Over 2,000 books, selected with the theme of "selling curiosity." You can read your purchases right there. World cuisine at weekend lunchtimes, spirits and cocktails in the evenings. ●3-4-25 Takaban, Meguro City ☎No phone number. 12 p.m. to 11 p.m. (from 10 a.m. on Sat., Sun., and holidays). No closed days.

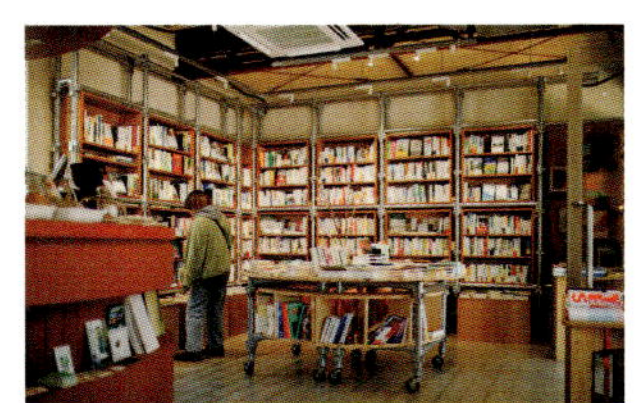

Chinese Cuisine Mimi 5

Chinese cuisine by a Taiwanese owner who's traveled the world sampling food. Packed with plenty of its eponymous herb, the chive ramen is hailed as a Gakudai specialty. The boiled dumplings with their chewy coating are also highly recommended. ●3-7-17 Takaban, Meguro City ☎03-5721-0082. 5:00 p.m. to 1:00 a.m. (from 11:30 a.m. to 1:30 p.m. on Sun.). Irregular closed days.

Byaku 6

An izakaya that uses fresh vegetables sourced from a long-running greengrocer in Akita Prefecture, where the owner's wife comes from. Designed to have a teahouse vibe all the vegetable side dishes are delicious. ●3-8-10 Takaban, Meguro City, One Bldg. 2F ☎03-6303-3789. 5:00 p.m. to 11:30 p.m. (from 4:00 p.m. on Sat., Sun., and holidays). No closed days.

Songkran 7

The owner lived in Thailand and has researched its cuisine extensively, tailoring it to Japanese taste buds. The interior is inspired by Thai food stalls, giving it a friendly atmosphere that also wins it lots of regulars. ●3-7-4 Takaban, Meguro City ☎03-5721-2139. 11:30 a.m. to 3:00 p.m. and 5:30 p.m. to 11:00 p.m. Irregular closed days.

biji Takaban 8

The restaurant's name means "seed" in Indonesian. Asian food with plenty of vegetables and spices. You can also get the bento boxed lunches and deli dishes to go, so you can relish them at home as well. ●2-5-17 Takaban, Meguro City, Corpo-Marumoto, Room 102 ☎03-3794-6606. 12:00 p.m. to 3:00 p.m. and 6:00 p.m. to 9:00 p.m. Closed on Thu.

 Photos: Koh Akazawa Text: BRUTUS

KICHIJOJI

Homes mixed into the downtown area—a local feel just 20 minutes from the heart of Tokyo.

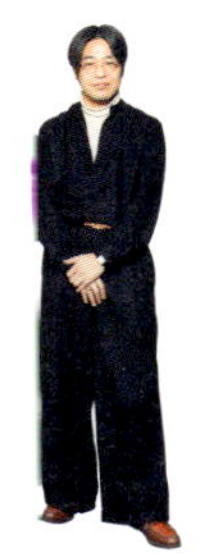

Daisuke Eguchi

●Owner of ***Eguchi Vintage Clothing, Watch & Watch Repair Shop SHOTO***

Daisuke Eguchi was born in Tokyo in 1980. In 2016, he opened ***Eguchi Yohin Ten Eguchi Watch & Clock Shop*** in Kichijoji. Since 2024, he's also been running a new store in Shoto, Shibuya that has a watch repair workshop as well. He's been an avid barhopper around Kichijoji for over 20 years.

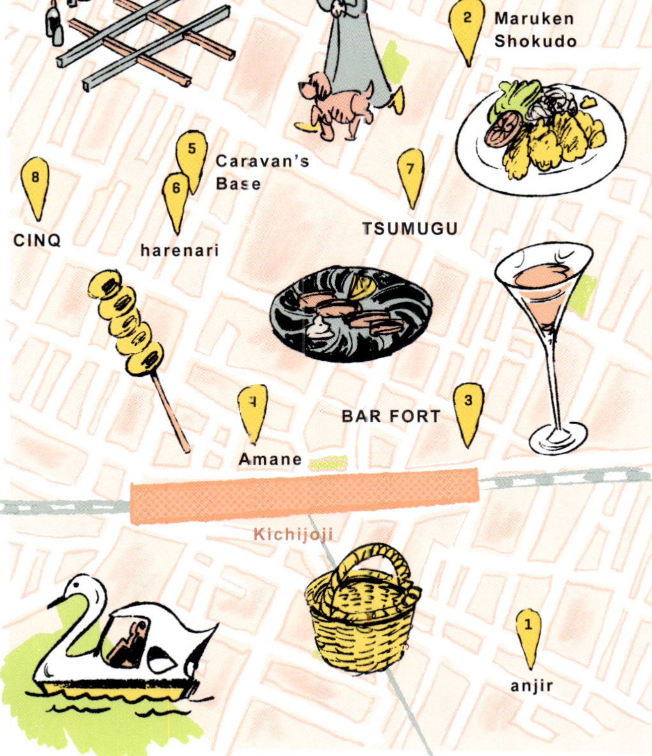

anjir 1

Small bistro with chef's choice courses only (mainly meat dishes that go with wine). Great for casually eating out or celebrating anniversaries, etc. It's also nice that you can chat to the chef as you order. Recommended: grilled Iberian pork. ●2-13-3 Kichijoji-Minamicho, Musashino City, Unius Shonan 1F ☎0422-29-8668. 6 p.m. to 12 a.m. Irregular closed days.

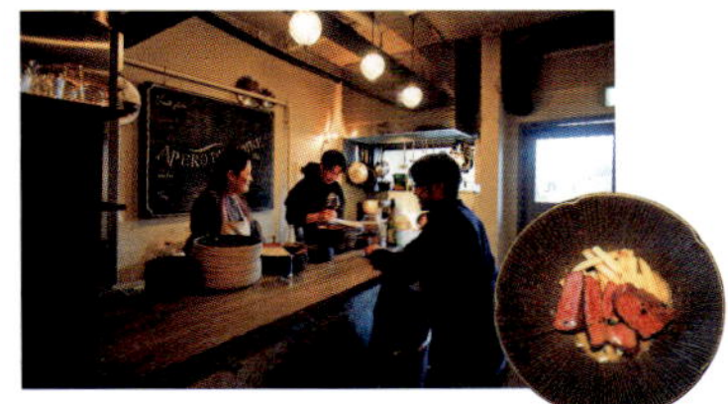

Maruken Shokudo 2

Set meal place founded in 1960, run by a brother and sister (after their parents). Low prices for 60+ years—loved by students, too. The daily special alternates between meat and fish. Minced meat cutlet meal: ¥570. ● 1-6-14 Kichijoji-Higashicho, Musashino City ☎0422-22-4250. 11 a.m. to 3 p.m. and 5 p.m. to 9 p.m. Closed on Sun. and Mon.

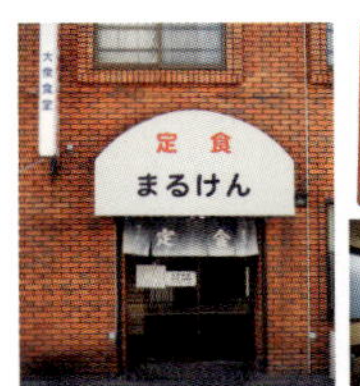

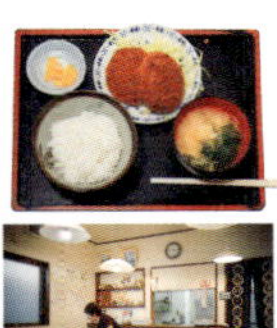

BAR FORT 3

Bar with jazz background music and a focus on whiskey. Rare original cocktails like "Porcini and Tea Sweet Cocktail" (¥1,760). Handmade raw chocolate with four kinds of sake (¥990) is very popular. ●1-31-3 Kichijoji-Honcho, Musashino City, Misono Bldg. 2F ☎0422-27-6126. 7 p.m. to 3 a.m. (last orders). (Sun. last orders: 11 p.m.) Irregular closed days.

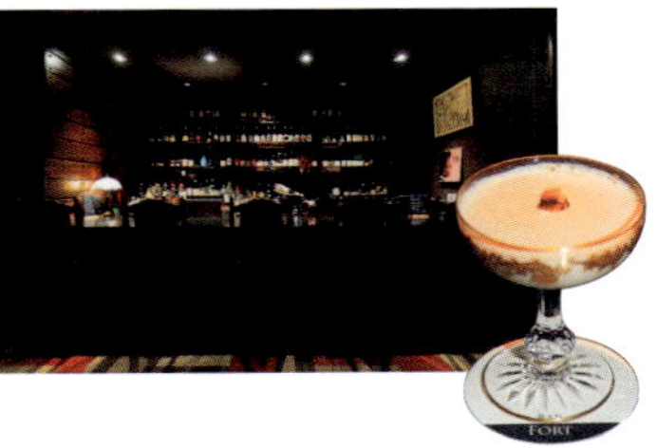

What first prompted me to open a store in Kichijoji was its wealth of places to go for a drink. Being 23 at the time, I went out for drinks after work practically every day. Twenty years have passed since then, and the town as a whole has gotten more popular, with more big-name stores. But even so, there are still lots of store owners and local customers who have a strong affection for Kichijoji. There are family-run places like ***Maruken Shokudo*** and ***anjir***, too, so it's a place anyone can feel at home. I often become friends with people I meet in stores. Even though it's a compact town, there are still lots of old places left—something that can conversely feel new to younger people. It was just an ordinary shopping district in the old days, so it's great that it's now somewhere that attracts all kinds of people.

Amane 4

Harmonica Yokocho taiyaki shop. Long lines. Winged taiyaki with Hokkaido red beans has brown sugar in both skin and filling—gently sweet! Sometimes custard and matcha ones, too. Great chewy dumplings. Walnut sauce & grilled soy sauce: ¥160 each. Winged taiyaki: ¥240. ●1-1-9 Kichijoji-Honcho, Musashino City ☎0422-22-3986. 11 a.m. to 6 p.m. Irregular closed days.

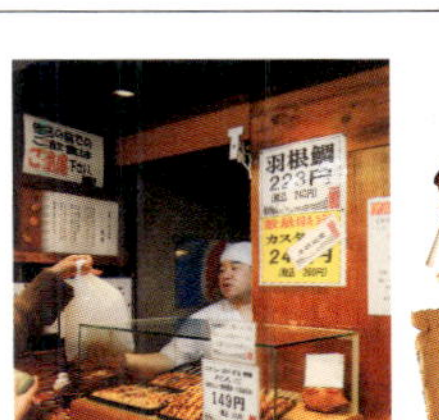

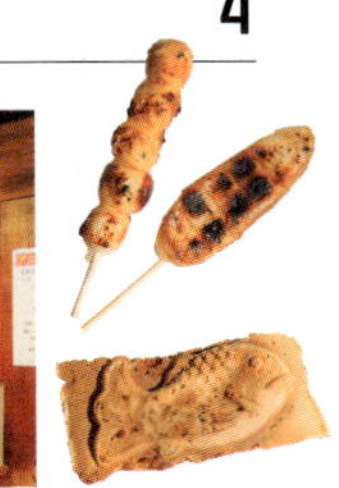

Caravan's Base 5

Commonly known as "Carabe," this is a café where you can play board games from all over the world. They explain the rules to you, so beginners can feel at home, too. You can also bring your own games. ●2-7-13 Kichijoji-Honcho, Musashino City, Ladybird Bldg., Room 302 ☎0422-27-2720. 1:00 p.m. to 11:00 p.m. Closed on Mon.

harenari 6

Creative izakaya in a semi-basement. Dishes with seasonal vegetables and fish reflect the owner's experience from work in various restaurants after university. Wide choice of alcohol. The likable owner keeps people coming back, too. ●2-8-10 Kichijoji-Honcho, Musashino City ☎080-5096-8070. 5:30 p.m. to 12:00 a.m. Irregular closed days.

TSUMUGU 7

Eatery at the end of Sunroad. 100%-buckwheat noodles and "hometown food," plus plenty of snacks and sake. ●1-6-1 Kichijoji-Higashicho Musashino City, 2F ☎0422-77-7428. 11:30 a.m. to 3:00 p.m. and 6:30 p.m. to 10:00 p.m. (5:00 p.m. to 10:00 p.m. on Fri., 11:30 a.m. to 10:00 p.m. on Sat., Sun., and holidays). Closed on Mon. and Tue.

CINQ 8

This store is lined with European kitchen and daily necessity goods bought in by the owner. The original wallets have a simple, high-quality design that can be used for a long time, making them perfect gifts, too. ●2-28-3 Kichijoji-Honcho, Musashino City, Greeny Kichijoji 1F ☎0422-26-8735. 11:00 a.m. to 7:00 p.m. No closed days.

HIGASHI-NIHOMBASHI

The "Residential area in Chuo City" Is now in full bloom.

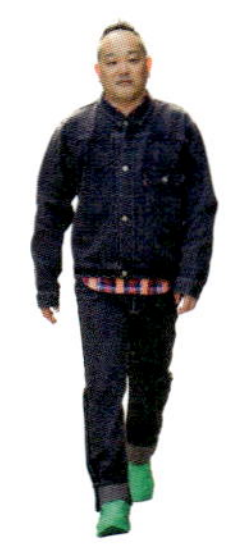

Kenichi Warita

●Owner of ***BEAVER BREAD*** and ***bouquet***

After working at ***Bigot's Shop Printemps Ginza***, Kenichi Warita went on to serve as the chef at ***Ginza L'écrin***. He founded his own shop in Higashi-nihombashi in 2017. Today, he's in his beloved ***COMME des GARÇONS*** shirt and shoes.

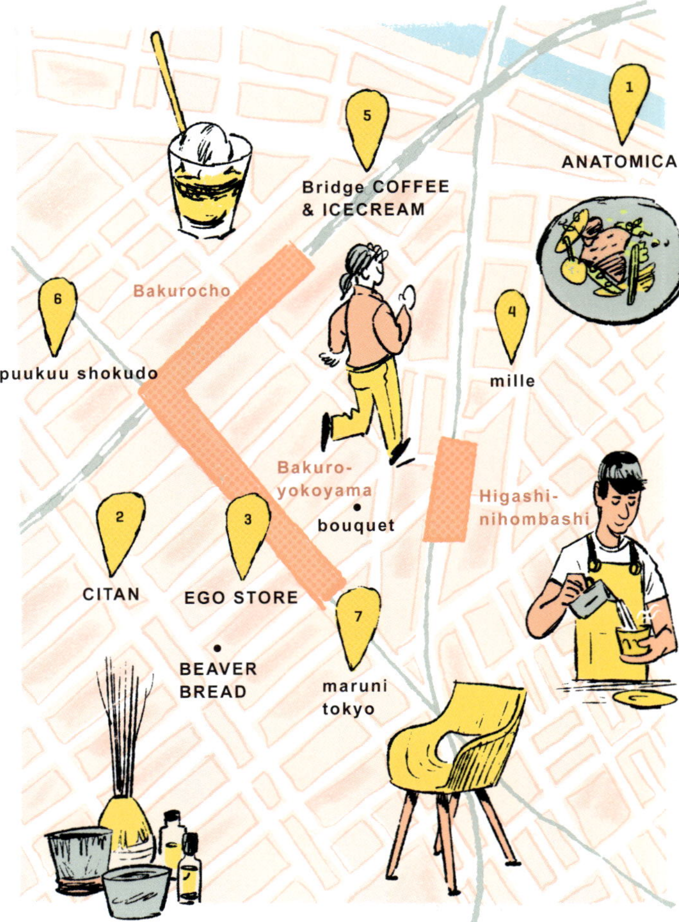

ANATOMICA 1

The Tokyo store of the brand founded in Paris in 1994. Inspired by traditional European fashion's "anatomical" explorations and sometimes recreated from the threads and weaves, the collection captivates fashion lovers with its enduring comfort and beauty. ●2-27-19 Higashi-Nihombashi, Chuo City, S Bldg. 1F & B1 ☎03-5823-6186. 1 p.m. to 8 p.m. Closed on Tue.

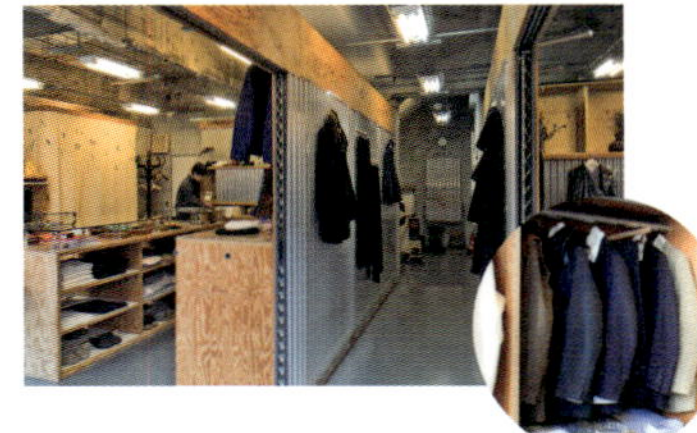

CITAN 2

Pioneering next-gen. hostel, opened in 2017. 1F has coffee stand ***BERTH COFFEE***. B1 has cash-on-delivery bar & diner with a range of craft beers and spirits from East Tokyo. ● 15-2 Nihombashi-Odemmacho, Chuo City ☎ 03-6661-7559. 8 a.m. to 6 p.m. for 1F and 6 p.m. to 11 p.m. (last orders) for B1 (Fri. & Sat. last orders: 11:30 p.m.). Irregular closed days.

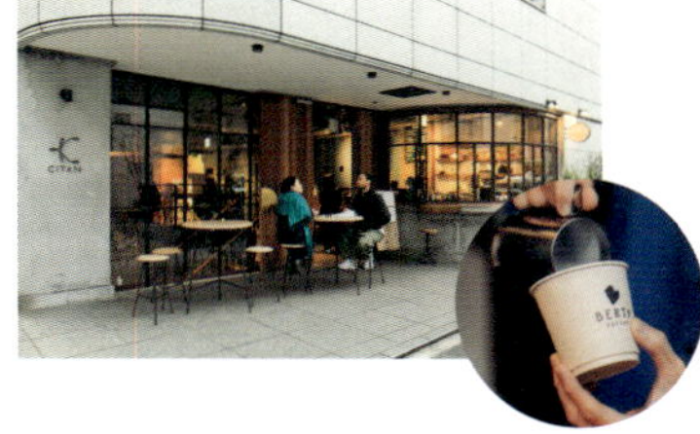

EGO STORE 3

An owner with select shop roots, Satoshi Hashimoto opened this lifestyle store last December. Tableware, fragrances, and local toys. Reflecting the owner's refined taste, the selection includes the "Ego" Arita ware series and works by popular artists like Nobuyuki Ishioka. ●3-3-14 Higashi-Nihombashi, Chuo City, 1F ☎03-6661-1279. 12 p.m. to 7 p.m. Irregular closed days.

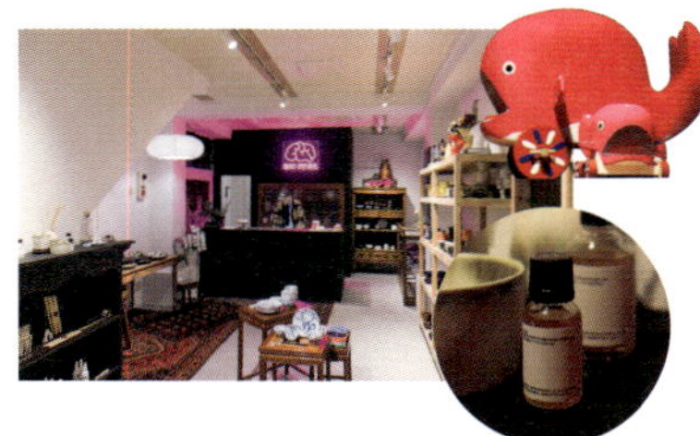

When I opened my store in Higashi-Nihombashi after 20 years in Ginza, it was just before the redevelopment boom breathed new life into the area. I'd often gone to ***Fukumori*** and ***ANATOMICA*** in Bakurocho, but I was curious to see how opening a bakery in a town that didn't have one would change things. Now, there are seven or eight bakeries within just a few kilometers, and neighborhood kindergartens use our eco bags to put the kids' indoor shoes in. So, eight years on from opening, it feels like we're really part of the neighborhood. This area has an image of being a wholesalers' district, but it's actually residential. It's easily accessible and safe, and the residents have fine taste. So, nice shops have gathered here and created a new neighborhood naturally, with no major revitalization drives required. I hope I've played my own humble part in that.

mille 4

Bistro (rare in Higashi-nihombashi). Chef Toshio Chiba showcases his experience and skills from Tokyo and France. Food is seasonal à la carte dishes based on authentic French cuisine. All wines are natural. Start with the blissful selection of appetizers. ●2-8-1 Higashi-Nihombashi, Chuo City, 1F ☎03-5829-8138. 6 p.m. to 11 p.m. (last orders). Closed on Sun.

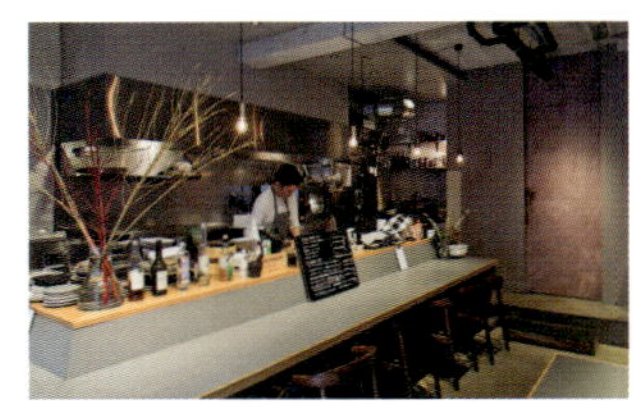

Bridge COFFEE & ICECREAM 5

City icon on 1F of the historic Eagle Building, which has stood in Bakurocho for over a century. Delicious original blends roasted by ***Little Nap COFFEE ROASTERS*** and ice cream from affiliated store ***Bole***. ●1-13-9 Nihombashi-Bakurocho, Chuo City, 1F ☎03-3527-3399. 8 a.m. to 5:30 p.m. (last orders: 9 a.m. on Sat., Sun., and holidays). No closed days.

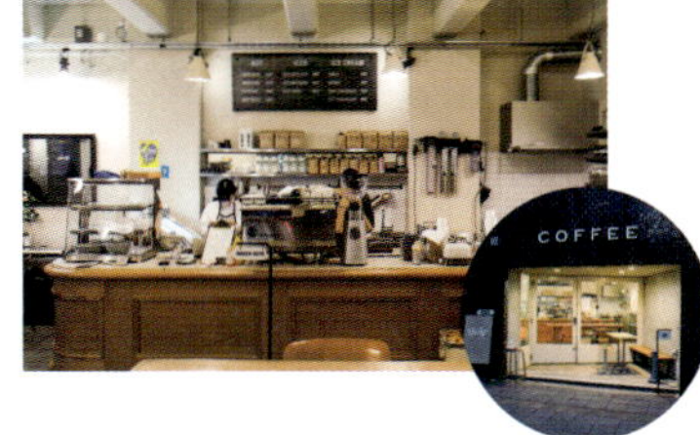

puukuu shokudo 6

A restaurant that opened in 2020 and is run by ***minä perhonen.*** Organic vegetable soup, curry, coffee, and natural wines await your daily delectation. ●1-2-11 Higashi-Kanda, Chiyoda City, Room 202 ☎03-6820-8837. 11:00 a.m. to 2:00 p.m. (to 5:00 p.m. on Sat., last orders in both cases). Closed on Sun. (unless there's an exhibition on) and Mon.

maruni tokyo 7

A Tokyo store run directly by ***MARUNI WOOD INDUSTRY INC.***, the historic wooden furniture maker that was founded in Hiroshima in 1928. Get to experience its signature series in-store. ●3-6-13 Higashi-Nihombashi, Chuo City ☎03-3667-4021. 11:00 a.m. to 6:00 p.m. (from 10:00 a.m. on Sat., Sun., and holidays). Closed on Tue. and Wed.

Photos: Kazuharu Igarashi (p. 36), Yu Inohara (p. 37) Text: Yoko Fujimori

NISHI-OGIKUBO

The "counter spirit" is still alive and well in the Reiwa-era.

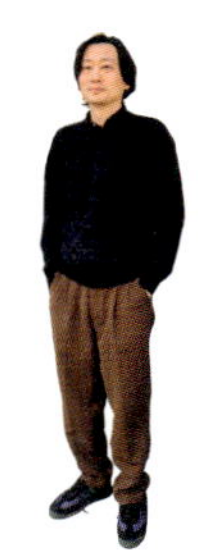

Teruoki Mishina

●Owner of *FALL*

Worked part-time at a bookstore after university. Opened lifestyle shop ***FALL*** in Nishi-Ogikubo in 2005. Holds some 50 pottery and other exhibitions a year. Active writer. Latest book: ***Searching for Things in the Surf*** (Shobunsha).

SUTOA 1

"Made in Japan" stripe specialist. T-shirts, baby clothes, and more, made from over 100 fabrics cut into 10-cm-wide strips. Endless color combinations. Based in Nishi-Ogikubo since art university, designer Makoto Kunitoki also started up the popular event ***NISHIOGI CHA SAMPO***. ● 5-7-19 Nishi-Ogi-Kita, Suginami City ☎03-3397-1791. 11 a.m. to 6 p.m. Closed on Mon. and Tue.

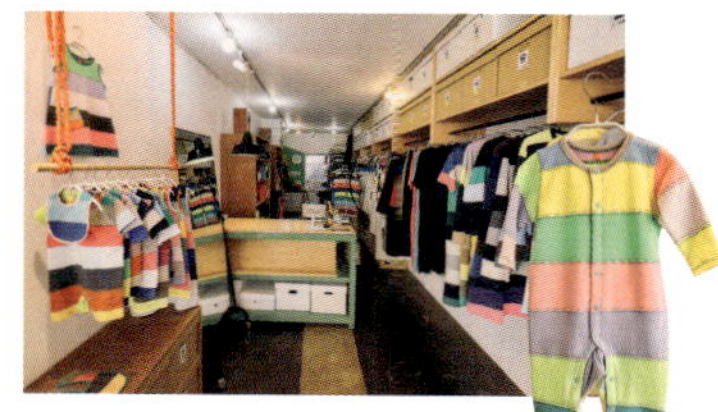

Hobbit-mura 2

Est. 1976. Nishi-Ogikubo hippie culture pioneer. 1F: organic vegetable store ***Nagamoto Kyodai Shokai***. 2F: restaurant ***BALTHAZAR***. 3F: bookstore & free school. Bookstore ***nawa prasad*** is run by Yuriko Takahashi. Famous for books on Buddhism and natural farming. ● 3-15-3 Nishi-Ogi-Minami, Suginami City. Opening hours and holidays vary by store.

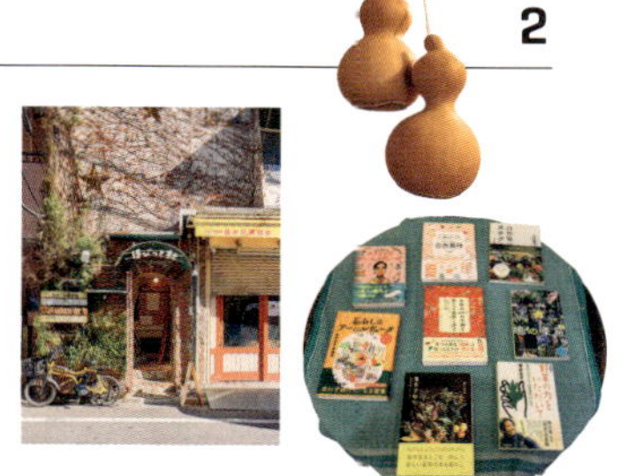

Sanninto 3

Books, food, and alcohol. Opened by owner Tsuyoshi Mizukoshi in 2005. Reclaimed-wood counter, vintage furniture. Sika deer venison from owner's native Yamanashi. Activist owner (chair of "Heiwa-dori Ave. Shopping Street"). ●3-17-5 Nishi-Ogi-Minami, Suginami City ☎ 03-5346-2892. 6 p.m. to 12 a.m. (last food orders at 10 p.m.). Closed on Tue. and Wed.

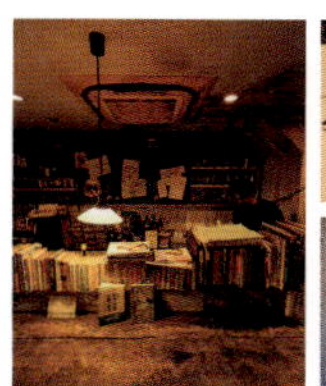

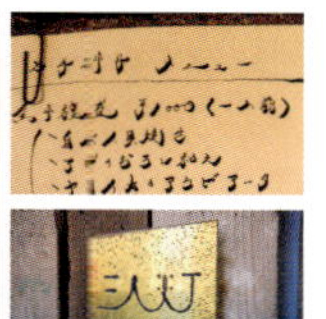

Secondhand Books Otowakan 4

Beloved "neighborhood secondhand bookstore," est. 2000. Rich selection on philosophy, music, film, etc., so clientele ranges from students to businesspeople. Owner "sells books slightly cheaper than elsewhere, and buys them at a fair price." Local writers and manga artists often drop by. ●3-13-7 Nishi-Ogi-Kita, Suginami City, 1F ☎ 03-5382-1587. 11 a.m. to 8 p.m. Closed on Tue.

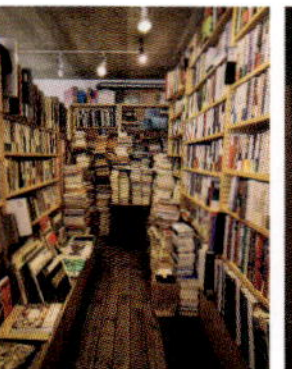

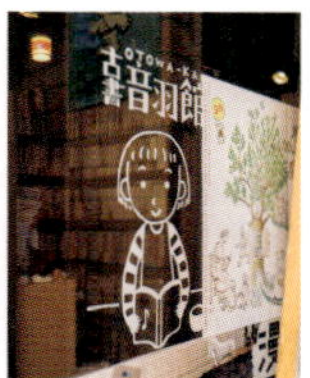

poubelle 5

The store's name, ***poubelle***, means "trash can" in French. Owner Tsuyoshi Yazawa curates and arranges vintage tools, contemporary art, and art books. He's sometimes repaired the items on display as well. A shop that'll sharpen the "resolution" you see and perceive with. Opened in 2014. ●3-42-5 Nishi-Ogi-Kita, Suginami City ☎090-1540-7133. 12 p.m. to 7:30 p.m. Closed on Tue.

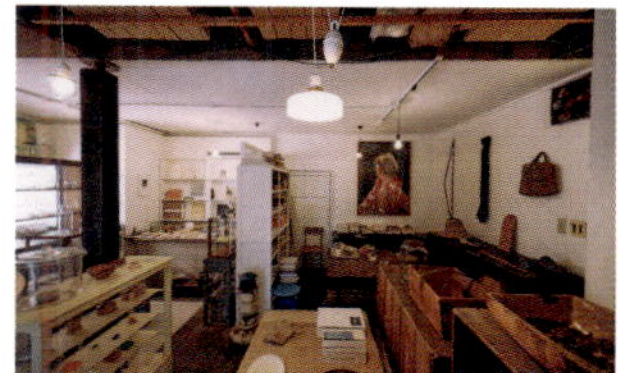

JUHA 6

A coffee shop that roasts its coffee by hand. Its name is from the title of a movie by director Aki Kaurismäki. With the pre-war jazz and blues as well, this is a haven for lovers of records and dark-roast coffee. ●2-25-4 Nishi-Ogi-Minami, Suginami City ☎050-3562-0658. 1:00 p.m. to 8:00 p.m. (from 12:00 p.m. on Sat., Sun., and holidays). Closed on Mon. and Tue.

Konno Shoten 7

Founded over 50 years ago, this is the last remaining purveyor of new books in Nishi-Ogikubo—a true neighborhood bookstore. The staff's love for books and keen selection sense really stand out. They hold author talks and signings, serving as a hub for knowledge in Nishi-Ogikubo. ●3-1-8 Nishi-Ogi-Kita, Suginami City ☎03-3395-4191. 10:00 a.m. to 9:00 p.m. No closed days.

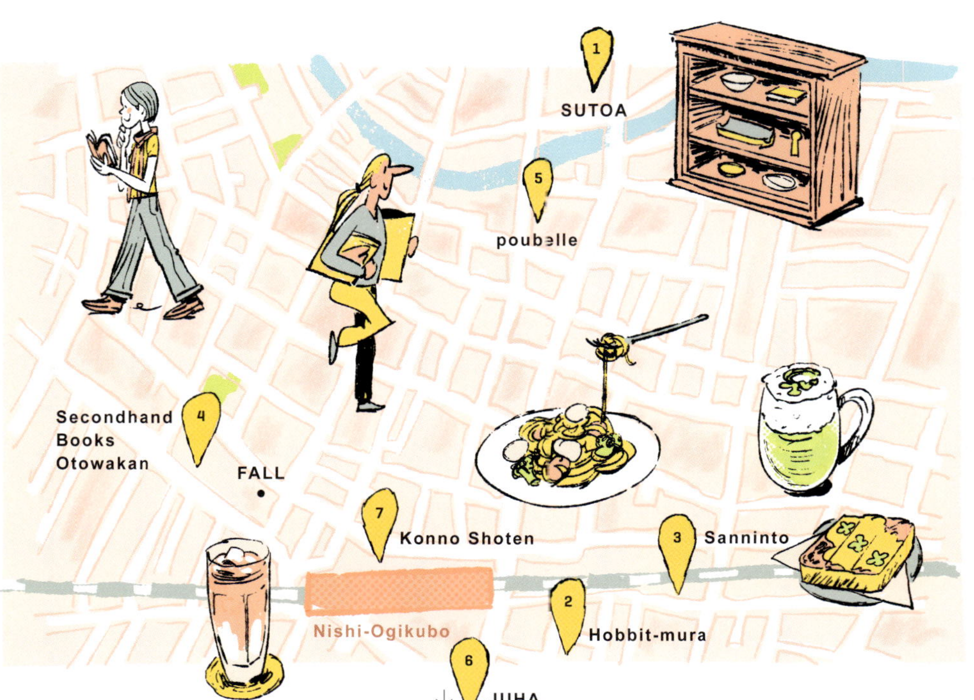

Suginami has had a literature and antiques culture since the birth of the Asagaya Literary Village in the 1920s. Counterculture like ***Hobbit-mura*** sparked a rise in antique shops, secondhand bookstores, and cafés—the bedrock of today's Nishi-Ogikubo. The lack of any major urban development could explain all the unique independent shops. The ones I've selected here are all "hardcore" (laughs).

There are many more overseas tourists now than when I opened my shop 20 years ago. I'm glad the area has gotten brighter and more livable, but it's its sense of being closed off that makes Nishi-Ogikubo really interesting. After all, if everything got opened up, the hardcore stuff would disappear. Maybe the next generation will find the right balance there.

OMOTE-SANDO

A potpourri of old and new creativity east of Meiji Jingu.

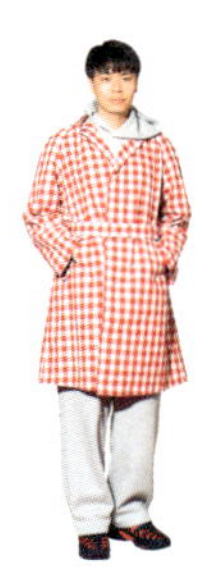

Yasutaka Ochi

●Representative of ***DILIGENCE PARLOUR***

Yasutaka Ochi was born in Saitama in 1989. He's a florist and the CEO of Europe Inc. and has been running a store in Omotesando Hills since 2016, designing flowers for ads, exhibitions, and events. His genre-crossing activities encompass writing, photography, painting, and more.

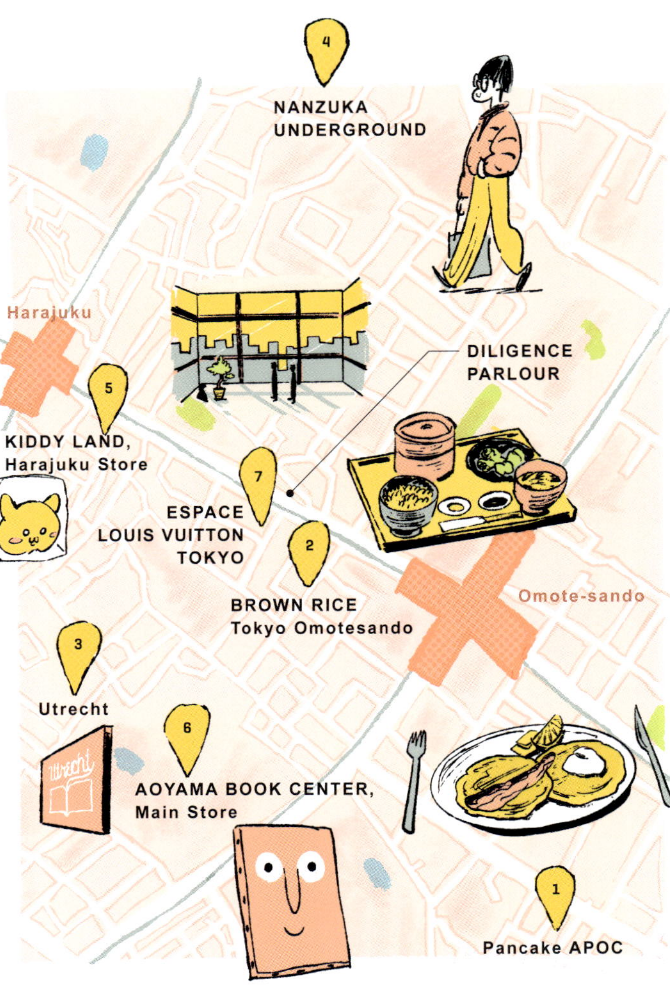

Pancake APOC 1

Specialty store run by Masako Okawa. Pancakes made with organic maple sugar and palm oil. ***a Piece of Cake*** in the Taro Okamoto Memorial Museum is its sister store. Set A: ¥2,550. ●5-16-3 Minami-Aoyama, Minato City, 2F ☎No phone number. 12:00 p.m. to 5:00 p.m. (to 3:30 p.m. on Fri. and 4:00 p.m. on Sun., last orders in all cases). Closed on Mon., Tue., and other irregular days.

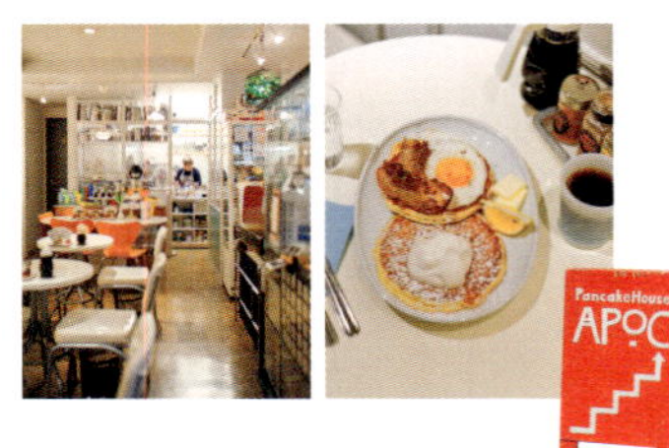

BROWN RICE Tokyo Omotesando 2

Japanese cuisine using brown rice, fermented foods, and seasonal organic, pesticide-free ingredients. Organic restaurant going since 2003. Set meal with soup & three dishes: ¥2,500 weekdays, ¥2,900 Sat., Sun., holidays. ●5-1-8 Jingumae, Shibuya City, 1F ☎03-5778-5416. 11:30 a.m. to 6 p.m. (Last orders: 5 p.m. for food and 5:30 p.m. for drinks). Closed on 1st Tue.

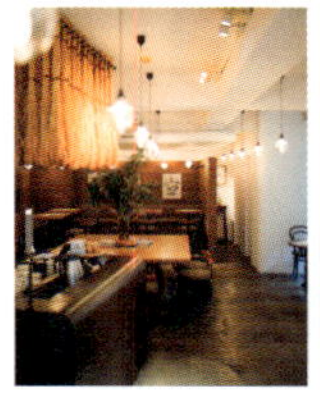

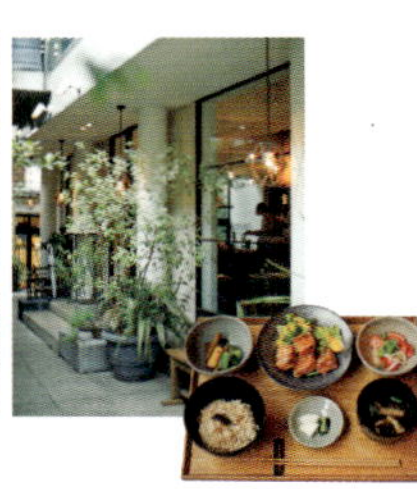

Utrecht 3

An art book specialty shop that opened in 2002 and has been at its current location since 2014. Mainly handles books on art, design, and fashion. Also holds book launch exhibitions and many other events. ●5-36-6 Jingumae, Shibuya City, KARI Mansion 2C ☎03-6427-4041. 12:00 p.m. to 7:00 p.m. Closed on Mon. (or the next day if Mon. is a holiday).

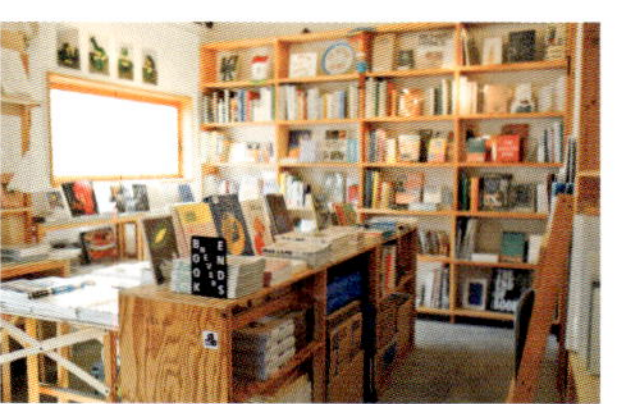

I've been commuting to Omotesando since my early 20s, and running my own shop there for the last nine years. Amid its mix of old and new high and low culture that reflects the times, I've found many spots that are a real fit for me. I go to ***Utrecht*** to discover the unknown, ***AOYAMA BOOK CENTER*** for foreign magazines and books, and ***KIDDY LAND*** for "Chiikawa" goods. I really feel the creators' will in places like ***ESPACE LOUIS VUITTON*** (which I've been frequenting since seeing an Ernesto Neto exhibition there in my student days), ***NANZUKA UNDERGROUND*** with its humorous contemporary art, and favorite cafés ***APOC*** and ***BROWN RICE***. They're cherished places that always inspire me.

NANZUKA UNDERGROUND 4

NANZUKA flagship gallery. Connects pop cultures like illustration, manga, fashion, and music with contemporary art, and spreads them worldwide. Simultaneous ***Hiroo Kikai and Toshio Saeki solo exhibitions*** to be held from April 4 to May 2. Logo is by Hajime Sorayama. ● 3-30-10 Jingumae, Shibuya City ☎03-5422-3877. 11:00 a.m. to 7:00 p.m. Closed on Sun. and Mon.

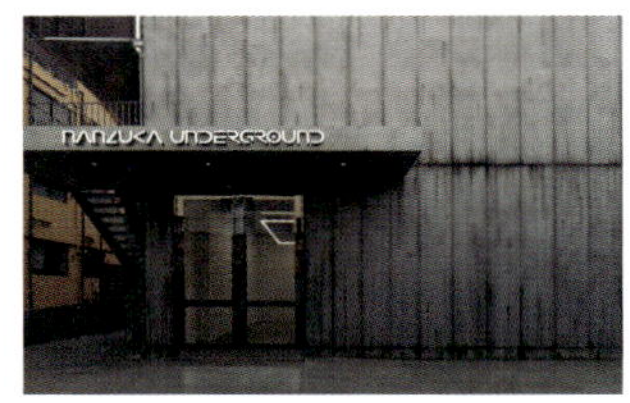

KIDDY LAND, Harajuku Store 5

Floors 1 to 4 have a vast range of Chiikawa Land goods, character goods from miffy, Sanrio, Pokémon, Studio Ghibli, and Disney, and toys like TOMICA and PLARAIL. B1 has a Snoopy Town Shop. Chiikawa Mochitto Plush S: ¥2,090. ●6-1-9 Jingumae, Shibuya City ☎03-3409-3431. 11:00 a.m. to 8:00 p.m. No closed days.

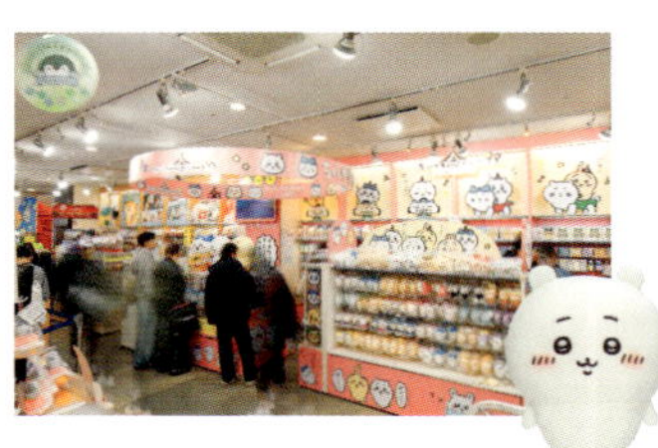

AOYAMA BOOK CENTER, Main Store 6

Commemorative talks, signings, and original art exhibitions are held regularly, including events for Tsuzui's ***Jump Out! Tsuzui-san 2*** on April 5 and Machi Tawara's ***Living Words*** on April 19. ●5-53-67 Jingumae, Shibuya City, Cosmos Aoyama Garden Floor B2 ☎No phone number. 11:00 a.m. to 9:30 p.m. (from 10:00 a.m. to 9:00 p.m. on Sat., Sun., and holidays). No closed days.

ESPACE LOUIS VUITTON TOKYO 7

Introduces the collection of Fondation Louis Vuitton. The next exhibition is planned for fall 2025. ●5-7-5 Jingumae, Shibuya City, Louis Vuitton Omotesando Bldg. 7F ☎ 0120-00-1854. 12:00 p.m. to 8:00 p.m. Irregular closed days. (Open only during exhibitions.)

Photos: Koh Akazawa (p. 38), Kazuhiro Shiraishi (p. 39) Text: Hikari Torisawa (p. 38), Shoko Yoshida (p. 39)

HIGASHI-GINZA

From Showa-dori Avenue eastward—the expanding Ginza tourism zone.

Yoshiyuki Morioka

●Owner of ***morioka shoten*** bookstore

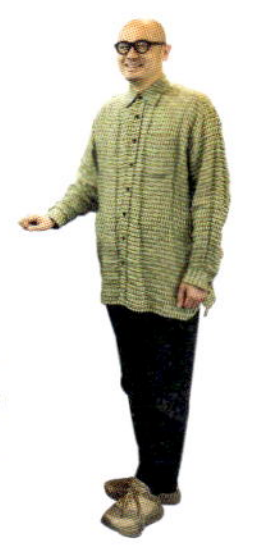

Yoshiyuki Morioka was born in Yamagata in 1974. Besides heading the bookstore ***Morioka Shoten***, he's also a writer, with ***Forgiving Shortcakes*** (Raichosha) and numerous other books to his name. He also hosts the GINZA SIX Podcast ***Ginza Is Six O'Clock at Night***.

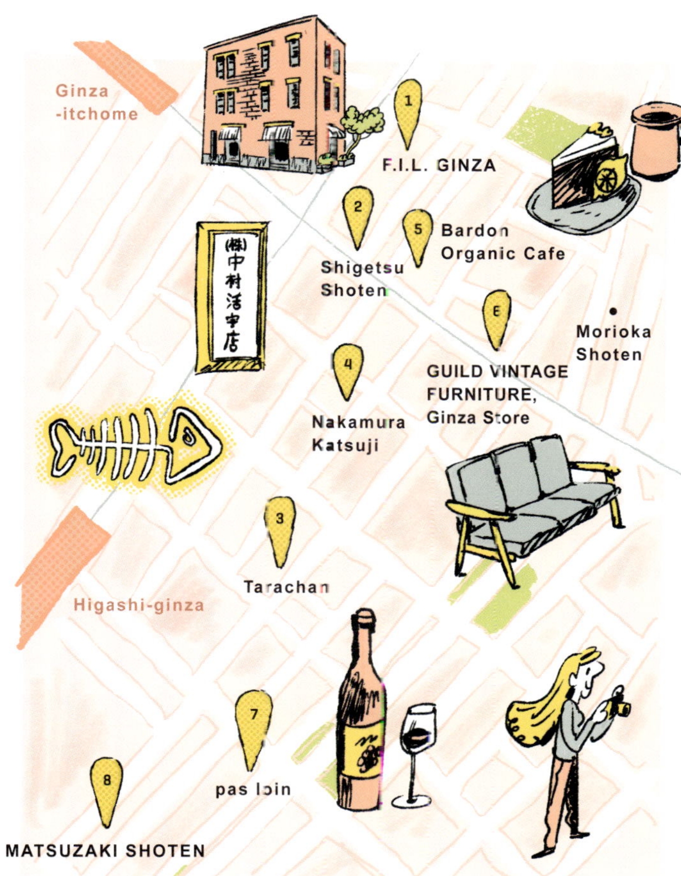

F.I.L. GINZA 1

Store directly run by ***visvim*** in a small building that's over 90 years old. The original fixtures are as impressive as the clothes, but the standout is the seamless carpet on 2F. A single piece cut to fit the space and floor details, it's simply breathtaking. ●1-20-17 Ginza, Chuo City ☎03-3528-6500. 11:00 a.m. to 8:00 p.m. No closed days.

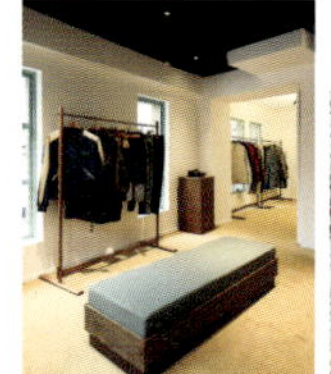

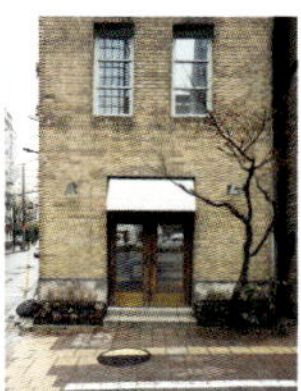

Shigetsu Shoten 2

Natural food store run by a hairstylist. Dried mullet roe from the owner's native Karatsu in Saga, plus organic ingredients from all over Japan. Kitchen set up to combat food waste. Set meals and takeout bento made by hand every day. Recommended: dried mullet roe rice ball (¥580). ●1-20-11 Ginza, Chuo City ☎None. 11 a.m. to 7 p.m. (6:30 p.m. on Sat. and Sun.). Closed on Tue.

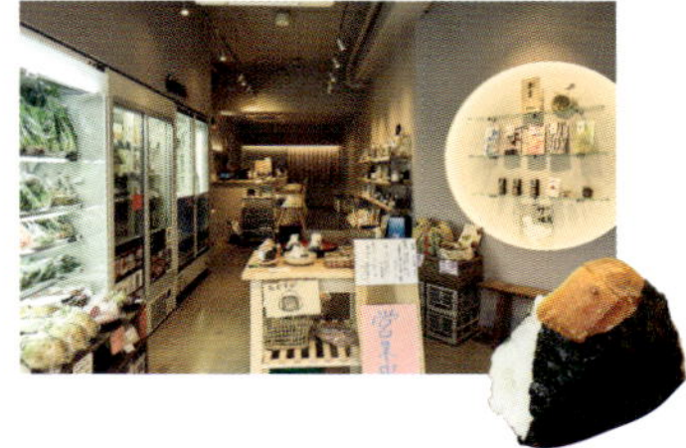

Tarachan 3

Run by a Korean lady. Specializes in "pugok," a rich soup made by simmering dried cod. Hangover staple in Korea, its gentle flavor being good for no-appetite days. Set with three kinds of kimchi, salted shrimp, and rice: ¥1,300. ●3-13-5 Ginza, Chuo City, Suzuki Bldg. 1F ☎03-6278-7780. 7 a.m. to 7 p.m. (to 4 p.m. on Sat.). Closed on Sun. and holidays.

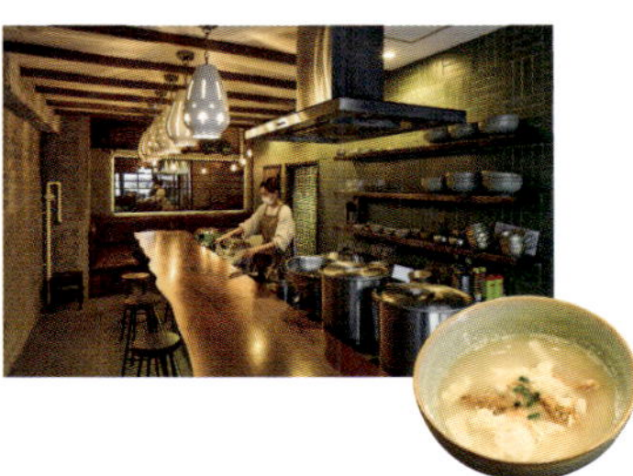

Higashi-ginza was once called Kobikicho. Today, charming long-running shops share its streets with various new ones. I was surprised to learn that besides ***MATSUZAKI SHOTEN*** and ***Nakamura Katsuji***, the six other places are all from after post-pandemic 2021! Old or new, everywhere is easy to drop into and offers high quality. In fact, I have a touching story. I wrote about ***Nakamura Katsuji*** in my book ***800 Days Around Ginza***. A man who read it in prison went there right after getting out and said, "I want to make some name cards and start over." It made me wonder if there's something about this high-quality town that helps people back to the straight and narrow. Higashi-ginza could be "a town for people who want to be grown-ups."

Nakamura Katsuji 4

Letterpress company. Est. 1910. Sole craftsperson is 5th-gen. owner Akihisa Nakamura, who's in his 70s. "Ye olde shoppe" vibe can be intimidating, but the owner says, "I want people to know about letterpress printing," and welcomes all comers (including orders for name cards). ●2-13-7 Ginza, Chuo City ☎03-3541-6563. 8:30 a.m. to 5:00 p.m. Closed on Sat. and Sun.

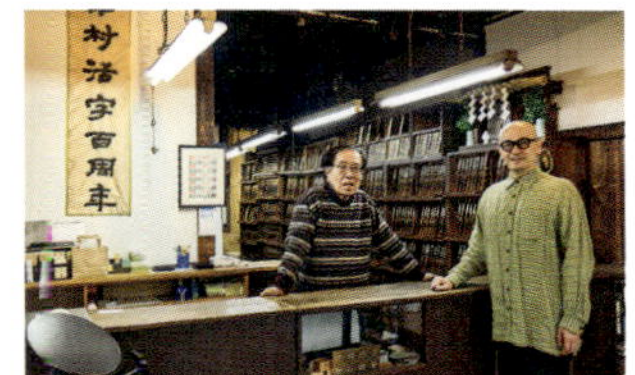

Bardon Organic Cafe 5

An organic café offering vegan cakes and sweets made with carefully selected nuts. Also has dried fruit & nut bars that make the perfect light snack. ●1-21-12 Ginza, Chuo City, Blue box Bldg. 1F ☎03-6228-7133. 11 00 a.m. to 6:00 p.m. Closed on Thu.

GUILD VINTAGE FURNITURE, Ginza Store 6

Handles Scandinavian furniture from Denmark. The quick product turnover and knowledgeable service are why everyone wants to keep coming back again and again. ●1-22-10 Ginza, Chuo City, Ginza Sutoku Bldg., Room 102 ☎03-6263-2122. 12:00 p.m. to 7:00 p.m. Closed on Thu.

pas loin 7

A standing wine bar run by ***bistrosimba***, a popular spot in Ginza that's fully booked day after day. So of course, the snacks are top-notch, too. ●4-14-2 Ginza, Chuo City, XCD Ginza Bldg. 2F ☎080-5828-4141. 8:00 p.m. to 1:00 a.m. (to 12:00 a.m. on Sat.). Closed on Sun., Mon., and other irregular days.

MATSUZAKI SHOTEN 8

Ginza Matsuzaki Senbei, a 200-year-old shop that relocated and reopened in 2021, switching its name to the alphabet in the process. Besides offering Japanese snacks like kawara senbei, soka senbei, arare, and okaki, the on-site café's summer-only shaved ice is also a hit. ●4-13-8 Ginza, Chuo City ☎03-6264-6703. 10:00 a.m. to 7:00 p.m. No closed days.

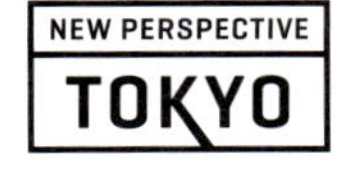

Tokyo Strolls with an Overseas Perspective.

HELSINKI

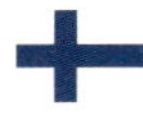

LOTTA MAIJA

● Textile designer and illustrator

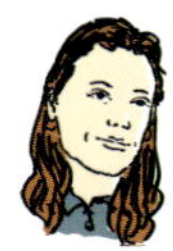

Marimekko textile designer Lotta Maija is a colossal Tokyo fan who's worked as an intern here and studied as an exchange student at Tama Art University.

Two special spots for savoring Tokyo with all five senses.

I'm from a sauna country, so I love Japan's bath culture. (I'm making my very own sento map). Of the 20+ I've been to, my favorite is the modern-feeling ***Koganeyu***. As the hot water engulfs you, it's sublime! Recommended by a dear Japanese friend, long-running senbei shop ***Daikokuya*** is a special place whose yesteryear vibe contrasts with the modern bustle. Savoring the senbei, I'm glad of the effort put into baking each one with such care. I go for the sweet "sugar-coated" ones.

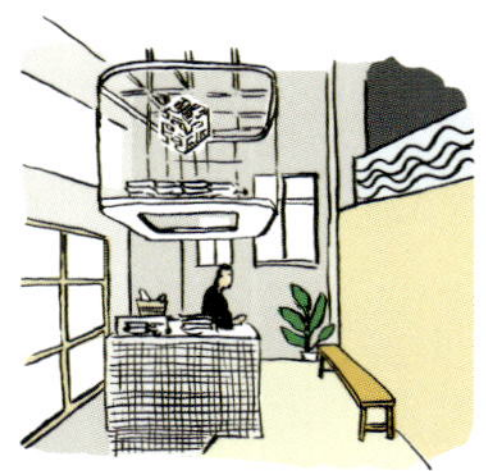

Koganeyu

Sauna, cold plunge, löyly, and outdoor bath. Plus, there's homemade craft beer at "Bandai Beer Bar." ●4-14-6 Taihei, Sumida City ☎03-3622-5009. 6:00 a.m. to 9:00 a.m. and 11:00 a.m. to 12:30 a.m. (from 6:00 a.m. to 9:00 a.m. and 3:00 p.m. to 12:30 a.m. on Sat.). Closed on the 2nd and 4th Mon.

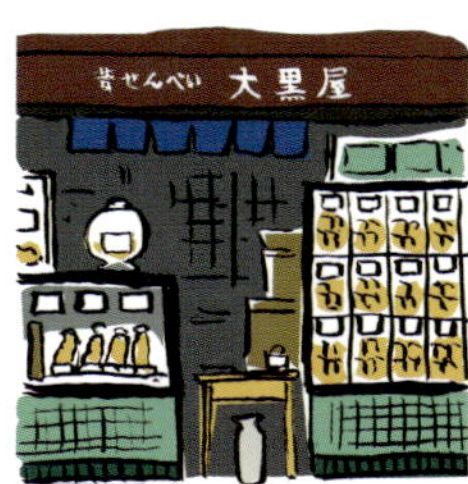

Daikokuya

Long-running senbei shop that uses carefully selected rice and brewed soy sauce, and carefully hand-bakes each one over Kishu Binchotan charcoal. The shop's classic look cuts a fine figure in the downtown shopping district. ●1-3-4 Yanaka, Taito City ☎03-3821-7000. 10:30 a.m. to 6:30 p.m. Closed on Thu.

Text: Kitsune

LONDON

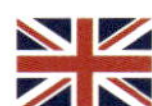

JAKE TILSON

● Artist

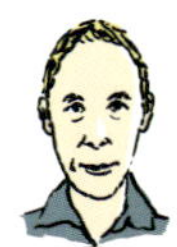

London-based artist Jake Tilson first visited Japan in 1994. Captivated by Tsukiji Market and downtown Tokyo, he's published several books on them, ***Finding Tsukiji*** to name one.

What fuels my creative drive is the Tokyo that still hasn't had a chic makeover.

Tsukiji Market was my top spot in Tokyo, so it's a shame it closed. Fortunately, ***Kitsuneya*** in the outer market is still open, so I go there for "Offal Donburi." The joy of rice topped with stewed offal and a raw egg, while standing. The once-thrilling ***Hands*** has turned into a lifestyle store, so for the last decade, I've switched to ***VIVA HOME Toyosu Store***. A vast floor that's all DIY, with nary a whiff of chic. A high risk of buying more than your suitcase can hold.

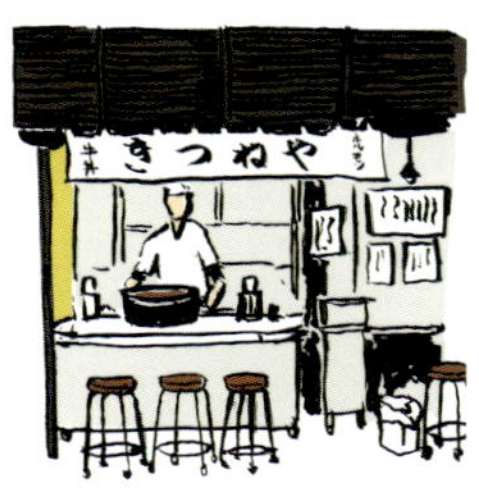

Kitsuneya

The signature dish is "Offal Donburi," for which fresh beef offal is slowly stewed in Hatcho miso. The "Beef Donburi" and "Meat & Tofu Set" are popular, too. ●4-9-12 Tsukiji, Chuo City ☎03-3545-3902. 6:30 a.m. to 1:30 p.m. Closed on Sun., holidays, and the market's closed days.

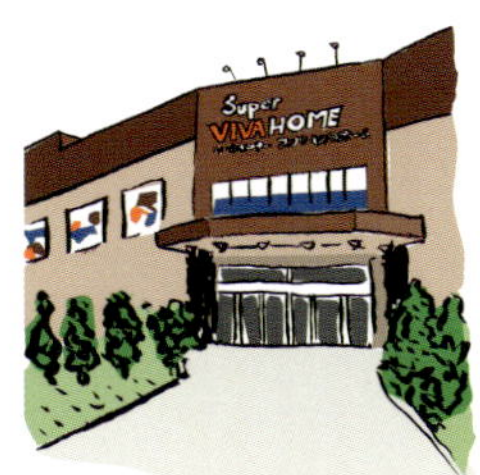

VIVA HOME Toyosu Store

Gigantic DIY store (one of the largest in Tokyo). Stocks everything from professional tools to everyday DIY essentials and gadgets. ●3-4-8 Toyosu, Koto City ☎03-3536-9611. 9:30 a.m. to 9:00 p.m. in the lifestyle section, and from 6:30 a.m. to 9:00 p.m. in the materials section. No closed days.

Text: Megumi Yamashita

TAIPEI

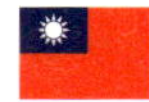

HALLY CHEN

● Designer and author

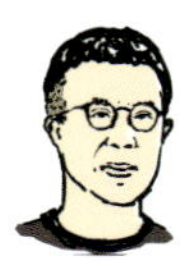

A lover of traditional sweet shops and cafés, Harry Chen has been hooked on Tokyo's cafés since 2007. In 2023, he published ***My Beloved Tokyo Cafés***.

Two traditional long-runners that captivate Taiwanese café enthusiasts.

Cafe de l'ambre has maintained consistent service over two generations, with no drop in quality despite the rise in tourists. I often order the "Amber Queen," but just gazing at the coffee is enough to satisfy my soul. ***Classics Café Lion*** has a ban on talking loudly and taking photos, so you get to immerse yourself in a private coffee-and-music time-out. The moment I do, it truly hits me that I'm back in Tokyo. The music playlists are so beautifully designed that I keep them as mementos.

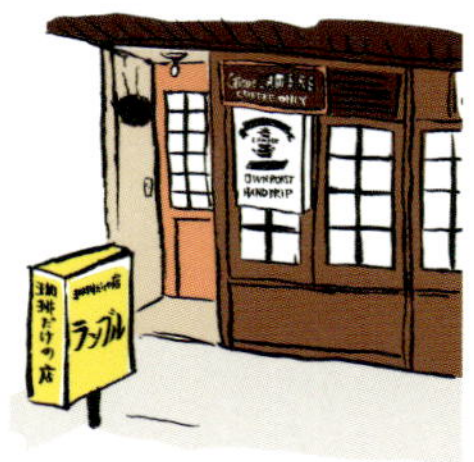

Cafe de l'ambre

The owner has been carefully selecting, roasting, and hand-dripping the beans ever since it was founded in 1948. Long-running café that's always just served coffee, with no light meals, etc. ●8-10-15 Ginza, Chuo City ☎03-3571-1551. 11 a.m. to 8 p.m. (to 6 p.m. on Sun. and holidays). Closed on Mon.

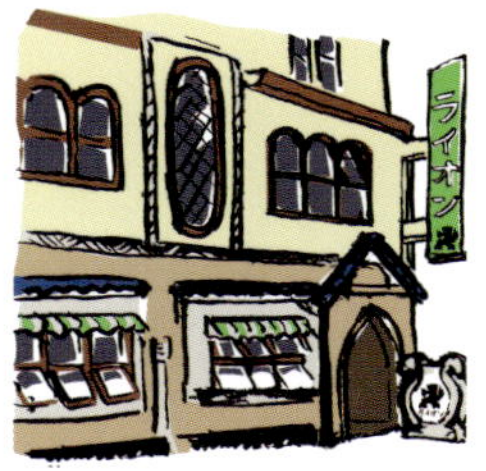

Classics Café Lion

A café where you get to enjoy classical music through large speakers. The selection is based on customers' requests, with staff-led ***Regular Concerts*** every day at 3:00 p.m. and 7:00 p.m. ●2-19-13 Dogenzaka, Shibuya City ☎03-3461-6858. 1:00 p.m. to 8:00 p.m. No closed days.

Text: Mari Katakura

VANCOUVER

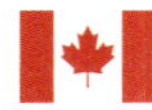

ARTHUR CHMIELEWSKI

● Founder and creative director of ***HAVEN***

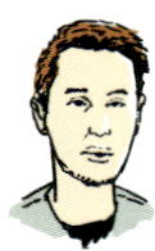

Arthur Chmielewski cofounded the select shop ***HAVEN*** with his brother, and also launched a brand with the same name. He's held exhibitions and pop-ups in Tokyo.

Tokyo shops and designs that update your aesthetic eye.

I've been coming to Tokyo and getting inspiration from its fashions, shops, and designs almost every year for 18 years now. ***TEENAGER*** is a favorite vintage shop for rare ***Patagonia MARS*** goods, military-spec items, and deadstock British military gear. ***21_21 DESIGN SIGHT*** founded by Issey Miyake is another inspiring spot. The exhibits that fuse the now and the traditional are teaching me how design influences daily life.

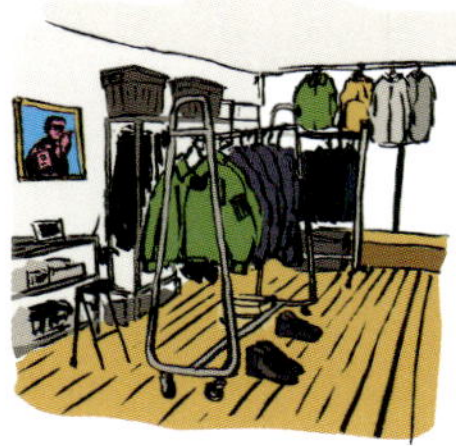

TEENAGER

Selects vintage and new clothes from all over the world. Stocks global military and workwear items, and rolls out original products as well. ●6-32-5 Jingumae, Shibuya City, Dorumi Harajuku, Room 203 ☎03-6804-7390. 1:00 p.m. to 8:00 p.m. Closed on Wed.

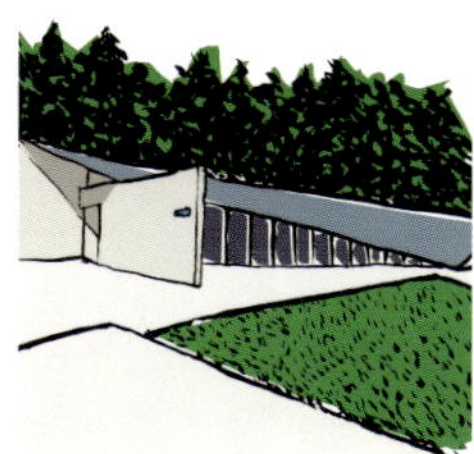

21_21 DESIGN SIGHT

An exhibition space that looks at "everyday life" from a design perspective. Holding the special exhibition ***The Art of the RAMEN Bowl*** until June 15. ●9-7-6 Akasaka, Minato City, Tokyo Midtown ☎03-3475-2121. 10:00 a.m. to 7:00 p.m. (last admissions at 6:30 p.m.). Closed on Tue.

Text: Kozue Sato

Illustrations: Akiko Maegawa Editing: Yuriko Kobayashi

NEW YORK

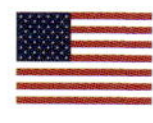

ARCHIE ARCHAMBAULT

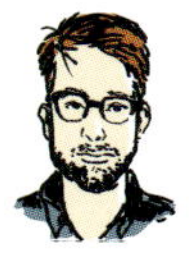

● Creator of ***Archie's Press***

Archie Archambault creates global city maps based on his backpacking travels. They're available to buy at the ***MoMA Design Store*** in New York.

A city that's like a convenience store for art discoveries.

Memories of Tokyo grow in my mind, and I sometimes wonder if I was dreaming. Like this time I was strolling around Yanaka, a stray cat caught my eye, and before I knew it, I was buying pottery at nearby ***Yanaka Warakuya***. The white plates that still lie on my table remind me it wasn't a dream. ***Strange Store***, a shop recommended by a friend, was like a fun convenience store full of wares that were nostalgic yet fresh, and childish yet charming. If only I'd bought something!

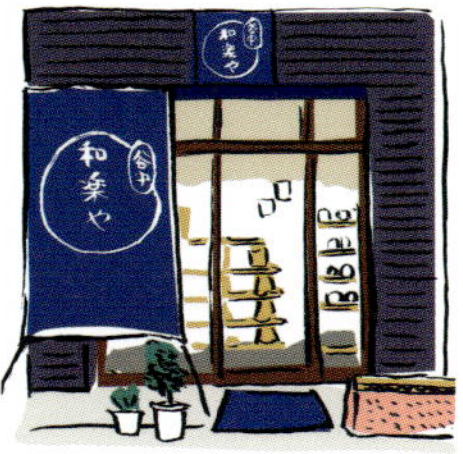

Yanaka Warakuya

In downtown Yanaka, you can get Japanese tableware and goods mainly by artists from western Japan. There's bound to be something that'll add some Japanese charm to everyday life. ●3-14-8 Yanaka, Taito City ☎03-5842-1917. 11:00 a.m. to 6:00 p.m. Closed on Wed.

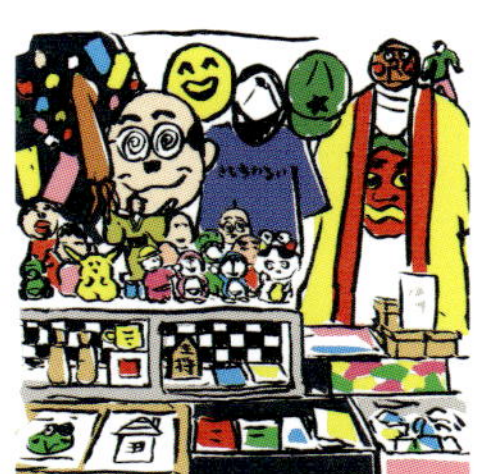

Strange Store

Shop in an apartment that sells items selected by contemporary artist Ken Kagami. Lots of irregular closed days. Check Insta to see when it's open. ●12-3 Uguisudanicho, Shibuya City, Room 301 ☎03-3496-5611. 3 p.m. to 6 p.m. (from 12 p.m. on Sat., Sun., and holidays). Irregular closed days.

Text: Natsumi Ohara

BANGKOK

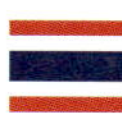

ANUPONG KUTTIKUL (PINTO)

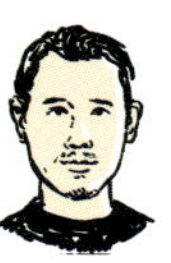

● CEO and cofounder of ***CARNIVAL BKK***

Anupong Kuttikul is CEO of ***CARNIVAL BKK***, a leading shop in Thailand's street culture scene. He's a sneaker collector who's been to Tokyo 20 times.

Tokyo is an endless "playground" that constantly fuels inspiration.

Sneaker Shop SKIT is a spot where I can find rare historic items, and I never miss it out. I was thrilled when I found a pair of early-2000s "Nike SB Dunk Low Paris" originals there. I grew up on Japanese games, and ***Super Potato, Akihabara Store*** is jam-packed with retro ones, so I get to revisit my childhood there. Sneakers, fashion, games, food, music...Tokyo is like a playground that's got everything I love. Its charm also lies in its perfect balance of futuristic elements and preserved traditional culture.

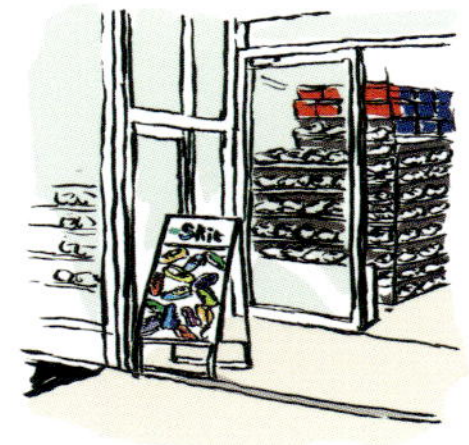

Sneaker Shop SKIT Tokyo Kichijoji Store

The keen-eyed staff select sneakers from all genres—new, used, the latest, and classic. You can also find items that weren't initially released in Japan. ●1-18-1 Kichijoji-Minamicho, Musashino City, D-ASSET Kichijoji 1F ☎0422-47-6671. 11:00 a.m. to 7:00 p.m. No closed days.

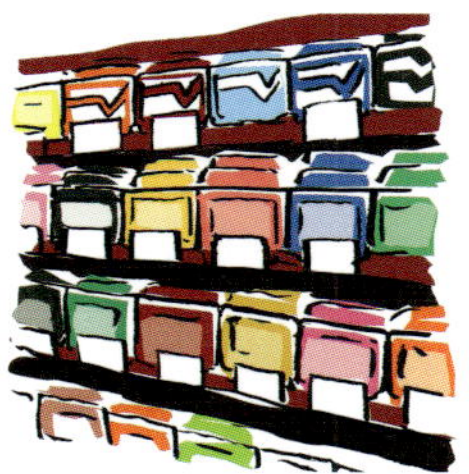

Super Potato Akihabara Store

A top-tier retro game shop with a peerless selection. The fifth floor is a game center where you can play nostalgic arcade titles. ●1-11-2 Soto-Kanda, Chiyoda City, Kitabayashi Bldg. 3-5F ☎03-5289-9933. 11:00 a.m. to 8:00 p.m. No closed days.

Text: Chinami Hirahara

MELBOURNE

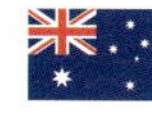

MICHELLE MACKINTOSH

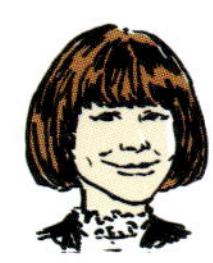

● Book designer and writer

Cofounder of Melbourne-based publishing studio ***Floating Books***. Since coming to Tokyo for her honeymoon, she's been back over 60 times.

A Tokyo destination that's away from the downtown hustle and bustle.

I first encountered ***CASICA*** through shimenawa decorations. I buy one enriching, special daily item there whenever I'm in Tokyo. The styling and attention to detail are so inspiring. I recreate the café's dishes at home. Visiting 120 hot springs nationwide for a book, I found ***Maenohara Onsen SAYA-NO-YUDOKORO***. Eating 100% buckwheat noodles in a private room while drinking Calpis and beer between baths—luxury. Hot springs, a garden, and farm-fresh vegetables—bliss.

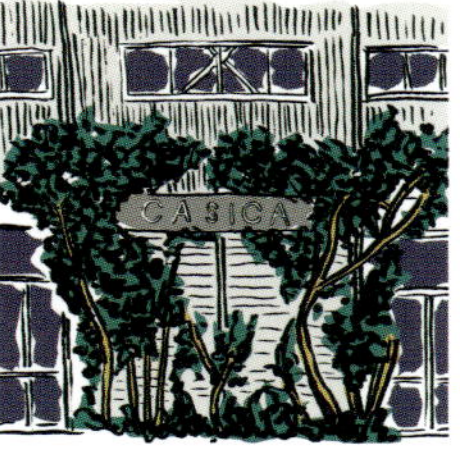

CASICA

Sells interior goods, tableware, and plants selected regardless of nationality or era. Also has Japanese antiques. The café's menu is based on medicinal cuisine. ●1-4-6 Shinkiba, Koto City ☎03-6457-0826. 11:00 a.m. to 6:00 p.m. Closed on Mon. and the 2nd & 4th Tue.

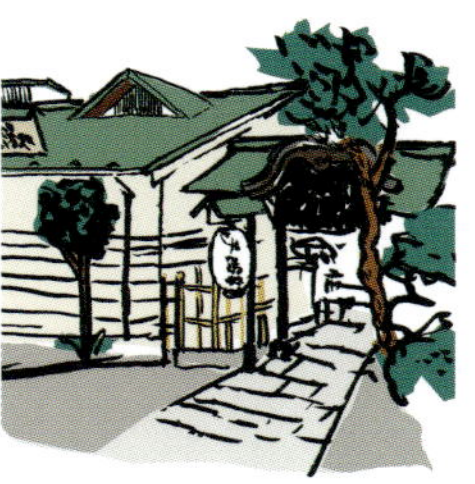

Maenohara Onsen SAYA-NO-YUDOKORO

Day-trip hot spring with all-natural water from 1,500 m underground. Restaurant with a moss garden serves soba made with 100% grown-in-Japan buckwheat. ● 3-41-1 Maenocho, Itabashi City ☎03-5916-3826. 9:00 a.m. to 12:00 a.m. (last admissions at 11:00 p.m.). No closed days.

Text: Mifumi Obata

MEXICO CITY

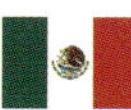

CARLOS ALONSO

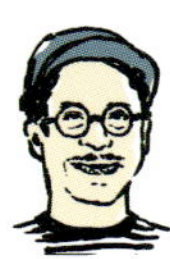

● Café owner, DJ, and lawyer

Carlos Alonso owns ***Fuzz & Brew***, a café in Mexico City that roasts its coffee in-house. He visits Tokyo at least once a year to enjoy music-bar hopping.

A place with great flavors and a real local vibe.

I love wandering the back alleys in Tokyo. Once, I found ***Hatos Outside***, a spot for delicious curry and craft beer. A magnet for cool youth, plus a DJ booth inside—really unique. I can get nicely drunk while talking with the staff. Despite being in a central residential area, it feels as open as a beach. ***Tonkatsu Taiho*** has a great nostalgic Showa atmosphere. I always have the "Special Premium Pork Loin Cutlet Set Meal." The meat's doneness and the side of fluffy cabbage are perfect.

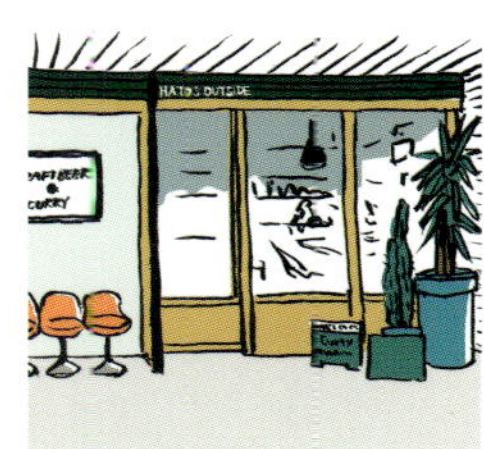

Hatos Outside

Spicy curry with rich vegetable flavors, plus vegan and kid-friendly options. ●4-22-5 Akatsutsumi, Setagaya City, Akamatsu Bldg. 1F ☎03-6265-8351. 11:30 a.m. to 3:00 p.m. and 5:30 p.m. to 11:00 p.m. (from 11:30 a.m. to 10:00 p.m. on Sun. and holidays). Closed on Mon.

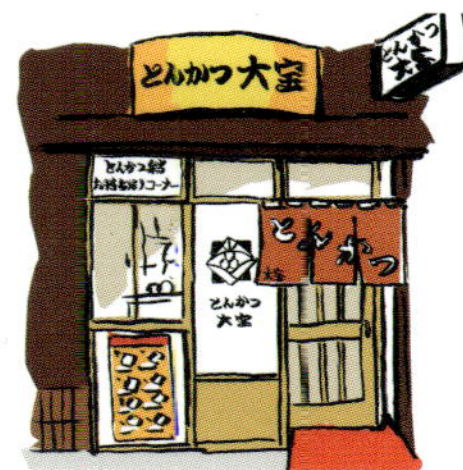

Tonkatsu Taiho

You can also try "TOKYO X"—Tokyo-raised pork with a fine texture and clean fatty flavor. Limited stocks, so get it before it sells out. ●1-6-15 Meguro, Meguro City, 1F ☎03-3491-9470. 11:30 a.m. to 3:00 p.m. and 6:00 p.m. to 10:00 p.m. Irregular closed days.

Text: Miho Nagaya

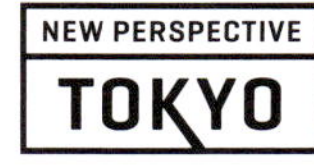

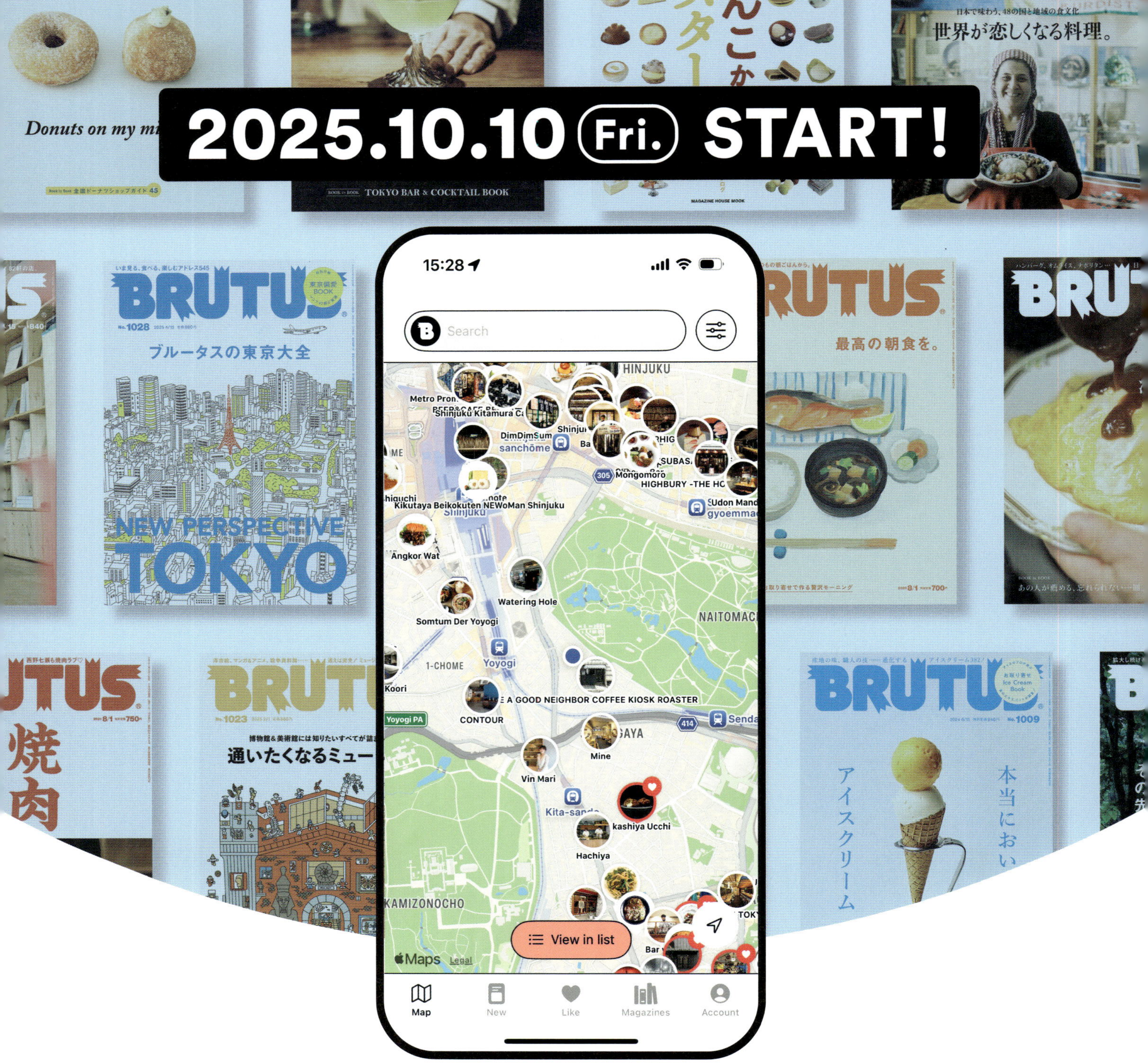
2025.10.10 Fri. START!
Donuts on my mi
TOKYO BAR & COCKTAIL BOOK
世界が恋しくなる料理。
BRUTUS
ブルータスの東京大全
NEW PERSPECTIVE TOKYO
最高の朝食を。
通いたくなるミュー
焼肉
アイスクリーム
本当におい
15:28
Search
View in list
Map
New
Like
Magazines
Account

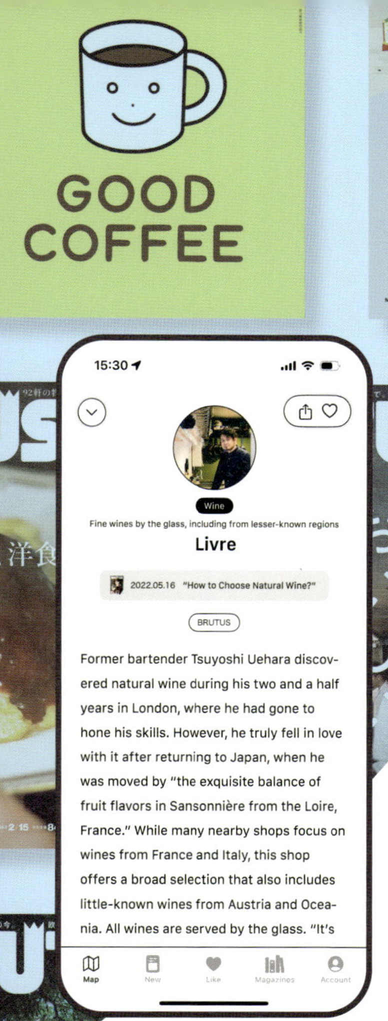

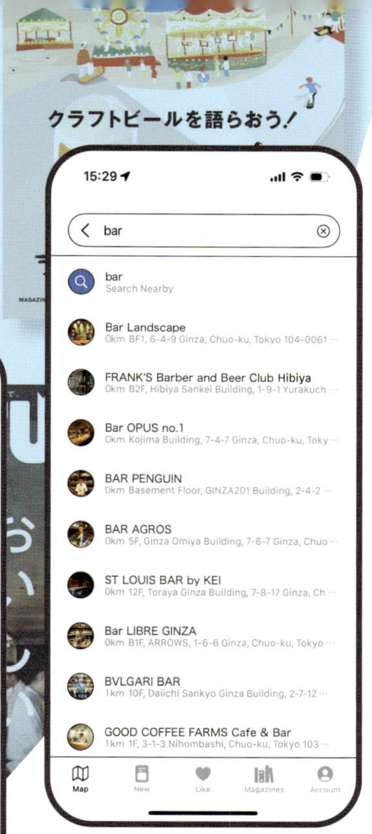

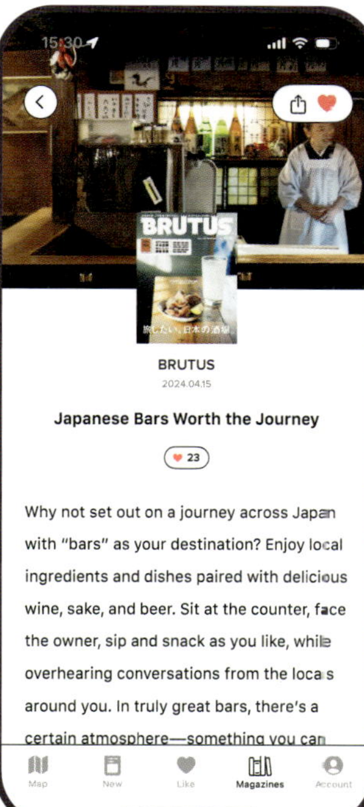

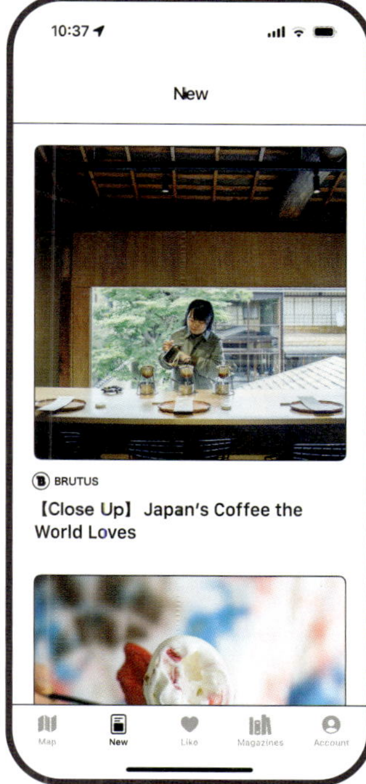

1

Read magazine articles!

As a new media platform from BRUTUS, past magazine featured articles are also available. The featured themes are also a trove of topics currently trending in Japan. You can save shops that catch your eye as a list on the "Like" screen by tapping the heart.

2

Search by keywords.

Let's say you suddenly want to go to a bar. You think, "If nearby, I'd like to go to one with nice vibes that BRUTUS chose." Well, just search by keywords using the search bar. It also shows the distance from your current location, so it's handy for deciding if you need a taxi.

3

Search by featured themes.

BRUTUS pays close attention to magazine features. For example, a feature on "Japanese Bars" would be quite useful for enjoying good food and drinks on your next vacation. Featured spots are listed and linked to a map, so you can search for places that catch your eyewhile checking their locations.

4

Heaps of original articles.

In addition to magazine features, it also links to articles on BRUTUS.jp, and mapzine original content that compiles interesting areas and keywords. The number of spots increases as you use it, and its enjoyable reading experience are charms you won't find in other search apps. You'll be notified of new content via push notifications.

map + magazine = mapzine. The map app you've always wanted!

Tokyo and parts of Japan are overflowing with visitors from overseas. While people are making use of social media to visit various attractive places, there are still many hidden, wonderful spots that aren't well known. At BRUTUS we've been reporting and editing articles on the culture of Japan since our launch in 1980. With this app, we hope you'll learn about spots selected by magazines in Japan to further enjoy your travels. The mapzine English version is a new magazine media platform, brought to you by BRUTUS, designed to be enjoyed by people worldwide.

We've partnered with whitemap, a company that developed a system engine which combines smooth UI/UX with easy-to-use maps and easy-to-read articles, resulting in outstanding operability. As a lifestyle magazine, BRUTUS covers more than just food. You can search for everything from used clothing and tableware to aquariums, zoos, and museums.

Also, since we're a media outlet, one charm of mapzine is that it's enjoyable to read. All mapped spots have articles introducing them, so you can see the perspective the editorial department took in their coverage. Original content will also be distributed within mapzine and linked to a map. Be sure to download it to enhance your experience in Japan!

Download now and have unlimited access for two weeks!

After buying a ticket you'll have full access for two weeks. You can start using it right away to check shops and spots you want to visit in advance, and then use the map when you head out. Scan the QR code for more details!

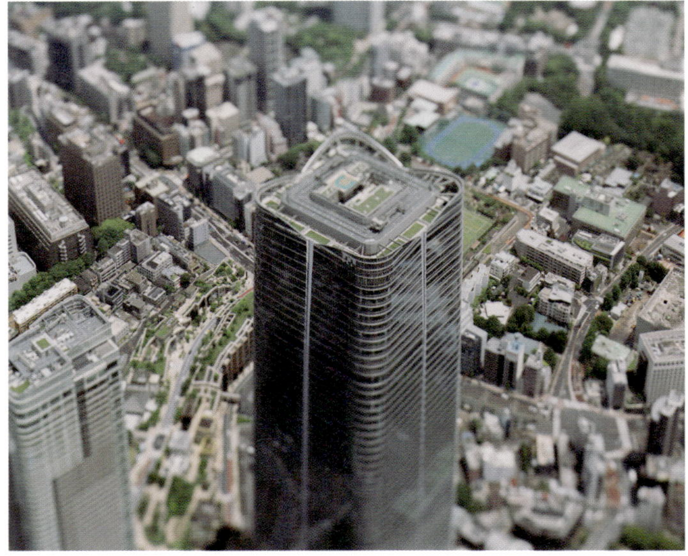

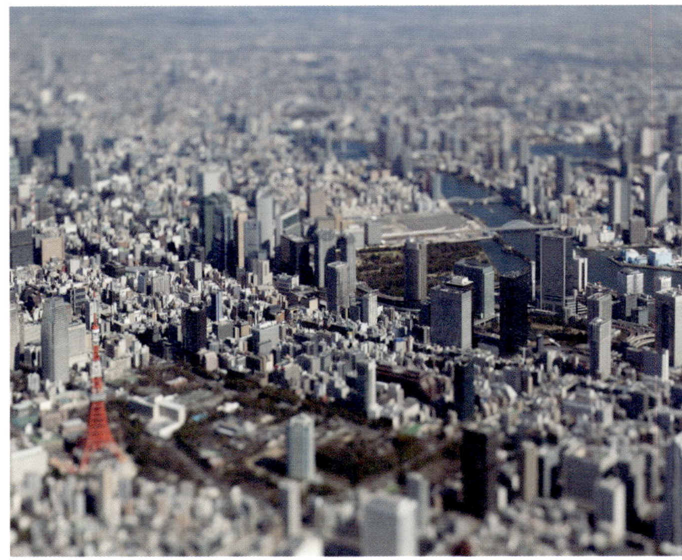

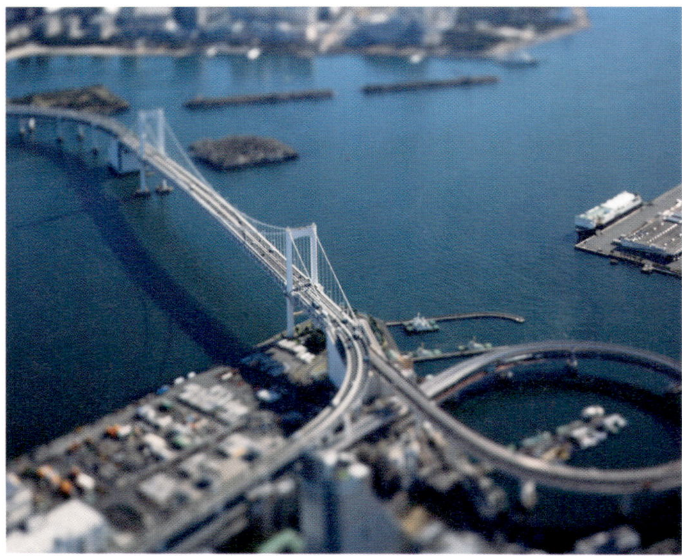

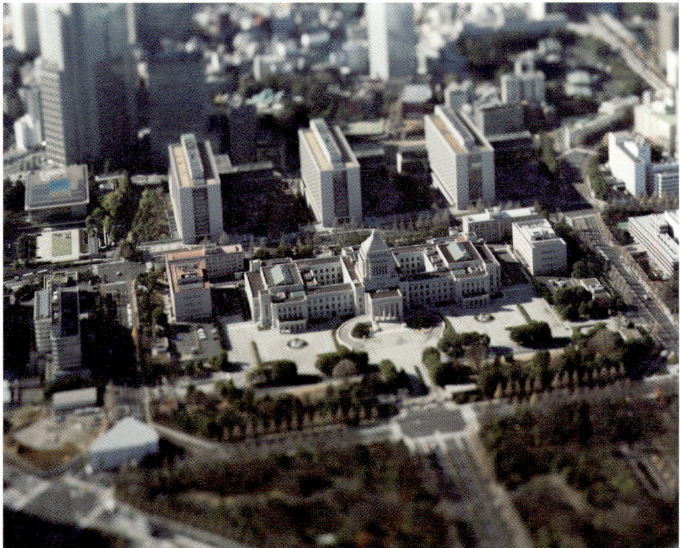

Naoki Honjo

● Photographer

Born in Tokyo in 1978, studied Media Art at Tokyo Polytechnic University Graduate School before developing a distinctive technique using large-format cameras with bellows to transform real landscapes into diorama-like miniature worlds. His 2006 photobook "small planet" won the Kimura Ihei Photography Award. His works are included in the permanent collections of the NYC Museum of Art and Tokyo Photographic Art Museum.

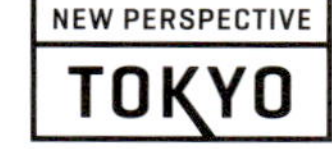

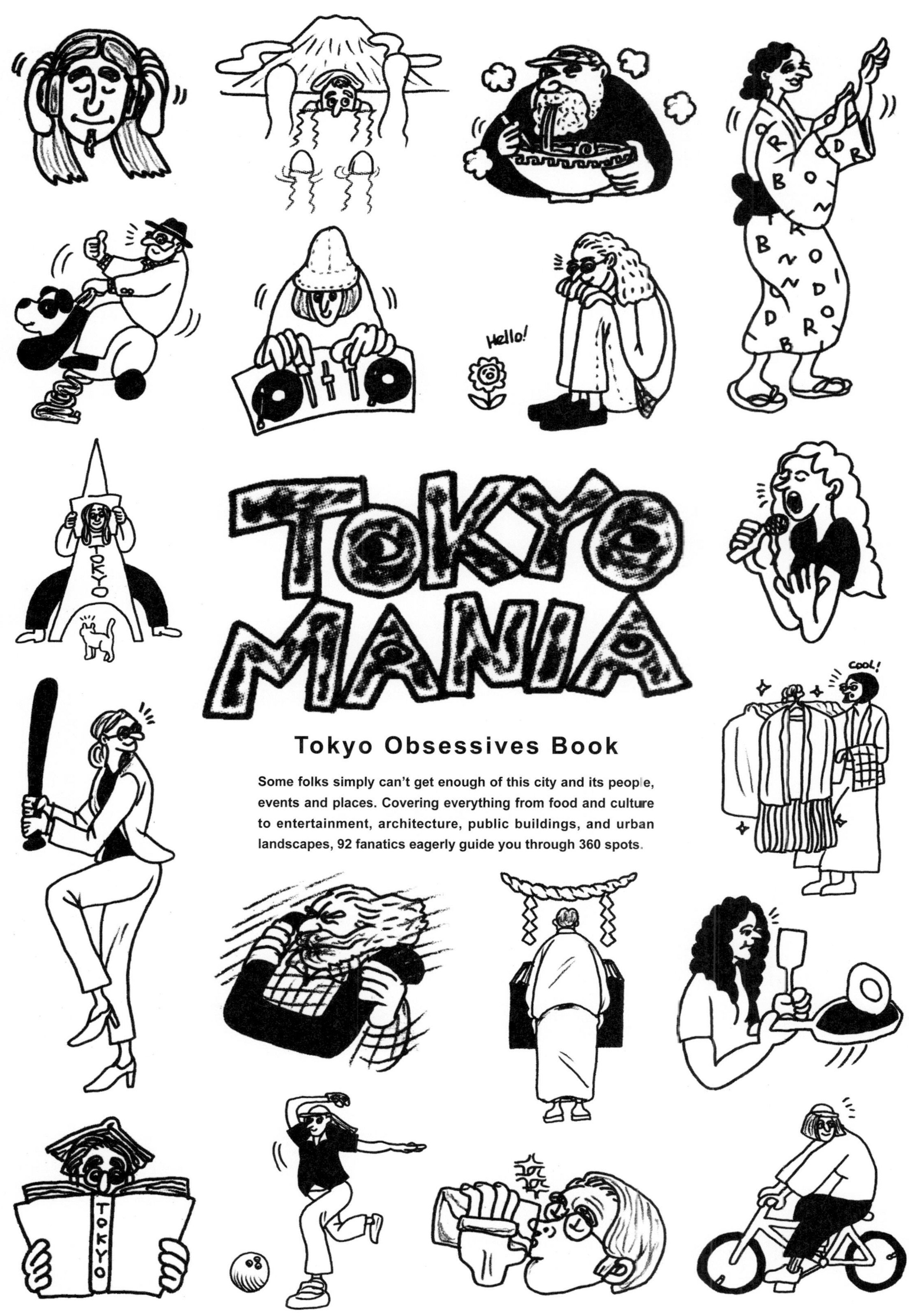

TOKYO MANIA

Tokyo Obsessives Book

Some folks simply can't get enough of this city and its people, events and places. Covering everything from food and culture to entertainment, architecture, public buildings, and urban landscapes, 92 fanatics eagerly guide you through 360 spots.

01 CURRY AT SOBA SHOPS

The Curry I Remember After over 300 Standing Soba Shops.

Seiji Nakazawa ●Writer and guitarist

Has a series ***Standing Soba Wanderings*** on the web media ***SORA NEWS24***. Casual maniac who's been to over 300 soba shops on interview trips and tours.

Morning in the entertainment district, where last night's dreams still linger. A bar hostess is seeing off some customers. Her cheerful voice rings out: "See you!" It's as if she's saying it to herself. Spring slumber knows no dawn. Not that I care. Even the dreams at my feet are spring in this world. The zombies yawn as they pass by, too. This is the route I always take. There's a shabby flower bed along that street. Dry, hard soil that barely soaks up any water. The boy finishing off his night shift has clearly watered them too much. As I jump over a puddle on the asphalt, I spot a flower in that hard, cracked bed. A difference I didn't notice yesterday. A boundary found in the cycle of repetitive days. Sometimes, a subtle difference catches you off guard, doesn't it? I think curry at standing soba shops is like a flower buried in a hard, everyday routine. For example, the nostalgic charm of ***Minogasa***'s curry, or the special vibe of ***Yomoda Soba***'s. Recalling these subtle, never-exaggerated details suddenly makes me crave some. What soothes passersby isn't flowers grown in hothouses, it's ones blooming by the roadside. Isn't this concept the very essence of a soba shop where you eat standing up? When that soba craving hits… Curry: adding extra color to standing soba shops. And the flowers will bloom today, too. And are sure to tomorrow and the day after that as well.

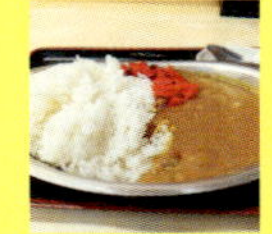

Sobayoshi, Nihombashi Main Store This soba shop's curry is all about the broth. Curry this flavorful is rare at a stand-up eatery. It's all down to being directly run by a wholesaler of bonito flakes: thinly shaved ones go into the curry. And the essence of those? Very thin bonito flakes, souvenirs of which are also sold near the ticket machine. ●1-1-7 Nihombashi-Honcho, Chuo City, 1F.

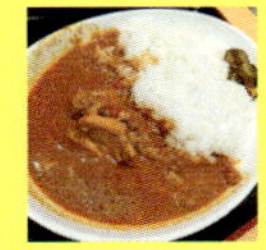

Yomoda Soba, Shinjuku Nishiguchi Store When it comes to curry at Standing soba shops, ***Yomoda Soba*** is a must-try. The curry at this hidden gem is authentic Japanese-style Indian curry. The flavor is light but goes perfectly with rice. Truly a curry you'll suddenly find yourself craving. ●1-15-7 Nishi-Shinjuku, Shinjuku City, 1F.

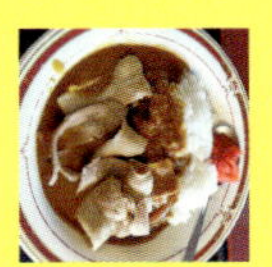

Tateshina With skyscrapers towering overhead, ***Tateshina*** at Akasaka-mitsuke Station serves curry with a rich, Western-food diner flavor. The varied options include curry rice, meat curry, meat-and-egg curry, and eggplant curry. In fact, this was once a curry shop. Even the curry at this eat-standing soba shop had a previous life. Ah, Akasaka—such flower-like charm! ●3-1-16 Akasaka, Minato City.

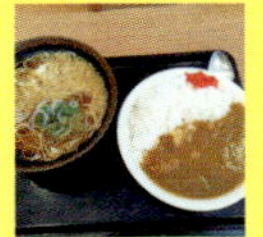

Okada ***Okada***'s curry can only be ordered as part of a set. Try it, and you'll definitely see why. The richness comes with a spicy kick. The nostalgic heat contrasts vividly with the soba in its hot, sweet broth. The soba is the weft, the curry the warp. Someday, the tapestry these sets weave could well heal your wounded soul. ●13-6 Nihombashi-Kodemmacho, Chuo City.

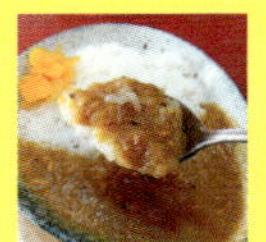

Tambaya Why does this eat-standing-up soba shop serve Indian curry? You might wonder at the "Indian curry: ¥460" on the sign, but actually, it's a recipe brought in by a Nepalese staff member. The fiery, spicy aftertaste is the real deal. This Indian curry has only gone up ¥10 in the last decade. ●2-16-1 Shimbashi, Minato City, 1F.

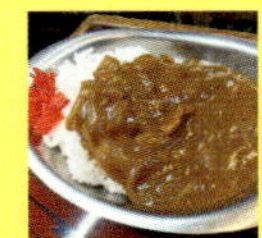

Minogasa Main Store Firstly, ***Minogasa***'s rice is delicious. The crisp, firm rice goes perfectly with how Japanese curry which brings out the sweetness of the onions. The more you chew, the more nostalgic it feels. Just as the morning dew tells of last night's storm, ***Minogasa***'s curry reveals the path it's walked. This curry has journeyed far. ●3-10-5 Iwamotocho, Chiyoda City.

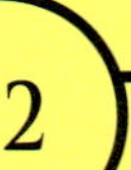

02 CRAFT COLA

Head into Town, and Have a Wonderful Encounter with Craft Cola.

Masayuki Koibuchi ●Craft cola peddler and meister

Has been heavily into craft cola since 2018, drinking some 3,000 cups of it a year. Runs the fictional select shop ***CRAFT COLA hour***, and does promotional and other activities all over Japan.

Craft cola culture dates back to the birth of ***Iyoshi Cola*** in 2018. The "arrival of so-called craft cola" on the scene sparked a major buzz, and new brands were soon appearing in quick succession, getting picked up in the media, and having fairs at malls and the like. Quickly growing into a boom, the genre went through a whirlwind of change in its early days. Things may seem a bit calmer now compared to the earlier momentum, but there are clearly areas where they've progressed, too. One of these is the richness and depth of chances to try them in various cities. While there are now more large malls, supermarkets, and so on where you can buy a range of craft cola brands, there's also been a rise in places where you can savor them deeply, such as stores run by ***Iyoshi Cola*** and wonderfully unique urban spots. Now the boom has passed, the places that still promote craft cola are all great spots that have discovered its potential for themselves, and offer unique and delicious ways to experience it. I've selected some particularly appealing spots offering just such experiences in the Shibuya, Koenji, and Shimo-Kitazawa areas. So, if you're out and about this spring or summer, why not sample some craft cola? You're sure to discover a new favorite brand or a fresh way to enjoy it. And I hope that one day, after you've had a wonderful urban encounter, you'll toast it with me and regale me with your tale. Have a nice CRAFT COLA!!

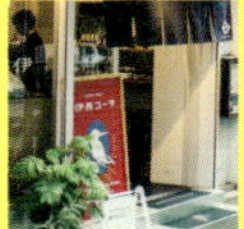

Iyoshi Cola Shibuya Jingumae ***Iyoshi Cola***—the pioneer and king of craft cola. Its second directly run store in Shibuya Jingumae bustles every day with Japanese and international customers alike. In addition to the classic flavors, the store offers seasonal ones and herbal extract toppings, providing a deep, exclusive experience. ●5-29-12 Jingumae, Shibuya City.

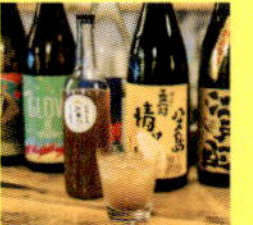

IGOR COSY SHINSEN One of my recommended craft cola cocktails can be had at ***IGOR COSY SHINSEN***. Made with "Asama Cola"—which features spicy Shinshu Korean ginseng—and "Bakkan Nasakeshima"—a shochu with a rich barley aroma—it has a flavor that's deeply redolent of popcorn. I really hope you give it a try. ●18-6 Maruyamacho, Shibuya City, 1F.

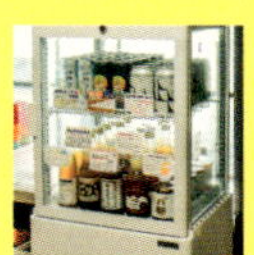

Kosugiyu After starting out with selling ***Iyoshi Cola***, the public bath Kosugiyu now offers some 20 different craft colas. Currently stocking four on a permanent basis, they hold an event called "Kosugiyu Craft Cola Fest" every summer. Above all, the baths are incredibly relaxing, and a craft cola after a soak at Kosugiyu is pure bliss. ●3-32-17 Koenji-Kita, Suginami City.

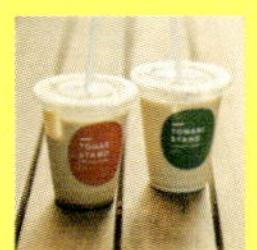

Kosugiyu Tonari A café & shared space next door to ***Kosugiyu***. Four to five craft colas to enjoy, changing with the season. On the café menu, the milk-based craft cola syrup is recommended. With its unique flavor that's like chai latte or fruit milk, it's a lovely shot of post-bath euphoria. ●3-32-17 Koenji-Kita, Suginami City.

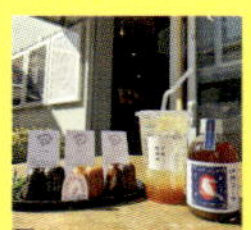

Shimokita Genzojo A café and bar that opened in December 2024 and spreads movie culture through scripts and 8 mm films. Six carefully selected craft colas from across the country, offered as new movie-watching drinks to enjoy with milk, in cocktails, and more. As you sip your cola, you can also sate your hunger with popcorn and canelés, too. ●2-36-13 Daita, Setagaya City.

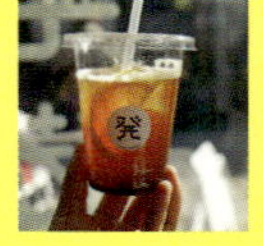

Hakko Department Many shops don't handle commercial brands, only offering their own homemade craft colas. A standout drink is "Yamabuki Cola" from ***Hakko Department***. They use vinegar in their craft cola, giving it a mellow and refreshing tang that permeates your whole body. Perfect for outings in the warmer months. ●2-36-15 Daita, Setagaya City.

03 MOUKO TANMEN NAKAMOTO

As Many NAKAMOTO Experiences as There Are Shops.

Zuketogo ●MOUKO TANMEN NAKAMOTO enthusiast

"Just a customer" who got hooked on NAKAMOTO after first having MOUKO TANMEN in 1989. Admin of the fan site ***The Way of MOUKO TANMEN NAKAMOTO***.

MOUKO TANMEN NAKAMOTO (hereafter, ***NAKAMOTO***) is a famous ultra-spicy ramen chain with 29 locations nationwide, 12 of them in Tokyo alone (as of April 1, 2025). NAKAMOTO continues to captivate fans with its extremely spicy ramen, but its true value goes much deeper than just being a super-spicy ramen shop. It's been 36 years since my first taste of NAKAMOTO's ramen, and I've been hooked ever since. For the past 15 years, I've been visiting every location, and have eaten NAKAMOTO practically every day. Why am I so drawn to it? Well, it started with the "joy of overcoming insane spiciness," and eventually, I discovered the infinite depth beyond that. Besides the menu items common to all shops, each location also offers unique exclusive ones created by the staff, so there are new flavors to discover everywhere. The spiciness varies widely, and surprisingly, there are even dishes that aren't spicy at all. Realizing that this is NAKAMOTO's true charm—that it's not just a spicy ramen shop but a delicious one as well—changed my view of it completely. "The spiciness fades away, and all I can feel is the deliciousness." This is the moment when you truly experience the essence of NAKAMOTO. As you discover its deeper charm, NAKAMOTO transforms from just a ramen shop into an endless journey of new discoveries.

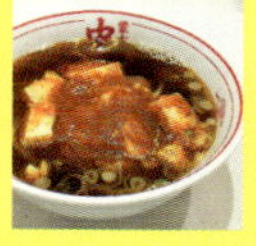

MOUKO TANMEN NAKAMOTO Kami-Itabashi Main Store The main store in Kami-Itabashi, which founder Tadashi NAKAMOTO ran out of his own home. A "sacred place," this store offers exclusive dishes like the early days' "Karafuto Ramen" and "MOUKO Ramen." Savor a bowl of NAKAMOTO's history, and connect with its roots. ●4-33-3 Tokiwadai, Itabashi City, Room 201.

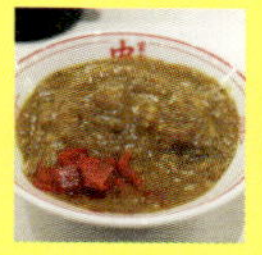

MOUKO TANMEN NAKAMOTO Shinjuku Out of all the stores, this is the only one that always serves curry. NAKAMOTO's curry has an image of being extremely spicy with heavy use of chilis, but it's actually mild. A surprisingly popular dish with a stew-like flavor. Located in a relatively quiet area along Otakibashi-dori Avenue away from Kabukicho, it's a calm place to visit. ●7-8-11 Nishi-Shinjuku, Shinjuku City, B1.

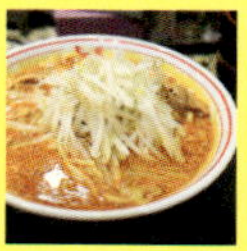

MOUKO TANMEN NAKAMOTO Shibuya Recommended for the spicy-averse is the milder, sesame-flavored "Sesame Osa," devised to acclimatize Shibuya's youth to the ultra-spicy "Hokkyoku Ramen." A here-only dish that was created as a trial one, then won so many fans it became a permanent fixture. ●2-6-17 Dogenzaka, Shibuya City, B2.

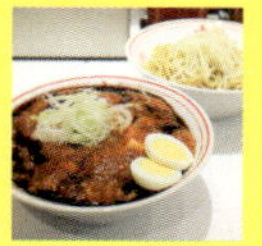

MOUKO TANMEN NAKAMOTO Kinshicho A store known for its wide range of exclusive dishes created by its ramen-loving manager. Different dishes appear every day, with weekly specials on weekends to boot. Awaiting you in Kinshicho is a variety of flavors so wide you'll never tire of them even if you come every day. ●3-14-5 Kinshi, Sumida City, 1F.

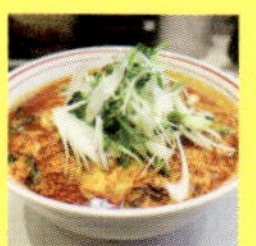

MOUKO TANMEN NAKAMOTO Akitsu Features seasonal limited-edition dishes called "North Pole Four Seasons," through which NAKAMOTO fanatics are said to feel the changing seasons. Famous for her friendly manner and wit, the owner-manager's wife serves up a lovely mood to go with the ramen. ●5-7-8 Akitsucho, Higashi-Murayama City.

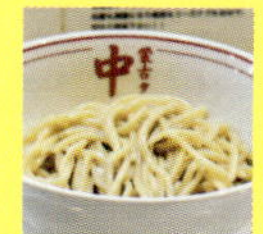

MOUKO TANMEN NAKAMOTO Tachikawa You can customize the noodle thickness with all the noodle dishes. Changing the standard medium-thick noodles to thick ones makes for a chewy, udon-like texture. Experience a different side of NAKAMOTO through a menu that offers something a little unusual. ●2-2-33 Nishikicho, Tachikawa City, 1F.

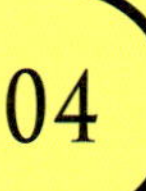

04 CROISSANTS

The Delightful Texture of Croissants.

Hiroyo Ishibushi ●President of the Panzuki Kyokai (literally, "Bread-Lovers' Association")

Organizes events to connect people through bread, and scours the whole nation in search of the very best bread.

Croissants are made by layering dough with butter folded into it, resulting in a texture not found in Japanese bread. Without a doubt, their greatest charm lies in their texture. The outside is a crisp honeycomb of crunchy layers that pop with every bite, while the inside is soft and fluffy, with a richly buttery flavor and a melt-in-the-mouth moistness. It's this gradation of textures that makes croissants so special. The texture varies widely depending on the techniques and ingredients used. The key factors in a croissant's texture are layer thickness, cavity size, baking level, and buttery flavor. After enjoying its visual beauty and aroma, the first sensation you get when you bite into one is the texture of the layers. Very thin layers create a delicate, melt-in-the-mouth bite, while thicker ones make for a strong, crunchy one. Cavity size also affects texture. Croissants with large cavities feel light and airy, while denser dough is moist and rich. The temperature they're baked at is also important. A high one creates a crisp texture, while slow baking at a low one enhances the buttery flavor and gives a moist finish. These combinations mean that far from being the same everywhere, croissants are unique to each store. Enjoy the individuality of croissants as you savor their different textures and features.

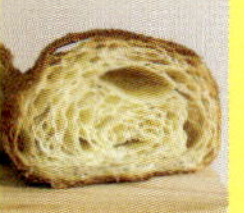

TOLO PAN TOKYO A bakery inspired by an American garage. The croissants have a crunchy outside and soft, chewy inside, with a rich, milky butter flavor and firm texture. Slowly fermented at a low temperature, the dough has a charming, handcrafted texture and aroma. ●3-14-3 Higashiyama, Meguro City.

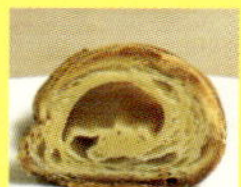

Zuckerbäcker Fukui A confectioner that carries on the flavors of ***TOKYO FREUNDLIEB***, a bakery that ran for 50 years. The ends have a light, crunchy, pie-like texture while the center has moist layers with a rich buttery flavor, making for a variety of textures in a single croissant. ●1-11-10 Fukasawa, Setagaya City, 1F.

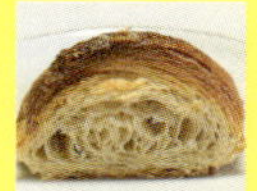

Jujiya Seipanjo A bakery that only uses Hokkaido wheat. The croissants here use a large amount of whole wheat flour. The dough is folded into 16 layers and goes easy on the butter, so you get to fully savor the wheat's flavor. The beet sugar syrup brushed onto the surface exquisitely complements the moistness inside. ●1-35-13 Daita, Setagaya City, 1F.

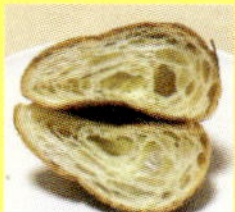

「TATSU」 A small bakery specializing in croissants and other Viennoiseries. These croissants have a crunchy outside and an unexpectedly soft, airy inside, and fill your mouth with the rich aroma of butter. The nine-layered dough creates a perfect contrast between the outside and inside. ●1-11-6 Toyotamanaka, Nerima City.

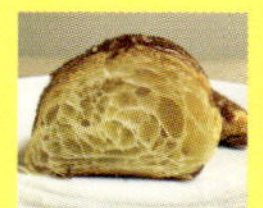

Bäckerei-Cafe Linde A German bread specialty shop in Kichijoji Sunroad Shopping Street. Formed into round shapes and baked by hand, the croissants get a unique crispy texture by being brushed with a lye solution before baking. The balance with the moist inside is exquisite, and the fragrant, sweet-and-sour flavor highly addictive. ●1-11-27 Kichijoji-Honcho, Musashino City.

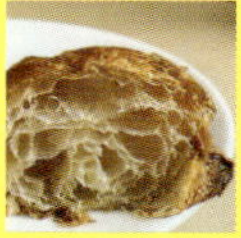

La Pâtisserie by Aman Tokyo ***Aman Tokyo***'s pastry shop. Made with French AOC-certified fermented butter, these croissants have a smooth, melt-in-the-mouth texture and a refined, richly buttery flavor that grows with each bite. ●1-5-6 Otemachi, Chiyoda City, Otemachi Tower, OOTEMORI B2.

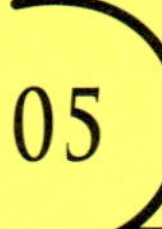

05 SPRING ROLLS

Welcome to "Wrapped Cuisine"—A World of Endless Possibilities.

Tomohiro Hisamatsu ●Scriptwriter

Scriptwriter for the shows ***AniReco TV, Kitano Makoto no Zubari***, and more. Also eats over 1,000 kinds of spring rolls every year, a feat for which he's appeared on ***Matsuko no Shiranai Sekai***.

Japan is currently going through something of a "spring roll civil war." In fact, spring roll shops are popping up rapidly nationwide. Examples include ***Fukuoka Harumaki Buru*** in Fukuoka, ***Sayonara Ten San***, ***Onigiri to Harumaki Kiyoshi***, ***Mamehachi, Shunshindo***, and ***THE HARUMAKI CLUB KOBE*** in Kansai, ***Harumaki Shokudo Dekoboko*** in Aichi, ***Spring Roll Specialty Shop Harumaki Baton*** and ***Tokyo Harumaki*** in Tokyo, ***Harumakiya*** in Ishikawa, and ***HARUMAKI GALAXY*** in Hokkaido. That gives you an idea of just how many spring roll shops there are here. However, just because specialty stores are opening up everywhere, that doesn't mean the spring roll scene is booming among the general public. One fried food ranking even had them below "daigaku imo"—a fried dish that hardly feels fried at all. And even when they got a spot on ***Matsuko no Shiranai Sekai***, they were described as a "lackluster dim sum." Feeling sympathy for spring rolls for being an underdog like myself, I travel the country eating and promoting them as a self-styled "spring-rollist." When most people hear "spring roll," they tend to think of "gomoku harumaki." I've picked out shops that showcase the infinite possibilities of spring rolls as well as this variety, and show that no matter what you wrap in them, its flavor will explode as it gets steamed within. So, let's get started. "Spring roll wrappers harbor a microcosm?! Rare spring rolls you won't find in any Chinese restaurant."

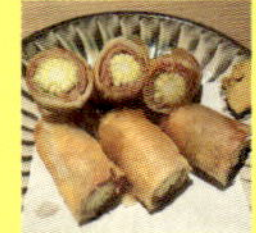

Shuko Aomon Creative izakaya-like places often serve spring rolls, too. This one has a "Prosciutto and Baby Corn Spring Roll." Great cross-section, and the salty prosciutto and sweet baby corn (corn silk and all) blend perfectly! The crispy-then-crunchy corn makes the texture fun, too! And don't miss the famous fried horse mackerel, either! ●2-31-4 Nishi-Gotanda, Shinagawa City, B1.

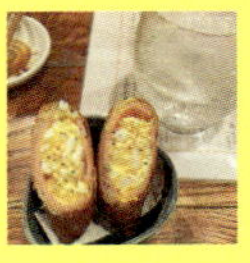

Kazamido This Japanese restaurant-style shop unexpectedly serves "Ham and Egg Spring Rolls." Despite the kid-friendly-sounding name, they're packed with black pepper and go great with beer. Owner Noriaki Yokota says the key is a perfect slatiness, achieved using just eggs and ham. ●3-1-14 Kami-Meguro, Meguro City.

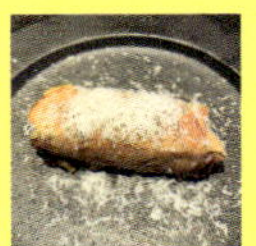

BRASSERIE by plein A casual French bistro inside TORANOMON HILLS. At first, you might be like, "Spring rolls? Here?" But then, you'll discover a really chic one: "Yezo Venison Ragout Spring Roll. The vibrant spinach and tender, slow-cooked venison are divine—but beware, it's hot. ● 2-6-2 Toranomon, Minato City, Toranomon Hills Station Tower 4F.

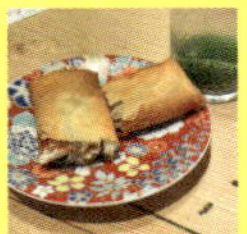

Sumibiyaki Lily A reward for making the steep climb up Shibuya's "Wave Street": "Spring Roll with Eel Cream Cheese." Tasty enough with eel alone, these have rich cream cheese in them to boot. Besides drinks, you'll be craving white rice, too—so much so that you'll want an "Eel & Cream Cheese Spring Roll Topped Rice Bowl." ●1-14-9 Dogenzaka, Shibuya City, Room 102.

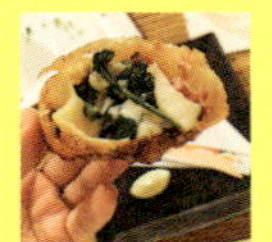

Ebisu Rakkyo A hidden gem and city staple, running between Ebisu and Shibuya for over 25 years. The must-have is the "Matsutake Mushroom & Wagyu Beef Spring Roll" (plus other fillings that vary by season). Aromatic matsutake and savory wagyu. Steaming the ingredients inside the wrapper brings out their full glory. Make that first bite condiment-free. ●2-8-9 Ebisu-Nishi, Shibuya City, 2F.

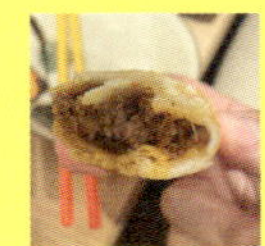

Aozora Spring rolls are also found at Okinawan restaurant. "Taco Cheese Spring Rolls." In a nutshell, fried tacos. The spring roll wrapper makes them really crispy, and the juicy meat and rich cheese inside fully satisfy palette and appetite alike. The happy surprise of finding spring rolls at an Okinawan place is also a big plus. Reservation/referral required. ●5-1-3 Akasaka, Minato City, 2F.

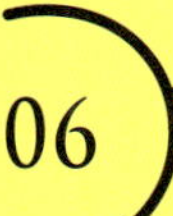

06 EXTREME RAMEN

Enter the World of Extreme Ramen!

Kiriwo Kei ●Ramen Instagrammer

Likes ramen with a "strong" look and large portions. Consciously limits his annual ramen intake to 300 bowls. Regularly holds ***Kirio Meshi***, a food event in the craft beer industry.

I'm a nerd who hangs out at casual bars that serve strong liquor, hookah lounges, and dusty record shops. Consequently, I did wonder if I'd be out of place as a selector for this project. However, when I was asked to write about "extremeness," I got straight into it, and now, the introduction alone looks set to blow the 600-character limit for the whole thing. Well, as I near 40, I think I'll lift the lid on my full-on extreme ramen lifestyle. Age has reduced my stamina and brought complaints like indigestion and shoulder pain that have forced me to eat less. On top of that, they've made me travel a lot less, too. The me of a few years ago would cry to see the me of now, ordering small servings even at ramen chains that do bumper ones. Even so, I can still tell you about plenty of shops that have an extreme presence, flavors, and character. If you can't eat big, just enjoy the uniqueness instead! So, what is "extreme ramen" anyway? Well, it's not just about quantity, and that's for sure. Actually, it's more about strong individuality, long lines, and above all, flavor. Here are some shops yours truly, Kiriwo, confidently recommends. What's that, you say? The distribution of areas seems a bit biased? Well, that's no big deal, though, is it? I mean, I did use to call myself "From Musashino," after all...

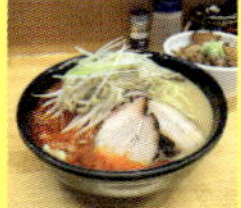

Misokko Fukku "One of Tokyo's most popular miso ramen shops," and that's no exaggeration. Strong yet mellow, mellow yet with a deep core. The flavor is enjoyed by all ages and genders, as is clear from the diverse crowds lining up for it. I particularly recommend the spicy miso ramen and tantammen. ●2-40-11 Kamiogi, Suginami City.

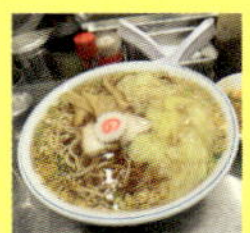

Chukasoba Mitaka A skilled shop said to "carry the genes of Tokyo's oldest ramen eatery." Its extremeness lies in the high rate of beer orders, the "white powder" that sharpens the flavor, and the way the owner's gentle outward manner hides an inner boldness. Roast pork, Red Star beer, and a large bowl of abura soba are what I want. ●3-27-9 Shimorenjaku, Mitaka City, B1.

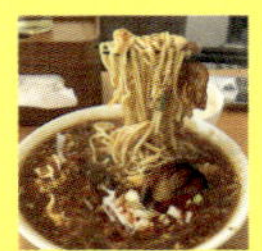

Yokohama Chukasoba Kamiyama The sudden move from Kyodo to Mitakada was the talk of Tokyo's ramen scene in summer 2024. Sanmamen noodles with real Chinese food sense, and powerful meat and garlic chive stamina noodles that grab Musashino ramen fans by the stomach and don't let go. The weekday-only offerings are also worth a look. ●2-7-6 Inokashira, Mitaka City, 1F.

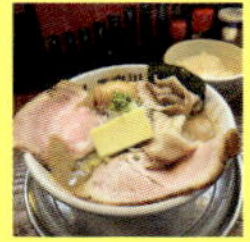

Ganso Ichijo-ryu Ganko Ramen, Tamayakata Store A family-oriented town with cinemas, malls, entertainment places, and even an IKEA, Tachikawa is also a hub for horse racing, bike racing, and subcultures. Try the rich, cloudy soup at this standout shop in Tamayakata, the food court north of WINS Tachikawa. ●1-2-16 Nishikicho, Tachikawa City.

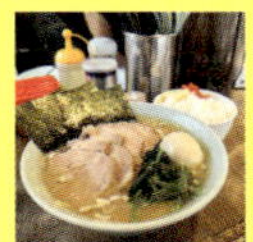

Ramen Chop Into its third year in 2025 and already looking set to be a leading ie-kei ramen shop in west Tokyo, this place has strong momentum. Powerful umami, generous rice portions, and thick, dark seaweed adds satisfying volume. The ¥300 kids ramen for preschoolers is a family-friendly touch, too. ●5-8-15 Hoyacho, Nishitokyo City.

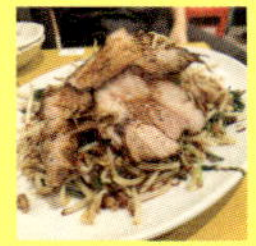

Tamagawaya Saketen Beer at a ramen or Chinese restaurant feels like a reward in a hard life. The popular fried rice is a must, but the dry Taiwanese noodles—a.k.a. "sara Taiwan"—are exceptional. Washing down sara Taiwan, fried rice, and char siu with gallons of beer qualifies as extreme, surely? ●7-34-1 Nishi-Kamata, Ota City.

07 PANCAKES

Pancake Boom Originals Where Long Lines Still Form Even Today.

Mr. Kuroneko ●Writer on sweets and gourmet food

Visits over 1,000 cafés and pancake and sweet shops every year. Hailed by magazines as "Japan's top pancake eater." Shares info with some 80,000 followers on social media.

A café-lover since my school days, I have a particular penchant for pancakes. Here are my pick of the "spots that sparked the pancake boom and still draw long lines today." Back when I first began café hopping, a few pancake places had already opened ahead of the boom—and if you ask me, they also paved the way for it. First, ***Coffee Tengoku*** opened in 2005 on Asakusa's Rokku-dori Avenue. Baking carefully on a copper griddle, it quickly became a popular spot with long lines outside. The next year saw ***Pancake MaMa Cafe VoiVoi*** open in Sangenjaya. This stylish pancake-only café—something that was a completely new concept at the time—appeared in many café guides, and attracted pancake fans from far and wide, too. Then, ***Eggs 'n Things*** (founded in Hawaii in 1974) and ***bills*** (founded in Sydney, Australia in 1993) hit Japan at long last. The start of the pancake boom more or less coincides with the opening of ***Eggs 'n Things, Harajuku Store*** in 2010 and ***bills Omotesando*** in 2012, these two neighboring areas even being described as a pancake mecca. There were lots of new pancake shops opening up around then, but ***Chaka*** in Kitasenju (2010) and ***Rainbow Pancake*** in Harajuku (2011) became especially popular for their unique batter.

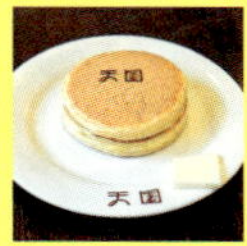

Coffee Tengoku A shop on Rokku-dori Avenue in Asakusa. The name means "heaven," a striking choice owner Rumi Ueno, being a fan of witty comedy like rakugo, hit upon thinking it'd been fun to hear lines like "I'll be waiting for you in Heaven." The hotcakes lovingly baked on a copper griddle are stamped with the "Tengoku" logo. ●1-41-9 Asakusa, Taito City.

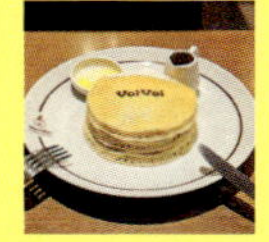

Pancake MaMa Cafe VoiVoi A pancake shop a two-minute walk from Sangen-jaya Station. It wins hordes of repeat fans with its buttermilk pancakes made from a unique blend of wheat and rice flour with added local Japanese buttermilk. Besides the simple plain ones, the seasonal varieties are also popular. ●1-35-15 Sangenjaya, Setagaya City.

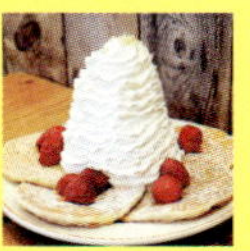

Eggs 'n Things, Harajuku Store The popular Hawaii-based shop's first overseas branch. Eye-catching pancakes topped with familiar whipped cream. The generous mound of whipped cream might look rather daunting, but its light sweetness and smooth texture make it a breeze. ●4-30-2 Jingumae, Shibuya City.

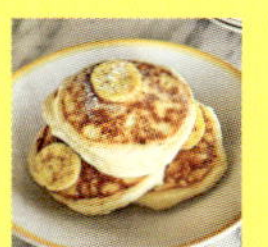

bills Omotesando An all-day-dining restaurant from Sydney, this is a popular spot that's lauded for serving "the world's best breakfast." The pancakes made with fresh ricotta and whipped egg white and topped with homemade honeycomb butter and maple syrup offer a perfect balance of sweet and salty. ●4-30-3 Jingumae Shibuya City, Tokyu Plaza Omotesando Harajuku 7F.

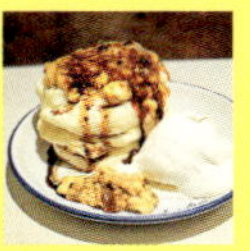

Chaka A pancake shop in a Kitasenju residential neighborhood. So popular it gets fully booked as soon as online reservations start. Refined to perfection, the pancakes with fluffy whipped egg whites have a unique melt-in-the-mouth texture. Focusing on seasonal fruits, the monthly limited-edition pancakes offer a new pleasure every time. ●31-7 Senju-Kotobukicho, Adachi City.

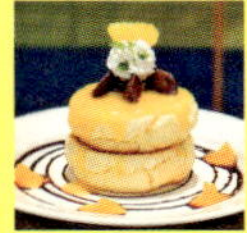

Rainbow Pancake A Hawaiian rainbow-inspired pancake shop in Ura-Harajuku. Owner Dai Iwaki apparently launched it to offer pancakes that would bring fun and happiness to everyone. The thick, fluffy pancakes were revolutionary when the shop first opened. So delicious you'll be beaming after just one bite. ●4-28-4 Jingumae, Shibuya City.

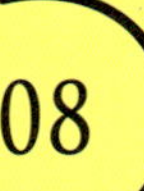

08 OHIYA

World-Class Hospitality! Glasses of Chilled Water Brimming with Kindness.

Chikako Tsuruta ●Ohiya researcher

A writer from Iwate who's currently residing in Chiba. In 2015, she started putting posts on Instagram with the hashtag "#お冷研究家(IceWaterResearcher)." An ohiya enthusiast who's collected over 1,000 photos.

It's so par for the course that it's usually overlooked, but take a closer look at the ohiya (chilled water) served in restaurants and cafés, and you see it's actually a concentrated dose of the "spirit of hospitality." Nice to meet you. I'm Chikako Tsuruta, an ohiya researcher who's been sharing photos and info on ohiya served in cafés and restaurants on Instagram for around 10 years. When I first started researching it, "Instagrammability" was all the rage, and no one spared ohiya so much as a glance. When I first started posting, even I jokingly called it "lousy Insta" myself. But then as I carried on, I realized how wonderful and charming ohiya really is—and before I knew it, 10 years had flown by. Underpinning this ohiya culture is Japan's safe tap water—but ironically, that's probably also why so many people leave without finishing it...! Such a pity. Despite it being a free service, so many shops go to the extra expense of special glasses, high-quality water, and so on. I really do appreciate all the effort they put into it. Many come up with creative ways to delight customers with ohiya. For example, ***Kazuma Coffee Ten*** serves it in original glasses crafted by a Japanese glass atelier, and ***Matryoshka*** in Ueno puts rosemary in it. It's just chilled water, but there's more to it than that. Stop just taking free ohiya for granted and start appreciating all the heart that goes into it as well, and I bet you'll find it hard to leave unfinished.

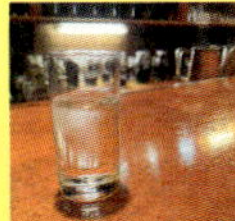

Juichibo Coffee Ten A café tucked away along Sotobori-dori Avenue, five minutes' walk from Yurakucho Station. As you stroll past the roaster, you'll be struck by the jazzy atmosphere. Sipping ohiya at the counter as you wait for a nel drip coffee, you'll forget all about the urban bustle and the stresses of daily life. ●2-2-19 Ginza, Chuo City.

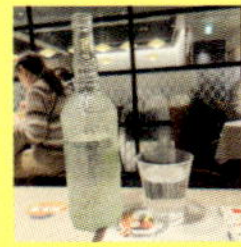

Matryoshka, Ueno Store A Russian restaurant on the ninth floor of Ueno Marui, two minutes' walk from Ueno Station. Adding a touch of elegance in the cozy interior, there's ohiya with rosemary served in a bottle. The sign at the entrance also advertises its love of ohiya. ●6-15-1 Ueno, Taito City, Ueno Marui 9F.

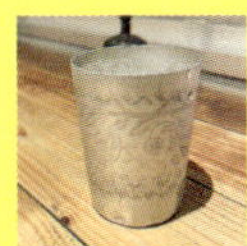

Soup Curry Ponipirika A Shimo-Kitazawa soup curry shop near the Honda Theater and The Suzunari. The steep stairs lead to a blissful space filled with a curry aroma. Sipping ice-cold ohiya from a delicately patterned aluminum cup as you choose your curry is pure bliss. ●2-8-8 Kitazawa, Setagaya City, 2F.

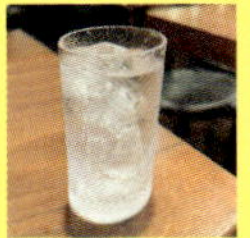

Kazuma Coffee Ten, Harumi-dori Store A café with locations in Jimbocho, Ginza Namiki-dori Avenue, and Harumi-dori Avenue. You can buy original ohiya glasses at the Harumi-dori Avenue one near the Ginza 4 intersection and at the two other stores as well. Perfect for entertaining guests at home, and as gifts for coffee-lovers. ●5-7-19 Ginza, Chuo City, Tokyo, 4F.

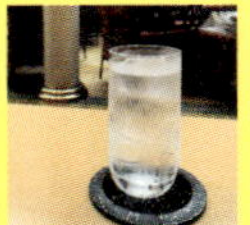

Café Lounge "Pandora" Three minutes down Gyoninzaka from Meguro Station. A lounge in Meguro GAJOEN, which will close temporarily starting in October 2025. The spacious area with a waterfall view makes you feel like you've climbed several steps toward adulthood. Enjoy an elegant pause with ohiya served on a beautiful coaster that's like a night sky. ●1-8-1 Shimo-Meguro, Meguro City.

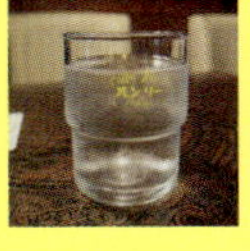

Oyasumidokoro Only A historic coffee shop in the thriving tool district of Kappabashi. Boasting over 70 years of history, ***Only*** is run as a multipurpose rest area. The ohiya has switched to self-service, but the irresistible coffee and the ohiya glasses are still just as loved as they've always been. ●2-22-8 Nishi-Asakusa, Taito City.

09 BUTCHER SHOP CROQUETTES

Strolling Around Downtown, Croquette in Hand.

Misako Kobayashi ●Croquette enthusiast

Born in Tokyo. Has lived in Kanda for 20 years. Into croquettes ever since she was walking along with one and someone informed her her birthday (May 6th) is "Croquette Day."

On my days off, I walk about 20,000 steps, and go in search of croquettes. I often visit east Tokyo—the so-called downtown area—and love how when I cross a bridge on the way, I get a different view every time. Famous tourist spots and entertainment districts thronging with visitors from all over. It could be a residential area or a temple district. Just as you're thinking there'll be lots of trendy restaurants there, you find bustling everyday eateries. In Tokyo, the city flows seamlessly, and I love that the scenery changes in just a short walk. While walking around these downtown areas, you'll notice that there are surprisingly few local butcher shops. Another sad discovery is that some have stopped offering fried foods and side dishes, or even closed down altogether. Here, I'll introduce croquettes that can be bought at downtown butcher shops that are still going strong. But what is it that makes fried foods from butcher shops so lovely? While on a walk, I stop by and browse the shop front showcases. The joy of biting into fried food right there on the spot! Now I'm a grown-up, it's a slightly guilty but irresistible pleasure. Perhaps this way of enjoying food has stayed the same since the Edo period, when people grabbed a bite of sushi or tempura at street stalls. Maybe it's exaggerating to call it a tradition from Edo, but I mean to go on and on enjoying freshly fried shop front croquettes.

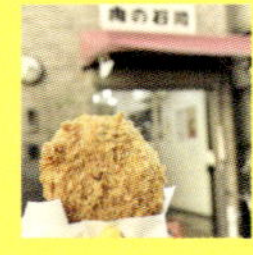

Niku no Ishikawa A butcher shop in the traditional-feeling Iriya area. The food made with homemade lard and a cherished infrared fryer doesn't absorb too much oil, so it stays crisp and light even after some time. The homemade croquettes with carefully debittered onions come in two types. And do try the popular fries, too. ●1-3-8 Iriya, Taito City.

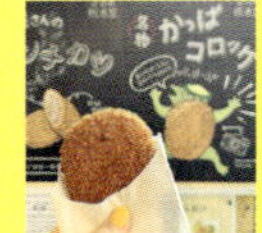

Tochigiya Kappabashi, Japan's top tool district, draws attention from foreign tourists, too. Leave the bustling main street, and a residential area unfolds. The scent of grilled yakitori led me to a butcher shop with a sign advertising the famous "kappa croquettes." As big as a ***kappa's*** shell, and incredibly satisfying. The perfect mid-walk snack. ●3-7-1 Nishi-Asakusa, Taito City.

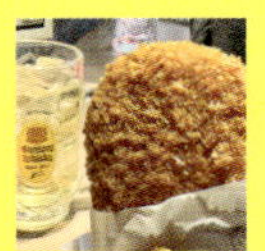

Niku no Oyama, Ueno Store In the lively Ueno Ameyoko area, there's a corner with bars that are busy from the afternoon onward. Inspired by the people enjoying fried food and yakitori, I had a drink at a shop front. The irresistible croquettes are a must with a mug of beer. Also great to stop by between museum visits or on a walk. ●6-13-2 Ueno, Taito City.

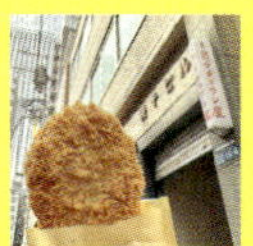

Choshiya A shop behind the Kabukiza that always has a long line. There are always freshly fried croquettes to be had. The sandwiches are excellent, too, and I also recommend buying extra to pop in the freezer. It's great to have a place to enjoy a croquette in the city center. ●3-11-6 Ginza, Chuo City.

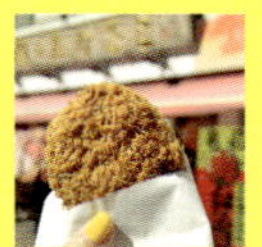

Niku no Takasago That familiar Oedo Line announcement as the train stops at Tsukishima Station! The shop front is lined with tempting meats and eats. Among these, the hearty roast pork croquette made with the famous Tokyo roast pork is a perfect souvenir or gift. A standout item is the luxurious curry croquette filled with rich Wagyu beef tendon curry. ●2-21-6 Tsukuda, Chuo City.

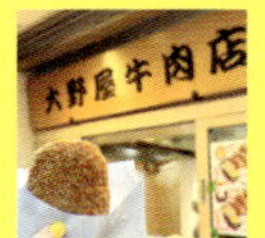

Onoya Gyunikuten Just outside downtown, but perfect for a stroll around old samurai homes, alleys, shrines, and an entertainment district. On a slope that's bustling day and night stands a butcher shop with an attractive fried food display. It offers four kinds of croquettes fried in homemade lard. My favorites are the mild-flavored corn and chicken cream ones. ●6-8-58 Kagurazaka, Shinjuku City.

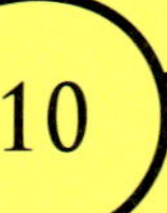

10 YAKIIMO

How About a New Wave Yakiimo?

Sota Amaya ●Writer

Eats yakiimo (roasted sweet potatoes) every day. Produces many urban yakiimo events, e.g., ***Shinagawa Yakiimo Terrace*** and ***Otemachi Tower Mori no Yakiimo***.

The days of "yakiimo...how nostalgic" are long gone. Here are six Tokyo shops offering some all-new, never-even-imagined-before ways to have them. Nerima's ***Hibi Yakiimo*** is a pioneer of the hearty "meal-style" ones. Its signature "Butter Yakiimo Curry" is an irresistible dish you'll want to pour over rice. ***Yanagiya*** is a mobile vendor around Ikebukuro that offers innovative "flavored yakiimo" made by aging "Tomitsu Kintoki" brand sweet potatoes from Awara City in Fukui Prefecture in liqueurs and syrups. The aroma and bliss the moment you crack it open and take a bite will change your view of yakiimo dramatically. ***Chomitsu® Yakiimo pukupuku*** near Chikatetsu-akatsuka Station offers the best "honey-drenched yakiimo" in Japan. The glittering, juice-like honey spills from the sweet potato, making it nothing short of fruity. ***OIMO cafe*** in Zempukuji serves "steak-style" yakiimo with a knife and fork in a house that's like a French restaurant. Moist yakiimo served with French rock salt, the "salted yakiimo" at ***Oimoya Noka no Daidokoro*** in Hamura City are tasty down to the skin. ***Imoyasu, Asakusa Store*** across from ASAKUSA HANAYASHIKI has created a hit with its "Sweet Potato Juice Fresh Caramel." Rare yakiimo varieties make surprise appearances, too, so keep an eye out for lucky finds!

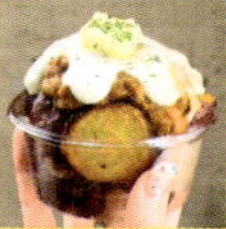

HIBIYAKIIMOTokyo The 2025 ***National Yakiimo Grand Prix*** champion. With its signature "Butter Yakiimo Curry," curry sauce and butter accentuate the aged yakiimo, creating a rich flavor that begs to be poured over rice. It's pioneering the world of gourmet-level "meal-style yakiimo". ●3-17 Nerima, Nerima City.

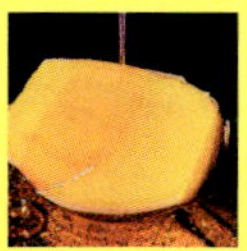

Yanagiya A mobile yakiimo vendor that sets up at events across Ikebukuro and Okachimachi. The owner used his bartender experience to evolve a version soaked in liqueurs and syrups: "flavored yakiimo." These preserve the sweet potato flavor while offering a vibrant, aromatic yakiimo experience. ●Ikebukuro and elsewhere in Toshima City.

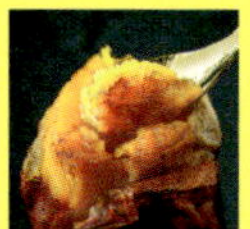

Chomitsu® Yakiimo pukupuku, Shimoakatsuka Store Developed over 15 years by the president using his own unique techniques, the "Chomitsu Yakiimo" is so moist that honey floods out of it like fruit juice. Other unique delights include a potage made with Chomitsu Yakiimo and "Imokawayaki," a dish made with a paste of silk sweet potatoes. ●8-27-7 Kitamachi, Nerima City, 1F.

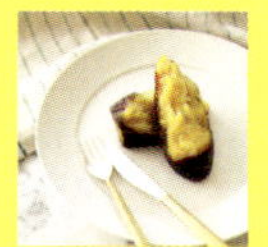

OIMO cafe ZENPUKUJI A sweet potato café directly run by a farm with 300 years of history stretching back to the Edo period. In the French restaurant-style shop, you can enjoy clay pot-roasted yakiimo with a knife and fork. Also serves stylish dishes like "Yakiimo Brûlée"—caramelized sweet potatoes with sun-dried salt. ●2-24-8 Zempukuji, Suginami City.

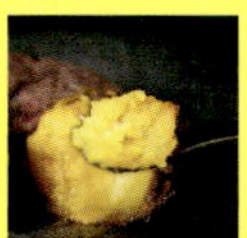

Oimoya Noka no Daidokoro A yakiimo specialty shop run by Kunitachi Farm. It's popular for its "salted yakiimo" made with a blend of French Lorraine rock salt, and Beni Haruka sweet potatoes from Ibaraki, the latter selected for its superior flavor. A key feature is that as well as the inside, the oft-overlooked skin is roasted to perfection, too. ●1-11-7 Gonokami, Hamura City, 1F.

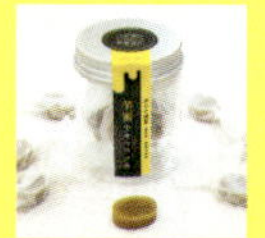

Yakiimo Semmonten Imoyasu, Asakusa Store Yakiimo shop near the retro amusement park ***Hanayashiki***. Spreading new sweet potato ideas like "Imo Mitsu Nama Caramel," which is made by simmering "syrup" extracted from sweet potatoes over three days. Sometimes has yakiimo with rare sweet potatoes that aren't on the market yet. ●2-7-24 Asakusa, Taito City.

11 "NOKKE" BEN

Unique Stores, Ultimate "Nokke Ben"!!

So Ishikawa ●Founder of ***Kurumeshi Bento***

So Ishikawa is a bento fanatic who sometimes eats bento from over 300 stores a year. In 2008, he founded Japan's first-ever bento delivery site: ***Kurumeshi Bento***.

We call bento whose side dishes are on the rice "nokke ben." Their main appeal is their packed look and flavor gradations. As you savor every last grain, you get to enjoy overlapping flavors of the rice and sides. The no-dividers high plating freedom also makes stores' individuality easy to showcase. The heart of global bento culture, Tokyo is home to "nokke ben" from astonishing places ranging from renowned and impossible-to-book spots like ***Torishiki*** and ***Sanomatsu*** to Michelin-starred restaurants.

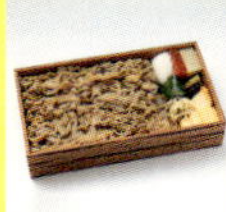

Sanomatsu Owner Yukinori Kikuchi's ultimate beef nokke ben is made using Japanese techniques and ingredients from his native Iwate. Its sukiyaki-style beef is tender even when cold, and seasonal ingredients like burdock and konjac hidden beneath add fun textures. The decorative knife cuts and grill marks on the side dishes are a delight to bento-lovers. ●2-21-4 Takaban, Meguro City, Room 102.

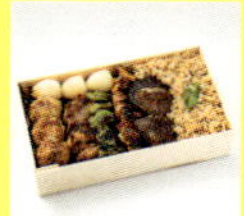

Torishiki Exquisitely grilled, jaw-droppingly fragrant skewers, and a perfect balance of chicken soboro, moist seaweed, and sauce-soaked rice. A secret joy is the aroma of the grill when I go in to get my order. The "yakitori bento" is also available at the ***Torishiki ICHIMON*** branches ***TORIOKA*** and ***TORIKAZE*** (order in advance required). ●2-14-12 Kami-Osaki, Shinagawa City.

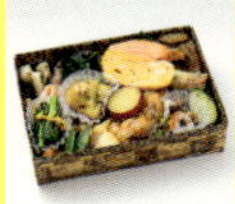

Sotomeguro Only open on Friday and Saturday. "Sotomeguro Wabento PRO" is a bento of the week that's only sold for one hour starting on 5 p.m. on Saturdays. The "Okazu-Zukushi" line features all your bento sides piled on rice—over 20 in all, ranging from standard ones like salt grilled salmon and karaage to unusual ones like smoked potato salad. ●4-14-5 Meguro, Meguro City.

12 PARFAITS

Places to Enjoy the Latest Parfaits.

Onoya ●Parfait critic

Actively shares the charm of parfaits through magazines, radio, and talk events. Authored works include ***Parfaits Are the Greatest*** and ***A Date with Parfait***.

Parfait culture is spreading nationwide, but Tokyo has the widest variety. Parfait-serving shops are rapidly increasing, many offering truly astonishing examples. They create visual impact with innovative 3-D forms, complex aromas using tea, alcohol, herbs, and spices, and wide-ranging flavors that even include vegetables, meat, and fish. I contend that more than just a food experience, parfaits are also a stimulating form of entertainment to be enjoyed with all five senses.

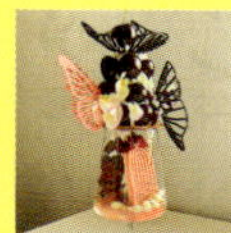

Ameniji With the "Dark Cherry Parfait" (mid-April 2025 onward), the langues de chat atop the glass dish and butter sandwiches inside it form a fascinating geometric pattern. This shop always serves parfaits that look like surreal museum objects, and this one is a stunning example that combines potatoes, black sesame, and dark cherries. ●2-12-6 Imado, Taito City, 2F.

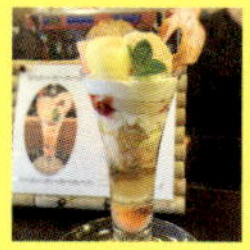

CAFE CUPOLA mejiro Serves parfaits with layers of aromas that form a "concert of scents." The "Flower Moon-Ripened Apple Parfait" (ends in March 2025) is a masterpiece of unfolding fragrances including bourbon raisin Assam tea, white balsamic vinegar, Earl Grey, chinoiserie spice, and dill. ●3-21-7 Shimo-Ochiai, Shinjuku City, 1F.

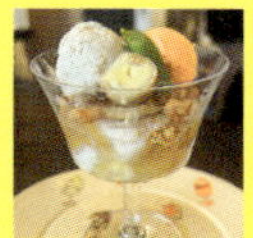

Typica A shop that proves there's no ingredient you can't put in a parfait. The "Waiting-for-Spring Parfait" (until early April 2025) features shiitake mushroom ice cream, carrot cumin ice cream, seasoned quail eggs, hot pepper crumble, boiled chicken, lotus root butter, and flying-fish-stock jelly. As you savor the spiciness and umami, muse on what a parfait is. ●3-18-10 Nishi-Ogi-Minami, Suginami City.

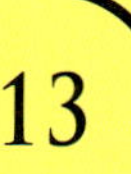

13 CLEAR BROTH RAMEN

Thin Noodles in Clear Broth.

P ●Food writer

A true gourmand who delights in both delicious and not-so-delicious foods. Traveled the world in search of good eating, only to end up in Japan. Currently writes food columns for various magazines.

"Ms. Koizumi Loves Ramen Noodles" is great, but "P Loves Ramen Noodles" works, too (self-praise). But I'm not an otaku, just a hedonist. Oh, maybe not. I've loved ramen since I was a kid. Instant or premium, cheap or pricy, it's all good as long as it's ramen. My current fave is no-additive light broth. The combo of clear broth and thin noodles. Saltier the better. So smooth that on a good day, I can easily go two bowls in a row. Feels like eating it cleans my stomach. Hope you find beautiful ramen like that, too.

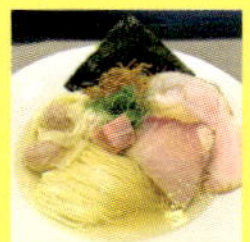

Ramen Break Beats A quiet residential area about 10 minutes' walk from Yutenji Station. Switching from a waiting list to reservations was widely met with cheers. The ramen is like a work of art—clear broth, beautifully arranged noodles, and pale pink char siu. The chef's aesthetic sense makes you sit up straight. Listed in the 2024 Bib Gourmand. ●4-21-19 Meguro, Meguro City, 1F.

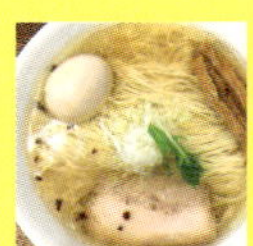

Tombo A 13-minute walk from Kichijoji Station. Long lines at lunchtime, and a broad customer base. From the counter, the chef is a picture of concentration and dedication to the noodles. Simple yet powerful bowls. Flecks of fried green onion on the surface boost the broth's savoriness. Noodles that give the perfect slurp length. ●4-16-12 Kichijoji-Minamicho, Musashino City.

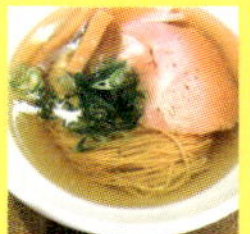

Shibasakitei Main Store The roots of light-flavored ramen. A popular spot with long lines. Many customers come for the weekend specials. The basic noodles look beautiful and clear. A few people find it daunting at first, but once they start, they often finish in no time. Tranquil ramen a minute's walk from Tsutsujigaoka Station. ●3-25-52 Nishi-Tsutsujigaoka, Chofu City.

14 "NOKKE" PUDDING

The New Idol: "Nokke Pudding."

Kosuke Ikehata ●Pudding prince

Office worker and pudding researcher. Has over 800 puddings a year. Pudding journalist whose activities include magazines, TV, events, and more.

Do you know what a "nokke pudding" is? When a dessert consisting of a pudding put on a Danish went viral in Taiwan in 2024, it sparked a boom in Japan of tall "nokke puddings"—puddings placed atop fruit and sweets. Besides their look being so cutely innovative, the very idea of them is so infectiously mold-breaking and free-spirited... A pudding on top of something is simply adorable (sigh). "Nokke puddings" have brought yet more fun and flavor to the pudding world, and I still can't take my eyes off them.

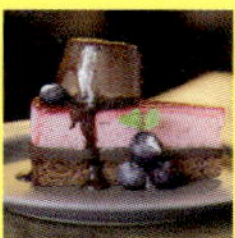

cafe omotenashamoji This shop in Takadanobaba serves delicious nokke puddings that change every month. Their dark look is unbearably cute. The bouncy chocolate pudding and rich chocolate cake are incredibly intense. An exquisite balance created through the sweet tang of cassis. Simply divine. ●3-28-1 Nishi-Waseda, Shinjuku City, 1F.

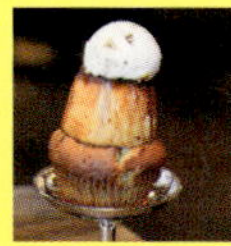

beans farm Available only when the owner whimsically decides to bake muffins, the tall "Whimsical Muffin Nokke Pudding" is a cream cheese pudding and ice cream atop a hot muffin. Rich, chewy pudding, buttery muffins, and ice cream. This is a truly sinful delicacy. ●468-6 Okuramachi, Machida City.

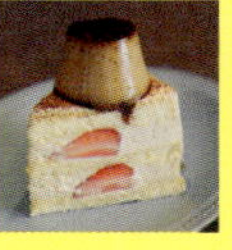

TSUBASA COFFEE "Pudding Pudding Short" is a shortcake with seasonal fruits and a small pudding on top. The cream made by mixing pudding into the shortcake cream creates a perfect unity. A truly blissful way to sate your pudding craving! ●1-15-12 Shinjuku, Shinjuku City, 1F.

15 EGG SALAD SANDWICHES

Masterful Sandwich Shops in Downtown Alleys.

Qoo Murasaki ●Illustrator

An illustrator who eats egg salad sandwiches on strolls. Regularly issues self-published magazine ***A Sandwich for Every Meal***. Hosts food channel ***Qoo Murasaki & Carbohydrates***.

I moved to the downtown area 12 years ago. I'd long loved reading historical markers on strolls, and was now living somewhere brimming with historical trivia. My strolls still yield fresh finds even after 12 years, like famous graves in small temple cemeteries or hidden shops in narrow alleys that make me wonder, "Is this really a street?" These "discoveries" are a charm unique to a built-up downtown. And there's nothing quite like finding a shop that's a perfect match. Let me share some great sandwich shops I've found on my strolls.

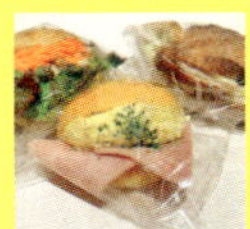

TEA wiz Sandwich A tea, scone, and sandwich shop in a residential area near Yanaka Cemetery whose streets are lined with old houses. With a wide variety of fillings and bread options that include croissants and baguettes, you're sure to find a unique sandwich. Also has a vending machine out front that sells sandwiches when it's closed. ●2-1-14 Yanaka, Taito City, 1F.

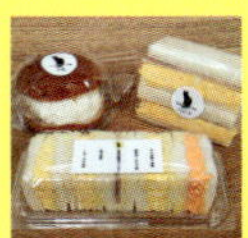

tamagetta A brand-name egg salad sandwich shop on Yokozuna Yokocho-dori Avenue. All the egg salad sandwiches are packed with egg salad and very filling. They also sell brand-name eggs, which you can even buy just one of. I recommend walking the short distance to the terrace by the Sumida River to eat your purchases in open surroundings. ●3-23-8 Ryogoku, Sumida City, 1F.

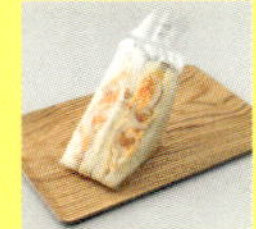

Canaria Sandwich, Hikifune Store Hikifune flagship store, plus branches in Kameido and in Kinshicho Station's building (TERMINA). Traditionally triangular shape, but the display case presents an impressive variety of fillings, from deep-fried cutlets to fresh fruit. Recommendation: seasoned boiled egg salad sandwich. ●1-43-4 Kyojima, Sumida City, 1F.

16 KARAAGE—FRIED CHICKEN, JAPAN STYLE

A Karaage Maniac's Top Picks!

Iku Arino ●Best-karaagenist

MC and radio personality Iku Arino has sampled over 3,500 karaage shops' wares and eats karaage every day (as part of a balanced diet, mind you).

Karaage is a universe unto itself. The crispy coating, the juicy meat, and the aroma of the garlic and soy sauce are sheer bliss. A miraculous mouthful where everything has been calculated. The maker's passion takes form as flavor, stirring the eater's emotions. Besides everyday karaage, there's high-end karaage as well. Experience a supreme one, and there's no turning back. Karaage is a priceless treasure given birth to by Japan. I've chosen my favorite spots based on the theme of "hospitality." Welcome to a karaage abyss.

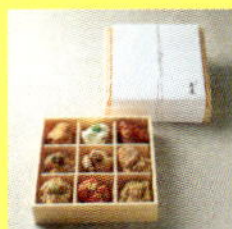

Kagurazaka Karaage Saitou, Kagurazaka Main Store The specialty is the "Karaage Gift" with nine kinds of karaage. Delicious even when cold and made so as to excite the eater, the colorful karaage are like a "jewel box." Based on the flavors of the owner's native Kyushu, the shop uses young chickens from Miyazaki. ●2-12-1 Kagurazaka, Shinjuku City, Line Build Kagurazaka 1F.

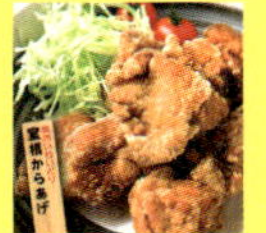

Karaage-ya Oshu Iwai, Akihabara Main Store Uses the Iwate brand chickens "Oshu Iwaidori." The secret soy marinade is garlic-free and uses ginger and onion, producing a fragrant, refined flavor. The irresistible juiciness is the appeal here. The carefully crafted flavor is a culinary masterpiece. I recommend the "Iwai Bento" with three pieces each of thigh and breast. ●4-16-5 Asakusabashi, Taito City.

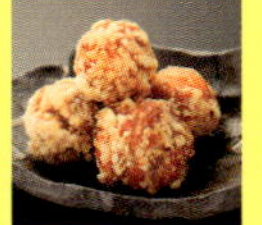

Kichigo, Sugamo Store Takeout shop with a range of alluring karaage flavors. Key feature is tailoring the cooking and seasoning to the cut of meat used in each karaage. E.g., "Soy Sauce Karaage [Thigh]" is rounded to seal in the juice. Karaage that convey an oil-hot passion to fully bring out the ingredients' flavor. ●1-2-1 Sugamo, Toshima City, 1F.

17 DRAFT BEER

Angel Rings Atop Superb Beers.

paricco ●Bar writer

Avid drinker paricco began writing articles about booze and bars in the 2000s. His books include ***Barfly Kid***, ***Drinking in Moderation***, and ***Heavenly Bars***.

When it comes to how draft beer tastes, an extremely important part is played by factors like how clean the beer taps are, the temperature, the management of the glasses, and how it's poured. The joy of serendipitously finding a perfect beer in a place you just happened to drop into at random is simply unmatchable. One sign of a good beer is that with each sip, you get an "angel ring" of foam inside the glass. Beer like that is hard to find, so you'll definitely want to remember its blissful taste.

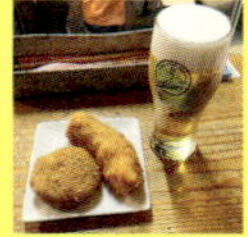

ebian The story goes that this shop was born when a long-running fried food shop closed down and the current owner inherited its recipes and location, then added a standing counter as well. Snack on crispy minced meat cutlets and croquettes as you savor ice-cold, angel-ring-forming beer. ●2-29-5 Taishido, Setagaya City.

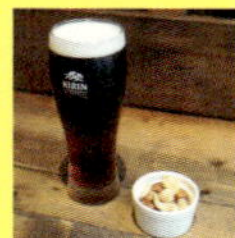

BOQUERIA Bar on the street called ***Nakano Renga Zaka*** near Nakano Station South Exit. Drinks and an international range of snacks. Creative ideas like the "Urchin Pudding" with fresh sea urchin are also fun. Has top-quality beers "Ichiban Shibori," "Ichiban Shibori Black Draft," and "Half & Half," and a spacious interior to sup them in. ●3-35-6 Nakano, Nakano City.

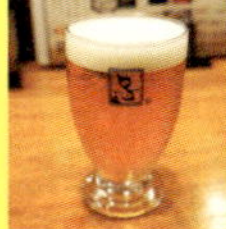

Yakitori Daikichi, Shakujiidai Store A yakitori chain that nevertheless serves draft beer so delicious you'll find yourself sitting up straight for it. The homey service is also unique. Even though it's a chain, each store sources its meat differently, so there's fun to be had seeking out your favorite ***Daikichi***, too. ●6-19-3 Shakujiidai, Nerima City.

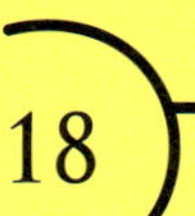

18 TOFU

Tofu Crafted from Artisans' Top Soybeans.

Shiori Kudo ●Tofu meister

A picky eater and tofu-lover since childhood, Shiori Kudo is the author of ***A Tofu Recipe for Every Day*** and director of ***Tofu Restaurant Yomoyamo*** in Ningyocho.

We tend to think "tasty tofu" is all about smoothness and richness, but listen to artisans talk about their "favorite soybeans," and it'll be like you had your blinkers on the whole time and they just got ripped off. Japan has over 300 varieties of soybeans, and a different kind of tofu for each technique of the artisans who handle them. "Single-origin" tofu highlights one soybean variety, while "blended" tofu combines several for flavor and ease of preparation. When we tour around a town's tofu shops, maybe we're on a quest to find our own "favorite soybeans"...!

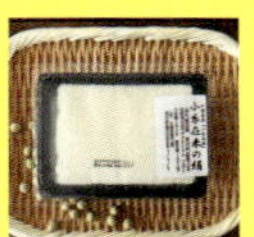

Miyoshi Tofu Workshop Since 1967. 2nd-gen. owner Shingo Hirata's silky tofu of "Koito Zairai" beans has such a refined sweetness and smoothness that people call it a "fine lady." Tofu born from love of soybeans, deepened by visits to the farmers. Mobile sales van on weekdays. ●3-22-11 Kyojima, Sumida City, Shitamachi Ninjo Kirakira Tachibana Shopping Street.

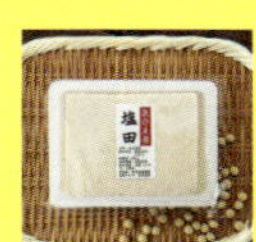

Kiai Tofu Saitamaya Since 1952. "Tamahomare" soybeans were once deemed unsuitable for making tofu, until 3rd-gen. owner Hiroyuki Arai fell in love with them and opened everyone's eyes. Using thick soy milk and a minimum of water, silken tofu "Enden" has a rich flavor that shows artisanal dedication. Tofu from different soybeans as well. ●2-9-14 Takaramachi, Katsushika City.

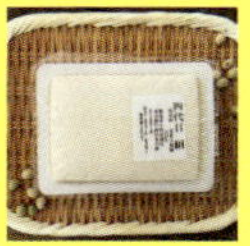

Onoda Tofu Store Est. 1905. 4th-gen. owner Shigeru Onoda is a former chef. "Yondaime Kinu" uses sweet, isoflavone-rich Hokkaido "Otofuke Osodefuri" soybeans. Melt-in-the-mouth with a rich soybean aftertaste. Limited batches of sesame-scented "Rikyu Tofu" on Fri., and unpressed tofu with blue soybeans and rare varieties on Sat. ●5-25-6 Higashi-Nakano, Nakano City.

19 SNACK BARS

Deep Nightlife with Snack Bars Old & New.

Koichi Taniguchi ●Professor at Tokyo Metropolitan University

Koichi Taniguchi was born in Oita. The representative of the Snack Bar Studies Group, his books include ***The Public Sphere in Japan's Nightlife*** and ***Night Entertainment in Japan***.

This year marks the 100th anniversary of the Showa-era. Snack bars are a symbol of that period. Recent years have seen growing isolation and avoidance of dining out with others become concerns in the US, but in contrast, Japan's communication-oriented snack bars seem to be thriving. Snack bars, where opening the door will lead to a comforting conversation with someone. A new trend of "community building" has also emerged. It might seem like a curveball, but I'll introduce some snack bars, including some authentic and famous ones.

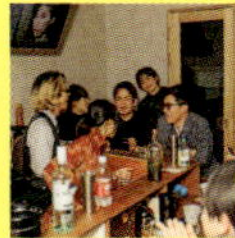

Snack Suichu Look for the glowing blue sign at the end of an alley a short walk from Yaho Station. Light spills out from the semi-basement interior. The friendly atmosphere welcomes is neighborhood regulars and newcomers from afar alike. Enjoy conversation and karaoke with strangers. No smoking. ●1-17-12 Fujimidai, Kunitachi City, 1F.

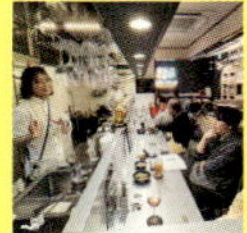

Machinaka Snack, ARAKAWA LABO Main Store Bus from Tabata Station, or a short walk from Odai Station on the Toden Arakawa Line. Lively interior. Customers of all genders and ages. Space designed to spark conversation even with strangers, with toast glasses and shared bottles. No karaoke—perfect for chatting. No smoking. ●2-37-6 Nishi-Ogu, Arakawa City.

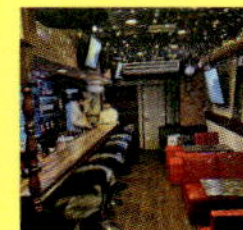

Caseiro Bar A classic snack bar in Shinjuku 2. A mixed clientele, so everyone is welcome. A stylish, calm interior, with witty talk from handsome manager Nobu. The diverse customer base makes for multicultural and multidisciplinary chats. Has karaoke. Non-smoking except for e-cigarettes. ●2-7-3 Shinjuku, Shinjuku City, Room 305.

20 HAMBURG STEAK

Top Hamburgs Made by Total Pros.

Teppei Goto ●Hamburgs fanatic and surveyor

Teppei Goto has being sampling hamburgs while working as a surveyor in Tokyo for 17 years now. He spreads the appeal of unique ones on social media.

Hamburgs are a beloved national dish and home staple. Crafted with professional skill and through trial and error, restaurant hamburgs offer deeper flavors than homemade ones. Highly particular about ingredient selection and cooking methods, these restaurants offer blissful dishes that bring out the meat's umami and care deeply about texture and aroma—and you can tell with just one bite. The more effort is put into them, the tastier hamburgs get! Experience their infinite possibilities.

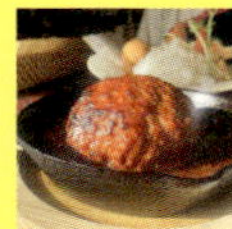

Cool Cafe The signature "Ultimate Salted Rice Malt Fluffy Hamburgs" has an incredibly soft patty. Blended with 60% A5 Wagyu beef and 40% Japanese pork, it's a concentrated dose of umami. The demi-glace is simmered with beef tendons and vegetables, with ripe tomatoes and red wine added for richness. ●8-38-1 Nishi-Ogu Arakawa City.

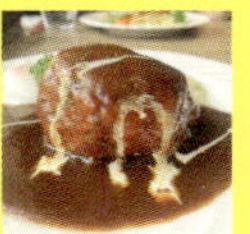

Hashiguchitei The signature hamburgs features a fluffy, tender texture. After searing the surface for aroma, they place it in a fond (broth) and slow-cook it in a pizza oven to finish. The marriage with the rich, exquisitely flavorful demi-glace sauce is simply irresistible. ●1-11-13 Kyodo, Setagaya City, 1F.

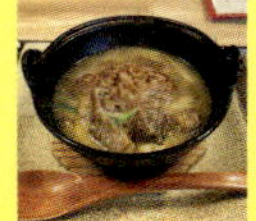

Syu Don't miss the "Wagyu Soup Hamburgs" served in a cast-iron pan. The umami-packed patty is topped with rich Kuroge Wagyu beef soup. Savor every last drop. Finish with a light ochazuke-style dish of shredded hamburgs and soup. Sprinkle on red pepper at the end for a flavor twist. ●4-[illegible]-24 Ichinoe, Edogawa City.

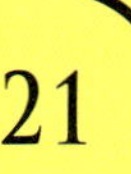

21 YOGURT

In Search of Yogurt Craftsmanship.

Chika Mukai ●Yogurt fanatic and representative of Yognet

Chika Mukai researches yogurt production and food culture at farms and factories nationwide, and penned ***The Book of Yogurt***. She posts detailed product reviews daily on social media.

Yogurt is often only talked about for its lactobacilli these days, but its true essence is more multifaceted. The cows' breed, feed, and environment, the raw milk's sterilization method, the lactobacillus strains, the fermentation, the post-processing, the serving container, and the toppings. Each yogurt reflects countless choices and tremendous craftsmanship on the part of the farmers and producers. Even in Tokyo—far removed from its primary sector—there are still a few farms and specialty shops that respect tradition, offering deeply refined yogurt.

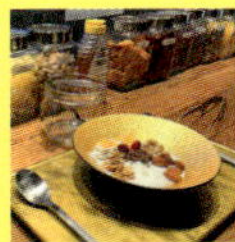

BioGaia daigo A shop specializing in BioGaia's ***L. reuteri***. A shop that has the founder of Japan's first-ever yogurt maker as its representative and offers raw milk-based yogurt from its own farm in Hiroshima, based on the philosophy that a healthy diet leads to a healthy you. I recommend the plain yogurt sold by weight with all-you-can-eat toppings. ●5-15-1 Hiro-o, Shibuya City, 1F.

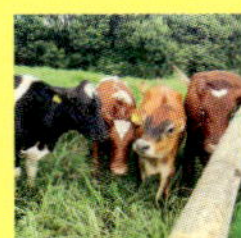

Isonuma Milk Farm Ranch raising seven breeds of dairy cow. Committed to animal welfare and using eco-feed. Contributes to the community through hands-on experiences. Jersey cow milk yogurt, with 200 times more lactobacilli than usual. At ***TOKYO FARM VILLAGE***, enjoy dairy products while admiring the pasture. ●1625 Kobikimachi, Hachioji City.

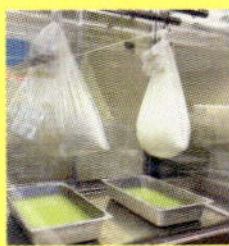

Greek day Omotesando The top brand that created a Greek yogurt boom in Korea landed in Japan in September 2024. The traditional Greek method of straining yogurt in cloth is a must-see. The "Combination Yogurt" topped with fruits and granola is wonderful. ●6-7-15 Jingumae, Shibuya City.

22 SAKE

Sake Bars with Simple Edo-Style Snacks.

Kiyoko Yamauchi ●Drinker, writer, and sake sommelier

Interviews and writes about breweries and sake bars nationwide. Books include ***Taking over a Storehouse, All About Sake All the Time, Late Night Sake Reviews***, and ***Have Sake, Will Travel***.

When I drink sake, I prefer "low-key" snacks. Ones with simple, understated tones like brown and gray are the best. Stylish, eye-catching dishes are nice sometimes, but their focus on appearance cramps their sake pairing potential. Kind of like how humble people who can get along with anyone, modest snacks can go with any kind of sake. So, with simple snacks, I can freely enjoy my sake without worrying about what it'll go with. Humble snacks tend to be found more in sake bars in Edo-Tokyo than in the provinces. Experience the pleasure of having your sake go down easy.

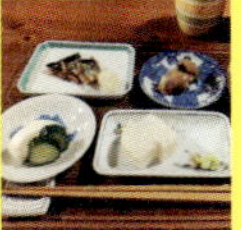

Teppa Bankara Treasure trove of humble snacks that make sake flow. Owner: "They're nothing to look at." Simple yet quality snacks like homemade pickles, kamaboko fish sausage with wasabi, simmered clams, and minced sardine balls. Sake is mostly mellow and food-friendly. Great to relax and enjoy all kinds, from chilled to warmed. ●1-25-7 Tsukishima, Chuo City, 2F.

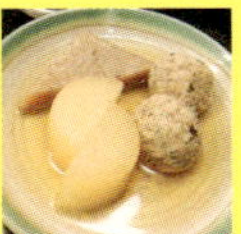

Jokanya Tomikyu Est. 1972. Oden soup and warmed sake. Inheriting the oden recipe from the previous gen., the ladies make a subtle broth using kelp, bonito flakes, and chicken wings. Perfect with warmed sake. Unique large, aged sake-warming jug keeps the sake flowing. I also recommend the proprietress's simple side dishes. ●3-12-4 Shinjuku, Shinjuku City, Room 107.

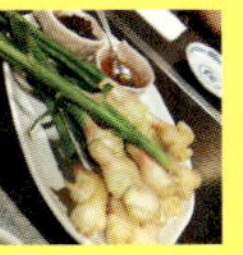

Oshiage Yoshikatsu Don't underestimate Tokyo's food-producing prowess. Enjoy simple snacks made with Tokyo ingredients like fresh fish from the Izu Islands and Ogasawara, Tokyo Shamo, Edo vegetables, and Edo miso. Also appealing is the vast array of little-known Tokyo sake. You're sure to get a true sense of what a fertile land Tokyo really is. ●5-10-2 Narihira, Sumida City.

23 FRIED RICE

Fried Rice Fanatics Drool Over.

Juri Sato ●Fried rice nutritionist

Juri Sato is the most fried rice-loving nutritionist in all of Japan. She's currently working out so she can have it even more. Her mission is to promote health through entertainment.

I'm Juri Sato, Japan's biggest fried rice fan nutritionist. Fried rice is a simple dish, yet has so much depth. Adjusting things like the rice's fluffiness, the amount of stir-frying, the ingredients' chunkiness and the sauce's thickness makes for endless variations. Every bite brings a new fried rice discovery—that's part of the charm. Here are my top fried rice picks that made me think, "I'm definitely having that again!" All of them are guaranteed to draw you in with their deliciousness.

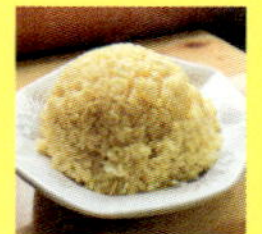

Choutoku Simple, salty egg fried rice that's just rice, egg, and green onion. This is the ultimate fried rice. Just perfect. The simple yet rich flavor fills your mouth, and the rice's lightly crumbly texture sets it apart from other restaurants. Best eaten with the popular fried gyoza. ●1-10-5 Mukogaoka, Bunkyo City.

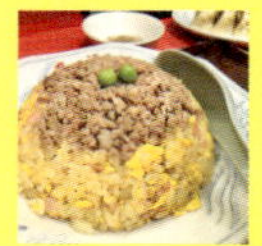

Chinese Cuisine Marufuku The chopped char siu and green peas add vibrant color. The base fried rice uses ham, onions, and eggs. The onions' crispness adds an accent that goes great with the savory char siu. Also, the crisp bite from the pepper adds extra depth. Utterly addictive. ●4-17-2 Maenocho, Itabashi City.

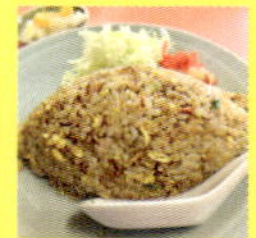

Shichimencho A long-running Chinese restaurant in Koenji. The fried rice has a striking omelette-like appearance. Take a bite, and a perfect savory soy sauce aroma fills your mouth, whetting your appetite for more. The cabbage, red ginger, and pickles make a perfect palate cleanser. The way those deep flavors unfold will make you crave it again and again. ●4-4-15 Koenji-Minami, Suginami City.

24 DEEP-FRIED NOODLES

The Chinese Food That Time Forgot.

MARUOSA ●Musician and deep-fried noodle researcher

MARUOSA is an extreme musician who studies deep-fried noodles' history and does field work on them every day, all while giving live concerts in 20+ countries.

Among neighborhood Chinese places, deep-fried noodles reign as a particularly mysterious dish. Said to have originated in America around 1900, it came to Japan as one of the so-called "American Chinese" dishes. This unassuming dish of fried noodles topped with mixed vegetable sauce has quietly survived on menus for over 100 years virtually unchanged. In an era where everyone is calling for food culture diversity, I really hope it gets reappraised now.

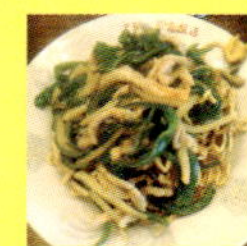

Shikin Hanten, Harajuku Main Store Flagship of new-wave neighborhood Chinese cuisine, collaborating across various genres like apparel and music. Long-runner full of uniquely playful variations on deep-fried noodles. Deep-fried noodles that preserve tradition while being new-era pioneers. Chinese pepper steak deep-fried noodles: ¥1,200. ●2-35-9 Jingumae, Shibuya City.

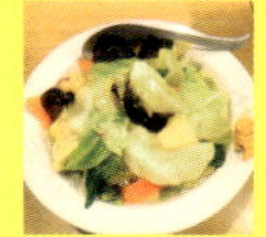

China Yatai Juhachiban, Shinkawa Store A name familiar to everyone: "Juhachiban." At the directly run store, the founder's sons serve light, salty deep-fried noodles. Their special noodles are fried in high-quality lard, and give a rich flavor with every bite. Deep-fried noodles: ¥1,020 (¥980 at lunchtime). ●2-7-7 Shinkawa, Chuo City.

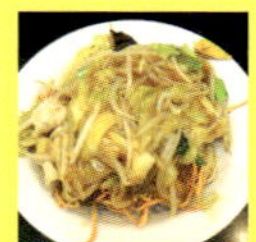

Manraku Hanten Long-running Chinese restaurant, serving Jimbocho (the world's largest used bookstore district) since 1912. A classic taste only orthodox deep-fried noodles can deliver. This "delicious in a normal way" flavor is rare now, making it all the more cherished. Deep-fried noodles: ¥900. ●3-5-1 Kanda-Ogawamachi, Chiyoda City.

25 GYOZA

Good People Vibes = Happy Gyoza.

Ai Yoshida ●Editor, and founder of the HAPPY GYOZA CLUB

Formerly a women's magazine editor, now an independent editor and writer. Since 2024, she's been spreading the joy of gyoza as the leader of the HAPPY GYOZA CLUB (***Raifuku Gyoza Club***).

Gyoza make people happy. And if their shop is filled with "good vibes," everything is perfect. For example, the boiled gyoza ***Yoshiharu***'s sibling owners serve bring people unmatched joy when they're served them, and unmatched bliss when they eat them. ***Gyozakan***'s gyoza shine with family teamwork and good vibes, and ***yum***'s are crafted by a dim sum master and bring an instant smile with the very first bite. No matter how down you're feeling, these gyoza will instantly lift your spirits.

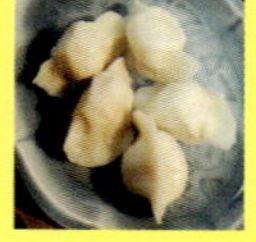

Yoshiharu Place an order, then watch them roll out the dough, wrap the filling, and carefully craft each gyoza. Shiny, delightful boiled gyoza so blissful that you'll want to share the joy with the people around you. Lots of seasonal gyoza as well, so visit throughout the year and enjoy the menu with all five senses. ●8-1-14 Kokuryocho, Chofu City.

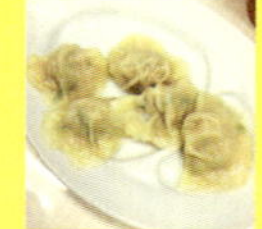

Gyozakan A gyoza specialty shop run by a husband and wife. After getting an order, the wife rolls out the dough, then the husband quickly serves the gyoza with great timing. It's also exciting to watch the family teamwork while you wait. Of their 10 simple gyoza varieties, the boiled ones with celery and bell peppers are the most popular. ●4-29-19 Kami-Kitazawa, Setagaya City.

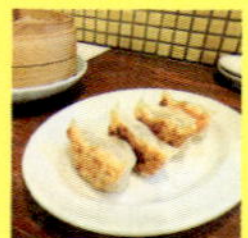

yum A spot for enjoying dim sum crafted by chef and dim sum master Minori Nishihara, paired with wines selected by sommelier Kumiyoshi Watanabe. The dim sum and Chinese dishes in this cozy space are sheer bliss—especially the spicy "Lamb Gyoza" made with dried tomato! ●1-6-5 Hatagaya, Shibuya City, 1F.

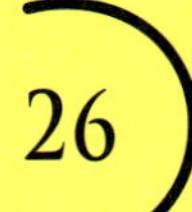

26 SHUMAI

Shumai Means It's a Top Shop.

Shumai Jun ●Representative director of the Japan Shumai Association

Shumai Jun is a shumai researcher who's eaten over 10,000 shumai of 2,000 different kinds. He's written ***The Shumai Book***, and has also supervised "Tokyo Shumai."

Alas, shumai are now a minor food. However, their rarity means that places that serve them are very likely to be great shops. Shumai are often either a hidden popular dish at great restaurants (and not just Chinese ones), or at shumai-focused shops that also serve other outstanding stuff. In short, "where there are shumai, there's a great shop." Tokyo is crammed with diverse stores, and searching for shumai here often leads to discovering great shops or dishes. That's why I never tire of going on shumai walks.

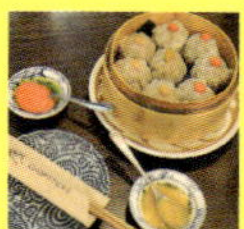

Shumai Bar Ogawa One of the pioneers of the "shumai izakaya" style, known for its signature shumai and tamagoyaki omelets. The signature "Iwachu Pork Special Shumai" are medium-sized and chunky, richly savory, and satisfyingly meaty. Also does lamb, chicken, duck, and fried shumai. ●3-1-10 Shibuya, Shibuya City, 1F.

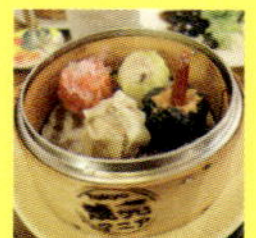

Tokyo Shumai Mania Always offers more than 10 kinds of shumai, plus other Asian Chinese dishes. The basic "Mania Shumai" convinces with its juicy pork flavor and firm texture, while the "Grilled Shumai" and "Fried Shumai" have different tastes and textures to enjoy. They also develop new shumai every month. ●4-21-7 Shimbashi, Minato City, 1F.

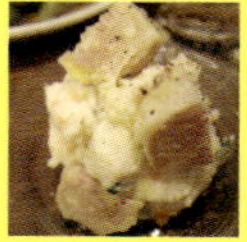

Orenchi Here, they liken shumai to a French-style pâté, creating meat dishes that are distinct from Chinese cuisine. "Chilled Shumai" and "Smoked Shumai" are exactly the kinds of dishes you'd find at a French bistro. The "Shumai Potato Salad" with chopped shumai mixed in is both innovative and delicious. The pairing with the premium tequila highball is perfect. ●6-16-3 Soto-Kanda, Chiyoda City, 1F.

27 LEMON SOURS

No. 1 for Lemon Sours: Setoda Lemons.

Lemon Zamurai Yoshihiro Suzuki ●Lemon sour maniac

Lemon Zamurai Yoshihiro Suzuki runs lemon sour focused social media and a specialty shop, and wholesales and develops lemons. He's also appeared on ***Matsuko no Shiranai Sekai***.

Over 90% of people have never had a "truly tasty lemon sour." When I asked myself, "What makes a truly great lemon sour?", I realized that it's the maker's passion—their commitment to quality ingredients and that "extra bit of care." Here, I'll introduce some shops that serve one-of-a-kind lemon sours made with my beloved "Setoda lemons." These will make you one of us lemon sour freaks, too—and we're less than 10% of the world's population. Time to sally forth into the world of truly tasty lemon sours.

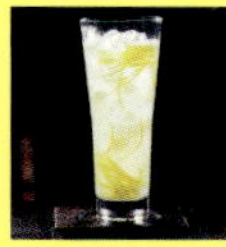

Nanritei A Japanese sake bar that serves lemon sours and takoyaki. Among the vast choice, the must-try is the "Special Nanritei Lemon Sour." It goes perfectly with the homemade syrup, filling your mouth with an impressively rich flavor. Connoisseurs drink it while nibbling thinly sliced lemon peel. ●2-14-20 Jiyugaoka, Meguro City, 2F.

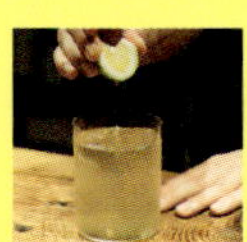

OPEN BOOK A bar specializing in lemon sours made with carefully selected shochu. The top pick is the lemon sour consisting of the Amami brown sugar shochu "Ryugu" infused with Setoda lemon peel. The shochu's sweetness really shines, and is balanced by homemade lime syrup. A must for lemon sour fans. ●1-1-6 Kabukicho, Shinjuku City, Golden Gai 5 bangai.

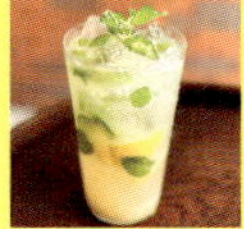

Aimaijiku URBAN LEMONERY A craft lemon sour specialty shop that uses Setoda lemons. The signature "Zamurai Lemon Sour 'Shutsujin'" is made by blending vodka with lemon juice and other ingredients, then leaving it overnight. The result is a balanced, cocktail-like drink. ●6-33-14 Okusawa, Setagaya City, 1F.

28 INDIAN CURRIES

Eye-Opening Indian Curries.

Yukon Yagi ●Company employee

Yukon Yagi has sampled the Indian cuisine at over 1,000 restaurants in Japan and abroad, shares info on it on social media, and also hosts social events based around it.

When it comes to Indian curries, Northern ones like butter chicken and light Southern ones with coconutty sweetness are popular these days, but I'm currently most interested in Eastern and Western ones. Through dishes like the Eastern mustard fish curry and Western chicken broth soup curry, they offer flavors that defy Indian curry stereotypes. Tokyo is in fact home to some top Indian restaurants, so you can enjoy the "real deal" without having to go all the way to the subcontinent.

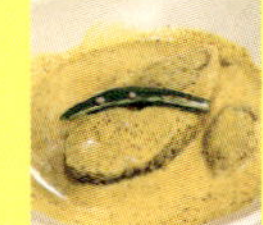

Puja A rare spot where you can enjoy cuisine from Eastern India and West Bengal. The mustard curry made with the river fish ilish features the sharp acidity of mustard and the spicy heat of green chilis. The blend of those with the sweet, boiled-to-tender river fish creates a unique flavor that truly defies typical Indian curry expectations. ●3-2-1 Machiya, Arakawa City, B1.

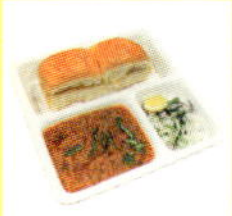

Tokyo MithaiWala A place to enjoy Indian sweets and Western Indian dishes from Mumbai. Offers many street foods that are still rare in Japan, showing that there are other depths to Indian cuisine besides curry. If you want to go to India, first, come here and sample its street food among Indian customers. ●6-8-5 Nishi-Kasai, Edogawa City.

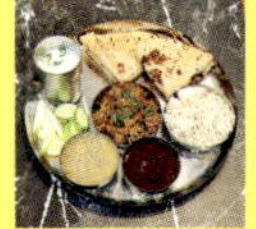

Desai's A hidden gem specializing in Western India's Maharashtra cuisine. The renovated house looks like a hideaway, and the chicken thali set's red and white soup curry offers the perfect chicken umami and mild spiciness. Powerful spices in the chicken curry follow, elevating the aftertaste to the highest level. ●1351-3 Ukitacho, Edogawa City.

29 COLLEGE CAFETERIAS

3rd Boom! Top "New College Cafeterias."

Akira Karasawa ●College cafeteria expert and university lecturer

Akira Karasawa has sampled the menus at 350+ campuses, and also helps to plan them. He's supervised numerous books, one being ***Cheap and Tasty College Cafeterias.***

College cafeterias' third boom is seeing a lunch revolution in Reiwa, too! Showa-era college cafeterias competed based on volume and low prices, Heisei-era ones based on flavor and quality. In the Reiwa-era, many are competing based on stylishness and visual impact. From cafeteria, to restaurant, to gourmet spot. Some offer original lunch menus that kindly show the calories—student-first in every way. Japanese, Western, Italian, Chinese, salads, desserts, freshly baked bread…today's college cafeterias are turning into popular oases. So, enjoy!

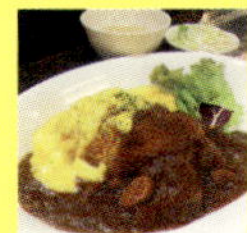

Aoyama Gakuin University "Affordable, tasty, handy, bright, and open to the public"—no wonder ***Ichinana Shokudo*** is in the college cafeteria hall-of-fame. Changes-every-other-day "Aoyama Monogatari" and set-meal-of-the-day "Omotesando" mean you'll never get bored. The exquisite Ichinana Curry also comes in a boil-in-the-bag pouch. ●4-4-25 Shibuya, Shibuya City.

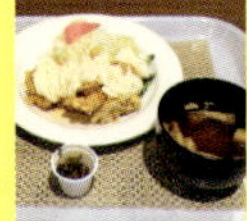

Taisho University The famous campus restaurant ***Za Gamall Classic Kamodai Shokudo***. Run by a former Prince Hotel chef, the cafeteria is open to students and non-students alike. It serves seven affordable "one-tray lunches." Another attraction is the full-on cuisine that offers fresh ingredients at low prices. ●3-20-1 Nishi-Sugamo, Toshima City, Bldg. 5 gokan 8F.

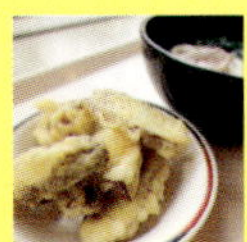

Tokyo University of Agriculture ***Cafeteria Green*** impresses not just with its flavors but also with its variety, volume, and novelty—it'll never get boring. With daily and weekly specials, a variety of item-rich bento, and more, there's plenty to choose from. Uses ingredients grown by students in agriculture projects and the like. ●1-1-1 Sakuragaoka, Setagaya City.

30 TO-GO FOOD

Delicacies from Independent Shops.

KAORU ●Food director

Dress the Food founder Kaoru is an active food director for ads, magazines, TV commercials, and more, and editor-in-chief of the food art book ***shichimi magazine***.

I like buying food and ingredients at small local shops. As soon as I buy something special that's full of the shop's warmth, I want to bite into it right there. The mixed sandwich at ***Buruku*** with its fluffy bread, not-too-childish egg salad, and delicate potato brings me a feeling of childhood peace. The shumai at ***Iseya*** are best enjoyed sitting on a bench in Inokashira Park. These juicy delights taste even better with mustard. The strawberry daifuku at ***echigo tsuruya*** has been my top choice for over 20 years.

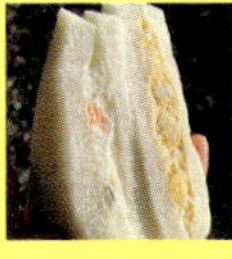

Buruku A Japanese-style bakery founded in 1951. Long loved by locals, it has a nostalgic atmosphere and offers simple, comforting food typical of the Showa-era, like cream buns, yakisoba buns, and sandwiches. The egg-and-potato-salad mixed sandwich is a classic that should definitely be passed down. ●4-33-10 Nishi-Ogi-Kita, Suginami City.

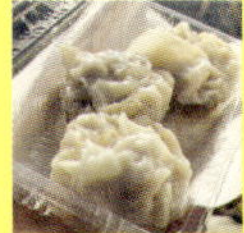

Iseya, Koenten Opened in 1960, this iconic yakitori shop in Kichijoji has fragrant smoke hanging in the air, but its hidden gem is the shumai. These are large in size, meaty, and very juicy. The subtle flavors and high quality are thanks to the shop's meat wholesale background. ●1-15-8 Kichijoji-Minamicho, Musashino City.

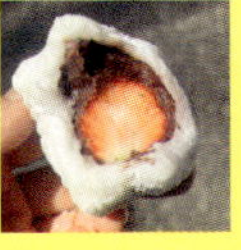

echigo tsuruya A mochi shop founded in 1985. Additive-free, freshly pounded daifuku rice cake, mitarashi dango dumplings, and more. A long-time bestseller, the strawberry daifuku are made to order, with a limit of 300 a day. Watching the craftspeople shape freshly made rice cakes into daifuku in the snug interior is lovely, too. ●3-38-20 Shoan, Suginami City.

31 DONUTS

Legendary Shops Behind the Donut Boom.

Hitomi Mizorogi ●Donut explorer

An illustrator, graphic designer, and donut explorer, Hitomi Mizorogi eats over 500 kinds of donuts every year and researches them as food culture.

The donut boom has been going on since 2022. Love donuts? Then head to three shops that built the Tokyo donut scene in its five central cities, and savor their delights. ***haritts*** pioneered fluffy, chewy donuts, ***GOOD TOWN DOUGHNUTS*** brought America's "daily treat" to Japan, and ***DUMBO Doughnuts and Coffee*** serves oversized donuts as if they're "normal." All are long-runners that have been loved by many for years. Just as there are masterpieces to read and mountains to climb, there are donuts to eat.

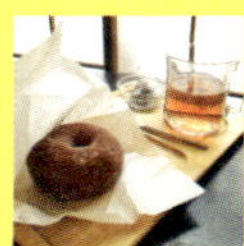

haritts, Uehara Store A top Tokyo shop that's been running in Yoyogi Uehara since 2006. Praised even by peers for their incredible texture and cited as an inspiration, it has hordes of followers. The fluffy, feather-like bounce and chewy texture captivate all who try them. The gentle-flavored donuts are true masterpieces that blend into daily life. ●1-34-2 Uehara, Shibuya City.

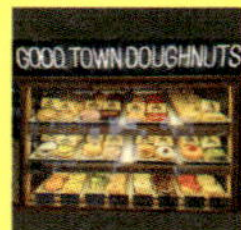

GOOD TOWN DOUGHNUTS A key player in spreading American "donut culture" in Tokyo. Since opening in Harajuku in 2015, it's continued to lead café trends. Bright and pop-y in true American style, the donuts are free of artificial flavors and colorings, and have a chewy, delicate taste. Currently sold at ***The Little BAKERY Tokyo***. ●6-13-6 Jingumae, Shibuya City.

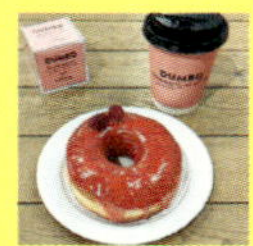

DUMBO Doughnuts and Coffee, Azabu-Juban Main Store Opened in 2016 with its iconic pink motif, this place rolls out big, colorful NY donuts in Japan. Surprisingly large but with a soft texture, pleasant sweetness, and hint of spice, you'll finish it all before you realize it. ●2-17-6 Azabu-Juban, Minato City 1F.

32 BUDGET MEGA NOODLES

Untapped Bumper Budget Noodles.

Shinichiro Nojima ●Writer and manga artist

Budget food researcher Shinichiro Nojima is well versed in local and convenience store gourmet eats. He also publishes numerous original recipes.

Casual yet unique, with bumper portions and a great taste. Ah, budget cuisine. Within that genre, noodles offer a particularly wide variety and lots of hidden gems. At ***Handmade Udon Rikimaru***, extra-thick, firm noodles get a surprising Jiro-style twist, boldly expanding udon's possibilities. ***Miyuki Shokudo***'s Soramen uses somen rather than Chinese noodles, and has a gentle flavor. The perfect end to a night's drinking. ***Spice***'s chilled noodles topped with fried pork loin karaage somehow grow on you. Budget noodles' diversity could well be ahead of its time.

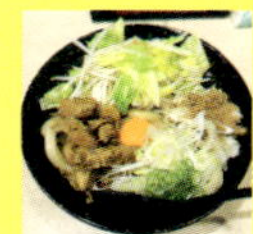

Handmade Udon Rikimaru Serves authentic Yoshida udon, a traditional dish from Yamanashi. Their hard texture and thickness call to mind Ramen Jiro, but the truly Jiro-style "Abura Udon" is an absolute gem. Rich broth with pork fat and heaps of veggies. Add garlic to make them explosively powerful. ●2-18-9 Fujimidai, Nerima City 1F.

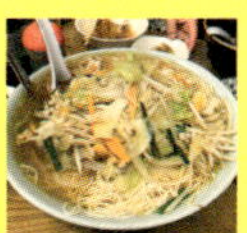

Miyuki Shokudo Some 250 menu items. Good prices and amounts (two portions of noodles even for regular size). Go in with no advance info and you'll surely be overwhelmed. "Soramen" has a huge portion of somen, and saltiness that really suits the light broth. Perfect for sharing among mates. Three flavors: soy sauce, miso, and salt. ●1-9-18 Matsuyama, Kiyose City.

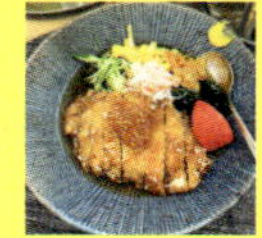

Spice Refreshingly seasoned chilled Chinese noodles—the iconic antidote to summer's heat. But these have a whole slice of fried pork loin karaage on top. Contrastingly light and heavy. Yet strangely, the karaage tastes like sweet Chinese fried chicken, blending in to become an essential ingredient. ●4-6-13 Honcho, Higashi-Murayama City.

33 ICE CREAM

Nostalgic Legendary Ice Cream.

Iceman Fukutome ●Ice cream expert

Eats over 1,000 varieties of ice cream a year. Founded Japan Icecream Mania Association (2014). Book: ***Encyclopedia of Nostalgic Japanese Ice Cream***. Has a sensitive stomach.

Tokyo is brimming with sweets, and "legendary" ice cream shops loved across generations thrive there. From Meiji's stylish ice cream to Showa's simple soft serve and overseas flavors, each shop has its own story. Founded in Ginza in 1902, ***Shiseido Parlour*** pioneered Western culture as Japan's first-ever soda shop. Its ice cream has been loved by many great writers, and changed Japanese people's view of sweets. Long-running ***Omiya Yougashiten*** serves its signature homemade ice cream all year round. Known for pioneering photogenic culture, ***Daily Chico*** in Nakano offers colorful eight-tier soft serve—a must-try for ice cream fans. ***Mikado Coffee***'s "Mocha Soft Serve" was created in 1969 by blending coffee and ice cream, and has become a store specialty everywhere from Tokyo to Karuizawa. ***SOWA*** is loved by locals for having stuck to its egg-free gentle flavor since before Tokyo Tower was built. The revolutionary ***B-R 31 Ice Cream*** was born in 1974. They popularized the innovative chocolate mint flavor called "hakka," bringing flavor diversity to Japan's ice cream. These legendary shops are landmarks in the history of the food culture revolution. Since prewar times, these shops have evolved while keeping their essence, concentrating Tokyo's memories and flavor revolution. Visiting these "living pieces of food culture heritage" will etch rich flavors into your memory.

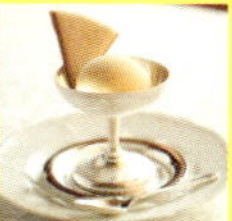

Shiseido Parlour, Ginza Main Store Salon de Café Founded as Japan's first-ever soda fountain, then revamped in 1928 as ***Shiseido Ice Cream Parlour***. Being served at a Ginza restaurant really raised ice cream's status. The classic flavor has been praised by great novelists and loved for generations. ●8-8-3 Ginza, Chuo City, Tokyo Ginza Shiseido Bldg. 3F.

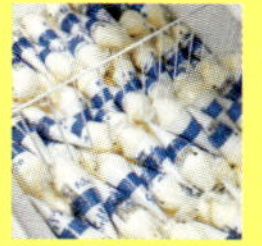

Omiya Yougashiten A long-runner that's been going since the Meiji-era, and has kept its unique "chilled and set soft serve" style. The distinctive paper sleeve covering the entire cone is a unique visual identity unseen elsewhere, notable even in the history of ice cream design. ●2-4 Kanda-Awajicho, Chiyoda City.

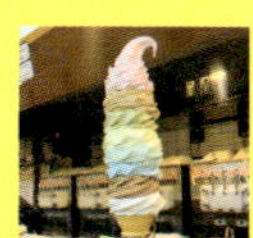

Daily Chico An iconic spot that blends Tokyo subculture with ice cream. Ever since its foundation in 1966, its unconventional eight-tier style has been forging new links between youth culture and ice cream. This visual impact pioneered today's photogenic sweets. ●5-52-15 Nakano, Nakano City. Nakano Broadway B1.

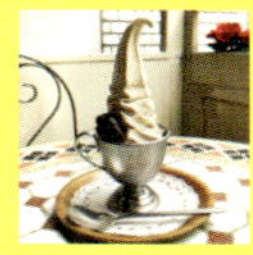

Mikado Coffee, Nihombashi Main Store "Mikado Coffee's Mocha Soft" pioneered a new frontier by blending coffee culture and ice cream. A legendary flavor that also captivated John Lennon and Yoko Ono in Karuizawa. Getting even non-coffee drinkers to enjoy the flavor pioneered soft serve diversity. ●1-6-7 Nihombashi-Muromachi, Chuo City.

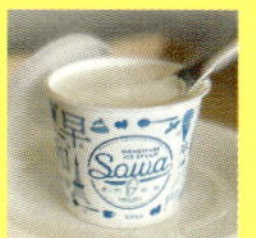

SOWA This historic ice cream shop dates back to before Tokyo Tower was built, and is well known for its unique egg-free recipes. It was renovated in 2021, keeping its original flavors while updating its logo and containers. This has boosted its historic value even further. ●3-19-10 Toranomon, Minato City.

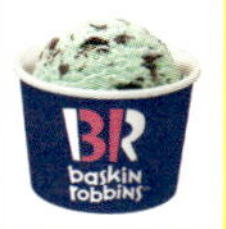

B-R 31 Ice Cream The chain known worldwide as ***Baskin-Robbins*** has been localized in Japan as "31." When simple flavors were dominant in Japan, bold overseas ones made a big impact, shaping the diverse ice cream market the country has today. ●3-1-1 Kami-Osaki, Shinagawa City.

34 SECOND-RUN THEATERS

Favorite "Second-Run Theaters."

Tadamasa Okamura ●Former director of the cinema ***Stranger***

Tadamasa Okamura founded the cinema ***Stranger*** in Kikukawa, Sumida City, in 2022. He stepped down as director in 2024, and is currently a director at a branding design company.

Like a vintage clothing or book store, a favorite cinema makes movie-watching a daily and fulfilling habit. There are three kinds of cinema: first-run theaters for new releases, classic theaters for old films, and second-run theaters for movies after their first run has ended. Second-run theaters are what I love. They have a relaxed atmosphere you won't find at first-run or classic theaters. Yet they still offer the thrill of new releases. The cinema I founded, ***Stranger***, was also a hybrid of a second-run and special-screening theater. Find your favorite second-run theater, too.

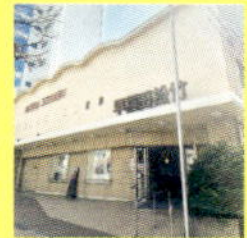

Waseda Shochiku A traditional second-run theater where two films are shown, changing every week. Tickets are only sold at the box office on the day, not online. Seat availability info is updated nearly in real-time on the official website. After deciding on a seat at the box office, the "I'm about to watch a movie" excitement starts to build. ●1-5-16 Takadanobaba, Shinjuku City.

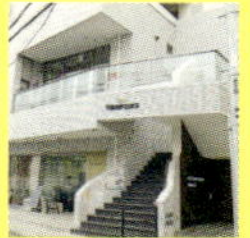

Shimotakaido Cinema Shows five to six semi-new films every day, along with special screenings. This theater satisfies my movie cravings to such an extent that I'd advise anyone looking to move to the west side of Tokyo to "live along the Keio Line or Setagaya Line, near the Shimotakaido Cinema." A super-value membership service is also available. ●3-27-26 Matsubara, Setagaya City, 2F.

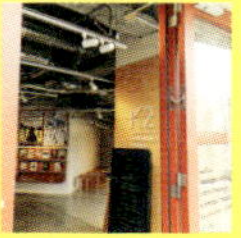

Shimo-kita Ekimae Cinema K2 ***K2*** is almost directly connected to Shimo-kitazawa Station, making it one of Tokyo's best-located theaters. Japanese films often feature guest events, bringing the audience closer to the work. Being a newly opened theater in 2022, it of course has online reservations and so on as well. ●2-21-22 Kitazawa, Setagaya City, (tefu) lounge 2F.

35 MINI THEATERS

Adventurous Mini Theaters.

Sawako Omori ●Film critic and journalist

Sawako Omori won the Japan Film Pen Club Award for ***Mini Theaters Revisited: City and Cinema Stories 1980-2023***. She has also published translated works.

The early decades of the 21st century have seen cineplexes, streaming, and the pandemic lead to the closure of some old mini theaters, but some still thrive. The three theaters below are independently run rather than being owned by large corporations, and showcase their commitment with bold programming that's unique and slightly adventurous—only intended for true movie buffs. If that's the true spirit of mini theaters, then it's reassuring to see them sticking to that mentality.

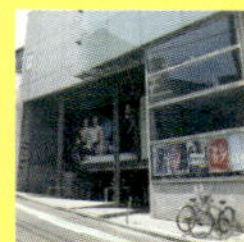

EUROSPACE A pioneering mini theater in Tokyo that opened in the 1980s. Also involved in the production of works by Leos Carax. With an eye on film history, they actively discover new directors both locally and internationally. Aki Kaurismäki is one of the signature directors of the theater, which continues to screen his works. ●1-5 Maruyamacho, Shibuya City, KINOHAUS 3F.

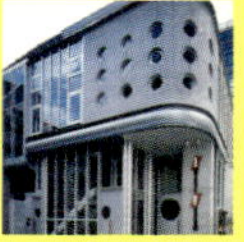

Image Forum This theater used to screen experimental films and run a film school near Yotsuya-sanchome Station, but fully relaunched in the 2000s to become a mini theater of the 21st century. Committed to screening films that only it can, including long ones. Excels at screening avant-garde art films and ambitious documentaries. ●2-10-2 Shibuya, Shibuya City.

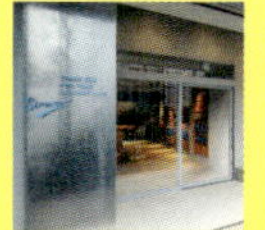

Stranger An ultra-mini theater that opened in 2022. The seating is limited, but this enables it to show unprofitable works. Also screens unreleased works by directors like John Huston and Hal Ashby who are less known in Japan. It also produces handmade original magazines. ●3-7-1 Kikukawa, Sumida City, Kikukawa Kaikan Bldg. 1F.

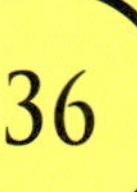

36 FOLK SONGS

Folk Songs: the Flavor of the Land.

Hajime Oishi ●Writer

Writer who specializes in local regions and climates. Many books: ***Touching Another World, The Postwar History of Bon Dances, Visiting Inner Tokyo People, Japanese Festivals***, etc. Cat-lover.

Folk songs are like local cuisine. Each region has its own songs just like it has its own flavors. I've traveled Japan to discover folk songs like that, but my hometown of Tokyo has lots of places to enjoy them as well. Examples include Asakusa's ***KAZUNOYA OIWAKE*** (a leading folk song izakaya), ***Bookboo*** (which handles folk song records in Jimbocho), and the live performances at ***Nakano Station Bon Dance Festival***. Savor the rich flavor of folk songs in the midst of a concrete jungle. This kind of fun is also part of Tokyo's charm.

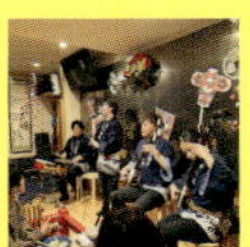

KAZUNOYA OIWAKE "Folk song izakaya" abounded in Tokyo during the economic boom. ***KAZUNOYA OIWAKE*** is a renowned spot that succeeded ***Asakusa Oiwake***, Tokyo's oldest folk song izakaya. Enjoy Japanese cuisine and drinks while listening to Tsugaru-jamisen music and folk songs from all over the nation. ●5-37-7 Asakusa, Taito City.

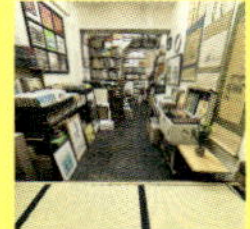

Bookboo A newly opened shop in Jimbocho, a town famous for its secondhand bookstores. It sells folk song records, old books, and vintage lifestyle items collected by the owner. The raised tatami floor creates a calm atmosphere. They're open irregularly, so check their Instagram (@bookboojimbocho) to see when. ●1-1 Kanda-Jimbocho, Chiyoda City, 2F.

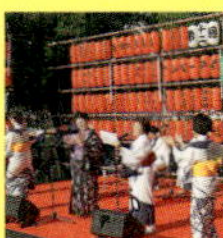

Nakano Station Bon Dance Festival While it's famous for the DJ bon dance with Bon Jovi songs, the main event is the traditional bon dance with live music by the Nakano Folk Song Association. The association performs Japanese folk songs from far and wide. Check the event dates on X (@nakano_bonodori). ●4-10-2 Nakano, Nakano City, Nakano Central Park.

37 GOOD MUSIC

Enjoy a Timeless Space with Good Music.

MAYU KAKIHATA ●DJ and record shop staff

Mayu Kakihata mainly listens to '60s and '70s rock—which first sparked her love of music—plus soul, funk, and rare groove.

I've been into music and records from the '60s and '70s since my student days. I feel a kinship with people of all ages and genders who share my interests—beyond music as well—even without exchanging many words with them. Here, I'll introduce some shops with a timeless charm and style that I've loved going to for years, regardless of the genre. In places like this filled with love for music, you'll enjoy good music in warm surroundings even 10 or 20 years on.

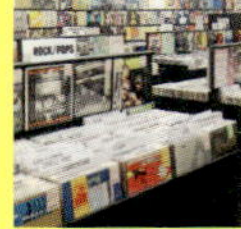

diskunion ROCK in TOKYO A record shop that every record-lover should visit. It has stores in many cities, but each one has a unique selection and staff, giving it its own charm. This shop has Shibuya's largest selection of rock CDs, records, and goods, from standard rock to subgenres. ●32-7 Udagawacho, Shibuya City, B1.

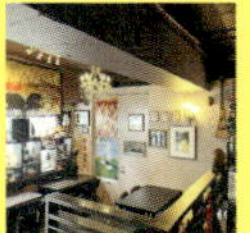

Marielranganee A curry shop just near the site of the former Tokyu Department Store Honten Store. Enjoy delicious Sri Lankan curry surrounded by records, music books, instruments, and figures. The curry's simple yet profound flavor is the art of subtraction. I also recommend it for a break when record-shop hopping. ●34-6 Udagawacho, Shibuya City, 5F.

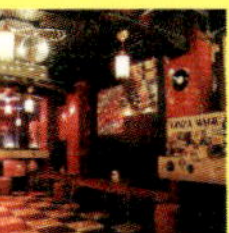

GINZA MAGIC A DJ bar in Ginza with a classic disco vibe. You can drink or dance while listening to skillfully played soul and funk, and even get your favorite song played by writing it on a request sheet. Learn the steps from regulars, and feel a nostalgic vibe you'll only find here. ●7-7-9 Ginza, Chuo City 1F & 2F.

38 FAMILY MUSIC

To Listen to the "Family Music" Around You…

Kazunoko Music Mate ●Family music collector

Kazunoko Music Mate is probably the only person in the world who collects family music. He's based in Arakawa City and does DJing, talk events, and more, working mainly in Tokyo.

Family music means recordings of ordinary people singing and playing. Choir CDs or piano recital records—maybe you have some at home. You can also find them at thrift shops, or record stores like ***manual of errors SONOTA***. I'm currently sharing recordings I've collected on ***SUPER DOMMUNE***. Community halls like ***Move Machiya*** offer local music recitals by neighborhood residents. Family music is being created right there in your own town!

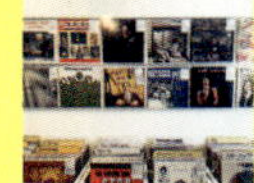

manual of errors SONOTA A record store that mainly sells online. They have lots of family music records, including unique categories like "students," "private local," and "off-key." Perfect for people seeking great music they've never heard before. They also occasionally sell things in-store. ●10-7 Moto-Yoyogicho, Shibuya City, Room 201.

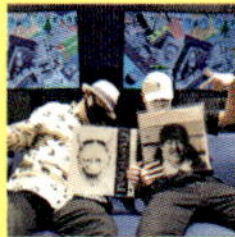

SUPER DOMMUNE Live streaming studio "currently" run by artist Ukawa Naohiro. In popular show ***Family Music All Day!***, family music collector Kazunoko Music Mate shares his collection while chatting with Ukawa Naohiro. Running for seven years. Can see it live in Shibuya PARCO 9F studio. ●15-1 Udagawacho, Shibuya City, Shibuya PARCO 9F.

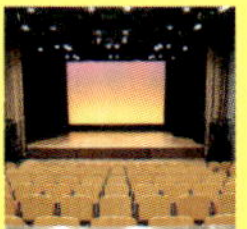

Move Machiya (Move Hall) A multipurpose hall in Arakawa City. This is a great place to encounter musical activities with the broadest base, like children's piano recitals and senior citizens' karaoke contests. Every town has a richness of everyday music you won't feel with pro performances. ●7-50-9 Arakawa, Arakawa City, Center Machiya 3F.

39 CLAW MACHINES

Retro Claw Machines That Hook Adults.

Let's Go Yoshimasa ●Impersonator

Rose to fame through his "Off-stage Ken Shimura" impersonation. Loves claw machines, and works both as an impersonator and an amusement company employee.

I loving hunting for retro claw machines. The motor sound of the Chansler machines at ***Candy Store Game Museum*** takes me back to my childhood, when I'd go there with my kid brother and a fistful of coins. The same machines are to be found at ***Omocha no Fukushima***, where the retro capsule toy machines and whole atmosphere are pure nostalgia. Playing retro games to a soundtrack of bowling noises at ***Hyper Lane*** is great, too! These places "grab" my heart like it's a prize in one of my beloved retro claw machines.

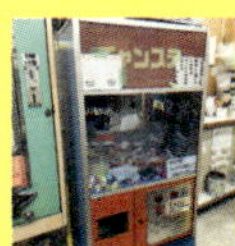

Candy Store Game Museum This place doesn't just have claw machines but dozens of other retro games running as well—and you can actually play them. It's lined with tons of rare machines that are now hard to come by. Especially nostalgic are the "¥10 coin flicking games," whose prize payout sounds bring back lots of memories for many. ●17-8 Miyamotocho, Itabashi City.

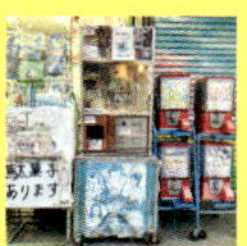

Omocha no Fukushima Old-school toy shop in Kirigaoka Central Shopping Street. Nostalgic games out front, and packed with extremely rare toys inside. While nearby shops are closing down, this toy store is still going strong. With its retro vibe, this is a must-visit gem for nostalgia-lovers. ●1-9-1-9, Kirigaoka, Kita City.

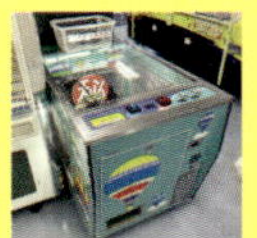

Hyper Lane A classic bowling alley and a hidden gem for game-lovers. Rare early machines like "Capriccio" and "Wonder Hunting" used to be running here, and simply gazing at them was pure joy. Even now, just hearing "game corner in a bowling alley" makes my heart flutter. ●1-43-6 Higashi-Ikebukuro, Toshima City, 3F & 4F.

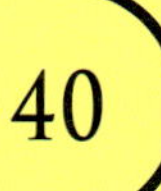

40 RAKUGO

Explore Edo Culture with Rakugo.

Edanoshin Katsura ●Rakugo performer

Edanoshin Katsura is the head of ***Z Rakugo***. He presents a wide variety of projects, including visual rakugo shows using LED screens, and rhythm units who blend rakugo with techno.

The Japanese storytelling art of rakugo is divided into Edo and Kamigata, east and west. Likewise, Tokyo shows clear east-west cultural splits, too. Walking around Tokyo's east side while listening to it on YouTube or a podcast will immerse you in rakugo even more. You'll feel like a character from the rakugo could jump out from a soba shop or public bath at any moment. Wrapped in the town's charm, you'll be able to feel the passage of time. Here, I'll introduce some specialty shops that are steeped in that Edo charm and frequented by rakugo performers.

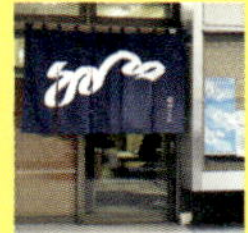

SHINEDOZOME Marukyu Shoten A wholesaler of chusen-dyed hand towels and yukata robes, founded in Nihombashi-Horidomecho in 1899. Committed to reviving classic patterns and creating new designs, they also run TEWSEN, a stylish shirt brand that uses yukata fabric. They're also a go-to for rakugo performers looking for original hand towels. ●1-4-1 Nihombashi-Horidomecho, Chuo City.

Asakusa ISAMI-DOU The place to go for rakugo and rokyoku records. A collection like a museum archive, with everything regardless of fame, going all the way back to Japan's first-ever entertainment records from the Meiji-era. Old records bring back the voices of masters who recorded rakugo on phonograph. Romantic and captivating. ●6-5-2 Asakusa, Taito City.

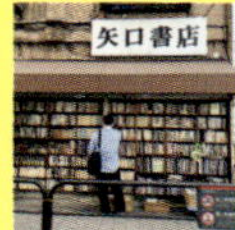

Yaguchi Shoten Famous Jimbocho secondhand bookstore. Besides lots of old movie and TV drama scripts, it's also keen on rakugo-related books and goods. "Sokkibon" (verbatim transcriptions of rakugo performances) were apparently popular in the Edo-era. Reading rakugo lets you enjoy it at your own pace, so I recommend that as well. ●2-5-1 Kanda-Jimbocho, Chiyoda City.

41 COMEDY THEATERS

The Miracle of Sharing Mirth with a Crowd.

Tokio Shiratake ●Broadcast writer

Tokio Shiratake is a writer for the TV show ***Downtown no Gaki no Tsukai ya Arahende!!*** and Shimofuri Myojo's YouTube channel, ***Shimofuri Tube***.

When comedians who are out to shake up the world start to exude the energy needed to compete at the top, they really begin to shine. Have you ever watched a comedy contest on TV and thought, "That guy shouldn't have won!"? The volume is getting adjusted, and the camera crew decides what's shown. You'll miss so many great moments if you aren't actually there. I always look forward to witnessing those miraculous moments when a real live person does something incredibly funny right before my eyes.

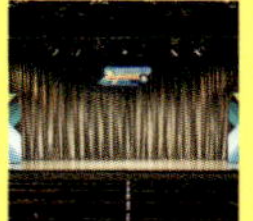

Lumine The Yoshimoto A comedy theater run by Yoshimoto Kogyo. Offers top Japanese comedy live shows featuring TV stars practically every day. With some 500 seats, you can hear the audience's laughter loud and clear, producing a wonderful feeling of unity. Note: Ticket prices vary depending on the performance. ●3-38-2 Shinjuku, Shinjuku City, Lumine 2 7F.

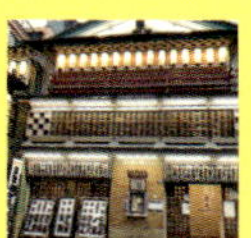

Shinjuku Suehiro-tei Three or so minutes' walk from Shinjuku-sanchome Station. One of four regular rakugo theaters in Tokyo. 79-year-old historic theater, and "Shinjuku City Cultural Property No. 1." Rakugo, plus comedy and folk songs. Interesting place where audiences range from seasoned rakugo fans to curious youngsters. ●3-6-12 Shinjuku, Shinjuku City.

Euro Live A theater in Shibuya City's Maruyamacho that offers unconventional experimental comedy shows like the beginner-friendly ***Shibuya Rakugo*** and the monthly comedy event ***C-buya Conte Center***. Watching comedy shows in an intimate 178-seat space is exceptionally exciting. ●1-5 Maruyamacho, Shibuya City, KINOHAUS 2F.

42 ELEPHANT PLAYGROUND EQUIPMENT

Searching for Elephants in the Concrete Jungle.

Asamin ●Playground equipment maniac

Nagoya-based writer Asamin loves finding interesting playground equipment lurking in urban parks, and searches for unique and charming examples countrywide.

Most playground equipment is mass-produced for safety and durability, but I just can't stop touring around parks looking for unique pieces. What's the classic motif for playground equipment? Having been all around the country nationwide, I found it's elephant-shaped slides. However, in Tokyo, I've found some elephant slides that are quite unlike what I'd imagined. They're basically elephant slides, but their designs are so alluringly offbeat. What surprises me are their designs and functionality. Their uniqueness makes them even more lovable.

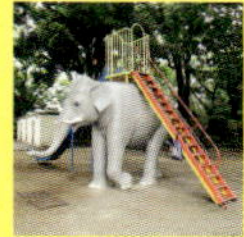

Asukayama Park At Asukayama Park, the elephant slide differs so much from the typical image that you might doubt if it can really be the one they ordered. It's definitely an elephant slide, but the overly realistic elephant supporting the slide is unlike anything else. ●1-1-3 Oji, Kita City.

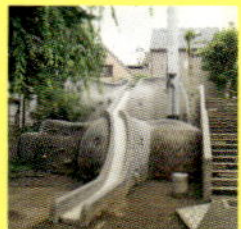

Akagi Children's Park Hidden away in a dense residential area in Kagurazaka, I found a massive elephant slide that uses the limited urban land and height difference really well. Consisting of two elephants with their trunks forming a slide, it's also designed so kids can climb up the ears. It's like an art piece while still being flawlessly functional. ●21-21 Akagi-Shitamachi, Shinjuku City.

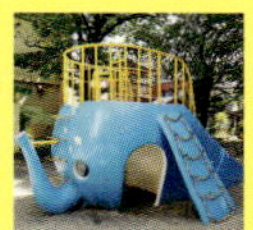

Machiya 3 chome Children's Park In this park, the huge elephant slide overturns the usual notion that an "elephant slide's slope must be the trunk." The elephant's trunk isn't used at all, while the back of its head is made to form a large slope—in fact, it's tempting to ask, "Is there really any reason for it to be an elephant at all?" ●3-27-6 Machiya, Arakawa City.

43 ROLLER COASTERS

Beyond the Thrills Lie Superb "Jet-Scapes."

Roller Coaster Man ●Roller coaster maniac

Roller Coaster Man is an influencer who travels the world to share the thrill of roller coasters. X: @jetcoasterotoko

My love of roller coasters has led me to conquer every single one in Japan! Plus, I've ridden around 800 in 20 different countries. No matter how many times I ride them, the free-fall and high-speed thrills are unbeatable. While traveling the world, though, I discovered the allure of "jet-scapes"—breathtaking views from roller coasters. (We call them "jet coasters" in Japan.) For example, the magnificent view of Mount Fuji from Fujikyu Highland's FUJIYAMA is a uniquely Japanese "jet-scape." Tokyo also has various "jet-scapes" in its city center, downtown areas, and suburbs.

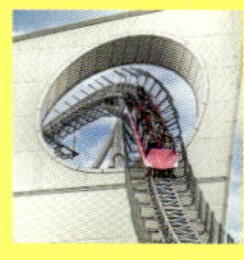

Thunder Dolphin (Tokyo Dome City Attractions) An amusement park surrounded by Tokyo skyscrapers. Thunder Dolphin is a rare roller coaster in the world that goes over buildings and passes through a Ferris wheel like a dolphin. Riding it at night is recommended for the sight of Tokyo Dome and the high-rise buildings all lit up. ●1-3-61 Koraku, Bunkyo City.

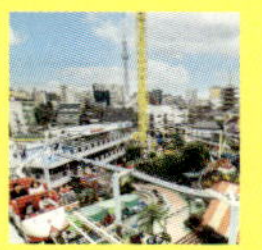

Roller Coaster (ASAKUSA HANAYASHIKI) A historic amusement park that's affectionately known as "HANAYASHIKI." Although it's small, Japan's oldest extant roller coaster is a super-exhilarating ride that whooshes right by buildings and nearly crashes into houses. Offers views of Senso-ji and TOKYO SKYTREE®—a unique contrast of traditional and modern. ●2-28-1 Asakusa, Taito City.

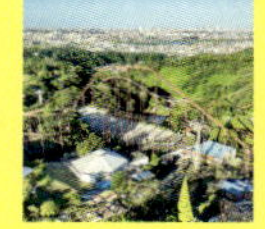

Bandit (Yomiuriland) A nature-filled amusement park up on high ground in the Tama Hills. Riding Bandit through the park's forest, you can see the lush greenery of Tama and the skyscrapers of Shinjuku. You get to enjoy "jet-scapes" that change with the seasons, from cherry blossoms in spring to illuminations in winter. ●4015-1 Yanokuchi, Inagi City.

44 KARAOKE

Memories of Tokyo Intertwined with Karaoke.

Yukkyun ●DIVA

Holds a graduate degree in Comparative Arts from Aoyama Gakuin University's Graduate School of Literature. Launched ***DIVA Project*** in 2021. Second full album ***You'll Never Be Reborn*** is on sale now.

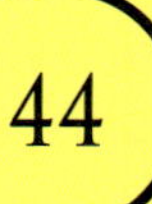

After moving to Tokyo for university, I spent my most of time going to karaoke in Shibuya. The best part about being a student was that I could go in the daytime when it's cheapest. ***Karaoke Rainbow*** in Shibuya Modi is a true hidden gem. Even after my student days, I'd still travel all the way from Shibuya to ***Best 10*** in Sangenjaya for its "cheap" prices and sing there till dawn. Unforgettable Tokyo nights! Now I'm older, I go to ***KaraokeKan*** in Ginza—the adult's playground. Taking someone along who rarely goes to karaoke is great fun.

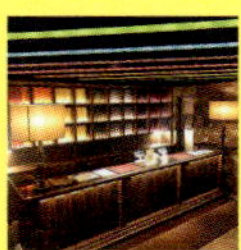

Karaoke Rainbow Shibuya A karaoke on the eighth floor of ***Shibuya Modi***—a prime location just 5 minutes from Shibuya Station Hachiko Exit. It's inside a commercial complex, so it's an unexpected hidden karaoke spot. On weekdays until 7 p.m., the first hour is free—a stunning deal. The unique interior is also a highlight. ●1-21-3 Jinnan, Shibuya City, Shibuya Modi 8F.

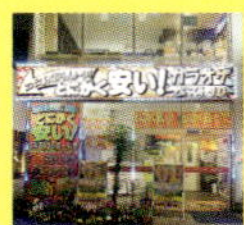

Best 10, Sangenjaya Store Unbeatable late-night free-time rates: from 9 p.m., up to 8 hours with self-service drinks for ¥2,080 (Mon. to Thu. and Sun. only). The go-to place for karaoke till dawn. You can bring in your own food and drinks, so stocking up at the supermarket in front of the station is fun, too. ●2-14-5 Sangenjaya, Setagaya City, 2F.

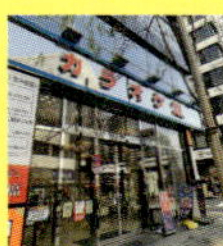

KaraokeKan, Ginza Sohonten Located in a large building near Sukiyabashi Intersection. Within a 5-minute walk from Ginza, Yurakucho, and Hibiya stations. There's a wide range of rooms, from party ones for large groups to solo karaoke ones. The rooms facing Sotobori-dori Avenue offer sweeping views toward Hibiya, and even glimpses of Tokyo Tower. ●4-2-17 Ginza, Chuo City.

45 UP-AND-COMING COMEDIANS

Discover Up-and-Coming Comedians.

Larry Toda ●Comedy critic

Worked at a TV production company, then became a freelance writer. Actively works as a comedy critic in a wide range of fields. His many books include ***Matsumoto Hitoshi, Comedy, and Television***.

You can enjoy comedy content anywhere on TV or online these days, but live comedy still has a special charm. There are lots of funny professional comedians, regardless of fame. Live shows are unique places to spot rising comedians before they hit it big. Agency-organized live comedy shows and independent ones have both been on the rise recently, which is energizing the whole scene. Be sure to take in a live show and find your own favorite comedian.

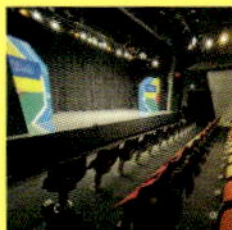

Jimbocho Yoshimoto Manzai Theater A theater where rising Tokyo Yoshimoto comedians like Nightingale Dance and ***M-1*** laureates Elf and Evers compete fiercely. Many fresh newcomers perform here, so expect lots of sharp new jokes. The audience is mostly young as well, so it's a lively, energetic atmosphere. ●1-23 Kanda-Jimbocho, Chiyoda City, 2F.

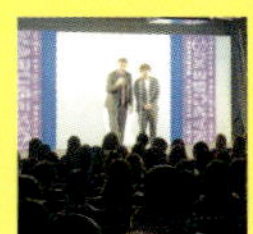

Nishishinjuku Narugeki Permanent theater opened in 2021 by comedy live show production group K-PRO. Live shows featuring top comedians from various other agencies as well as K-PRO. Getting to check out comedians from all kinds of agencies all in one place is very handy. Welcoming atmosphere for comedy live show beginners as well. ●7-21-20 Nishi-Shinjuku, Shinjuku City, B2.

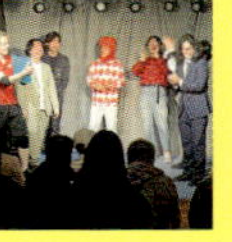

BeachV A theater run by Sony Music Artists (SMA), just a 30-second walk from Senkawa Station. The numerous popular comedians it's produced include Hollywood-Zakoshisyoh, Baking, Nishikigoi, and Yasuko. The stage is close to the audience, creating a homey atmosphere. You can get so close to the comedians you can even see their spit fly. ●3-11-3 Kanamecho, Toshima City, B1.

46 A Catalog of Hotels with Outstanding Diversity.

Nobuaki Takizawa ●Hotel critic

Nobuaki Takizawa reports on hotels in Japan from a users' perspective. He's highly trusted by the media when it comes to the subject.

Hotels come in a diverse range of forms, and offer services ranging from luxury to low-cost. A city that's lived in and visited by legions, Tokyo is packed with hotels—a veritable hotel catalog. For example, the ***Grand Hyatt Tokyo*** is an entirely foreign-owned hotel. Passing through the porte cochere takes you into an extraordinary world. The ***Shinjuku Prince Hotel*** towers over the bustling nightlife, offering a sanctuary-like escape with stunning city views from the upper floors. Tokyo hotels are highly diverse and trend-sensitive. Reflecting the sauna boom, ***hotel hisoca Ikebukuro*** has a sauna in every room. Business hotels are impressive as well. ***Quintessa Hotel Tokyo Haneda*** lobby boasts 8,000 comics that guests can take to their rooms. Another draw is the 24-hour curry rice and udon service. For meals, breakfast at ***Vessell Inn Takadanobaba Station*** is a must-try. From Hokkaido to Okinawa, breakfast menu items from group hotels nationwide offer a "tour of Japan" experience. Sweet-tooths should visit the ***HOTEL COCO GRAND KITASENJU*** with its outlet shop for popular sweets. As it's run by a confectionery maker, guests can enjoy luxurious sweets in their rooms without having to wait in line. The fun of Tokyo hotels doesn't just lie in the stay, but in the extra experiences they offer as well.

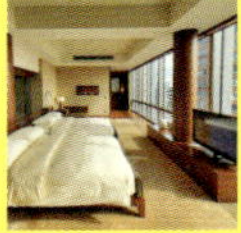

Grand Hyatt Tokyo A foreign-owned luxury hotel in Roppongi Hills. It has a contemporary urban atmosphere and is full of art, making it a cultural hub for the big city. The diverse dining options include ***The French Kitchen***'s high-quality buffet, plus Japanese, Chinese, and steakhouse cuisine. ●6-10-3 Roppongi, Minato City.

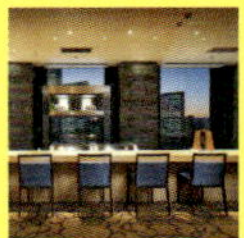

Shinjuku Prince Hotel Conveniently located with direct access to Seibu-Shinjuku Station. The market-inspired buffet dining is popular, but ***Japanese Dining and Bar FUGA*** also offers great views and atmosphere. ***The Station Café & Bar*** has a casual atmosphere and a Seibu Shinjuku Line departure board—a real "station." ●1-30-1 Kabukicho, Shinjuku City.

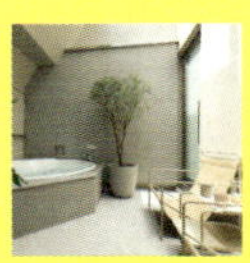

hotel hisoca ikebukuro Just a 2-minute walk from Ikebukuro Station West Exit. The average room area is a spacious 37 m². For the limited-to-one-room-per-day anniversary plan, they decorate your room with balloon art and lights. Options like a whole cake, champagne, and bouquets of flowers are also popular. ●1-10-4 Nishi-Ikebukuro, Toshima City.

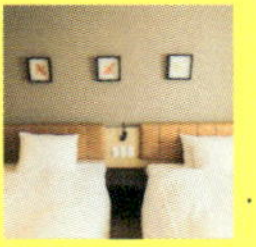

Quintessa Hotel Tokyo Haneda Comic & Books Just a 5-minute walk from Keikyu Kamata Station East Exit, with great access to Haneda Airport. The rooms have a natural atmosphere, and Simmons beds to relax on. Some rooms offer views of the high-speed Keikyu Airport Line, which is popular with train enthusiasts. ●1-25-3 Minami-Kamata, Ota City.

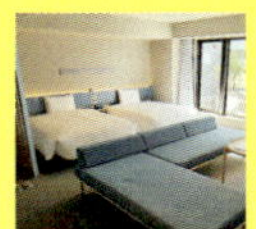

Vessel Inn Takadanobaba Station Directly connected to Takadanobaba Station on the subway's Tozai Line, with rain-free access. The 3rd floor has two "BABA Suites" with a massage chair, a steam sauna, and a balcony with BBQ options—a relaxing urban retreat that draws many repeat guests. ●2-17-4 Takadanobaba, Shinjuku City.

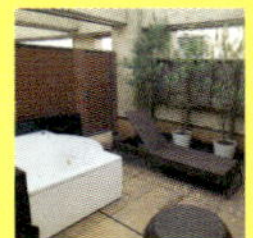

HOTEL COCO GRAND KITASENJU A 3-minute walk from a station with a nostalgic post-town vibe. The spacious bathhouse includes a men's dry sauna, an outdoor bath, and a women's bedrock bath. The diverse rooms include the Bali and Monaco Suite Twins, each with a balcony, outdoor bath, and massage chair. ●3-40-2 Senju, Adachi City.

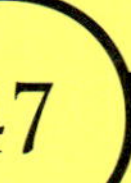

47 Great Neon Signs That Spice up City Strolls.

Daisuke Matsumura ●Book designer

Worked at an advertising agency and a printing company, then joined the publisher ***PIE International (PIE Graphics)***. Has also published a compendium on signboards and other "urban lettering."

Neon signs on nighttime streets evoke nostalgia, their soft light producing a unique atmosphere. First used in outdoor advertising during Japan's economic boom in the early years after the war, neon signs have long been cherished, with nightlife districts still being called "neon towns" even today. Neon signs have declined due to the rise of LED tube lights and the shortage of skilled craftspeople, but the recent trend for all things retro is boosting their popularity again, especially among young people. In addition, Japanese city pop's recent recognition around the globe has seen "neon" drawing attention worldwide, with it even featuring in artwork and lyrics. Neon signs use gas sealed in a vacuum inside a glass tube, and are powered by a transformer to produce the light. "Neon gas" glows red and "argon gas" glows blue, and coloring the inside of the tube enables various other colors to be produced. Neon signs are weather-resistant, energy-efficient, and cost-effective. What's more, they have a lifespan of around 10 years. As Tokyo's spring grows warmer day by day, rather than being fooled by LED impostors masquerading as neon, how about finding some real neon signs? Here are six iconic examples in Tokyo, ranging in scale from small eyewear shop ads to signs for huge stores.

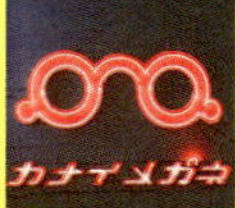

Kanai Megane Eyewear shop founded way back in 1933, located in front of Otsuka Station. Its walls bear two big red neon signs like round glasses. The red neon light reflected beautifully in the buses at the stop across the street momentarily wraps the town in a mysterious atmosphere. A formative part of the cityscape. ●2-45-4 Minami-Otsuka, Toshima City.

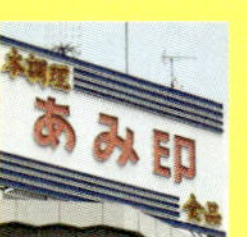

Ami-jirushi Shokuhin Kogyo ***Ami-jirushi*** offers fried rice bases, soups, and seasonings. The large neon sign (which also appears in Makoto Shinkai's ***Weathering with You***) is impossible to miss as soon as you leave Tabata Station. Also must-sees are big signs on company rooftops along railroads and highways that can be seen from inside the vehicles. ●1-6-2 Higashi-Tabata, Kita City.

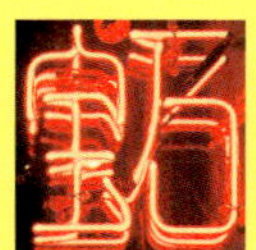

Jewel Uhara Neon signs are often used for store names or brands, but this jewelry shop's one reads, "We'll design and create a unique gem that's just for you." Various other eye-catching neon signs also adorn the dazzling facade, with designs such as pictograms of jewels. ●3-27-3 Nishi-Ikebukuro, Toshima City.

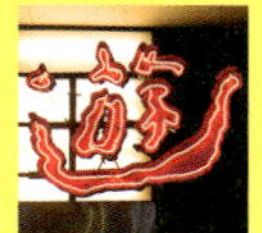

Yuboku Shinjuku Store Neon signs look really great in Kabukicho. The facade of yakiniku restaurant ***Yuboku***'s Shinjuku Store features a bold neon sign with the store name written in free brushstroke characters. The way the final brushstroke of the "⻌" sweeps naturally skyward is beautifully captured in the neon tubing. ●2-26-3 Kabukicho, Shinjuku City.

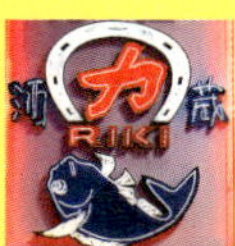

Sakagura Riki, Ikebukuro Nishiguchi Store A popular izakaya chain in Saitama whose main store is in Urawa. The Ikebukuro Nishiguchi Store features a dynamic neon sign depicting a cow, a pig, a chicken, and a fish. After some exquisite skewers and simmered offal, you'll want to enjoy the fun neon sign in a tipsy mood. ●1-15-3 Nishi-Ikebukuro, Toshima City.

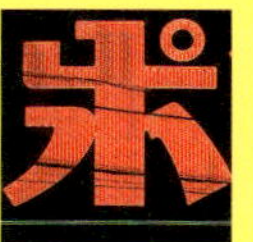

Neon ad for POM Juice The giant "POM Juice" neon sign is visible through the train window at Tokyo Monorail Tenkubashi Station. Put up in July 1975, it'll soon be celebrating its 50th anniversary, having been through repeated revamps. Stand below it and you'll be transported to another world—one that's wrapped in red. ●15-6 Haneda-Asahicho, Ota City.

48 MOUNTAIN TRAILS

A Physical and Mental Escape from Reality on an Easy Trail in Tokyo!

Atsushi Ishihara ●Photographer

Atsushi Ishihara does the photography for the "Trail Running" series in the magazine ***Tarzan***. He takes his equipment along to interviews, mainly in the Kanto area mountains. He's also a trail runner.

I've finally finished submitting the data. My eyes are bleary and my back is stiff from sitting too long. The morning sun streams in. What a beautiful morning! If I jump into bed now, I won't wake up until dusk. How many mornings in my life have I had a premonition of such a "wasted holiday"? So, I grab my already packed bag and head out on a small trip. (Readers are advised to get enough sleep before doing this). The trailhead is just a train or bus ride away. It's not a race, so I can turn back if I get tired. I run along leisurely enjoying nature. I don't run uphill, and I don't have to. Downhill slopes make me run automatically. The fresh greenery soothes my eyes and the birds and rustling trees calm my mind. It's nice to be somewhere with no signal. You swap convenience for freedom from work and personal matters. Be sure to take a mountain map with you. Another hiker once asked me over 2,000 m up mountain, "My mountain map app has stopped working. Do you know this route?" Smartphones are handy, but take a spare battery just in case. Having a headlamp, portable food, and emergency gear could save your life. These places are home to monkeys, deer, and Asian black bears as well. Letting them know how far away you are with a bear bell is also important. Despite my hay fever, I don't care about getting covered in pollen and dust. That's why I love routes with a hot spring to wash off in afterward.

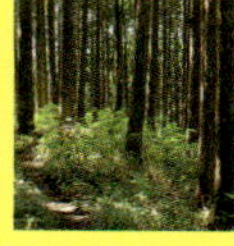

Kompira ridge trail About 15 km. JR Mitake Station (by Nishi Tokyo Bus) → bus stop under the cable car (Takimoto Station) → cable car's Mitakesan Station → Mt. Hinode → Kompira Ridge → Mt. Kompira → Musashi-Itsukaichi Station. Cable car skips most of the climb up to the trail. Afterward, wash off the sweat at ***Tsuru Tsuru Onsen***. ●Near 17 Mitakesan, Ome City.

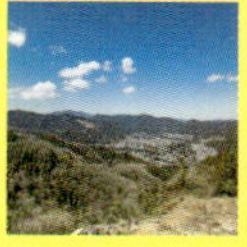

Akabokko trail About 10 km. JR Miyanohira Station or Hinatawada Station → Tengu-iwa Nature Trail entrance → Mt. Yogai → Tengu Rock → Akabokko → Tenso-jinja Shrine trail entrance → JR Ome Station. Walk from Ome Station to Kabe Station and you can wash off at ***Kabe Onsen Umeno Yu***. Akabokko's fantastic vista is great for lunch. ●Near 2 Wadamachi, Ome City.

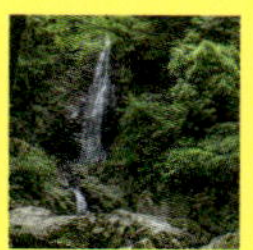

Mt. Sengenrei trail About 12 km. JR Musashi-Itsukaichi Sta. → Nishi Tokyo Bus Sengen-one Ridge Trailhead bus stop → Mt. Sengenrei → Hossawa no Taki Falls → Musashi-Itsukaichi Sta. (by Nishi Tokyo Bus). Colorful Sengen-one Ridge soothes the eyes, and refreshing Hossawa no Taki Falls the body. ●Nr. Sengen-one Ridge trailhead, Hinohara Village, Nishitama County.

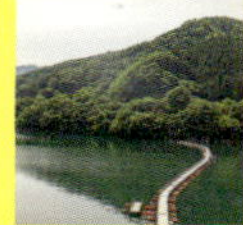

Lake Okutama trail About 23 km. JR Okutama Sta. → Ogouchi-jinja Shrine / Mugiyama Ukihashi bus stop (Nishi Tokyo Bus). Cross Mugiyama Ukihashi Bridge. Follow lakeshore (lovely scenery and path). Finish at ***Okutama Mizu-to-Midori no Fureaikan***. Bus back to Okutama Sta. Bath at ***Okutama Onsen Moegi-no-Yu***. ● Near Mugiyama Ukihashi Bridge, Kawano, Okutama Town, Nishitama County.

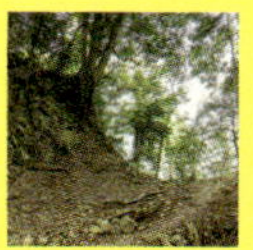

Hachioji Castle Ruins trail About 10 km. JR Takao Station → Nishi Tokyo Bus Miyanomae bus stop → Taiokokuruwaone ridge trailhead → Hachioji Castle Ruins → Mt. Takao entrance. At this Odawara-Hojo clan castle ruin, you can reflect on the scale of Hideyoshi's conquest of Odawara. It's also a well-known haunted spot. ●Near 3 Moto-Hachiojimachi, Hachioji City.

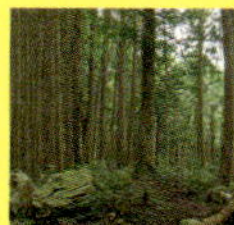

Mt. Takamizu trail About 10 km. Walk from JR Ikusabata Sta., follow Hiramizo River (on your right) to Kogenji Temple. Mt. Takamizu trailhead starts here. No view at Mt. Takamizu, so rest at Mt. Iwatake-ishiyama summit and admire the Oku-Musashi mountain range. From Mt. Sogaku, it's a few more climbs up and down to the goal—JR Mitake Sta. ●Near 1 Sawai, Ome City.

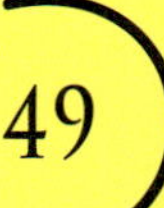

49 PLACES TO READ

Places That Make You Want to Go Out Just for a Read.

Mitsuhiro Kumagai ●Owner of ***twililight***

Owner of ***twililight***, a bookstore, gallery, and café in Sangenjaya. Also a publisher (e.g., Hiroko Oyamada's ***Small Lunch***). Other activities include writing, curating, and planning.

Setagaya Park's fountain and ***twililight's roof*** are perfect spots for a thoughtful walk after a read. That's because you can entrust your thoughts to the breeze, shifting light, and clouds. A coffee shop at a station you're getting off at for the first time on some errand is also great for reading—***cafe angelina*** is a prime example. Rather than taking the shortest route, I stop by a coffee shop, open a book, and let my mind, excited at the unfamiliar town, devour the words. The words I read become a staff, guiding my thoughts inward and toward the future. When I leave the shop, I feel in tune with the town. A library like ***Musashino Place*** is the perfect spot for reading that stimulates a chain of thought. I open a page, hit upon an idea, then browse the shelves of eye-catching books as I look for one on it. A heaven I could spend eternity reading in. Speaking of heaven, ***Kosugiyu Harajuku*** is just like that, too. In the heart of Harajuku, I wash away my outward self and loosen my cold, stiff body and mind. What I read in the waiting room is pretty much always poetry. Transcending their meaning, the poems' words spread throughout my refreshed soul. In the sense of refreshment, a travel destination also suits reading. That's because it lets me break free from daily life and take a look at myself. At a window seat in ***Royal Host Haneda Airport Store***, I read as I watch the planes coming and going, and let my thoughts take flight. As long as I don't forget my curiosity, then even though I'm not getting on a plane, I can still fly anywhere. In my book.

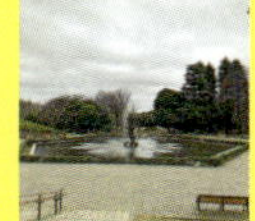

Setagaya Park's fountain A lush green oasis in the urban sprawl, Setagaya Park is 18 mins' walk from Sangen-jaya Sta. Surrounded by benches and grass, the fountain is perfect for a relax. The play park is great if you have kids with you. ***Setagaya Future Peace Museum*** shows the horrors of war and the value of peace, and is free. ●1-5-27 Ikejiri, Setagaya City.

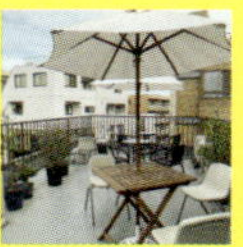

twililight's roof A bookstore, gallery, and café just a 5-minute walk from Sangen-jaya Station. Buy a book or order something from the café menu, and you're allowed to go on the roof. I always pick a book, admire the art, have a coffee, then daydream up on the roof. It lets me catch my breath and reconnect with myself. ●4-28-10 Taishido, Setagaya City, Suzuki Bldg. roof.

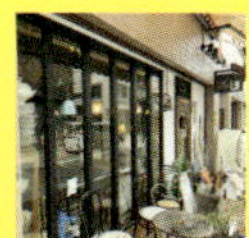

cafe angelina A 2-minute walk from Setagaya Station. It's been around since 1990—35 years, now—and as you cross the threshold, you'll instantly feel at ease. Dim lighting and well-worn tables. It's a precious place where you can get food and coffee anytime from when it opens at 11:30 a.m. until it closes at 2:00 a.m. ●1-15-12 Setagaya, Setagaya City.

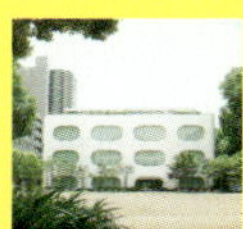

Musashino Place - People, Town, and Information Creation Center Unique rounded white public library with rows of oval windows. Open to 10 p.m., so perfect for after work. Can read the books in its comfy café. Can borrow only if living/studying/working in Musashino City, or living in an adjacent one. ●2-3-18 Kyonancho, Musashino City.

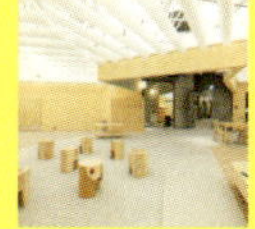

Kosugiyu Harajuku 4-min walk from Harajuku Sta. Floor B1 of "Harakado" at Harajuku's Jingumae intersection. Unwind in a bath in the heart of town. Towels sold, so empty-handed is OK. Milk, hot, and cold baths to switch between. Lovely artistically crafted wooden buckets and stools, too. ●6-31-21 Jingumae, Shibuya City, Tokyu Plaza Harajuku, "Harakado" B1.

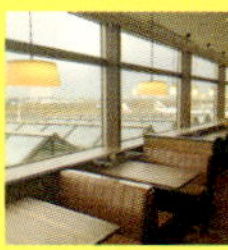

Royal Host Haneda Airport Store This is in the pre-check-in area, so anyone can use it. Another key point is the runway view from the window seats. The seats are comfortably wide apart—presumably because lots of customers bring big luggage. Savor your journey's prologue and epilogue in relaxing style. ●3-3-2 Haneda Airport, Ota City, Terminal 1 Bldg. Marketplace 4F.

50 CYCLING

Escape the City Noise and Relax at a 24-Hour Free Bicycle Rest Spot.

YUKI (YUKHINX) ●Messenger

Since graduating from Musashino Art University, YUKI has placed in races all around the world, and cycled 3,000 km across Europe. Now, she channels these experiences into her works.

When I'm riding along on my bicycle, I get to feel the towns and nature change around me as scenery that's from my everyday sphere of life flows past my eyes. I make sure I keep moving through different landscapes so that my blood keeps flowing and my head doesn't stop thinking. A bicycle has no roof or walls to keep you safe like a car does, so in Tokyo's car-dominated traffic, the faster I ride, the more I need to sharpen my senses so that I can quickly assess my surroundings and protect myself from danger, and not cause anyone else any harm, either. As I go on using my body in this way, I start to feel a primitive sense of freedom, even within the whirlwind of modern society. When I've finally achieved this new perspective, if I slumped down in some closed-in space made of concrete, it'd make me reluctant to go back outside. On top of that, paying ¥100 at a bike rack would drag me back to the capitalist world. If I need to take a break, it might seem wasteful to some, but I'd much rather take one in a place that gives me freedom and room than somewhere that feels overly efficient and cramped due to too much marketing. Far away from any thoughts of money and the urban hustle and bustle, as I grip the handlebars of my own free will rather than doing it because someone else has told me to, I begin to see quiet landscapes emerging within the urban sprawl.

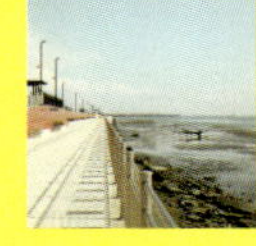

Soramunado Haneda Green Space The terrace at the cycling road's end presents the Tokyo Wan Aqua-Line Expressway, the opposite shore, and planes flying overhead. A thrilling spot. It's lovely to get off the bike and walk the 2 km path surrounded by river and sky, watching the birds and driftwood. ●2-8-1 Haneda Airport, Ota City.

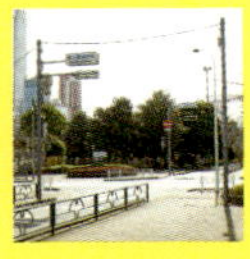

Central intersection at Aoyama Cemetery The central intersection with its wide sidewalks, restrooms, and vending machines makes you completely forget bustling Roppongi and Aoyama-dori Avenue. Some messengers affectionately call it "Bochiman" and use it as a resting point. In spring, the cherry blossom trees come into full bloom. ●Near 2-32 Minami-Aoyama, Minato City.

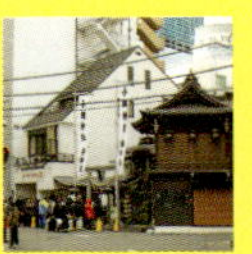

Koami-jinja Shrine This wooden shrine survived WWII air raids and is famed for protecting soldiers—its reputation as a good-luck deity sealed by an anecdote that all who had amulets from it came home safely. A certain messenger company's exorcism at the shrine is also said to have stopped bike thefts and accidents. ●16-23 Nihombashi-Koamicho, Chuo City.

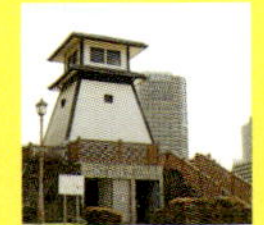

1 Tsukuda About 2 km from Ginza. Tsukudajima has traces of the Edo-era fishing town, offering a calm atmosphere that evokes the past and gives you a moment of respite. It's a place where you can hop off your bicycle for a leisurely stroll, visit the tsukudani shops and Sumiyoshi-jinja Shrine, and eat on a bench by the Sumida River. ●1 Tsukuda, Chuo City.

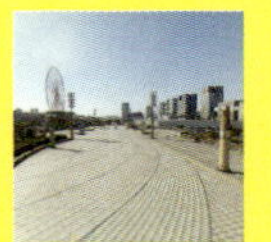

Yumeno Ohashi Bridge At 360 m long and 60 m wide, this the widest pedestrian bridge in Japan. This spot has also been used as the finish line for group rides. It's very quiet because it's far from the station, very few people come by, and no vehicle traffic is allowed. With buildings, a Ferris wheel, and a lit-up bridge around, it's a great spot at night. ●Near 3-1 Ariake, Koto City.

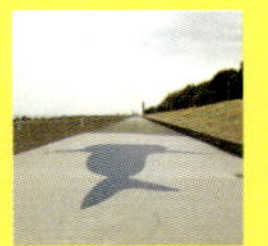

Wakasu Seaside Park There's a 6 km cycling course, a campsite, a free fishing spot, and daytime bicycle rentals. Since no vehicle traffic is allowed, you can have a relaxing bike ride or sunbathe on the lawn. If you cycle, you can see expansive scenery, including Tokyo Gate Bridge. ●3-1-2 Wakasu, Koto City.

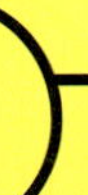

51 ESCALATORS

Enjoy the Futuristic City from Escalators.

Miha Tamura ●Escalator maniac

An escalator maniac ever since moving to Tokyo for college and being captivated by the cityscapes seen from them. Book ***Amazing Escalators*** was published by X-Knowledge in 2020.

When I was a child, I was thrilled by the "futuristic cities" depicted in manga and anime. I was particularly fascinated by the depictions of new vehicles racing through the sky and people traveling around through tubes. What excited me when I moved to Tokyo was the glimpses of a "futuristic city" that I could already see right there on its streets. One example is the escalators in ***TOKYO Solamachi®*** at Oshiage <SKYTREE> Station, which crisscross each other up in the air. The tube escalators at ***LIVIN OZ Oizumi Store*** glow mysteriously at night like it's some secret society. While the Oedo Line is famous for its depth, the long escalators at Iidabashi Station with their winding green lights feel like an entrance to a mysterious world. On the rooftop of ***SHIBUYA SKY***, you can experience briefly floating in the air on escalators that seem to rise straight up into the sky. ***Izumi Garden Tower*** offers the thrill of moving through a beautiful glass-walled tunnel. The newly renovated ***Kabukiza*** has red steps that look like a carpet but move as you step on them. Escalators themselves aren't a new invention, and are probably regarded as ordinary, everyday things by most people. But in Tokyo, there are already so many places where you can enjoy them as "vehicles that move through the air," and experience a futuristic city.

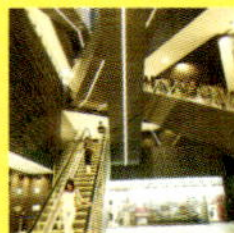

TOKYO Solamachi® ***TOKYO Solamachi®*** opened at the foot of TOKYO SKYTREE®. The open space at the entrance connected to Oshiage <SKYTREE> Station is a stylish, 21st-century place. The long escalators intersect at an angle, and the lines of light in the outer panels make you want to endlessly snap photos. ●1-1-2 Oshiage, Sumida City.

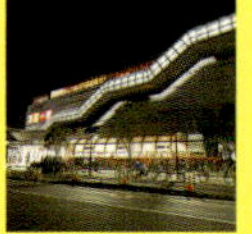

LIVIN OZ Oizumi Store An impressive shopping building with tube escalators attached to its exterior wall. It closely resembles the famous architecture of the Centre Pompidou in Paris. At night, it's lavishly lit up, turning it into such a work of art that you can easily forget it houses a supermarket and cafés. ●2-10-11 Higashi-Oizumi, Nerima City.

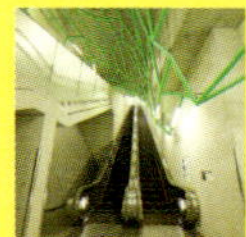

Oedo Line Iidabashi Station The Metropolitan Subway's Oedo Line has public art at all of its stations. The squiggly green pipes on the ceiling in Iidabashi Station are "Web Frame" by Makoto Watanabe. Riding the escalator through a space that's like an alien plant invasion is a surreal experience. ●4-9-5 Iidabashi, Chiyoda City.

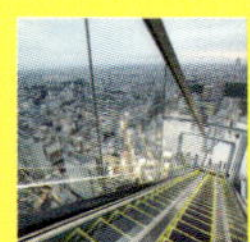

SHIBUYA SKY The escalators at the 47-story ***Shibuya Scramble Square*** are among the tallest outdoor ones in Japan. No roof, just a glass fence on one side. Incredibly open. You feel like you're floating in the air as you look down at the city below. ●2-24-12 Shibuya, Shibuya City, Rooftop.

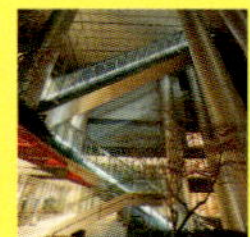

Izumi Garden Tower A glass-walled building directly connected to Roppongi-itchome Station. Enclosed in the same glass as the exterior, the escalators are luxurious tunnels. The long escalators from the 4th to 7th floors feel like you're being sucked into the air, and their solemn arch-shaped supports resemble rows of torii gates. ●1-6-1 Roppongi, Minato City.

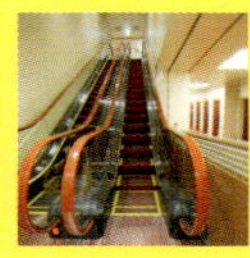

Kabukiza Reopened in 2013. The escalators were custom-made for accessibility, and the first to ever be installed in the theater. "Red" is used for the escalator steps and landing plates, matching the red carpet in the hallway and the red pillars and creating a seamlessly unified space. ●4-12-15 Ginza, Chuo City.

52 MUSEUMS

Feel the Ultimate Love of Collectors.

Toshiki Tanji ●Museum maniac

Museum writer and "rediscover Japan" blogger Toshiki Tanji has covered over 2,500 spots, including odd attractions, red-light districts, museums, and public baths.

When it comes to Tokyo museums, many might think of the National Museum of Nature and Science, Tokyo National Museum, local history museums, and the like. Lots of people visit museums every day to admire exhibits like Jomon pottery, precious art, and national treasures they learned about in history class.

However, Japan has literally thousands of museums, and some have imagination-defying niche collections that often make visitors think, "There's even a museum for that?!" They're run by companies, individuals, and various other parties. Here are six museums with niche collections. ***World Bags & Luggage Museum*** is a company-run one with bags from all around the world. The ones for train timetables, jade, anime ***Candy Candy*** goods, water supply outlets, and extinct media devices are all privately run. Be overwhelmed by jade stones huger than any you've ever seen before and get nostalgic over extinct media devices you once used, like flip phones and MD players. These rare items you don't see every day will move you deeply time and again. All these collections were amassed by individual enthusiasts. "Why did you keep on collecting them?" "What drives someone to do that?" Glimpse a way of life defined by sticking to your passion in the face of such criticism. How about spicing up your daily life with a trip to these maniac museums?

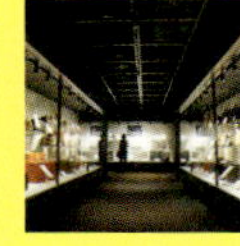

World Bags & Luggage Museum A corporate museum run by bag trading company ***Ace***. It exhibits bags from all around the world, include Madison ones with sales of over 20 million including fakes, and bags owned by celebrities like Nagashima and Inoki. There's also a must-see memorial hall dedicated to the founder, Ryusaku Shinkawa. ●1-8-10 Komagata, Taito City.

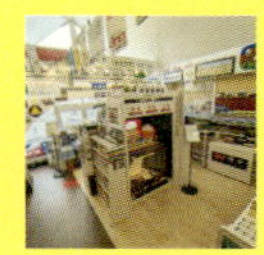

Tetsu-Tetsu Timetable Museum Some 900 timetables from Taisho-era to present, packed into one room along with other railroad goods. Even includes mock train platform. Privately run by railroad-crazy director. Admission: ¥3,000 for 45 min. More per minute than Disneyland, but director's warm hospitality is well worth it. ●5-23-11 Nakano, Nakano City.

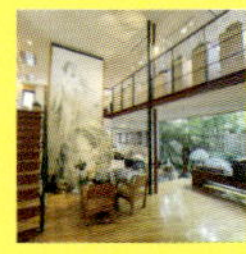

Jade Ore Museum With over 100 jadeite stones on display, you won't find a quirkier museum anywhere in the world. The spacious glass-walled atrium overwhelms with its vast array of jadeite stones, huge mosaic art, and jadeite stone bath carved from a giant boulder. ●4-5-12 Kita-Shinagawa, Shinagawa City.

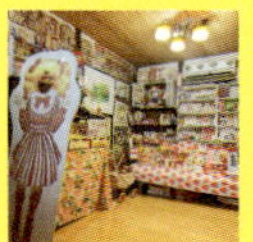

Candy Candy Museum Upstairs in a Showa-retro café, there's a wall full of anime ***Candy Candy*** goods that'll bowl you over. This private museum is run by Candy H. Milky, who's also a renowned fan of cross-dressing. Candy's love for chatting adds to the charm. ●7-4-11 Shibamata, Katsushika City, Showa Retro Kissa Sepia.

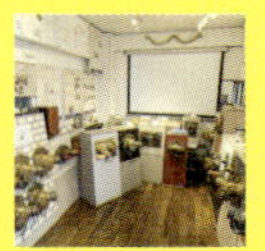

Sosuiko Museum The 5th floor of a building in Shimbashi is home to a niche museum full of water supply outlets. The deep world of water supply outlets—often seen but usually ignored. How about stopping by and letting director Yoshikazu Murakami tell you about their charms? ●2-11-1 Shimbashi, Minato City, 5F.

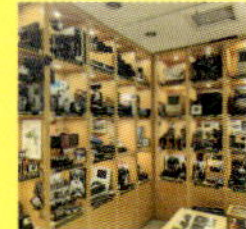

Extinct Media Museum A private museum displaying 1,500 media devices that have vanished or are going to, based on the idea that "all media go extinct except paper and stone." Looking at and handling the exhibits lets you reconnect with once-used-and-then-discarded bits of yesteryear. ●2-3-3 Uchi-Kanda, Chiyoda City, 1F.

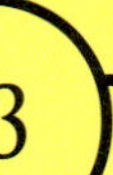

53 OUTDOOR ADS

Street Ads Reflect the Zeitgeist like a Mirror.

Seiya Kato ●Editor-in-Chief of Bizpa "Adcro"

After working in sales at a food manufacturer, Seiya Kato joined Bizpa in 2019. He handles content planning and production for the advertising and marketing media "Adcro."

Amid the hustle and bustle of Tokyo, I continue to search for "ads." Before I knew it, these "ad pilgrimages" of mine had entered their fifth year. From big screens at busy intersections to quiet signs in backstreets, my heart races at each new ad I find. What I value most is going there myself and verifying the ads with my own eyes. It's not just about taking photos, but also about finding out firsthand what kind of place the ads are in, and how people react to them. In trend hubs like Shibuya's scramble intersection, lots of ads feature hot-topic celebs. However, I also look at "what kinds of folks (fans) are showing interest." ...Maybe I derive joy from the very act of discovering something I didn't know. What I've come to realize as I've been doing this for five years is that ads differ enormously depending on where they are. For example, even though they have the same theme of "the wealthy," the Omotesando intersection with its brand ads and the Roppongi one with its flashy signs and ads for luxury items feel like different worlds. The spots I'm introducing here are ones my "ad pilgrimage" takes me to a lot, and some of my favorites. Ads aren't just promotional tools: they also serve as mirrors that reflect the city's "now." If you get a chance to stroll around the city, admire its ads as an integral part of its landscape.

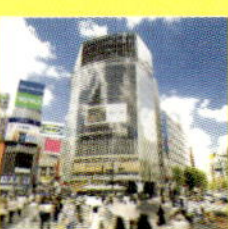

Shibuya scramble intersection This is an essential spot for my "ad pilgrimages." With all its large screens, billboards, flags, and advertisement trucks, it's a veritable advertising theme park. It's characterized by ads that reflect the latest trends, and there are new ones to discover every time you go there.

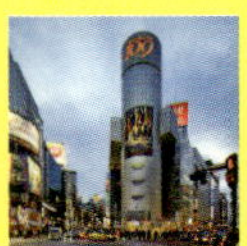

Intersection in front of SHIBUYA109's Shibuya Store This intersection is a must for staying up on the latest trends. In particular, the ads on the iconic 109 cylinder often feature trending celebs, reflecting what's "now" and making it a key spot. The spot offers a different vibe from the one in front of Shibuya Station.

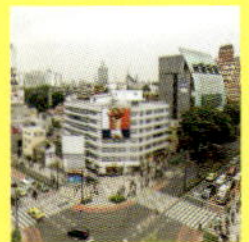

Omotesando intersection An area with lots of ads for high-end brands. This spot is surrounded by ads, and has a unique atmosphere thanks to the particularly high number of building signboards, which are presumably aimed at drivers. Luxury cars are often seen driving around. Recently, ads using box-shaped signage for 3D effects have also been appearing.

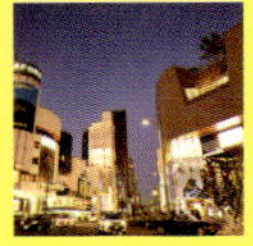

Jingumae intersection The ad trend here is like a blend of Omotesando and Shibuya. It's a place where there are more young people there for sightseeing and fun than folks there for business, so ads focusing on culture and fashion are a conspicuous presence. Impressive contents that simultaneously convey trendiness and luxury. Enjoy ads with a distinct flair.

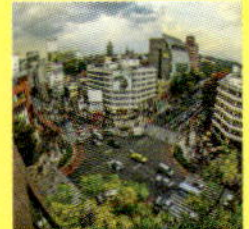

Near the Jingumae 5 intersection One block in from the Jingumae 5 intersection, there's a street lined with a whole host of "utility pole" ads. Its downtown vibe is completely different from Omotesando's boutiques and brand stores. The ads don't change often, but they still draw me there.

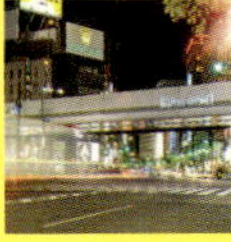

Roppongi intersection An area with lots of ads targeting affluent people. It's characterized by having lots of ads geared toward the vibe of the town, with ones to do with luxury goods, asset management, and investments standing out. The area has a bubble-era flashiness, with lots of cosmetic surgery and FX ads. They reflect the trends of their times.

Photos: iStock (53)

54 VISTA SPOTS

"Experience the City" from Train Viewing Spots.

Hiro Kaneda ●Observation deck maniac

Has visited over 400 observation towers and the like nationwide, and appeared on ***Matsuko no Shiranai Sekai***. Books include ***The Complete Guide to Observation Towers in Japan***.

Vista spots abound in Tokyo, notable ones being Tokyo Tower and TOKYO SKYTREE®. Enjoying views of beautiful streets, bustling crowds, and changing skies is delightful, but what truly stands out in Tokyo's scenery is the powerful trains running through the city. Here are some free train viewing spots near stations that are especially recommended for family outings. Watching Tokyo's streets from cultural spots will teach you more about them.

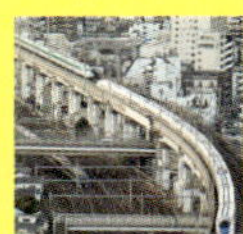

HOKUTOPIA A cultural complex in Kita City, Tokyo. From the free 17th floor observation lobby, enjoy cityscapes that feature TOKYO SKYTREE®, and also watch the Tohoku Shinkansen, limited express trains, freight trains, the Asukayama Park Monorail, and more. One of Japan's top train viewing spots with stunning views. ●1-11-1 Oji, Kita City.

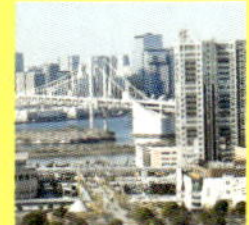

TOKYO PORT MUSEUM Offers great views plus the history and role of Tokyo Port and Tokyo Waterfront city. Also affords wonderful Odaiba views, with Rainbow Bridge and Tokyo Tower beyond New Transit "Yurikamome." Another highlight is watching the boats and planes around Tokyo Port, which add variety beyond trains. ●2-4-24 Aomi, Koto City, Aomi Frontier Bldg. 20F.

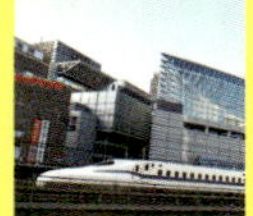

Tokyo Kotsu Kaikan 3F rooftop garden "Yurakucho Coline" A viewing spot for the relatively slower Tokaido Shinkansen, with elevated tracks nearby. Benches are also provided, making it a great spot to take a break. It's fun to watch people passing in front of Yurakucho Station from above. ●2-10-1 Yurakucho, Chiyoda City.

55 OLD BUILDINGS

Mosaic Art Adorning Showa-Era Buildings.

Nobuko Suzuki ●Writer

Former ***Tokyojin*** magazine deputy editor Nobuko Suzuki is currently writing about town walks and architecture. Her books include ***Vintage Buildings*** and ***Solo Tokyo Walks for Grown-Ups***.

Buildings from the high-growth era (the mid-1950s to mid-1970s) are now over half a century old and treasured as historic. Designs and decorations that reflected the styles of their times and materials that were once cutting-edge now feel unexpectedly fresh today. In particular, the many marble mosaic and tile murals that were created to add color and charm to edifices of steel and concrete are attractive highlights of these retro buildings.

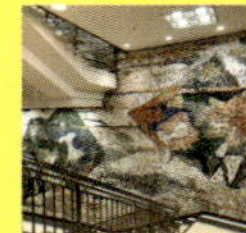

Tokyo Kotsu Kaikan Built in 1965. Rokuro Yabashi's marble mosaic murals span the stairwell wall from the first floor to the third. Yabashi also ran a family construction stone company, and created many mosaic works in Tokyo and across Japan. Seven of his works can still be seen in Yurakucho, Hibiya, and Marunouchi alone. ●2-10-1 Yurakucho, Chiyoda City.

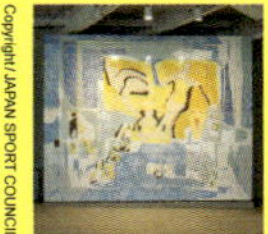

Murals at the Japan National Stadium Murals from the 1964 Olympics were relocated and preserved inside the new Japan National Stadium built for the 2021 Tokyo Olympics. They were created based on works by artists active at the time—Kazu Wakita, Saburo Miyamoto, and Shosuke Osawa. You can still feel the spirit of the 1960s in these works even today. ●10-1 Kasumigaoka-Machi, Shinjuku City.

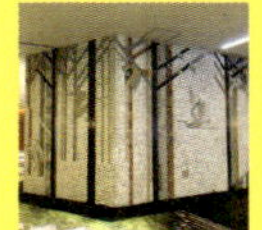

Hotel New Otani Tokyo The Main A luxury hotel opened for the Olympic Games tokyo 1964 to accommodate tourists come for the games. The lobby features a mural of a crane—a symbol of Japanese culture and good fortune. This mural is one of the few parts of the original interior remaining. ●4-1 Kioicho, Chiyoda City.

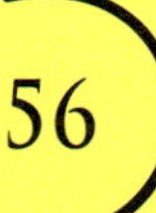

56 VINTAGE SHOP TREASURE HUNTS

Shops That Convey Their Owners' Character.

Daisuke Takashima ●Owner of the thrift shop ***FUNagain***

Daisuke Takashima opened furniture and miscellaneous thrift shop ***FUNagain*** in Sendagi in 2020. He also does styling work for hotels and private homes.

I believe a shop owner's keen eye for detail is synonymous with good shop direction. And visiting a well-directed shop motivates me to "work harder." Prices often depend on supply and demand, but shops that create value for items with no demand face less competition, so they're all the stronger. That's only possible if their character is well established. The following three shops are like mentors to me. Each visit greatly broadens my perspective.

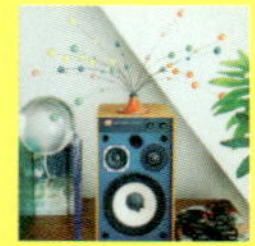

Ditty Tools. Deals in '80s goods, with lots of corporate-logo items and products of various styles. This is a shop that catches and highlights the charm of items that would otherwise be overlooked. Its non-nostalgic modern look is also great. The colorful objects change form depending on where they're placed. ●1-27-1 Komaba, Meguro City.

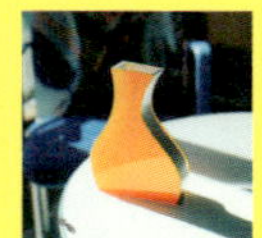

interior subtonez A shop made up of items the owner likes, whether they're well-known or not. It proposes new uses that are different from the original ones, teaching us the concept of "reimagining." A highlight is the '90s German acrylic vase with sharp edges that distort the traditional vase shape. ●4-1-1 Meguro-Honcho, Meguro City, Room C.

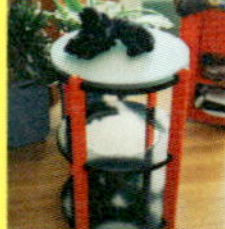

Graphio/büro-stil With 25 years of experience, this store's keen eye shapes a unique selection that focuses on products that are yet to be widely valued. The display stand was probably made in the 1980s, and has a richness simply because its role isn't clearly defined. ●2-32-7 Uehara, Shibuya City.

57 STREET GARDENING

Street Gardens on "Repurposed-Pot Streets."

Ayako Murata ●Street gardening enthusiast

Loves energetic plants on the street outside homes. Books: ***Looking at Fun Street Gardening*** and ***Overflowing Green: Twilight Street Gardening.*** Currently appearing on the show ***Love Botanical***.

In Tokyo's downtown areas, potted plants outside homes and shops are a delight for passersby. Sometimes, the plants are spilling out of their pots into cracks and gaps around them. "Street gardening" is all about enjoying the dynamics of plants placed out on the street. It makes me feel the rhythms of daily life and seasonal changes in the neighborhood. Particularly fun are containers reused as plant pots. Secretly studying them reveals their owners' lives, and makes Tokyo feel a little closer.

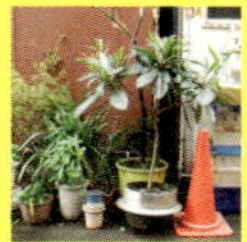

Tsukishima Monja Street One of Tokyo's famous culinary specialties—monjayaki. Residents carefully tend potted plants along Nishinaka-dori Avenue Shopping Street, a.k.a. ***Monja Street***. Lush greenery and a vibrant atmosphere. A treasure trove of repurposed pots: cup noodle containers, cooking pots, and even cookers. ●From 1 to 3 Tsukishima, Chuo City.

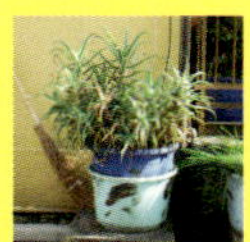

Fukagawa Edo Museum Street Fukagawa, home to many temples and shrines. Canals that supported Edo's logistics run everywhere. The street where ***Fukagawa Edo Museum*** is located is lined with shops that are full of downtown charm. Blue plastic barrels stand out among local tsukudani and Fukagawa cuisine shops. ●From 1 to 4 Miyoshi and from 1 to 4 Shirakawa, Koto City.

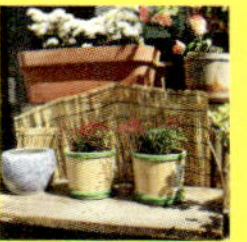

Yomise Shopping Street Now enclosed in a culvert, the Aizome River once ran from Komagome Somei to Shinobazu Pond. Street name comes from night stalls. Flowers brighten distinctive shop entrances. Unique repurposed pots line the street. Biwabashi Bridge Ruin, Snake Street, etc. tell of rivers past. ●Along the boundary between 3 Boundary of Sendagi, Bunkyo City and 3 Yanaka, Taito City.

58 BONFIRES

Fascinated by Camping's Highlight: Bonfires.

Bears Shimada Camp ●Outdoor cooking researcher

Bears Shimada Camp develops recipes while camping, mainly solo. His books include ***Bears Shimada Camp's Easy Eats***.

Bonfires are said to have a variety of benefits. These include calming effects, boosting communication, and relieving stress. They also provide warmth, light, and the joy of "outdoor cooking"—which is the true charm of camping. Captivated by these many benefits of bonfires, I go camping around 100 days a year, and enjoy their charm to the full. Here, I share with you some of my recommended bonfire spots, whose like you'll only find in Tokyo.

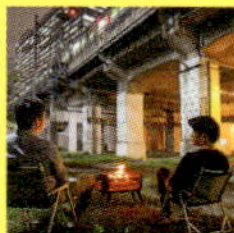

Camp practice site campass A camp practice site under the Yamanote Line's Akihabara Station. Located under elevated tracks, so you can camp there even in the rain. Get to enjoy bonfires and buildings' neon lights at the same time. A spot with a uniquely urban charm not found at typical campsites. ●4-9 Akihabara, Taito City.

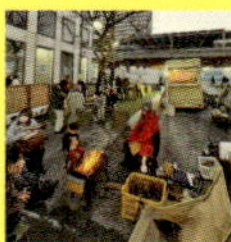

Higashi-Murayama Station Square A bonfire event is held irregularly here as a pilot project for developing Higashi-Murayama Station Square. It's based on the concept of "enjoying a bonfire casually on the way home," and has been held twice so far. In the future, maybe a permanent bonfire spot will be set up as a new, casual urban hangout. ●2-3-32 Honcho, Higashi-Murayama City.

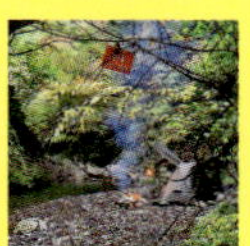

MOKKI NO MORI A members-only campsite in Hinohara Village, run by a forestry company. Camping here is basically without electricity or gas. Collect fallen firewood, light a bonfire, and enjoy a quiet time in the woods—a spot for feeling nature just as it is. Events that utilize the land are also held. ●654 Motoshuku, Hinohara Village, Nishi-Tama County.

59 WATER TOWERS

Extraordinary Symbols of Housing Complexes.

UC ●Company employee

UC claims to be the leader of the ***Japan Water Tower Party***, and writes for the coterie magazine ***Housing Complex Book***. X: @watertowerUC

Water towers are structures built to pump water into a large tank at the top and deliver it using gravity. They're most familiar in housing complexes, but also found at stations, factories, and the like. Colorful and uniquely shaped, they're veritable symbols of housing complexes, standing out with an extraordinary presence among their often monotonous, uniform buildings. Being off-limits like observation towers adds mystery. They're declining due to rebuilding and tech, so they're worth appreciating properly while you can.

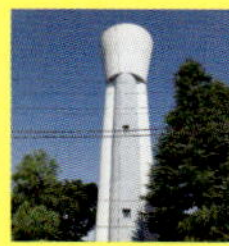

Tokyo Metropolitan Housing Supply Corporation, Soshigaya Housing Complex Built in 1955-56, this one stands north of Soshigaya-Okura Station along the shopping street. For the corporation's first water tower, its design with a bulge in the middle is exquisite and unique. ●2-5 Soshigaya, Setagaya City.

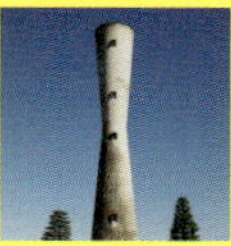

Tokyo Metropolitan Housing Supply Corporation, Tamagawa Housing Complex Four nearly identical towers in a huge complex of some 4,000 units in Komae and Chofu Cities. Photo: one near Building I (Komae City side). Appeared in many video works, including ***Ultraman*** and the video for BUMP OF CHICKEN's "Stargazing." ●1-5 Nishi-Izumi, Komae City.

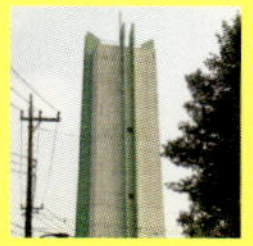

Tokyo Metropolitan Government Bureau of Waterworks, Atago Water Distribution Center This one with striking pale green lines is by Atago 2 Housing Complex. On water bureau land, but looks just like a housing complex one. There's one like it behind heroine Shizuku Tsukishima's housing complex in Ghibli's ***Whisper of the Heart***. ●2-51 Atago, Tama City.

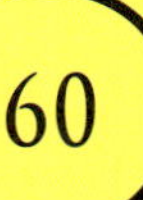

60 SLOPES

Slopes Are Journeys Beyond Time and Space.

Kota Sawamura ●Slope maniac

Kota Sawamura runs a site that rates slopes across Tokyo, Osaka, Nagasaki, and more using four Michelin-style criteria: gradient, length, history, and beauty.

When asked what they think of slopes, most people say "tiring." Even I used to think so, too. The slope I took to and from high school was pure hardship. But then, a topographical map of Tokyo changed my view. Though covered over with asphalt, the land beneath us has a fjord-like terrain, with a change in elevation of nearly 40 m from west to east within the sphere of the Yamanote Line. Slopes are just ways to move up and down, but thinking about the topography and residents around them turns them into journeys that go beyond time and space.

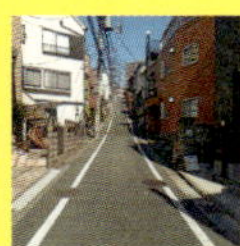

Fujimizaka A beautiful slope in Takada, Toshima City. The top used to offer a view of Mt. Fuji, but buildings block it now. The "atrium-like" U-shaped view of the sky from the top is blocked by condos. It also featured in Mamoru Hosoda's movie ***The Girl Who Leapt Through Time***. Nearby is "Nozokizaka," which is also a famously steep slope. ●Near 1-23-18 Takada, Toshima City.

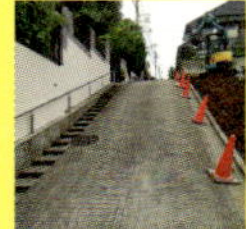

Slope with a 28% gradient sign in Sayama Hills A slope by Lake Tama, this is one of the steepest in Tokyo's suburbs. It climbs Sayama Hills (a remote-island-like hilly area on the Tokyo-Saitama border with Lakes Tama and Sayama within) from the south. Sometimes, cars get their front stuck on the way down and need to be rescued. ●Near 1-1004 Kohan, Higashi-Yamato City.

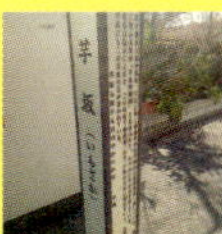

Imozaka A former slope near Nippori Station on the Yamanote Line, on the Arakawa-Taito border. Split by railway construction in the Meiji-era, it remains only in name in the "Imozaka Overpass." It was named after the wild yams (yamaimo) once harvested there. It appears along with dumplings in Natsume Soseki's ***I Am a Cat*** and a haiku by Masaoka Shiki. ●Near 7-11 Yanaka, Taito City.

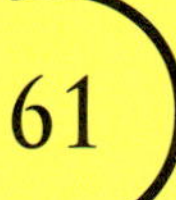

61 SHRINES

Blessed by "Beautiful Views" the Gods Behold.

Yuta Sasaki ●Modern-day shrine priest

Has visited over 15,000 shrines across Japan. Calls himself a "modern-day shrine priest," inspired by the Edo era ones. Actively involved in Shinto-related lectures and various media.

A shrine isn't a place for getting a wish granted, but for getting a message. That message comes after you've finished your visit, when you turn your back to the altar and feel the gods guiding you toward the view that unfolds before you. So, I really cherish the views seen from shrines. Tokyo is a bustling city, yet some shrines offer views that make you think, "The gods are beholding this beauty, too." This is either "despite being in Tokyo," or perhaps, "because it's Tokyo."

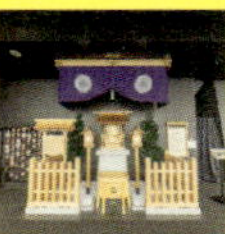

Tower Daijingu Shrine Established in 1977. Enshrines Amaterasu Omikami, invited from Ise Jingu Grand Shrine. The highest shrine in Tokyo's 23 cities, it's a place where you can pray while enjoying a panoramic view of the metropolis. A Tokyo-style shrine that overturns the traditional notions of what a shrine should be. ●4-2-8 Shiba Park, Minato City, Tokyo Tower Main Deck 2F.

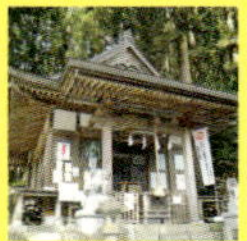

Kuzuryu Shrine A shrine in Hinohara Village—the only village in Tokyo apart from on the islands. It enshrines dragon god Kuzuryu Okami, and Ame-no-Tajikarao, who's said to have opened Ama-no-Iwato, the heavenly cave where Amaterasu had secluded herself. Beyond the shrine lies Kuzuryu Waterfall, offering refreshing air that's a rarity in Tokyo. ●7076 Kazuma, Hinohara Village, Nishi-Tama County.

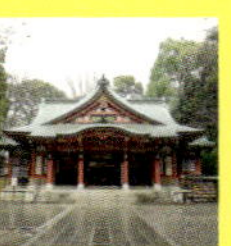

Setagaya-Hachiman Shrine The guardian of Setagaya, this shrine stands in expansive grounds thick with trees like a natural forest—not a man-made one, but one that grew over time (a rarity in Tokyo). Home to many small shrines, including Itsukushima Shrine (linked to the Year of the Snake). Be sure to visit them, too. ●1-26-3 Miyasaka, Setagaya City.

62 METROPOLITAN EXPRESSWAY

Unmissable *Kinuta Dental Clinic* Ads.

Soichi Shimizu ●Expressway maniac and car writer

Besides writing about cars, Soichi Shimizu is also an expressway maniac and traffic researcher, with ***Why Is the Metropolitan Expressway Always Jammed?*** among the books to his name.

The Metropolitan Expressway is the world's first urban expressway. Its design is reminiscent of Asian chaos—purely "Japan-original"—and driving on it offers a flight-like tour through the city center. The Expressway has many highlights, but here, let's focus on the billboards for ***Kinuta Dental Clinic***. The clinic spends ¥250 million a year on billboards like it's a hobby, and many of them are visible from the Expressway (especially on Shinjuku Route 4). Symbols of the Expressway, these billboards have hidden "features" that tickle fanatics' hearts.

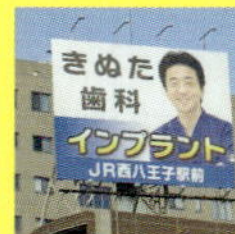

***Kinuta Dental Clinic* billboard, refined version** Near Shiba Park on the outer loop. Prime spot with views of TOKYO TOWER and Azabudai Hills. Right after that, this billboard appears. Their billboards basically show the director smiling eerily against a pink background, but this one's white-and-blue background looks refined. To suit the scenery? ●Near Higashi-Azabu, Minato City.

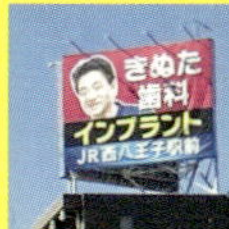

Kinuta Dental Clinic* vs. *ALBA Dental Clinic Shuto Expressway Route 4 is the clinic's billboard hub. Challenging its territory is up-and-coming billboard rival ALBA Dental Clinic. Near Shinjuku Route 4's Hatagaya Exit, ALBA is challenging Kinuta from right across the Expressway. The implant world's Godzilla vs. King Ghidorah? ●Near Sasazuka, Shibuya City.

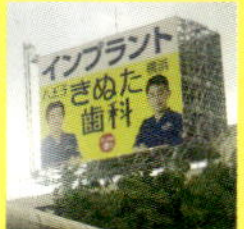

The Kinuta brothers' dream collaboration billboard Yokohama dental clinic director the elder Kinuta brother also puts up lots of billboards. Both brothers claim, "I was first." Sounds like bad blood, but then there's their dream collab one. The southbound Eifuku Exit on Route 4 is way too far from either clinic, though. ●Near Shimo-Takaido, Suginami City.

63 ZOOS

Casual Trips to Small Zoos and Aquariums.

Hirotaka Nozaki ●Video director and scriptwriter

Used to work in a company, but now creates music videos, films, dramas, etc. freelance. Also an illustrator—picture book ***Anteater*** out now. Often goes to zoos and aquariums.

Going to large zoos and aquariums first thing in the morning is great, too, but some might hesitate to do it. In that case, it might be a good idea to "drop by" while doing something else. One day, "dropping by" might become the main event. The three spots here are small but offer lots of learning and discoveries through various creatures. Why not drop by casually—after school, before or after work or shopping, or even for a nap break?

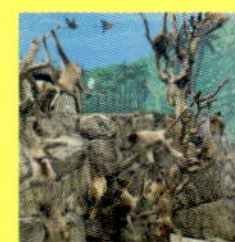

Edogawa Natural Zoo This zoo is home to sea lions, Humboldt penguins, endangered lesser pandas, giant anteaters, and two species of spider monkeys, which you get to see in groups. Nishikasai has lots of Indian restaurants, so I recommend eating there first, then hitting the zoo after. ●3-2-1 Kita-Kasai, Edogawa City, inside Gyosen Park.

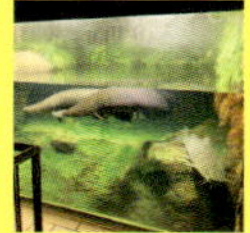

Adachi Park of Living Things Indoor park of living things with a giant goldfish tank at the entrance. Only place in Tokyo to see the newly arrived gundi. Compact, yet combines insect house, aquarium, zoo, and botanical garden elements. The tanks with pirarucu and jau are impressive. Relax like a catfish while you watch them. ●2-17-1 Hokima, Adachi City.

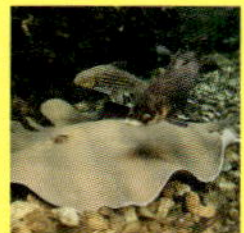

Itabashi Botanical Garden The name suggests plants only, but don't worry, there are other things, too. The largest tank holds a specimen of the world's largest freshwater stingray, ***Himantura chaophraya*** (whose name is Chao—acrylic stands available). Its size will truly amaze you. The café offers a "Funny Curry." ●8-29-2 Takashimadaira, Itabashi City.

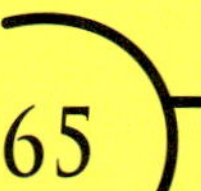

64 COMIC FOREGROUNDS

Hooked on Comic Foregrounds.

Tomoyuki Shioya ●Comic foreground enthusiast

Has stuck his face in 5,000 comic foregrounds. ***100 Comic Foreground Views*** currently being published as a series. A new look at comic foregrounds nationwide. X: @shioya20

Fascinated by comic foregrounds, I kept trying challenging situations and poses, and ended up loving them. Their simple design means anyone can easily try them, but for grown-ups, embarrassment and body size are barriers. However, when you overcome all that and just stick your face in, there's nothing like it. Comic foregrounds are also popping up at various events, making Tokyo a major hub for them. In the midst of the city's bustle, the very act itself is a challenge, but I'm going to keep taking on ever tougher comic foregrounds.

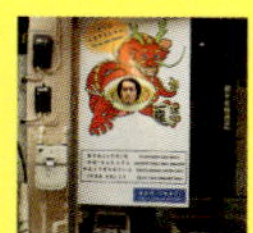

Mendokoro Ichiryu, Nakamise Store Popular beef bone ramen. Comic foreground picture is a ramen bowl. Noteworthy location: behind Nakamise Shopping Street, near Asakusa Kaminarimon—busy, with lots of tourists. Conquering the embarrassment and not caring if people stare, that's the trick. Choose a crowded weekend to be a true master. ●2-2-4 Asakusa, Taito City.

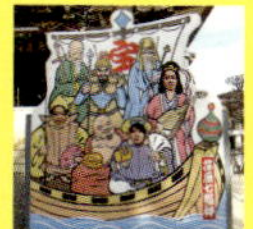

Horenji Temple A Nichiren Shu temple that's dedicated to Ebisu, one of the Ebara Seven Lucky Gods. It has a comic foreground depicting them. You can do it only from January 1 to 7 each year, so it's rare and tough. Getting a face in all three holes in this limited-period panel brings a special sense of achievement. ●3-6-18 Hatanodai, Shinagawa City.

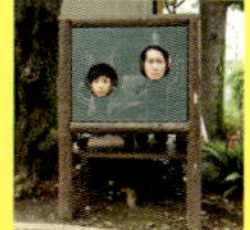

Ebisu Doronkoyama Play Park A comic foreground inside Ebisu-Minami-Ichi Park, which is a free play area for children. Standing on the platform makes the holes feel low, but sit on it with your feet under the board and the height's just right. Noticing the designer's intentions gives even greater satisfaction. ●1-26-1 Ebisu-Minami, Shibuya City.

65 WILD HERB WATCHING

Barometers of Urban Regreening.

Yuki Maeda ●Florist

Yuki Maeda worked at a TV station for 10 years, then went to study in the UK in 2013. She launched the flower brand ***gui*** in fall 2018 and opened ***NUR*** in Jingumae in April 2021.

"Aim to restore a nature-rich environment, starting with Tokyo." That might sound like a platitude, but to me, it's an achievable future. Here are three places where you can feel the cutting-edge of that spirit. Well worth a look is ***kaname no mori***, an organic spot where trees and wild plants grow vigorously on rainwater alone, with no irrigation. Where wild plants thrive, insects gather, birds come, and the cycle of life goes on. How about thinking about the future of environmental regeneration starting with some familiar wild herb spots?

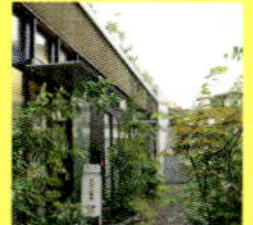

kaname no mori Created to serve as a "keystone" for environmental regeneration. Impressive exterior was made with no artificial materials, just organic and natural ones. The site has broadleaf trees like jolcham oaks and sawtooth oaks, there are pleasant fallen leaves underfoot, and various creatures visit it. A place where you can feel the future of Tokyo. ●3 Ebara, Shinagawa City.

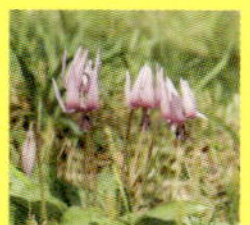

Institute for Nature Study Vast grounds nurturing a rich ecosystem: a forest, pond, wetland, and trail. Large trees, plus butterbur and witch hazel in early spring, dogtooth violets and akebi in high spring, then wild lilies, liriope, hosta, and loosestrife from early summer. ●5-21-5 Shirokanedai, Minato City.

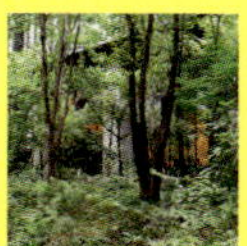

Otemachi Forest Despite being in Tokyo's business district, this place has natural, uneven terrain. When it was created, 117 plant species were planted here. By 2021, that number had increased to 208. Even rare species on the Red List (i.e., ones facing extinction) apparently appear. They say raccoon dogs come by occasionally, too. ●1-5-5 Otemachi, Chiyoda City.

66 GREENHOUSES

A Greenhouse to Settle In.

Chikako Miyauchi ●Botanical garden staff

Previously SHIBUYA CITY BOTANICAL GARDEN FUREAI's director. Now works at Mito Botanical Park. Hobby: touring botanical gardens in Japan and abroad like she's house hunting.

Since third grade in elementary school, I've been obsessed with "wanting to live in a greenhouse." A majestic one made of glass and steel and full of exotic plants. One where it's warm all year round, tropical fruits ripen, fish swim in ponds, and useful plants grow lush. Above all, one that's full of fresh oxygen. In a greenhouse like that, I think I could survive even if the world ended. I want to live in one like that! No, I want to go back to the wild and settle in it! I hope you visit the greenhouses I'm sharing here with that desire in mind, too.

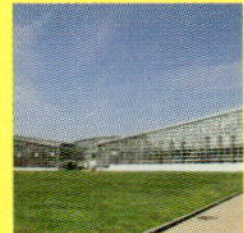

Jindai Botanical Park Spacious, one-story greenhouse. Perfect for "What would it be like to live here?" Each room differs in temperature and humidity, recreating each country. Air-conditioned begonia room is comfy even on hot days. Tropical water lily and arid plant rooms ease winter's cold. ●5-31-10 Jindaiji-Motomachi, Chofu City.

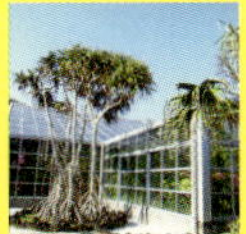

Hachijo Botanical Park Lower ceiling than mainland greenhouses, to withstand typhoons. Nevertheless, trees like papaya and mango stretch their branches high inside, and the cacao trees sometimes bear so many pods that you'll wonder, "Is that too much?" So, it's a hidden island paradise for chocolate lovers. ●2843 Okago, Hachijo Town, Hachijojima.

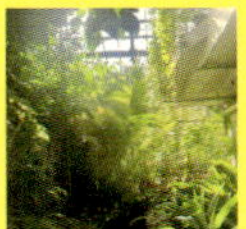

Medicinal Plant Garden, Showa Pharmaceutical University Compact, but full of medicinal trees and plants everywhere you look. Ferns grow on the stone wall on 1F, forming a stunning green curtain. Want wallpaper like this myself. On a university campus, so always check the opening days and hours in advance. ●3-2-1 Higashi-Tamagawa-Gakuen, Machida City.

67 SCENERY FROM TRAINS

Here Is the Origin of "Train Watching."

Masahiro Yoshikawa ●Comedian

Masahiro Yoshikawa is the funny man of the comedy duo ***Darling Honey***. He's a huge train fan, and actively appears on variety shows and writes columns about them.

I got hooked on trains after watching them from a bridge in Tokyo when I was around two. I was overwhelmed by the "number," "variety," and "aura" of the trains passing by. I went on to become a nationwide "train rider," but my roots are in "train watching." Tokyo has countless train-viewing spots that always satisfy my love of them. I like the slow-paced local lines, but the complex and busy Tokyo railroads are more my thing. Most of all, they bring back the thrill I felt as a child. I'll go on loving trains one-sidedly. Maniac mode engaged!

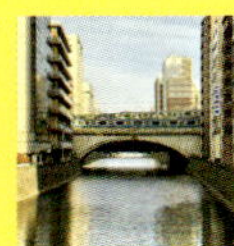

Mansei Bridge Bridge linking Akihabara Electric Town and Kanda. Surrounded by tracks on all sides. Shows sheer number of trains in Tokyo. Can see Chuo, Sobu, Yamanote, and Keihin-Tohoku Lines, and Ginza Line runs below. Plus some Tokyo history: Chuo Line once had a "Manseibashi Station." View of trains from former site of that is also superb ●1-2 Sotokanda, Chiyoda City.

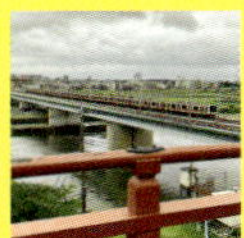

Tamagawa Sengen Shrine Atop an ancient burial mound—a rarity. See trains crossing the Tamagawa River from the observation deck. Train-lovers' highlight: the variety. Tokyo is famous for mutual through-services, and the shrine shows trains from eight companies. Fun game: "guess which company's train will come next." ●1-55-12 Denenchofu, Ota City.

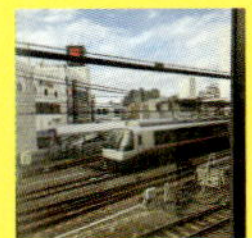

Tully's Coffee, Odakyu Marche Machida Store It's a store in the ***Tully's Coffee*** chain, but the trains run very close by. The sleek forms of Romancecars seen from there will utterly captivate you. A perfect spot for enjoying the beauty of trains' designs while reflecting on "Tokyo and tourism." ●6-1-1 Haramachida, Machida City, Odakyu Marche Machida 2F.

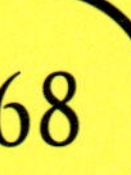

68 BATTING CAGE CENTERS

Casually Hit Some Baseballs Every Day.

Carlos Yabuki ●Writer

Popular culture specialist Carlos Yabuki's many books include ***Thoughts on Japan's Batting Cage Centers***. He became an ambassador for Oisix Niigata Albirex BC this year.

The image that many people have of batting cage centers is that they tend to appear suddenly and boldly along highways. While it's true that lots of them are like that, Japan's first one actually opened on the roof of the ***Rakutenchi Building*** in Kinshicho, in 1965. A batting cage center used to be somewhere you could just drop by on a whim in the heart of the city. It's perfectly fine to go in a suit or in sandals. Swing the bat whenever and however you like.

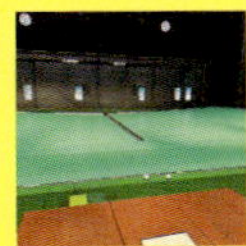

Ikebukuro Batting Center Now a rarity, this batting cage center is on a building roof, and is open all year round until 11:00 p.m. The building also houses Grand Cinema Sunshine Ikebukuro, home to Japan's largest movie screen. After a movie, go slug some baseballs back into the night sky. ●1-30-3 Higashi-Ikebukuro, Toshima City, grandscape Ikebukuro 14F.

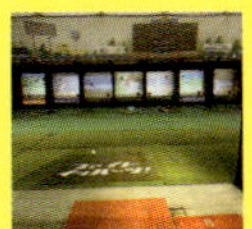

Jingu Batting Dome Fully indoor center inside Meiji Jingu Gaien. Has a batting cage where the balls come out in sync with footage of pros, letting you feel like one, too. Also has a strikeout game—great for practicing pitching. It's also perfect for warming up before amateur baseball games at the adjacent softball field. ●2-1 Kasumigaoka-Machi, Shinjuku City.

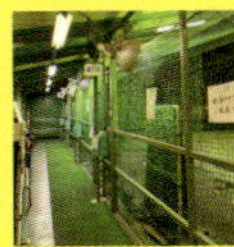

Waseda Auto Tennis Plaza Here, you can enjoy not only batting but auto tennis as well. Designed to suit women, this activity shoots tennis balls from a hole in the wall for you to whack with your racket. Though rare in Japan as a whole, it's a thriving entertainment in Tokyo's student districts. ●1-13-4 Nishi-Waseda, Shinjuku City.

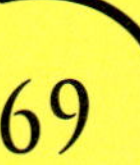

69 BOWLING GEAR

Boosting the Bowling Community.

Yoshihito Zaitsu ●Representative of ***Sasazuka Bowl***

Yoshihito Zaitsu is CEO of Keiokosan Inc., which runs the ***Sasazuka Bowl*** bowling alley, founded in 1973. It runs it with the motto of creating a wellness-focused society through bowling.

A long-running bowling alley that was founded in 1973. They have a signboard that says "long-running," but they don't stick to tradition. Instead, they aim to create a place where people of all ages can connect and smile together through bowling. They believe "true fun" comes from getting pros, shops, and the community involved. Here, I introduce some top spots that are energizing the bowling community—something that's essential for me as a bowling alley owner.

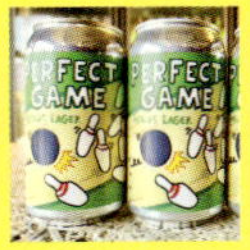

Manchin Liquor Store / MANGOSTEEN A liquor store with a standing bar that also supplies alcohol to ***Sasazuka Bowl***. They always recommend tasty mezcal. The signature Amaras Verde Mezcal is the most popular at the bowling alley. Have a collaboration beer developed for bowling while eating pizza, and enjoy a refreshing strike! ●4-29-14 Daizawa, Setagaya City, 1F.

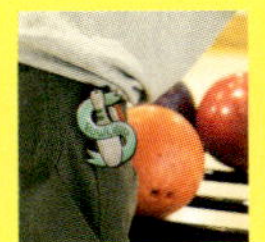

BLUE LUG Hatagaya A bicycle shop a 5-minute walk from ***Sasazuka Bowl***. The bicycles and parts from around the world are fun to see, and the neighborhood's working folk all want to commute on a BLUE LUG bike. The reflectors made in two collaborations with Sasazuka Bowl will look great on either your bicycle or your bowling bag. ●2-32-3 Hatagaya, Shibuya City.

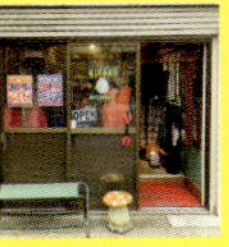

Kiraku A slightly unusual secondhand clothing store in Daitabashi. Sells American casual secondhand clothes and cool bowling goods that the owner bought from the US. At least five bowling-style shirts are always in stock. These clothes are good not only for bowling but as everyday wear as well. ●2-26-5 Ohara, Setagaya City.

70

SPECIAL SENTO

Feel the Extraordinary and Relax Your Body and Mind.

Tsukasa Shimokitazawa ●Sento guide meister certified by the Tokyo Sento Association

Tsukasa Shimokitazawa is a sento maniac who's been to over 3,500 public baths nationwide. He hosts the new sento culture event ***Tokyo Sento Night***.

Working in the city tends to make people settle into a routine where every day feels the same. Many want unusual experiences but, since travel takes time and money, they end up spending every day the same way. However, even in the city, there are affordable spots that offer an easy taste of the extraordinary. To wit, sento. Though their number has declined, there are still over 400 of them in Tokyo alone. They come in many styles, from retro Showa-era temple-like ones to ultra-modern stylish ones. The facilities in them now vary widely: some sento have trendy saunas and cold baths, while others offer natural hot springs, and medicinal, jet, electric (!), and open-air baths. Classic sento still have signature Mt. Fuji murals, verandas, and carp ponds. Some people might be worried about getting naked in an unknown sento or getting complaints from regulars, but following the posted rules means everyone can have a relaxing time regardless of age or gender. Even when the place is busy, you can still enjoy feeling "alone and naked" without disturbing anyone else. Soaking in a sento lets you escape from the everyday and feel your body really relax. Once you've been to one, it'll feel natural the next time, and being freed from the day-to-day could make your life deeper and richer.

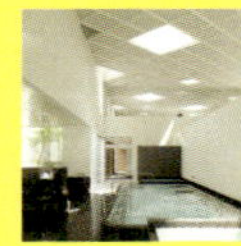

Hisamatsu-yu This place looks like a wonderful modern art museum—so much so that you'd never even guess it's a sento from outside. The clean bathroom features projection mapping visuals. Well-equipped with a strong saline open-air bath, sauna, cold bath, lukewarm carbonated spring, and electric bath. A satisfying sento I can recommend to anyone. ●4-32-15 Sakuradai, Nerima City.

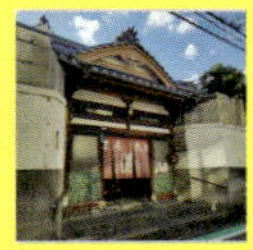

Teikoku-yu Prewar sento for rather hardcore fans. Name roughly means "Imperial," and it greets you with a dignified curtain. Plus a Showa time slip. Classic Mt. Fuji mural and carp tile art. Simple bath-only sento, but the water is as hot as you'd expect. Immerse yourself in the extraordinary. Also has a lukewarm herbal bath. ●3-22-3 Higashi-Nippori, Arakawa City.

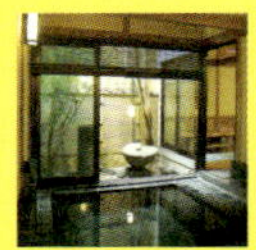

Tatsumi-yu Plain on the outside, but a somehow mysterious space. The tile mural also depicts a surreal landscape. Sauna, cold bath, and more. There's a large open-air bath, and beyond that, a hidden retreat—a spacious lounge filled with a vast manga library. Perfect for relaxing and easing away your fatigue. ●1-2-3 Miyoshi, Koto City.

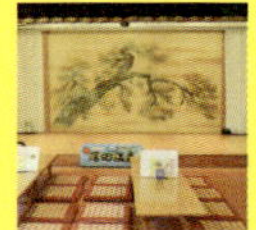

Kamata Onsen Full of Showa charm, this sento offers pitch-black natural alkaline hot water that smooths your skin. It has cold and hot baths, the latter being for maniacs. Has a sauna and cold bath. Open from 10:00 a.m. The 2nd floor is a nostalgic large banquet hall where even strangers bond over karaoke on the stage. ●2-23-2 Kamata-Honcho, Ota City.

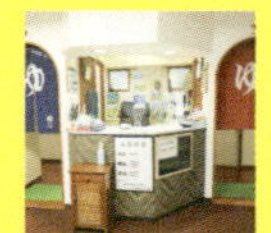

Tsukimi-yu A popular, clean sento loved by many locals. Relax in the lukewarm natural hot spring bath while admiring the large Mt. Fuji painting. There's a 45°C hot bath for hardcore fans, and going back and forth between that and the cold one feels otherworldly and invigorating. The spacious sauna is also clean, and the veranda is a popular "chill-out zone." ●5-36-16 Akatsutsumi, Setagaya City.

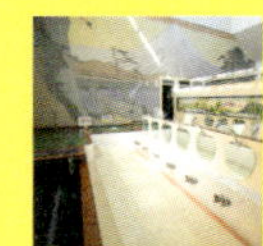

Showa Yokujyo It's a Showa-era sento, but its owner is a world-famous magician, and you can sometimes get to see pro magic there. The mural is a giant Mt. Fuji. The baths use smooth natural well water ranging from lukewarm to hot, and there's a cold bath as well. Open until 1:30 a.m., and has a sauna, too. ●5-21-12 Chuo, Nakano City.

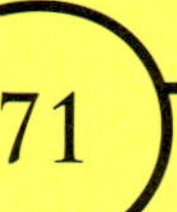

71

ELECTRIC BATHS

Touring Sento in Search of Electric Pleasure.

Kenchin ●Electric bath appraiser

Born in Osaka. Discovered the joy of electric baths in 2017. Has visited over 1,100 electric baths across Japan. Loves urban scenery, and housing complexes with shops on the first floor.

An electric bath is an amenity installed in a sento bathtub. It sends out a weak current from electrode plates, giving the bathers some electrical stimulus. I get the feeling many find them uncomfortable, though. There are two reasons for this. One is regional differences, the other is a lack of understanding of how to use them. Electric baths are more common in western than in eastern Japan. In Tokyo, about one in three public baths have them. In Osaka and Nagoya, that figure's 90%, and in Kyoto, it's 80%. In Kanto, the fewer chances to try one mean more people are uncomfortable about them. The key to using one very simple: keep your hands and feet away from the electrodes. Electricity flows through bones, so it's best to approach them thighs or hips first—i.e., parts with thicker layers of fat. Beginners should start with a mild current to get used to it. Once you get used to electric baths, soaking while pondering on the manufacturer adds to the fun. There are mainly two electric bath manufacturers in Japan: Konishi Denki in Osaka and Mizuno Tsushin Kogyo in Nagoya. Konishi's current feels like it hits you head-on, while Mizuno's feels like it melts into you. Konishi's electric baths are named "Pulse Massage" while Mizuno's are named "Jube." Being aware of the manufacturer lets you enjoy the current even more. I hope you check out my recommended sento with electric baths, and give them a try.

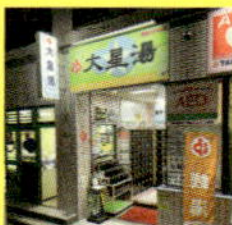

Taisei-yu Smooth well-water cold bath and relaxing lobby. Men's side has yacht-themed tiles and women's has Renoir-themed. Both very beautiful. Electric bath uses Konishi Denki's constant-current system, with a weak current from a long electrode plate. Very mild, so it's great for beginners. Has an AED that was carefully chosen by the owner. ●18-3 Ichigaya-Daimachi, Shinjuku City.

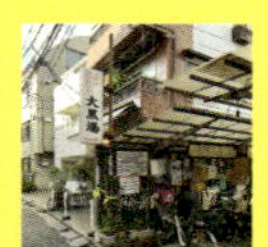

Daikoku-yu Entrance is lined with dozens of laundromat machines (a stark contrast to the upscale area). Electric bath uses Konishi Denki's constant-current system, and is in the mist sauna—surreal! Swapping between that and the spring-fed cold bath makes you all warm inside. Showa pop songs playing in the lobby and changing room are another plus. ●3-24-5 Nishihara, Shibuya City.

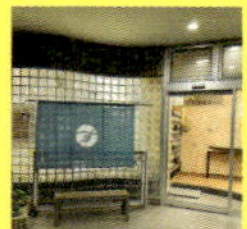

Suehiro-yu Distinctive octagonal washing area. Lie-down and microbubble baths, plus a relaxing craft-beer lobby. Electric bath uses Konishi Denki's constant-current system. Advice: stretch your legs out as you go between the electrodes. After three sets of swapping between the electric and cold baths, a cold drink is unbeatable. ●1-42-4 Oi, Shinagawa City.

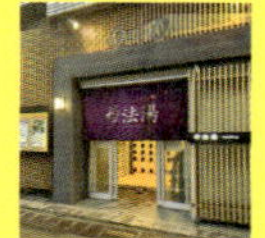

Myoho-yu A sento with lots of amenities and events carefully selected by the owner. The soft, carbonated silky bath warms you deep inside. The electric bath uses Konishi Denki's pulse massage system. It has Mizuno Tsushin Kogyo black electrodes—a puzzle, since it looks like a "Jube," but the electrodes don't match the brand. ●4-32-4 Nishi-Ikebukuro, Toshima City.

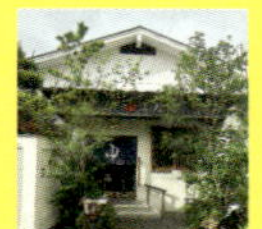

Yoshino-yu (Hirai) A sento with a wonderful veranda overlooking the courtyard in the lobby. The relaxing lobby time after the baths feels like a hot spring inn. The electric bath is a Mizuno Tsushin Kogyo "Jube." The massage currents push, knead, and tap your body—after which the cold bath feels good beyond words. ●4-23-2 Hirai, Edogawa City.

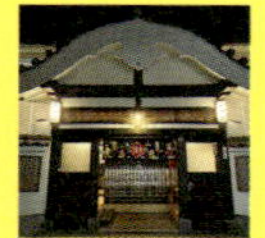

Tenjin-yu Enjoy a classic sento atmosphere with a Mt. Fuji painting and mosaic tiles. No sauna, but alternating between hot and cold baths is great. An electric bath was installed during renovations. It's a Mizuno Tsushin Kogyo "Jube" massage type. Enjoy pushing, kneading, and tapping courtesy of rhythmic currents. ●5-10-10 Nakano, Nakano City.

72 CULVERTS

New Landscapes for Experiencing "Evidence of Water."

Ankyo Maniacs ●Culvert enthusiasts

Ankyo Maniacs is a unit consisting of culvert enthusiasts Nama Yoshimura and Hideo Takayama. Their coauthored books include ***Culvert Maniacs! Expanded Edition*** and ***Culvert Paradise!***.

A culvert ("ankyo" in Japanese) is where a flow of water that had originally been a river or water channel has been moved underground. Here, we'll interpret culverts in a broad sense, and also include old river and water channel remnants. Tokyo abounded in water until not long ago, with natural rivers and irrigation channels flowing throughout. Post-earthquake and postwar "urbanization" and rapid economic growth saw many of these disappear. But look closely, and you'll spot evidence everywhere—and see that Tokyo is now a city of culverts. Since culverts were once rivers, many places feel oddly wide, narrow, winding, or surrounded by bollards, creating small oddities that often make them feel like portals to another world. They give a sense of stepping outside the city's everyday world a little. That's also the charm of culverts. Plus, traces of former waterfronts can also be found in culverts. For example, "bridges." Bridges on waterless street corners. They're probably overlooked by most passersby, but are conclusive proof that there was once a river there. Finding a bridge with its railings intact is certainly exciting, but even just the base pillars, nameplate, or even the bridge's name at an intersection feels like a treasure hunt. Such treasures are hidden all over Tokyo. Knowing that water once flowed there makes the usual cityscape look a little different. Let's enjoy letting culverts make little changes like that within ourselves, too.

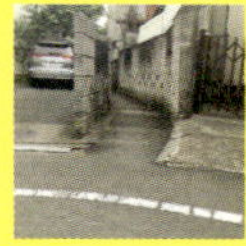

Otherworldly culvert 1 Walking through Asagaya-Kita, you'll suddenly find a culvert entrance around 1-21. Remnant of a branch of the Momozono River (which once flowed through rice fields). Like a maze inside. Verdant promenade nearby. Asagaya-Kita 1 is dotted with culvert entrances and quirky alleys. ●Near 1-21 Asagaya-Kita, Suginami City.

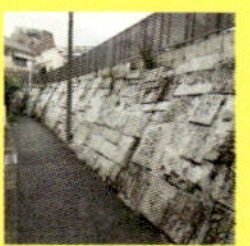

Otherworldly culvert 2 Myoshoji River tributary culvert running from north of Nakano Station and merging near Nakai Station on the Seibu Shinjuku Line. Strange white embankment with stacked stones appears along the dim alley. Look closely, and you'll see they're gravestones. Even deeper otherworldly vibe by night. ●Near 1-27 Kami-Takada, Nakano City.

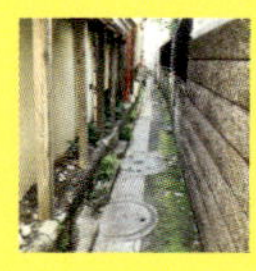

Otherworldly culvert 3 Alley built by filling in a stream. Too narrow for two people. That and the blind curves make it really thrilling, like entering another world. Remnant of a tributary of the Yabata River west of Mitake-dori Avenue in Ikebukuro 3. Even a river as small as this merges with many others and eventually reaches the sea. Romantic! ●Near 3-36 Ikebukuro, Toshima City.

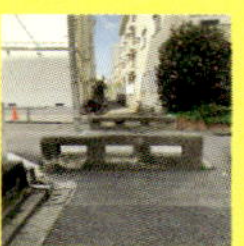

Treasure hunt culvert 1 Yamate-dori Avenue bustles with traffic, and the Metropolitan Expressway runs beneath. Slip into a quiet path, and you'll soon find the handrails of Hatsudai Bridge. Going further upstream along the Hatsudai River culvert, you can see clear spring water. A really rare find in the city center. ●Near 2-5 Hatsudai, Shibuya City.

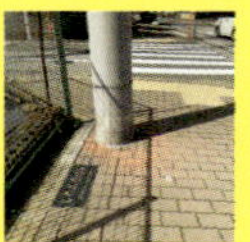

Treasure hunt culvert 2 Nishi-Ibori culvert runs from north of the Sobu Line's Shin-Koiwa Station to northeast Okudo. One of Tokyo's top "treasure hunt roads." Nameplates of many former bridges are embedded in the sidewalk. Photo shows Shitanda Bridge's. Try counting how many there are in all. ●Near 3-26 Okudo, Katsushika City.

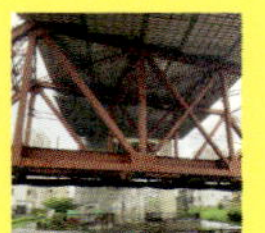

Treasure hunt culvert 3 Huge treasure. Where it once ran south of Kameido under Metropolitan Expressway No. 7, the Tatekawa River's former course is home to Tatekawa Bridge. "Forgotten freight line" of the Etchujima Branch. 1929 truss and brick piers remain even though there's no river, and an expressway above. Can view it from below in the park. ●Near 1-26 Kameido, Koto City.

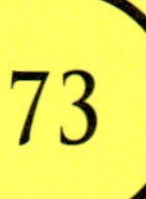

73 SHOWA-ERA SPOTS

Authentic Showa Landscapes Untouched by Tourism.

Yu Hirayama ●Showa maniac

Author of ***Living in Reiwa in a Showa Style*** and many other books on the Showa-era. Also currently has a series in the magazine ***Begin*** titled "Showa Stories That Resonate in Reiwa."

If the "Showa" era had carried on, this year would mark its 100th. It's a deeply special and meaningful year for people who remember the era. Tokyo's streets have changed enormously going from Showa to Heisei to Reiwa. Once standing proud as its tallest building, "Tokyo Tower" is now hidden by skyscrapers. What's more, neighborhoods around stations keep on and on getting redeveloped. Old shops like bookstores and butchers have vanished, to be replaced by modern chain restaurants and drugstores. It's natural for streets to change with the times, but each time I see transformations like these, they make me a bit uneasy. To be honest, I wish things would stay the same forever. The value of preserving old streets has deep roots in many places, like Kyoto, Kamakura, and Kawagoe. However, the focus there is on historic buildings, while everyday Showa-era shopping streets hardly get preserved at all. But isn't it those everyday streets, tied as they are to ordinary people's lives, that possess true cultural value? If things go on like this, a few decades from now, townscapes where you can truly experience Showa could very well have all vanished without a trace. Before they're gone forever, I want to visit as many Showa spots as I can, and engrave images of them deeply into my memory.

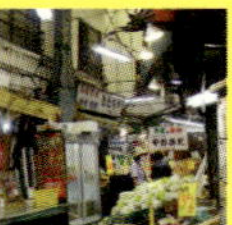

Kameari Food Market Strong postwar traces inside. Small, but lots of fruit and deli shops, and always bustling with locals. Two-story mortar buildings, once with homes upstairs. Covered by a corrugated roof, with countless wires passing overhead. Fluorescent lights along the passage add a nostalgic touch. ●Near 3-20-6 Kameari, Katsushika City.

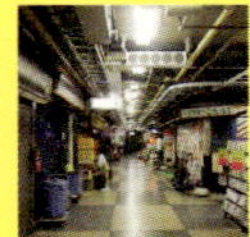

Asakusa Underground Shopping Street Japan's oldest underground mall. Low ceiling with exposed pipes and wiring evokes a bygone era. Underground malls are common now, but when this one was built, it must've felt like another world. Stand-up soba shops, izakaya, and yakisoba shops that serve beer—great for a pitstop after work. ●1 Hanakawado, Taito City.

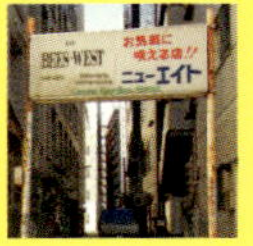

Green Garden Street This is right in the heart of Shinjuku. In a narrow alley between buildings, there's a lonely old gate sign for a former dining street. This is a remnant of "Ryokuengai," a cheap drinking alley and the origin of Shinjuku 2's gay town. Only a gate sign remains. ●2-5 Shinjuku, Shinjuku City.

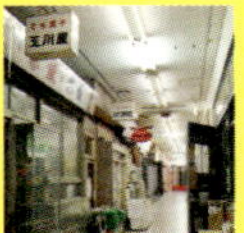

Ebisu Store Being inside a building, it feels like a Showa shopping street. Narrow passage and low ceiling practically scream "Showa," giving a strong sense of going back in time. Many shops have closed down, but some of the old ones are still there. (The photo is different from what's there now.) Right in front of Ebisu Station, so very easy to get to. ●1-8-3 Ebisu, Shibuya City.

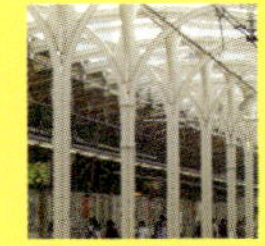

JR EAST Asakusabashi Station's steel pillars The gently rounded design of the steel pillars supporting the platform roof is simply fantastic. They were built by reusing old rails, and have remained in excellent condition since the station opened in 1932, over 90 years ago. Steel pillars with an aesthetic design like these are extremely rare even nationwide. ●1 Asakusabashi, Taito City.

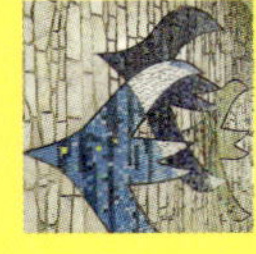

Mosaic mural in Metro Promenade Created by Tadashi Saji. Renovations at Shinjuku Station are erasing much of its Showa-era charm, but this piece in the JR-subway connecting passage has remained unchanged for over 50 years. The fish and bird shapes and the tiles' colors really capture the mood of the high-growth era. ●3 Shinjuku, Shinjuku City.

74 AMUSEMENT PARKS

"Weekday Night Amusement Parks"—Bliss!

369days ●Amusement park-loving duo

369days (read as "milk days") is a duo who share the charm of amusement parks through books and their website, the concept being "They're more fun as a grown up!"

You might think they're just for the daytime on days off, but going to "weekday night amusement parks" is great fun for grown-ups. Enjoy something extraordinary just beyond everyday life in Tokyo's unique amusement parks. A merry-go-round at night soothes tired souls with warm lights and gentle music. Find delicate decorations you overlooked when you were a child. A drink after work at an amusement park is special, too. Let's stroll around it a bit more before heading home. I mean, it's okay to get home late sometimes, right? We're adults now, after all.

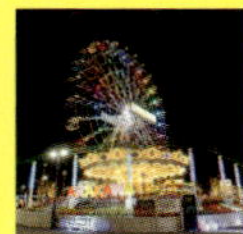

Arakawa Amusement Park The only city-run amusement park in Tokyo. Renovated in 2022, its attractions include a Ferris wheel, merry-go-round, mini train, and roller coaster. There's an animal park and Shitamachi Toden Mini Museum, which displays tram-related items. Friday and weekend nights have illuminations all year round. ●6-35-11 Nishi-Ogu, Arakawa City.

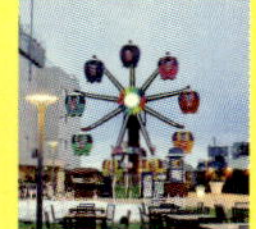

Rooftop amusement park Kamataen One of the few rooftop amusement parks with a Ferris wheel left in Japan. First one (1968) replaced in 1989 with current one, keeping name as "Ferris Wheel of Happiness." Usually open to 6 p.m., but in summer, there's a beer garden and you can see the Ferris wheel lit up. ●7-69-1 Nishi-Kamata, Ota City, Tokyu Plaza Kamata roof.

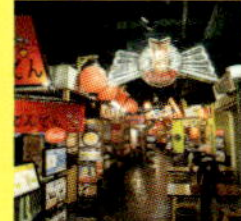

NAMJATOWN An indoor amusement park opened in 1996 with unique themes like ninja, sento baths, and a mosquito-catching attraction. The area themed on a 1950s town features gyoza and dessert shops. In the healing spot "Nyanja Town," you can pet real cats. ●3-1-3 Higashi-Ikebukuro, Toshima City, Sunshine City World Import Mart Bldg. 2F.

75 BEPOP

Bepop Signs "Popping Up" in Town.

Chikaku ●Bepop fan

Chikaku has begun photographing and collecting format-breaking station signs, calling them "stray signs." He also sells a Bepop-filled zine titled ***Bepop in Stations and Towns***.

Sold by office supplies maker ***MAX***, "Bepop" is a product specially designed for printing letters for signs. Its output feels like a giant version of "Tepra," "Name Land," and "P-Touch." Bepop is mainly used in factories and backyards, but if you look around carefully, you'll often see it popping up in everyday life, too. I love its strong presence and the awkward feel of its unique round gothic font, and always get excited when I spot Bepop signs around town.

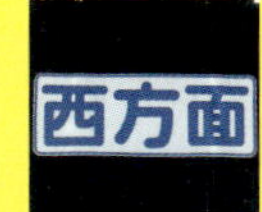

TOWER HALL FUNABORI A city-run cultural facility near the Shinjuku Line's Funabori Station. Many Bepop signs are on display, including direction labels in the 103-m-high observation room in ***Funabori Tower***. With Bepop signs displayed this high above ground, it can also be called the "highest Bepop spot." ●4-1-1 Funabori, Edogawa City.

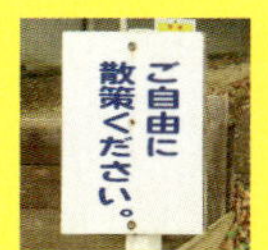

Saezuri no Mori A woodland near Nagayama Station (Keio and Odakyu Lines) where you can enjoy wild greenery. There are Bepop signs scattered around the entrance and along the walking paths. Text rarely seen elsewhere like "Strolling" and "Conservation" has been printed with Bepop, and can be seen alongside nature. ●2-1 Nagayama, Tama City.

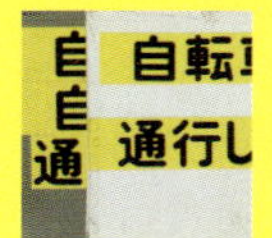

Akabane Station Out of all everyday places, train stations are where Bepop thrives the most. Several railway companies use it, including JR EAST. Akabane Station in particular has unique Bepop signs that are made with sheets and ink ribbons of various colors, and fun simply to look at. ●1-1-1 Akabane, Kita City.

76 CLUMSY-KID SIGNS

Risking All to Warn Us of Danger.

Toshiyuki Akanuma ●Clumsy-kid sign researcher

A keen walker, Toshiyuki Akanuma has been collecting clumsy-kid signs found on his strolls for around 19 years. He's amassed over 2,500 of them so far. X: @dozicollection

I collect warning signs featuring clumsy kids—"clumsy-kid signs," as I call them. Why do these clumsy kids end up in dangerous scrapes? Imagine a world with no clumsy-kid signs. We'd definitely have more careless accidents, right? Through their sacrifice, the clumsy kids make us think, "Mustn't end up like that," then take care not to. Consequently, they prevent accidents and save lives. In other words, we're alive thanks to them. Doesn't that make you feel a deep affection for them?

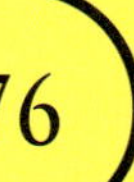

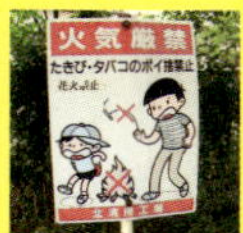

Clumsy-kid sign by the Kita Incineration Plant A sign prohibiting open flames on the greenway of an incineration plant in Shimo, Kita City. A clumsy kid hops about in agony, his butt ablaze. It immolates a child to warn people to be careful about cigarettes and bonfires. Note that the cigarette flung by the startled man is going to hit the boy. ●1-2-36 Shimo, Kita City.

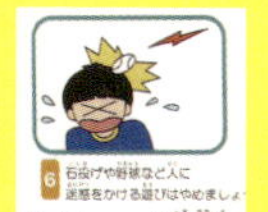

Clumsy-kid signs in Shiinoki Park One of the many "No XX" signs in Shinagawa City's parks. A lightning-fast ball hits a boy in the head. Pitching like that's too scary for a park! A child's sacrifice warns us of danger. "No stone throwing, baseball…" Huh? What's this "stone throwing" that even comes before baseball? ●5-5-12 Ebara, Shinagawa City.

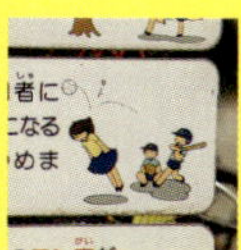

Clumsy-kid signs in Seika Park One of the many "No XX" signs in eastern Tokyo's parks. A boy has hit a baseball into a woman's head. She gets hurt, we get warned. Light gray blobs are shadows, and she isn't touching hers, so she's up in the air. Who'd jump up like that after a baseball to the head? Maybe she's trying to grab it. ●4-15-9 Kuramae, Taito City.

77 VENDING MACHINES

Street Corner Warmth at the Push of a Button.

Kenzaburo Ishida ●Vending machine maniac

Kenzaburo Ishida is a company employee who spreads the appeal of vending machines through TV appearances and social media. X: @jido__hanbaiki

Having been studying vending machines for over 15 years, I've noticed a few things about them. Japanese vending machines are "kind." The opening of the drinks is on the left when they come out, making it easy for right-handed people to just grab them and get started. Some vending machines sell room-temperature drinks for health reasons, and some even greet buyers with "Have a nice day." What should be just unfeeling boxes are watching over us with subtle kindness. With that in mind, I press another button today as well.

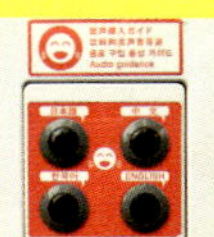

Chatty vending machines for overseas visitors Vending machines by DyDo DRINCO offer greetings and guidance in Chinese, Korean, English, and Japanese. They talk differently depending on the time, adding a playful touch. Japan's vending machines have recently been getting attention overseas, too, and their role is likely to grow. ●Near 1-21-5 Yoyogi, Shibuya City.

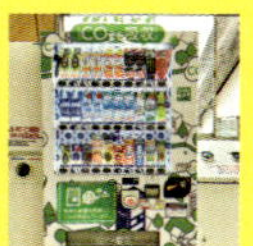

CO_2-gobbling vending machines Vending machines by Asahi Soft Drinks have special materials inside that absorb CO_2 from the air. They absorb as much CO_2 as around 20 cedar trees in a year, and it gets reused in asphalt and concrete. They also help restore blue carbon ecosystems, so they truly are eco-friendly. ●1-1-2 Oshiage, Sumida City, TOKYO Solamachi 1F.

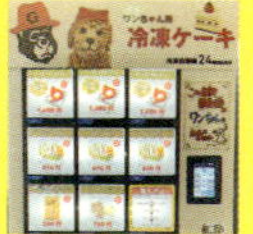

Frozen dog food vending machines These sell dog pizzas and birthday cakes made in collaboration with the famous PIZZA-LA chain. Japanese vending machines aren't just kind to people but to pets as well. Rows of these impressive vending machines can be found under elevated tracks in Asagaya. ●2-40-1 Asagaya-Minami, Suginami City, al:ku Asagaya, Units 9 and 10.

78 STORE-MINDING PLUSHIES

Little Clerks You've Definitely Seen.

Gome ●Store-minding plushie maniac

Loves photographing and looking at store-minding plushies (which she calls "misenui"—something like "shop + plushie = shplushie"). Shares photos of them on social media. X: @misenui

Plushies placed outside or inside stores as if they're holding the fort. I call them "misenui," and love looking at them. Their styles vary: some hold a sign showing the hours or menu, while others sit back and mind the store at their own pace. What especially catches my eye are the ones wearing clothes. How did the actual staff choose the clothes? Just imagining it warms my heart. Stores can run fine without them, but they're a soothing presence. I can't get enough of this playfulness.

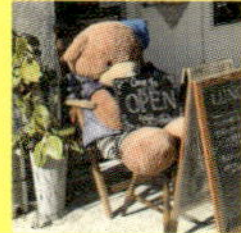

Café fuet A cozy café 5 minutes from Nishi-Ogikubo Station North Exit that's open from lunchtime to dinner. A large teddy bear at the front welcomes customers like a clerk. Its outfit regularly changes, revealing the owner's preferences and making it a comforting spot. ●3-42-13 Nishi-Ogi-Kita, Suginami City, 1F.

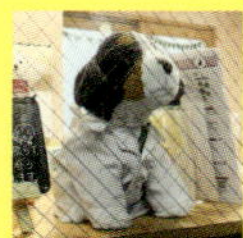

Ohana Animal Hospital In Koshin-dori Avenue Shopping Street, right by Koenji Station. A little plushie doctor welcomes you through the large window. Coolly sporting a white coat, the dog has a dignified yet kindly presence. He and some plushie friends warmly watch over shoppers and hospital visitors together. ●3-23-6 Koenji-Kita, Suginami City, 1F.

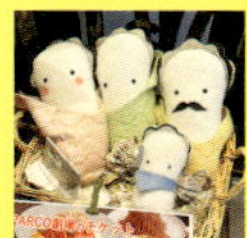

Shibuya Oyster Shop Shibuya Parco An oyster plushie family greets you at the entrance of this izakaya. Each colorful plushie has a unique look that gets you excited even before you're inside. Don't be fooled by their loose, relaxed look: they're actually old hands who've been working as misenui for eight years. ●15-1 Udagawacho, Shibuya City, Shibuya PARCO 7F.

79 STREET TANUKI

Tanuki Spots on Old Street Corners.

Muratanuki ●President of the ***Japan Tanuki Society***

A tanuki (racoon dog) researcher who posts photos of street-corner tanuki with "#街角狸 (StreetCornerTanuki)." Dream is to collect all tanuki scattered worldwide on social media.

Smiling tanuki in wicker hats holding a sake bottle and ledger. Called the "sake errand boy," these lucky-charm tanuki were first created by Meiji-era potter Tetsuzo Fujiwara. He opened the tanuki-only kiln ***Rian*** in Shigaraki in 1931, and the region became the center of tanuki statue production. "Street-corner tanuki" have evolved and changed. Modern ones are shifting to 2-to-3-heads-tall proportions, while old ones are slim, with patches around their eyes and bell-shaped bodies. Here are some old-tanuki spots in Tokyo.

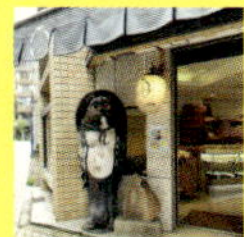

Tanuki Senbei ***Rian*** tanuki sitting under the eaves is the shop's symbol. More treasure inside: a tanuki by Edo-era master Dohachi Ninnami. (Usually, only replicas are put on display.) True to its name, the store sells tanuki-inspired rice crackers with a toasty flavor and crisp texture. Famous shop you don't need to be into tanuki to enjoy. ●1-9-13 Azabu-Juban, Minato City.

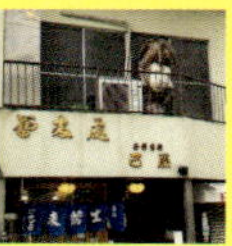

Tomoeya Ebisu On the veranda, a large ***Rian*** tanuki sits quietly watching over passersby. Its presence is breathtaking. How on Earth did they get it here? Tanuki line the entrance and inside, and at New Year's, visitors are warmly welcomed by ones clad in hakama pants. The traditional soba is also exquisite. ●2-2-1 Ebisu-Minami, Shibuya City, 1F.

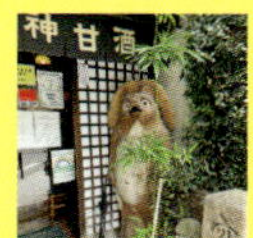

Amanoya Two ***Rian*** tanuki made in 1938 sit in front of the shop watching over visitors. Their weathered appearance evokes a real sense of history. What's more, there are lots of rare tanuki statues of all sizes inside as well, making this a must-see spot for tanuki-lovers. Enjoy Amanoya's sweets while immersing yourself in tanuki's charm. ●2-18-15 Soto-Kanda, Chiyoda City.

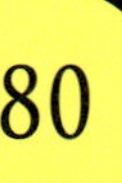

80 PARKS AND PLAYGROUNDS

Playgrounds Will Get Even More Fun.

Koro Fukazawa ●Park group representative

Born in Hyogo in 1982. Third-generation owner of ***KOTOBUKI***, established over a century ago in 1916. Promotes digital transformation of open spaces.

Playground equipment will get even more fun. I feel that more strongly every time I go to a park. Shadows of playground equipment make perfect hideouts, and forest paths make wonderful mazes. Play knows no bounds. But playgrounds are up against tough rivals—smartphones, video games, and after-school lessons. Always putting safety first, I constantly try to devise new kinds of fun. Parks are full of hints. Not all of them are cutting-edge. Actually, old games and equipment yield the most ideas. Let's think about how to play inspired by what we see.

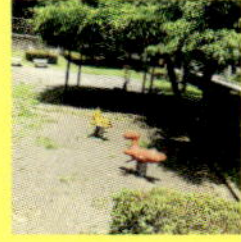

Hon-Machida Oyashiki Children's Park How easy should playground equipment be to understand? Children are more flexible than adults at accepting things they don't quite get. They interpret and ride this dog, horse, and sheep in their own way. Made of FRP (fiber-reinforced plastic)—rarely seen nowadays, and all the more charming for it. ●1143-5 Hon-Machida, Machida City.

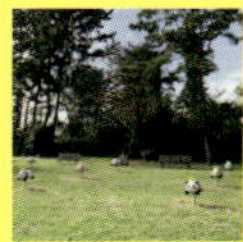

Tatsumi no Mori Greenway Park Installing copies of the same equipment can give it a different meaning. Intended for solo play, but having this many pandas to ride produces a veritable panda corps. And it's not mere repetition, either: the rare red panda at the core shoots the interest value through the roof. Let's all ride them together. ●Near 1-12 Tatsumi, Koto City.

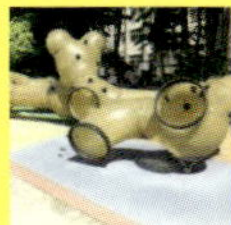

Oyata-Minami Park Besides being great for physically active play, there's also a hideout-like space. You can vaguely see that there's someone inside, but not who they are. That kind of vagueness makes for interesting playground equipment. It looks like a human organ or mole tunnels. ●4-42-1 Nakagawa, Adachi City.

81 SPIRAL STAIRCASES

Dramas Unfold on Spiral Staircases.

BMC ●Unit

Building Mania Cafe: five-member unit fascinated by '50s to '70s buildings. ***Good Staircase Photo Album: West*** published in 2014. Events, indie publication ***Building Monthly***, etc.

We've chosen spiral staircases built in the 1960s. The buildings from this era that us BMC members love often feature spiral staircase treasures. Their role was simply to be dramatic. In an age before 3D CAD, the architects did the drawings on paper by hand, then craftspeople built them, then made fine adjustments on-site or—if need be—started over from scratch. As you enjoy the depth and colors of beautiful spiral staircases created like this, we hope you'll spread the word about their charm.

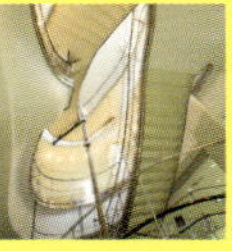

Meguro City Office Complex A magical spiral line runs through, creating stunning beauty. The pillars and handrails run alongside rhythmically. It starts with a floating feel, the midair turn is elegant, and the underside is a must-see. Its pure white surface forms lively curves that trace out the steps and connect the landings. ●2-19-15 Kami-Meguro, Meguro City.

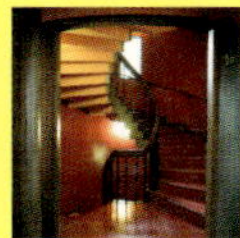

Tokyo Bunka Kaikan Crimson, perfectly round spiral staircase gets audiences all fired up for the show. Backstage has twin bright-blue, perfectly round ones that ease performers' nerves. Look down and it's like peering into an abyss, look up and it's like some higher plane. Stairs creating drama simply from going up and down them. ●5-45 Ueno-Koen, Taito City.

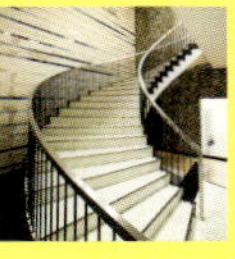

Kokusai Building Forming a whole with the Imperial Theater whose recent closure was a hot topic, this building has many great features, too. The stairs down to the basement have elegant curves and beautiful airborne, ribbon-like handrails. One background wall is marble and the other is striped tiles—a point that conveys the designer's feelings. ●3-1-1 Marunouchi, Chiyoda City.

Photos: Kiyoshi Nishioka (81)

82 LIVE MUSIC CLUBS

Always a Live Music Club Nearby.

Naonori Kuwata ●Live gig-lover and occasional organizer

Has visited 175 live music clubs across the country, and seen over 1,650 gigs. Favorite is shoegaze-style alternative guitar rock. Loves cutting-edge music.

I love music in general, and really love immersing myself in live performances. That's why I call myself a live gig-lover. About 90% of the live gigs I've seen were at live music clubs. I regularly add gig info for my favorite bands to my phone, get tickets, and go see them play. Chatting with band members at the ticket counter and on the floor builds closeness. It also feels like casually "going to hang out with them." Venues range from 20-seat solo performance spots to the largest—the 3,103-seater Toyosu PIT. The largest group in Japan is Sony's Zepp Hall Network. They run nine venues in six cities, including Odaiba, Haneda, and Shinjuku in Tokyo. PARCO's CLUB QUATTRO originated in Shibuya and has four venues nationwide. Shibuya is home to four O-Group venues named by Spotify, WWW/WWW X run by Space Shower TV, and nearby spots like Ebisu LIQUIDROOM and Daikanyama UNIT. All of them stand out. I often visit venues tied to the manga/anime ***Bocchi the Rock!***, including Shimokitazawa SHELTER and Shinjuku LOFT (LOFT PROJECT). Rinky Dink Studio (which runs 14 studios along with Shimokitazawa ERA, Kichijoji WARP, and Shinjuku NINE SPICES), and TOOS CORPORATION venues like Shibuya LUSH/HOME and Chofu Cross. Shinjuku MARZ, Koenji HIGH, Aoyama Tsukimiru Kimi Omou, and Shimokitazawa spots like DaisyBar, mona records, and LIVE HAUS are also great spots for live gig-lovers.

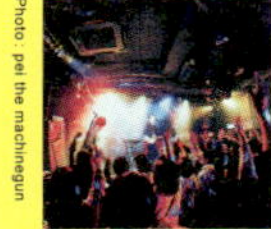
Photo: pei the machinegun

Shimokitazawa BASEMENTBAR Supporting the Shimokitazawa gig scene for many years. Plus there's THREE, run on the same floor. Fantastic staff—full of respect for the performers and organizers as well as the audience. Place that shows it's "people" who create "atmosphere." TOOS affiliate. ●5-18-1 Daizawa, Setagaya City, Calabash Bldg. B1.

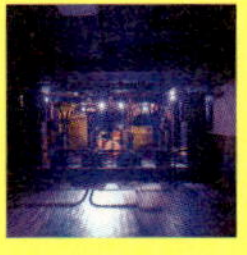

Shimokitazawa Chikamatsu Opened in June 2017 on the site of the former live music club Shimokitazawa CAVE-BE. A venue that spreads music, theater, film, and comedy cultures in Shimokitazawa. Its sister venue Chikamichi, which took over from the long-running GARAGE in January 2023, is also great. ●2-14-16 Kitazawa, Setagaya City, Kitazawa Plaza B1.

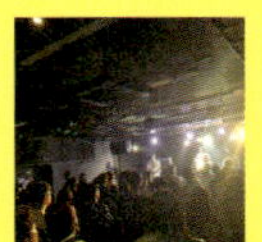

NISHIEIFUKU JAM Opened in June 2018 as a relocated Shinjuku JAM. Immersive, 250-capacity floor. Woofers embedded into both ends of the stage, giving excellent sound and visibility. Probably the only venue where you can pair lu rou fan from Jimbocho's ***Sangatsu no Mizu*** with craft beer. Rinky Dink affiliate. ●3-34-14 Eifuku, Suginami City, B1.

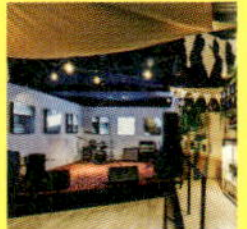

NEPO Kichijoji Opened in March 2019 next to Inokashira Park. A handy "next-generation live music club" with QR code wristbands for payment and live feeds on multiple stage wall displays. The first-floor food and drink area has an extensive menu and runs as a café during the day. ●1-17-4 Shimorenjaku, Mitaka City, B1.

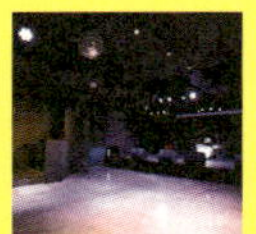

Shibuya TOKIO TOKYO Opened in March 2021 near Shibuya PARCO. Major artists have performed here since it opened, gaining it a reputation for unique bookings. The two-drink set ***FREE!!!*** leaves a strong impression of challenge and trial and error. Extensive drinks, including cold-brew coffee. ●3-7 Udagawacho, Shibuya City, B1.

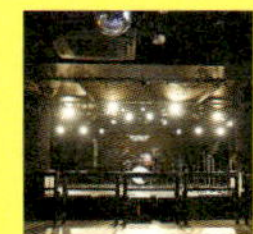

Shindaita FEVER Standout venue in front of Shindaita Sta., one stop from Shimo-kitazawa. Strong brand power, with top Japanese and international artists performing regularly. Bands often come out onto floor after, much to fans' delight. Shop ***pootle*** inside serves fried chicken in exchange for drink tickets. ¥300 lemon sours also a boon. ●1-1-14 Hanegi, Setagaya City, 1F.

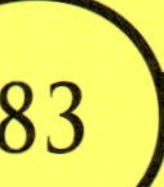

83 DAZAI OSAMU

A Musashino Literary Walk to Experience Dazai as a Painter.

Miyuki Daba ●Owner of the used-book café ***Phosphorescence***

Author of ***Dazai Marriage***. Original song CD and first mini album ***From a Window in Phos*** now on sale.

Here, I'll focus on Dazai as a painter, including his Reiwa-era revival. His self-portraits show a distinctive style with bold colors. He also painted people close to him. One was his close friend Jun Hiresaki. Hiresaki's former studio opened in 2023 as ***Niwaniha*** in Kokubunji, and has a wonderful "Dazai Room" with rare materials that reveal their bond. I recommend the nearby eel restaurant ***Wakamatsuya***, which is also linked to Dazai. ***Dazai Osamu Exhibition Room: This little house in Mitaka*** in Mitaka City Gallery of Art offers a special look at his works and paintings. (Some temporary closures.) Some pieces were created at a friend's studio. That studio's site was reopened in 2022 as the ***Hamae Sakurai Memorial Gallery***. Some floorboards stained with paint from that time are also on display. The Dazai Osamu Exhibition Room is nearby, so you can almost feel him painting. If you're in Mitaka around the anniversary of his death in June, the annual exhibition ***Do You Like Dazai?*** at ***Shirogane Gallery*** is a must-see. The diverse homage works to Dazai created by contemporary artists are truly inspiring. ***Dazai Osamu Literary Salon*** has postcards of self-portraits and handmade maps to buy. Even the rough sketches of the Tamagawa Aqueduct and bridges show artistic flair. Head to the bench by the pond in Inokashira Park, as if guided by Dazai. The view from his favorite spot remains unchanged even now. Here, you'll get a real picture of the man who lived here and gave his life to art and expression.

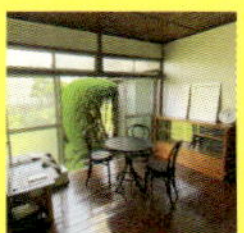

Niwaniha A spacious garden house opened in Kokubunji in 2023. It has a studio and learning space, and also serves as a local community hub. Originally his friend Jun Hiresaki's studio, its "Dazai Room" has valuable materials to see. Though still little known, its Showa-era building and garden are definitely worth experiencing. ●1-31-13 Higashi-Motomachi, Kokubunji City.

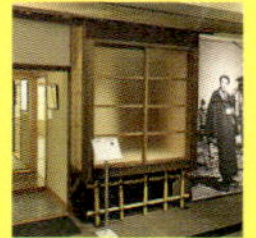

Dazai Osamu Exhibition Room: This little house in Mitaka Opened in 2020 to display valuable materials about him. Recreates his house full-scale. Also has an exhibit where you sit and write at his desk. The exhibits will make you lose track of time, so allow yourself plenty.* ●3-35-1 Shimorenjaku, Mitaka City, CORAL 5F, inside Mitaka City Gallery of Art.

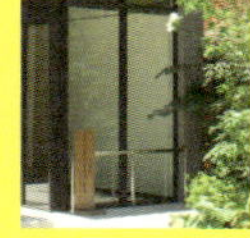

Mitaka City Hamae Sakurai Memorial Gallery In former studio of painter Hamae Sakurai (***Banquet Hostess*** model). Opened in 2022 for city residents to exhibit art and honor her artistic career. Hamae Sakurai exhibition shows strikingly powerful brushwork. Enjoy discovering the life and character of a painter who was inspired by Dazai's works.* ●3-42-3 Shimorenjaku, Mitaka City.

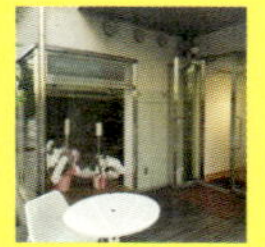

Shirogane Gallery Glass-walled building on Shirogane-dori Avenue. Participatory gallery that welcomes you anytime. Enlarged in 2021. Close to station, so it's good for shopping. ***Do You Like Dazai?*** exhibition in Mitaka every June is worth seeing. Standard route for fans touring Dazai sites on anniversary of his death. ●3-29-1 Shimorenjaku, Mitaka City.

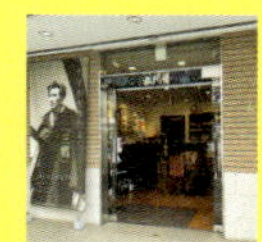

Dazai Osamu Literary Salon You can read Dazai's works here. Renovated in 2022 to include a book café. Enjoy Dazai coffee and Aomori apple juice while browsing the Shoshi Yamanouchi Library collection. You can buy "self-portrait" and "handmade map" postcards, plus original Dazai goods. ●3-16-14 Shimorenjaku, Mitaka City, Grand Argent Mitaka 1F.

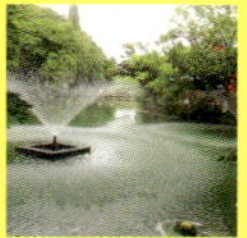

Inokashira Pond Dazai's oil painting "Portrait of Hisatomi-kun" is of Kunio Hisatomi, model for the artist in the novel ***Liz***. Hisatomi treasured it for the rest of his life. Inokashira Park appears in ***Liz***. The final scene with the mother's monologue to her new-to-Tokyo daughter is really colorful. Read it on a bench by the pond Dazai frequented for extra depth. ●4-1 Inokashira, Mitaka City.

*The Hamae Sakurai Memorial Gallery isn't a permanent feature, so you'll need to check the opening days. ***This little house in Mitaka*** will be closed until early June 2025. Photos provided by Mitaka City Sports and Culture Foundation: Dazai Osamu Exhibition Room & Dazai Osamu Literary Salon.

84 DEFORMED ARROWS

Beloved Road Signs Quietly Fulfilling Their Mission.

Gaku Yamazaki ●Road sign maniac

Has photographed over 4,000 road signs, covering all 47 prefectures. Runs the website "Road Sign Travels." Book: ***Unusual Arrow Signs***. X: @unusuarrows

Ever taken a close look at road signs? Coming across a traffic textbook when I was little, I got hooked on a page with a list of them. Been chasing around after them nonstop ever since. What especially piqued my mania was the "No Entry Except in Designated Direction" signs. Indicating permitted or prohibited directions, these come in unique varieties to fit the intersection shapes. I affectionately call them "deformed arrows," and go around photographing them. For example, the "deformed arrows" in Toshima, Kita City, are crazy complex! The "Yotsugibashi Minami" intersection in Sumida City has a bizarre, almost specter-like arrow. In front of Hibarigaoka Station in Nishitokyo, an arrow suddenly signals a U-turn! The more complex and bizarre, the more fantastic! Every time I see signs like these, I can't help but wonder how they got their shapes. Even more extreme are their curves and straight lines. My favorite arrows are either twisted or sharp—this is another point where tastes differ. The eerie twisted arrow at the "Yotsuya" intersection in Adachi and the sharp straight one at the "Shimurasakaue" intersection in Itabashi are must-sees. There are also times when I think, "This looks like something!" At Senju-Sakuragi in Adachi City, there are cute arrows that look like plants. Some also look like people or letters. They aim to be serious, but end up being oddly shaped—and that's their charm. These signs are still out there dutifully giving their all today, too.

Ultra-complex arrows North of Oji Sta., under Metropolitan Expressway's Oji-kita Ramp. Diagonal parallel roads are Metropolitan Road 306, split into two lanes due to expressway piers. Entering metropolitan road requires driving on left, so turns are restricted. Nearby alley is one-way exit. Complex intersection with restricted entry. ●Near 1-11 Toshima, Kita City.

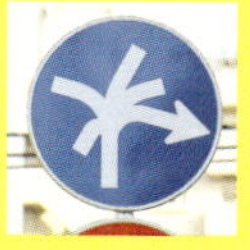

Bizarre arrow sign At the intersection south of "Yotsugibashi Bridge" over Arakawa River. From Kanegafuchi Sta., go straight southeast to reach this intersection with Route 6 (Mito Kaido). Sign is on narrow alley branching off street Kanegafuchi Sta. is on. Many roads cross here, but this sign makes only right turns possible. ●Near 5-39 Higashi-Mukojima, Sumida City.

U-turn arrow Beside the south exit rotary of the Seibu Ikebukuro Line's Hibarigaoka Station. Cross the station from south to north, and the road is blocked by a one-way exit. To reach Tanashi from there, you need to follow the sign, enter the station rotary for a U-turn, loop around, then exit into Yato Shindo-dori Avenue. ●Near 3-9 Sumiyoshicho, Nishitokyo City.

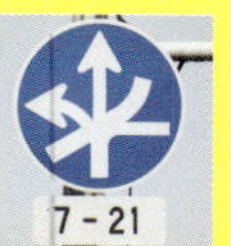

Squiggly arrows "Yotsuya" intersection, Adachi City. Head north from Gotanno Station, and this sign appears. The intersection is six-way and narrow, but the traffic is heavy. Right turns are banned from all directions during the day, resulting in each arrow having a slightly different shape. A very eye-catching intersection. ●Near 3-11 Chuo-Honcho, Adachi City.

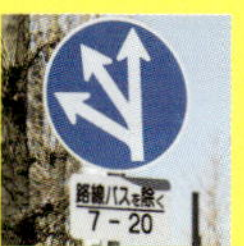

Sharp arrows Along Nakasendo road, at "Shimurasakaue" intersection in Itabashi City. Two left turns: one into Shiroyama-dori Avenue with Shimura Ginza Shopping Mall, one into old Nakasendo road and Shimizuzaka, which was once its "first tough slope." Azusawa Street extends off to the right, but this sign stops you from turning right into it during the day. ●Near 1-14 Shimura, Itabashi City.

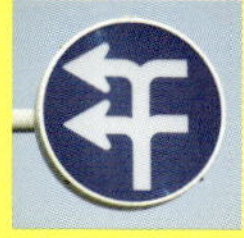

Plant-like arrows Northwest of "Senju-Sakuragicho" intersection in Adachi City, where road crosses Arakawa River levee, with parallel roads along top and bottom—hence this shape. Only left turns are allowed into either road. Lots of odd-shaped intersections dot this levee, so there are other "deformed arrows" to see as well. ●Near 2-14 Senju-Sakuragi, Adachi City.

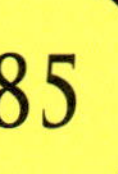

85 VINTAGE CLOTHES STORES

True Vintage Clothes-Lovers' Go-to Pro Store Owners.

Manabu Harada ●Vintage stylist

Has been working as a stylist for over 25 years. Author of ***The SUKIMONO BOOK***, and has also contributed widely to producing magazines and books about vintage items.

Someone bought some vintage clothes that are worth millions of yen? Vintage items are an investment? I'm not interested in any of that! I believe vintage clothes are for unconventional fashion tastes and maniac collectors. Sorry for the preachy start. The Tokyo vintage shops this loudmouth recommends are all pros—and always evolving. Like pro athletes who are surprisingly good at other sports besides their own, vintage stores that specialize in a particular thing are often also strong across the board. With the global vintage boom driving up prices, you can end up paying through the nose for shady goods from shops with neither knowledge nor taste! To avoid mistakes and disappointment from fading trends or getting fed up, I hope you head to the pro vintage shops I'm recommending here, get quality stuff, and stay hooked! So on that note, here are some professional shops for you. The level of professionalism in these six is undoubtedly world-class. Honestly. Lately, 20-somethings working in vintage shops are going to these to buy things for themselves. They're getting into vintage fashion pretty early for their age, but I couldn't be gladder. These shops might not readily share their knowledge. But if you keep loving it and keep going, you should definitely be able to get friendly with them and learn tons.

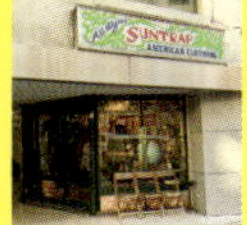

SUNTRAP Coveralls have surged in popularity and price lately. This is the go-to spot for vintage workwear pros. The real deal, it started collecting this stuff over 30 years ago, long before anyone else knew a thing about it. The most trustworthy shop, deeply knowledgeable about all things vintage down to the minutest details. ●4-23-5 Koenji-Minami, Suginami City, ACP Bldg. 1F.

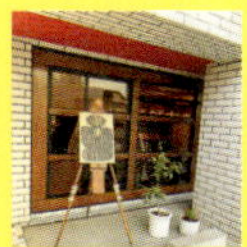

TORO Unique, high-quality vintage—flawless and long lauded by peers as "amazing." Owner Ikuko Yamaguchi is also a pro at vintage remakes, crafting them by hand at her in-store workbench. She says that when she finds nice materials on buying trips, she gets remake ideas in a flash! ●1-2-10 Jingumae, Shibuya City.

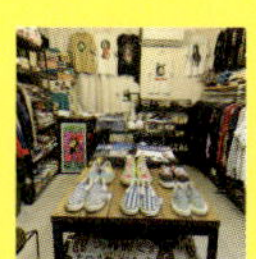

SKROVA Hanare Owner Yosuke Imaizumi is a vintage T-shirt pro. He loves skate and rock T-shirts, and has been selling them for years, unlike recently opened shops. The way he judges rarity based on his own values rather than the market's truly makes him the real deal. ●4-21-6 Koenji-Minami, Suginami City, Room 103.

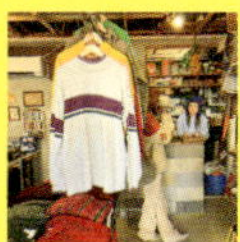

eel Owner Kyoko Yamaguchi is a styling pro. Before starting this shop, she worked at ***LONGABU*** in Koenji, and her styling skill was widely praised there. Her taste and styling will really teach you a lot. The cassette-tape DJ booth in the corner is also a nice touch. ●4-6-28 Asagaya-Kita, Suginami City, Tanaka Corpo 1F.

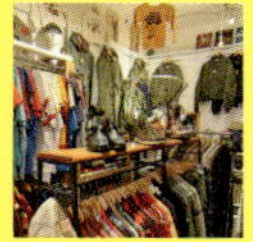

CA. A shop with a mania vibe where you'll find old books, catalogs, and clothes all under one roof. Owner Tadashi Sugiura is a vintage sweatshirt pro. He can tell you the brand, era, and color variation without needing the collar tags. His selection is currently leaning toward outdoor and military, with fewer sweatshirts. ●4-24-9 Koenji-Minami, Suginami City, Room 103.

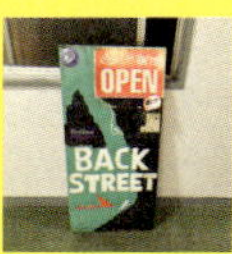

BACK STREET Outdoor vintage pro. GREGORY, patagonia, GRAMICCi, and more…the selection and knowledge are both unmatched. Worldwide collectors in this genre are watching this shop. Last year, it predicted a resurgence in vintage Patagonia for fall-winter 2024—and was spot-on. ●1-17-4 Nakamachi, Machida City, Machida Nakamachi Daiichi Bldg. 2F.

86 FLOOR TILES

Lovely Retro Floors Along Shopping Streets.

Akiko Imai ●Graphic designer

Floor maniac. Travels Japan in search of Showa-era floors. Also shares wonderful floors on X and Instagram (@eko_dacchiy). Coauthored book: ***Lovely Floors Underfoot, New Edition***.

I've loved floors ever since I glanced down and noticed the harmony of colors and patterns in them. Shopping streets are real treasure troves. Butchers often have great ones. Handmade ham and sausage shop ***Essen*** in Soshigaya Minami Shopping Street has a European tile one befitting of its name. Youth hotspots Shimokitazawa and Harajuku's Cat Street are also shopping districts. Some places have kept the old floor, while others have laid down a retro one on purpose. I walk along with my head down in search of miraculous encounters.

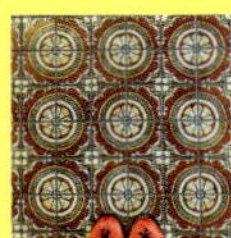

Handmade Ham and Sausage Shop Essen Ultraman Shopping district in Soshigaya-Okura, the birthplace of Ultraman. It's the collective name for three shopping streets. Essen is a 45-year-old shop in Soshigaya Minami Shopping Street. Exquisite handmade ham and sausages, and a very popular potato salad, too. ●6-28-5 Kinuta, Setagaya City.

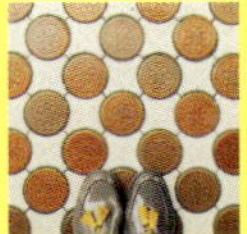

hickory Vintage clothing shop with 19 years of history in Shimokitazawa—itself one big shopping district. Also in the Shimokitazawa-set film ***Machi no Uede*** as the main character's workplace. American items from the '60s to '90s. Nice prices in line with today's trends. Charming cookie-like tile floor at the entrance, too. ●5-29-17 Daizawa, Setagaya City, Room 103.

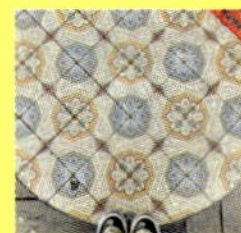

MR.BROTHERS CUT CLUB, Harajuku Store No. 2 A barbershop just off Cat Street. It's keeping classic barber culture alive while establishing a fresh new style. Beside the staff's skills, the antique-filled interior is also remarkable. They say the floor tiles are from an old European castle. ● 6-14-11 Jingumae, Shibuya City.

87 RUINS

The Past Remaining in City-Center Ruins.

Toru Kurihara ●Ruin & sea-of-trees explorer

Has explored over 2,000 ruins across Japan over about 30 years. Recent books include ***Mysterious Properties in Japan***.

"What's ruins' appeal?" It's a matter of taste and hard to explain, but I guess it's that they're "attractions built by humans and shaped by nature and time." People spend time and money to experience the "extraordinary" at theme parks. Former "stations" once busy with passengers and "bridges" once crossed by crowds. "Sluice gates" that held back water and let ships pass. Now, there's no one there, and the massive gates are still. Ruins have "extraordinary" appeal just like theme parks. I hope you go see that for yourself.

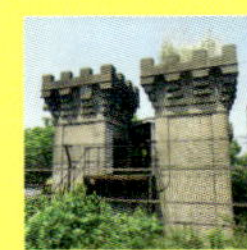

Former Komatsugawa Lock Gate Built in 1930 to balance water levels between the Arakawa and former Nakagawa Rivers. Closed in 1976. Beautiful, elaborately designed "lock gate" like a grand building. Not exactly a ruin, but something once used and now quietly displayed shares something with them. A treasure to be passed down. ●1 Komatsugawa, Edogawa City.

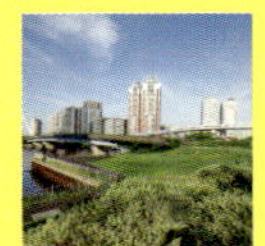

Aomi Bridge A bridge in Odaiba that vanished from the maps. Nevertheless, it once stood in a prime spot in the city. It was built in 1987 and closed in 1994. Several other bridges were built nearby, sharply reducing traffic—and that's why it was abandoned. A world destroyed, with all the humans gone. It feels like seeing just such a landscape for real. ●1 Aomi, Koto City.

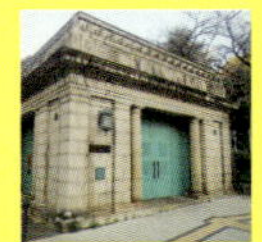

Former Hakubutsukan Dobutsuen Station A "phantom station" once stood next to Keisei Ueno Sta. Built in 1933 on hereditary land belonging to the Imperial family. Designed to be luxurious and grand. Fewer passengers led to suspension in 1997 and closure in 2004. An otherworldly station that should be busy, but only the staff remain. ●13-23 Ueno-Koen, Taito City.

88 GUARD PIPES

Cute, Pop, and Stylish Guard pipes.

Dai Okamoto ●Japan Guard Pipe Survey Team

Has been walking around photographing guard pipes for more than a decade, recording over 5,000 to date. Author of ***Illustrated Encyclopedia of Street Guard Pipes***.

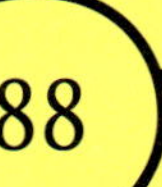

Guard pipes' manufacturers vary depending on who's in charge of the roads (the national, prefectural, or municipal government), and some create highly original examples. Many unnoticed everyday things can become objects of mania, and guard pipes are one of them. No one notices, but the way the pipes bend and the details on the plate give each its own unique character. They're technically called pedestrian guard fences, but I lump them all together under my own term of just "guard pipes (GPs)." Struck by a "Kita" fence in Kita City over 10 years ago, I began hunting for more—and so, this hobby of mine began. Since then, I've been steadily collecting photos of guard pipes, bollards, and guardrails everywhere, sorting them by look and shape. For this article, I was told I could pick six guard pipes from Tokyo—specifically, with a theme of my own devising. They're all dear to me, so it was a tough choice, but this time, I selected cute or charming ones. The happiest outcome for me will be if it makes you want to go see them, but I'm content enough just knowing you'll be a bit more aware of them. A fresh look at the ordinary—if you can recall what your own local guard pipes look like, then that's already something. Anyway, first of all, I'll be waiting at the usual spot on the way home today. Enjoy these cute, pop, and stylish guard pipes!

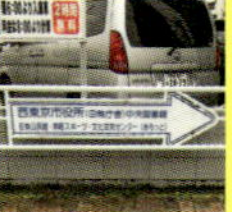

GP that tells you which way to go Nishitokyo City is a guard pipe paradise. A unique one appears as soon as you leave Tanashi Station South Exit. Don't be thinking it's just a firmly attached panel. The arrow-shaped plate is set into an arrow-shaped frame. Isn't this amazing? A lavish, one-of-a-kind fence, made just for this spot! ●Near Minamicho, Nishitokyo City.

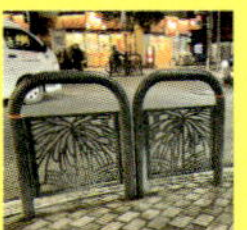

Itabashi Fireworks GPs Gate-shaped GPs on the four corners of the Takashimadaira 8 intersection, just past the shopping street coming from Takashimadaira Sta. Photo doesn't show it, but they're twice the normal size, and the large fireworks design really stands out—perfectly expressing the area's biggest summer event. ●Takashimadaira, Itabashi City.

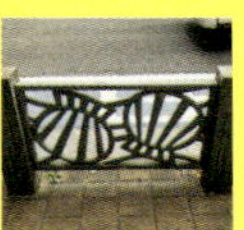

Shell GP This appears right outside "Omorikaigan Station," which is famous for the Omori Shell Mounds discovered by Dr. Morse. The wonderful fence evokes the coast and shell mounds with a striking relief design. The tiles also feature shells, and there might be other hidden details, too. ●Omori-Kita, Ota City.

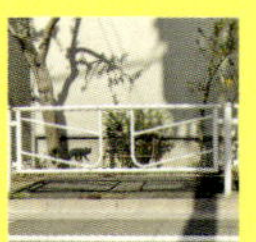

GPs in Kita City Your jaw will drop when you realize what the design is. It looks just like the kanji character "north." Three sizes, with the middle one pictured. Longest one is a stretched "north," so that's really cute, too. Designed to let people crossing the river from Kawaguchi know at a glance that they've entered Tokyo and Kita City. ●Nishigaoka, Kita City.

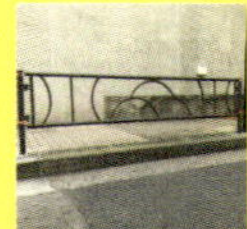

GPs in Shinagawa Though few in number, GPs in Shinagawa City have fun designs and plenty of variety. From afar, these ones look like the kanji "river," "goods," and "river" (read "kawa, shina, kawa," hint, hint). Talk about artistry—even seen from the opposite side, they still instantly tell you you're in "Shinagawa." A bona fide masterpiece. ●Near Nakanobu, Shinagawa City.

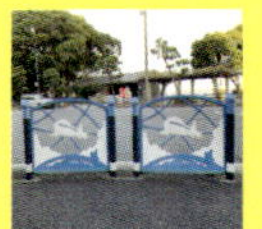

Airplane GPs Keihinjima, an island lined with industrial parks and warehouses. These cute GPs dot the roads around Tsubasa Park in overwhelming numbers. Compared with Haneda across the river with planes taking off nonstop, this landscape is a bit melancholic. The cute plane design definitely puts them among Japan's top GPs. ●Keihinjima, Ota City.

89 THE LOFT GROUP

Cultural Crossroads—The Loft Group's Revolution.

Yu Hirano ●Founder of the *Loft* live music clubs

Born in Tokyo in 1944. Opened five ***Loft*** live music clubs in Tokyo in the '70s and ***LOFT/PLUS ONE***, the world's first live talk venue, in '95.

Live music clubs are intimate spaces where the performers' and audience's deep passions intertwine. Paying to see niche bands and newcomers ignored by the media is the acme of music mania. Radical ideas and cutting-edge music arise in these venues. ***Shinjuku Loft*** at the dawn of punk was a haven for outcasts like The Stalin's Michiro Endo and the filth-throwing Hijokaidan. Being a taboo-free forum was a trait ***LOFT/PLUS ONE*** inherited as well, setting repressed voices free. I can proudly say that fostered Japan's talk culture.

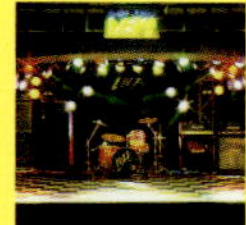

Shinjuku Loft Opened in October 1976 along Otakibashi-dori Avenue, Shinjuku. A leading live music club in Japan. Producing a whole parade of rock bands including the likes of Southern All Stars, BOØWY, Spitz, and Hi-STANDARD, it had a massive impact on the music scene. Moved to Kabukicho in 1999. ●1-12-9 Kabukicho, Shinjuku City, B2.

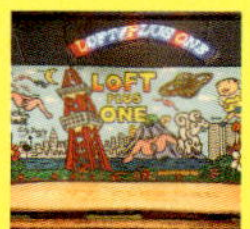

LOFT/PLUS ONE A live talk venue that opened in July 1995 in Tomihisacho, Shinjuku City, and moved to Kabukicho in June 1998. A subculture hub that hosts daily live talk events on every theme from culture and subculture to politics and underground topics, with guests from a diverse range of fields. ●1-14-7 Kabukicho, Shinjuku City, B2.

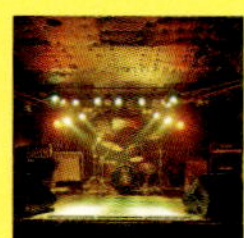

Shimokitazawa SHELTER Opened in October 1991 in Kitazawa, Setagaya City. When Shinjuku Loft was facing eviction, this live music club opened up as a "shelter" for it to evacuate to. Playing a leading role in the melodic hardcore and alternative rock scenes, it shaped a unique music culture in the youth culture hub that is Shimokitazawa. ●2-6-10 Kitazawa, Setagaya City, B1.

90 CONVENIENCE STORES

Exploring Chic Urban Convenience Stores.

Taiga Shirai ●Scenery freak and company employee

Zine ***Chic Convenience Stores Vol.1*** published in 2015. Travels Japan collecting landscapes. Latest book: ***Atmospheric Palm Trees***. Also compares mixed-juice drinks.

"Chic convenience stores" means ones with unique facade signs that are different from the ones major ones have. I collect and classify them into "urban," "tourist," and "facility" types. The term comes from their tendency to be found in so-called "chic" areas like Ginza and Roppongi. Exploring the reasons why they're chic (e.g., landscape regulations) is also interesting. Finding a brown convenience store in a tourist spot is one thing, but spotting a chic one in the city center is a truly special thrill.

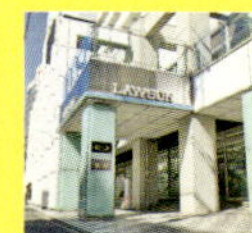

Lawson, Roppongi 3 Store Roppongi, a chic neighborhood known to all. The angular exterior and iconic facade sign feature Lawson's signature blue lines on a silver background, giving a sleek impression. The logo and lines softly glow like neon at night. Definitely worth seeing. ●3-17-10 Roppongi, Minato City.

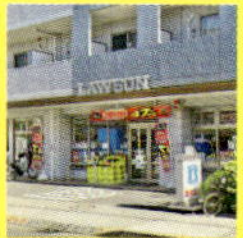

Lawson, Shimouma 3 Store A chic convenience store suddenly appears in a quiet residential area. The facade with its minimalist design and beautiful wood grain exudes elegance. A convenience store decked out like this is a very rare find. Located between Sangen-jaya and Gakugei-daigaku Stations, this one is well worth a visit. ●3-11-6 Shimouma, Setagaya City.

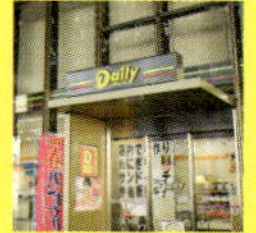

Daily Yamazaki, Roppongi 3 Store Two bold red and yellow stripes stand out against a silver frame. The urban mix of pop and stylish is even more endearing for the glimpses of the Bread Festival banner. One of the most stylish Daily Yamazaki stores you can find in all of Tokyo. ●3-7-1 Roppongi, Minato City, Unit 204.

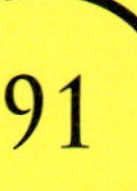

91 MANHOLES

Manhole Covers: History That's Within Reach.

Kohei Shirahama ●Manholer

On the exec. committee of Manhole Night. TV: ***Tamori Club*** and more. Articles: Japan Sewage Works Assoc. Journal, Japan Soc. of Civil Engineers Journal, ***Tokyojin***, etc.

Did Tokugawa Ieyasu really exist? Textbooks describe him in detail, but it's all secondhand info—not something you can check yourself. To put it in extreme terms, we can neither confirm nor deny if he existed, because it's hard to feel how he's linked to the world we live in now. In this context, manhole covers at least feel like links between ourselves and history. Scattered all across Tokyo and ranging from prewar "antiques" to newer painted ones, they all have carved into them history that's within reach.

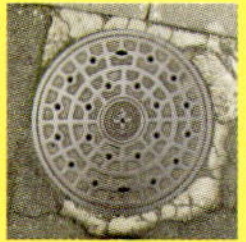

Manhole cover in Sendagaya Town, Toyotama County, Tokyo Prefecture Manhole cover with the emblem of Sendagaya Town, which disappeared in 1932 on merging with Tokyo City. Recognized by locals as well, this cover served as the model for confectionaries that symbolize the town. Still in use as part of the sewage system. ●4-13-1 Sendagaya, Shibuya City, in front of Takeda Clinic.

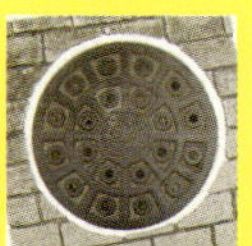

Manhole cover in Ogumachi, Kita-Toshima County, Tokyo Prefecture Bears emblem of Ogumachi, which vanished on merging with Tokyo City in 1932. Circle of 9 "wo" katakana are read as "Wogu," meaning "Ogu." Information panel on origins of cover and town. No longer in use (solely a monument). ●2-5-10 Nishi-Ogu, Arakawa City, by Yawata Children's Park.

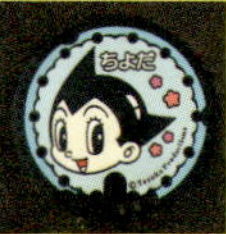

Manhole covers featuring Astro Boy Osamu Tezuka's ***Astro Boy***. The hero and his sister Uran are students at Ochanomizu Elementary. Also, their adoptive father is Dr. Ochanomizu. These manholes honor the "Ochanomizu" links. Three kinds of them along the street. ●1-1-1 Kanda-Surugadai, Chiyoda City, in front of Meiji University Liberty Tower.

92 GALLERIES

Galleries You'll Want to Linger In.

Shin Hamada ●Photographer

Mainly does portrait, documentary, and interview photography. Personal project HAMADA ARCHITECTS™ is also ongoing.

I do exhibitions so often that people ask me, "How many have you done this year?" Once I get an idea, I get an urge to make it real—give it form as an object or a space. This urge hasn't faded since I did my first zine at 20. Rather, 17 years on, I can tell it's getting stronger. I always regard the spatial design as also forming a part of the exhibition. While I do admire the white cube, the space must resonate more with the atmosphere of the work. Below are three venues I want to share.

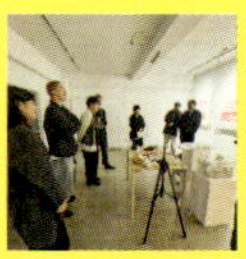

Midori.so Working space that anyone can visit freely, not just members. Gallery is on 3F of an old building. The white walls glow with natural light, and opening the dirty glass windows reveals the glittering surface of a murky pool. Comfy place with friendly, quirky people. That impression hasn't changed. Rather, it seems to be getting deeper. ●3-3-11 Aobadai, Meguro City.

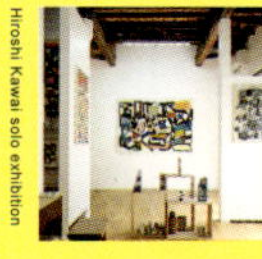

Hiroshi Kawai solo exhibition

Open Letter A house—I mean, gallery. Sunlight pours in, and the Yamauchi family's dining table is visible through the glass door. Rare space seamlessly tied to daily life, life and the exhibits interacting functionally. Aptly named, too: the modest bookshelves are bound to hold something that catches your eye. ●5-3-17 Shimo-Takaido, Suginami City.

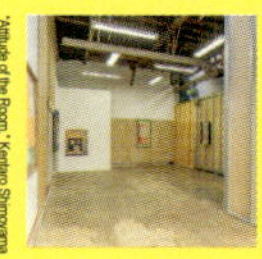

"Attitude of the Room," Kentaro Shimoyama

Higashikasai 1-11-6-A Warehouse Gallery run by two nice guys. Roughness and delicacy coexist here, and draw people in. Openness comes from the high ceilings and natural light—or maybe from the two guys casually greeting passing neighbors as they work outside. Ideal exhibition space—created through dialogue and collaboration. ●1-11-6 Higashi-Kasai, Edogawa City.

INDEX

ILLUSTRATIONS: KAZUMA MIKAMI TEXT: SELECTORS EDITING: MO-GREEN